NO OTHER NAME?

NO OTHER NAME?

A Critical Survey of Christian Attitudes
Toward the World Religions

PAUL F. KNITTER

SCM PRESS LTD

216211

334 02223 1

First published in Britain 1985
by SCM Press Ltd
26–30 Tottenham Road London N1 4BZ

Typeset in the United States of America
and printed in Great Britain by
Richard Clay (The Chaucer Press) Ltd
Bungay, Suffolk

To Cathy

Contents

Preface

All theology, we are told, is rooted in biography. This book confirms that statement. The theology behind the questions and the tentative answers to be examined in the following pages grew out of my own struggles as a Christian believer. The motivation to write this book, in other words, arose not only from the desire to explore a pressing theological problem but, more so, to arrive at a deeper integrity and commitment in my own Christian faith.

For the past twenty years or so, I have felt no small problem in integrating what I have learned and experienced from other faiths with what I have learned from traditional Christian doctrines, especially concerning the uniqueness and finality of Christ and Christianity.

From my experience in the classroom of a Roman Catholic university and in a typical Catholic parish, I know I am not alone; other Christians feel the same problems. This book, I hope, will help them, as it has helped me, to stare those problems in the face and search for new answers—answers that will be faithful both to contemporary experience and to Christian tradition.

The structure of the book reflects the path I have followed in confronting and trying to resolve the question of Christ/Christianity and other religions. Chapter 1 sets the problem: the new experience of religious pluralism in the world of today, the vision many persons have of a new kind of unity and dialogue among religions, and the perplexing questions Christians encounter when they feel themselves drawn toward such a unity and dialogue. Chapters 2 through 4 examine some of the popular attitudes as to why there are so many religions. To some extent, all of us share in or are affected by these widespread common sense opinions: "All religions are limited and cannot judge one another. They all share a common essence or a common source in the human psyche." There is perhaps much sense, common and theological, in these popular views, but they also seem too easy, too sure.

In chapters 5 through 7, I review the different Christian models for understanding and approaching other religions: the conservative Evangelical, the mainline Protestant, and the Catholic. Each is helpful in that each stresses central Christian beliefs that must be brought to interreligious dialogue. Yet none of these confessional models seems really able to listen to what the followers of other ways have to say. The problem, in all of them, appears to hinge on the traditional Christian claim for the superiority and normativity of Jesus Christ. Chapter 8 shows that a new, "theocentric" model for Christian encounter with other faiths is taking shape among a wide scattering of theologians (and, I suspect, among many of "the ordinary faithful"). This theocentric model seems to me to be the most promising avenue of Christian approach to followers of other ways. But it is new and, for many Christians, threatening to what they feel is the very foundation of their faith: the centrality of Jesus Christ.

So in chapter 9 I try to confirm the validity of this theocentric model by showing how a theocentric christology is consistent with the witness of scripture and with much of contemporary mainline Christian theology. Chapter 10 explores how a theocentric christology and theology of religions can be used in the actual task of dialogue. A theocentric view of religions and of Christ allows Christians to be fully committed to Jesus and fully open to other ways.

All this is the path I, with others, am exploring. It must win greater approval from "the sense of the faithful," before it can be called a valid Christian path. I hope this book will help promote such a validation.

A word about models. As is evident in contemporary theology, models (or "types" or "paradigms") can be very useful in mapping a complex, diversified theological territory. The danger, as the cliché has it, is that the map is taken for the territory. In their unavoidable generality, models cannot capture the exceptions and the diversity of opinion within the terrain they try to define. Therefore, when I speak of the "conservative Evangelical" or the "Catholic" models for understanding religions I am not saying that all Evangelicals or Catholics will fit snugly into these niches; also, many Catholics, for instance, feel more at home in the mainline Protestant model than in the Catholic. There is, happily, much ecumenical promiscuity nowadays. I give these models confessional names because the main proponents of each of them are located in a particular confession; each model is rooted in and sustained by the core claims of a distinct Christian tradition. Understanding the different confessional roots, we shall be better able to understand and evaluate the different ways Christians approach other faiths. The use of these models, therefore, should promote intra-Christian dialogue.

Because I wrote this book especially for the kind of intelligent, questioning laypersons I have met in the classroom and parish meetings, I have tried to keep the arguments as uncomplicated as possible and the technical, theological jargon as minimal as possible. Where technical language seemed necessary, I have tried to translate it. But I have also kept my theological colleagues in mind. In treating the question of the relation of Christ/Christianity to other religions, central Christian doctrines or convictions are at stake. I did not want to treat these doctrines cavalierly. I had to enter into "the theological discussion."

Though I have tried to keep footnotes to a minimum, I have also wanted to show that when I am presenting the views of others I am doing so accurately, or when I am advancing what might seem to be novel or unorthodox ideas (esp. in chap. 9 and 10), I am doing so in good theological company. Though this book is primarily a personal statement of faith for other faith-seekers, it is also intended to be a reputable theological contribution.

The book took shape in undergraduate and graduate courses at Xavier University in Cincinnati and at the Catholic Theological Union in Chicago. I have intentionally preserved its textbook design in the hope that other teachers will find it a useful tool in courses on interreligious dialogue, Christianity and world religions, and christology. The first eight chapters attempt an accurate presentation and a careful critique of current thinking on religious pluralism; the last two chapters try to break new ground. The ten chapters can fit neatly into a semester of fourteen weeks, or even more neatly into a quarter of ten weeks. (In a semester-long course, I found that students welcomed an additional week of discussion for the chapters on the Catholic and theocentric models and especially for the final chapters on christology and the practice of dialogue.) The supplementary readings for each chapter have been carefully chosen. They are brief and allow students to carry on further explorations into primary sources or differing opinions.

During the year preceding the final composition of this book, there was a small explosion of studies on the issue of Christianity and religious pluralism. They indicate, I believe, that after the intense discussion of a "theology of religions" during the 1950s, 60s, and early 70s,[1] the issue is becoming acute again. In fact, these books are perhaps signaling a *kairos*, a new context in which a revision of how Christianity understands itself and other religions is possible and necessary. A brief commentary on these recent publications can fittingly introduce and focus the intent of my study.

Willard Oxtoby in *The Meaning of Other Faiths* [2] offers a popular and clear introduction to the problems involved in the new Christian awareness of other religions; intentionally he stays on the surface of the issues. More penetrating analyses of needed changes in Christian attitudes toward other ways are offered by Walbert Bühlmann (*God's Chosen Peoples*), Arnulf Camps (*Partners in Dialogue*), John B. Cobb, Jr. (*Beyond Dialogue*), and Richard Drummond (*Toward a New Age in Christian Theology*).[3] All of them, however, as I shall indicate in the following pages, remain within the confines of what I call the Catholic model for a theology of religions.

Bühlmann and Camps presuppose and do not question the superiority and finality of God's self-disclosure in Christ. Cobb and Drummond are aware of the difficulties in traditional claims for Christ's normativity, and although they take up this question in their calls for a more authentic dialogue with other believers, they hold to a necessary completion of other religions in God's historical revelation in Jesus Christ.[4] Such claims, I shall argue, must be open to revision; if they are to be made at all, it must be with greater caution than is shown by any of these authors.

Alan Race in *Christians and Religious Pluralism* shows such caution.[5] He and I share many concerns and conclusions, especially regarding the uniqueness of Jesus. Although we differ in our readings of individual theologians (especially Raimundo Panikkar, Hans Küng, Paul Tillich, and John Robinson), Race's "types" (exclusivism, inclusivism, pluralism) and my models evince an amazing and confirming similarity. Our studies will complement each other. I have, however, tried to offer a broader and more nuanced perspective on the theological content of each model/type and on the theologians who represent them. More importantly, in chapters 9 and 10 I have tried to avoid the relativism that still clings to Race's conclusions.[6]

I cannot mention all the persons whose wisdom and support stand behind and within these pages. Phil Scharper, of Orbis Books, was with me from the very beginning, when I made my first outline of the contents of the book. Bill Danker and Jerry Anderson were instrumental in the decision of the American Society of Missiology to include my study in the respected ASM series; their critical comments on the entire manuscript were often disturbing and always rewarding. For their helpful evaluation of sections of the manuscript I am indebted to Raimundo Panikkar, Stanley J. Samartha, James Ebner, Monika Hellwig, William Collinge, Archie Nations, and Peggy Starkey. For reading the entire text and cleaning up both argument and style, I thank Coralyn Kendall, Dennis Doyle, and especially my wife, Cathy Cornell.

Chapter I

One Confronts Many

The title of this chapter might instill in the perceptive reader a sense of déjà vu. It sounds like another recycling of the old problem of the one and the many. The question of whether reality—atoms, human beings, gods—is ultimately one or many has taunted and teased the human mind from Heraclitus and Parmenides to Alfred North Whitehead, from the seers of the Upanishads to contemporary Zen Buddhists.

This introductory chapter does not offer another recycling of the problem; rather, in the light of the struggle of our twentieth century world to make it into the twenty-first century, it attempts a new and different rematch with the age-old question. Like all truly great questions, that of the many and the one continues to dog the human spirit, not to lead us to ever new confusions but to prod us to ever new insights into ourselves, our world, and how we are to live our lives.

I want to take up the question of one confronting many in the context of world religions—of the *many* world religions. From the clouded origins of the human species, as the spark of consciousness broadened and gave rise to the burning concern for the meaning of life, there have always been many religions, each with its own "ultimate" answers. Today our inter-communicating planet has made us aware, more painfully than ever before, of religious pluralism and of the many different ultimate answers.

Why painfully? Because the quantity and quality of this knowledge of many and other religions is today setting off a barrage of questions that religious persons of the past, secure in their own isolated religious camps, never had to face: Why are there so many different religions? If God is one, should there not be one religion? Are the religions all equally true, equally false? Do they all share in something common? How should they relate to each other? Are the many religions really one? More specifically, how should *my* religion relate to the others? Can I learn from other religions? Can I learn more from them than I can from my own? Why do I belong to one religion rather than another?

For anyone who takes religious faith seriously, these are painful questions.

1

More and more persons today feel that they cannot run away from such questions, not if their own faith is going to be honest. This is especially true for Christians—perhaps because they have always felt or been told that theirs was the only true religion, that the "many" other religions were destined by God's will eventually to become the "one" Christian religion.

The rest of this chapter will try to face and sound out all these questions about the one and many religions. Before we can really search for an answer, we must be well aware of the full content and urgency of the question. In order to do this, we shall consider: 1) the reality of religious pluralism in the world of today; 2) the new vision of religious unity that this reality is suggesting to many thinkers; and 3) the problems that all this poses for the concerned, intelligent Christian.

RELIGIOUS PLURALISM: A NEWLY EXPERIENCED REALITY

Many factors have worked together to make the age-old fact of religious pluralism a newly experienced reality for many today. The most significant factor is also the most obvious: knowledge. Today we in the West know more about other religions than ever before. The science of religions has come a long way since it was founded and given scientific respectability by Max Müller with his publication of *Comparative Mythology* (1856) and, especially, his *Introduction to the Science of Religion* (1873).[1] What was at first esoteric material for the delight of the ivory-towered philologist, lexicologist, phenomenologist, or comparative philosopher has become the popularly written and beautifully illustrated religious paperbacks that fill the shelves of American and European bookstores. Translations of the Bhagavad Gita, the *Tao-Te-Ching*, the *Dhammapada* are to be found alongside the Bible. Commentaries on the meaning and value of Hinduism, Buddhism, Taoism by Huston Smith, Alan Watts, Mircea Eliade are selling just as well—if not better—than the works of Christian theologians. More and more persons have more and more opportunities to learn about religions other than their own. And they are taking advantage of these opportunities.

In the desire to know more about others, Western Christians are motivated by the growing awareness that "they who know one, know none." Widespread interest in other religions has evolved, it seems, beyond its enthusiastic, less critical early phase, in the 1950s and early 60s, when many looked to the East as a panacea for all their personal and religious frustrations.[2] Today, for the most part, religious consumers are much more critical: they do not buy a new product without first carefully checking the ingredients. Yet the desire to learn about other products persists.

This is seen particularly in the continuing popularity of courses in the world religions on undergraduate campuses. Such courses continue to draw students at least as well as standard courses in Christian theology. Yet in studying other religions, students are generally not content simply to learn about teachings or practices—about nirvana, or *Karma* or *Brahman* or the

Tao. They raise, or force the teacher to raise, questions of evaluation, of truth, of comparison with Christian teachings. Even in Christian theology classes, students sense that to know only their own religion is not really to know it. Charles Davis reflects the experience of many a professor of undergraduate theology: "Increasingly it is difficult to raise any religious question among young people without discussing it against a background of all the World Religions . . . students want religious questions not only within the framework of Christian ideas. . . . Religious pluralism has undoubtedly entered into the consciousness of the younger generation."[3]

The knowledge that is making religious pluralism a newly experienced reality is not just a knowledge of other religious systems or ideas. It is also, and especially, a knowledge of other religious *persons*. It is one thing to confront a religious truth in the abstract—on the printed page or in a classroom lecture; it is quite another to see it enfleshed in the life of a friend. That is what is happening in our shrinking world. Not only are ideas migrating, but so are persons. One's neighbors today might be not only Baptists or Jews, but Hindus or Muslims:

> The religious life of mankind from now on, if it is to be lived at all, will be lived in a context of religious pluralism. . . . This is true for all of us; not only for "mankind" in general on an abstract level, but for you and me as individual persons. No longer are people of other persuasions peripheral or distant, the idle curiosities of travelers' tales. The more alert we are, and the more involved in life, the more we are finding that they are our neighbors, our colleagues, our competitors, our fellows. Confucians and Hindus, Buddhists and Muslims, are with us not only in the United Nations, but down the street. Increasingly, not only is our civilization's destiny affected by their actions; but we drink coffee with them personally as well.[4]

Because we are coming so close to each other, "We are learning each other's languages, both literally and figuratively."[5] Anyone who has had such experiences knows what they imply and the questions they raise. To have a friend, a colleague, or a neighbor who has found meaning according to a religious path that apparently is quite different from Christianity not only impresses but disturbs us. A Zen Buddhist who has found peace through a practice that does not even teach the existence of God, or a Hindu who has discovered "salvation" in the realization that there is no essential difference between her and other persons and a tree—what does this mean for *our* lives and *our* beliefs? Such friends, we know, are not religious fanatics. They are normal, happy human beings, getting their jobs done, raising their families as well, perhaps better, than we, and living lives of love, of service, of commitment. We cannot simply sit back and complacently conclude that that is fine for them; we want to learn more about them and about what their lives and beliefs mean for our Christian identities. In this way our "one" Christian religion is feeling the impact of the "many" others.

The impact becomes more pressing when we look carefully at what nineteen centuries of Christian missionary activity have actually accomplished. Certainly the achievements are extensive and laudable. Thanks to the blood and sweat of generations of missioners, the Christian church is "planted" and present on all continents and in almost every nation. Also, as Gandhi recognized, the vision and values of the Nazarene, as contained in the Sermon on the Mount, have notably influenced cultures that staunchly refuse to call themselves Christian. But if we consider the goal of Christian mission to be conversion, the picture becomes less impressive, in fact quite disheartening. After two thousand years of missionary labors, Christians number only about 31 percent of the world population. If present demographic trends continue, with the bulk of the population explosion taking place in non-Western, non-Christian nations, some experts predict that by the year 2000, Christians will number only 16 percent of the world population.[6]

We are confronted with further sobering reflections when we consider just who has been and is being converted to Christianity: "Superstitious folk religions and religious decadence were essentially what fell before Christianity's remarkable advance in the Mediterranean and European worlds when the faith staked its claim to what is now the seat of Christian cultural tradition. It is this kind of field that is always whitest for the Christian harvest."[7] Admitting the ethnocentric overtones in dubbing any religion "superstitious," we have to face the facts of the history of Christian missions: the vast majority of converts have come from polytheistic or animistic religions or from religions that had already lost their personal hold on the hearts of their peoples. When confronted by living religions, especially if they are undergirded by some kind of intellectual system, Christian missionaries have had practically no success at conversions.

A noted church historian sums it up: by the twentieth century, Christianity "had made relatively few converts from Islam, Hinduism, and Buddhism."[8] The major world religions continue to stand alongside Christianity as the many versus the one! What does this signify for a religion that has considered itself the one true religion, destined by God to embrace all peoples?

At the same time that Christians are admitting that centuries of missionary toil have not been able to remove the reality of religious pluralism, they witness, to their further dismay, a resurgence of missionary élan among these other religions. Hindus, Buddhists, and Muslims are claiming that their message, like that of Christianity, bears a "universal relevance." They want to make their own contribution to the unfolding modern world, and they feel that theirs might be more meaningful than much of what official Christianity has propagated and achieved. So other world religions are sending forth their own missioners to compete in the mission fields and even to take up their stations in the backyards of Christianity—in New York, San Francisco, Chicago, Cincinnati.

This missionary outreach was evidenced as early as 1893, at the World Parliament of Religions in Chicago, when Swami Vivekananda, a disciple of Ramakrishna, presented Hinduism as a universal faith for all humankind. His work and vision continue in the thirteen centers of the Vedanta Society spread across the United States. The same sense of universal relevance animates the neo-Vedantist reappraisal of Hinduism under the inspiration of the mystic-philosopher Sri Aurobindo and of the Oxford scholar and statesman S. Radhakrishnan.

The renewed intent of Buddhism to proclaim the universal *Dharma* for all was seen in 1952 when U Thaken Nu, prime minister of Burma, built the World Peace Pagoda in Burma and proclaimed that Buddhism had a message for the political woes of the world. The 1961 Conference of the World Federation of Buddhists manifested a missionary zeal that matches the great Christian missionary councils of this century. Today there are Buddhist or Zen centers in almost every major city of America. The founding of the Naropa Institute in Boulder, Colorado, in 1974, as an accredited institution of higher learning, attests to the intellectual and critical foundations of the Buddhist outreach to America.

Political and economic developments of recent years have given clear and perhaps disturbing witness to Muslims' renewed sense of Islamic identity and presence in the modern world. Behind the sometimes fanatical expressions of this Islamic resurgence, there are also the efforts of many Muslim scholars and faithful to work out a more dialogical, cooperative presentation of their message.

One should be slow to speak about Hindu or Buddhist "missionaries" here in the United States. As they would want to make clear, the purpose of their presence among us is primarily not to convert but to communicate—to add their melodies to the religious music of the West. Yet, the fact that they are among us with a renewed sense of purpose and the fact that we are hearing their voices constitute a new experience of religious pluralism that seems to be signaling a new era in the religious history of the world:

> The religious history of mankind is taking as monumental a turn in our century as has the political or economic, if only we could see it. And the upsurge of a vibrant and self-assertive new religious orientation of Buddhists and Hindus and the like evinces a new phase not merely in the history of those particular traditions, but in the history of the whole complex of man's religiousness, of which the Christian is a part, and an increasingly participant part.[9]

The new perception of religious pluralism is pushing our cultural consciousness toward the simple but profound insight that *there is no one and only way*. The force of this realization applies not only to religions but also to cultures, philosophies, economic systems. "Today, the universe of meaning has no center."[10] To put it more personally, we are facing the reality that "I (my reason, my consciousness, my being, my nation, my religion) do not exhaust the real nor am I its center—but only one of its poles, if anything at all. There are others.''[11]

The new awareness of multiplicity, of pluralism, is being felt not just as a provisional situation or a stopgap admission that we have to tolerate until we can come up with a masterplan that will herd all these "other" sheep into one corral. Pluralism does not result simply from the limitations of the human mind to "get it all together." Rather, pluralism seems to be of the very stuff of reality, the way things are, the way they function. Without multiplicity, without the many others, our world—from atoms to molecules to plants to bugs to humans—would not be able to function and exist. Reality is essentially pluriform: complex, rich, intricate, mysterious. "Pluralism is not the mere justification of opinions, but the realization that the real is more than the sum of all possible opinions.''[12]

In a sense, then, we shall never be able to get it all together. There can never be just one of anything. We sense this today. And this is why we are wary of any person or movement that presents itself as the one and only, or the final word. The one-way road is most likely the road to destruction. Perhaps this is the abiding meaning of the story of the Tower of Babel; the Lord God warned against the havoc inherent in all dreams or projects for a monolithic, one-way vision of reality.

And yet our new awareness of pluralism also makes us recognize that even though there can be no *one way*, even though there will always be *many*, nevertheless the "many" cannot simply exist as many. We feel that the many cannot exist in splendid isolation, yawning at each other in a kind of lazy, indifferent tolerance. Nor can they exist in angry opposition, confronting each other down the barrels of their guns or from behind the launch pads of their missiles. Somehow, they must meet each other and relate to each other, not in order to obliterate or absorb each other but to learn from and help each other. The words of the early American patriots assume a new and more urgent meaning in our pluralistic world: unless we—the many in our many-ness—hang together, we shall hang separately. So pluralism becomes not just a fact to be recognized, but a challenge to be achieved:

> Pluralism is today a human existential problem which raises acute questions about how we are going to live our lives in the midst of so many options. Pluralism is no longer just the old schoolbook question about the One-and-the-Many; it has become the concrete day-to-day dilemma occasioned by the encounter of mutually incompatible worldviews and philosophies. Today we face pluralism as the very practical question of planetary human coexistence.[13]

In our contemporary pluralistic world, therefore, we sense that if there cannot be *one* religion, neither can there simply be *many*. In the next section of this chapter I shall take a look at why many persons today are urging a new kind of unity among the many religions of the world—a *unitive pluralism* of religions.

THE POSSIBILITY AND NECESSITY OF A UNITIVE PLURALISM OF RELIGIONS

"Unitive pluralism" is a rather ambiguous term. Its meaning can be clarified by reviewing the reasons why many today are arguing that it is not only possible but necessary. The arguments for a unitive pluralism among religions can be summarized according to their basic starting points: philosophy, sociology-psychology, and politics-economics.

Philosophy: The Processive-Relational View of Reality

Today a major movement in philosophy is articulating, in typically complex jargon, a vision of reality that many ordinary persons sense to be true of their individual lives: that the world and everything in it is *evolutionary* or *in process*. The catch phrase is that we are not in a state of *being* but in a state, or better a process, of *becoming*. Nothing in the world is simply given, or prefabricated, merely to be assembled according to a predetermined plan. Rather, we and everything around us are caught up in a process of constant change, of movement, of exploration into newness. This is not a brand new insight on the stage of human thought; twenty-five hundred years ago, Heraclitus observed that "everything flows" and that we cannot step into the same river twice. Today modern thinkers are restating Heraclitus's theme more radically, and with greater clarity and persuasiveness. Among such contemporary restatements are Alfred North Whitehead's and Charles Hartshorne's vision of a world involved in an adventure of creativity through process; Teilhard de Chardin's universe evolving painfully but steadily from the biosphere to the noosphere to the unity of the Omega Point; Bernard Lonergan's "emergent probability of world order"; Aurobindo's Hindu vision of a world in evolution toward divinity.[14]

The vision these thinkers present is radically different from the worldview that guided the mind and imagination of Western civilization for most of its existence. For the majority of Europeans throughout the Middle Ages and into the Renaissance, creation came forth from the hand of God as a finished product, stable, and hierarchically ordered. One was not to tamper with this order. Humans were to keep their place in relation to God. Within the divinely constituted order of things, social classes were also to keep their places; God willed serfs to be serfs and lords to be lords.

Of course, change took place, but it was never anything radical or essential. Acorns became oak trees, children became adults. It was more a matter of natural growth of the given rather than evolution of the really new. Radical change in the world was reserved for the end of time. Even the first scientific model of the universe, that of Isaac Newton, viewed physical reality as a well-wrought machine, functioning according to definable and unchangeable laws. An unalterable, God-given "natural law" ruled over the world of humans and of atoms.

A confluence of many events and discoveries changed this image of an unchangeable world. The profound disruptions of the French Revolution and the industrial revolution set persons thinking that the social order might not be as unalterable and divinely established as they had thought. Even more disruptive of the stability of things was Darwin's discovery of biological evolution. His *Origin of Species* demanded that creation, if it was to be believed in at all, be seen not as a one-time event but as a continuous process, still unfinished and undetermined.

Then came the insights and discoveries of the "new physics," pioneered by Albert Einstein, which over a period of twenty to thirty years thoroughly remodeled the Newtonian universe. Reality was no longer seen as a well-ordered machine, made up of discrete parts neatly linked to each other. Rather, it was a buzz of activity, of constant process, in which the parts could not even be neatly determined and located. At its deepest, subatomic level, the world did not seem to show any "basic building blocks" or "beings," but rather an intricate, ever changing, and interrelating process of activity or becoming.

It was especially the new physics that prompted philosophers to a further insight into the way things are: if everything is a becoming rather than a being, the becoming takes place through *interrelating*. If we can be only if we become, we can become only if we reach out and relate. Nothing, whether an electron or a human being, can be "an island unto itself." Modern psychology is also trying to draw out the mind-boggling implications of this essentially interrelated quality of all reality. "We are our relationships" has become almost a cliché. It is difficult to grasp this as literally true, for we still look upon things as substances rather than events; we deem ourselves primarily individuals rather than partners.

The very structure of our language prevents us from grasping that we *are* our relationships. We begin our thinking and speaking with nouns that are then followed by verbs; the subject generally must precede the predicate. If we could speak and feel the language of the Hopi Indians, which is made up primarily of verbs that serve as nouns, we might be closer to the way we and the world really are. We are not first of all individuals who later relate; rather it is our relating—how we do it and with whom or what—that makes us (or gives us the semblance of being) individuals. We are not "becomings" but "becomings with." Cut off the "with" and we cease to exist. This interrelated quality of our existence is as real as it is beyond neat conceptual analysis and clear statement. In physicist David Bohm's terminology, we and the world are all part of an "implicate order," an infinitely complex and dynamic web of interrelationships.[15]

These thinkers view the multiplicity, the plurality, of creation as empowered with a potential for ever greater unity, even though many of them do not feel able to say just where this potential will end up. The many are called to be one. But it is a one that does not devour the many. The many become one precisely by remaining the many, and the one is brought about by each of the many making its distinct contribution to the others and thus to the whole. It is a process that aims at an ever more pervasive concentration of the many in each other and thus in a greater whole. Whereas individualization is weakened, personalization is intensified; the individual finds its true self as part of other selves. So there is a movement not toward absolute or monistic oneness but toward what may be called "unitive pluralism": plurality constituting unity. But is all this a dream, a product of poetic rapture? Perhaps. As we shall see, today we may have no choice but to dream this dream and try to make it reality.

All of the above is familiar to devotees of Teilhard and to readers of process philosophy/theology or of philosopher-scientists such as Fritjof Capra.[16] But what does it mean for the religions of the world? Anyone for whom this philosophical model of becoming through relating makes sense will find in it a lens to interpret the new experience of religious pluralism described in the first section of this chapter. The world religions are confronting each other as never before and they are experiencing a new sense of identity and purpose because they, like atoms and humans and cultures, are moving toward a more pervasive unity through better relationships with each other. They are being urged by what seems to be the creative lure within all reality toward a new form of unity, a unitive pluralism.

Unitive pluralism is a *new* understanding of religious unity and must not be confused with the old, rationalistic idea of "one world religion" in either of its alternate brand names. The new vision of religious unity is not *syncretism*, which boils away all the historical differences between religions in order to institutionalize their common core; nor is it *imperialism*, which believes that there is one religion that has the power of purifying and then absorbing all the others.[17] Nor is it a form of lazy tolerance that calls upon all religions to recognize each other's validity and then to ignore each other as they go their own self-satisfied ways. Rather, unitive pluralism is a unity in which each religion, although losing some of its individualism (its separate ego), will intensify its personality (its self-awareness through relationship). Each religion will retain its own uniqueness, but this uniqueness will develop and take on new depths by relating to other religions in mutual dependence.

Again, for the moment, we find ourselves asking whether this is but a fanciful dream.

Sociology-Psychology: Personal Identity through World Citizenship

The dream appears less fanciful in the light of new perspectives from sociology and social psychology. These perspectives emanate from a renewed grappling with the timeworn problem of the individual and society. How can individuals truly attain their own personal identity and at the same time be part of and conform to the demands of society? Today, thanks to psychologists and educators such as Lawrence Kohlberg, we are realizing the importance of moving from a "conventional" to a "postconventional" understanding of identity and morality.

Conventional personal identity is basically that of children: I obey, I take on rules or values in order to be rewarded with acceptance and mommy and daddy's love. The values, although they may be sound, are not truly my own. Neither is my identity. Postconventional self-identity urges persons to grow up and accept values and roles freely, intelligently, critically. The truth or goodness of what I choose to do and be will be determined not by its payoff or by its conformity to what the neighbors, boss, or parents expect; it will be true in itself. Truth and value will have a *universal* quality, independent of what society expects or demands of me. Recognized as universal by me, it will be my truth and value, my identity.[18]

Persons today, however, are realizing that such an understanding of postconventional identity is not enough. Social analysts such as those of the Frankfurt School of "critical theory" warn that within this new and needed stress on personal freedom and appropriation there lies the cancer of a destructive individualism, both personal and national. The danger is that in determining the true and good for and by myself, it becomes only *my* truth and *my* good, and loses its universal quality. The criteria for determining truth all too easily become how truth will benefit me, my identity; how it affects and possibly harms others is not considered. The possibility of self-deception and self-serving becomes all the more subtly pernicious when, with these criteria for truth, an individual nation seeks its own postconventional identity. What makes sense, what works for one nation or culture, all too readily is proclaimed universally true, binding for all other nations. The proclamation of such truth to other nations easily becomes a tool for exploiting them.

Charles Davis, following the critical theorist Jürgen Habermas, urges that if our postconventional personal identity is going to be genuinely based on *universal* values, our identities must be "universalistic." This means that in our contemporary world we cannot attain values that will be valuable for all if we stay only within the backyard of our own culture or nation. We have to step out of our backyard or neighborhood and, together with persons on the other side of the tracks or ocean, strive for values that can ground our collective identities. Without this effort at universal communication and cooperation, we cannot avoid deceiving ourselves and hurting each other:

> Human society today cannot achieve a rational identity within the boundaries of any permanent collective body, with its particular territory or organization. Our basic social identity cannot come from membership in a stable collective entity, confronting us as fixed objective reality. Such a social identity is incompatible with our universalistic

personal identity. Instead of consisting in membership of a fixed collective body, collective identity at its basic level lies in a process of universal communication, uniting human beings without distinction in the shaping of a new collective will, in the creation of new collective identities at the level of concrete action, in the formation of a new global order.[19]

This means that today, in order to be good citizens of any one nation we have to be *world citizens*.

Wilfred Cantwell Smith argues the same point when he insists that true knowledge, knowledge that will bring life, is not a matter of cold, individual objectivity but can result only from what he terms "critical, corporate self-consciousness." Self-consciousness, or personal identity, must be critical; we have to apply our intelligence and reason. But it must also be corporate, or what he calls "global" or "transcultural"; we also have to use the experience and intelligence of others. "True knowledge, in human affairs, is that knowledge that all intelligent men and women . . . can share, and can jointly verify, by observation and by participation. True human knowledge is disciplined and corporate self-consciousness."[20] Truth that is truth only for me, in which others cannot participate and thereby profit from, is a very suspicious truth. Smith puts it succinctly: "the truth of all of us is part of the truth of each of us."[21]

If we take these notions of "universalistic personal identity" and of "critical, corporate self-consciousness" seriously, we find that on the practical day-to-day level our attitude toward strangers is drastically changed. The stranger, the new face, the man with the turban or the woman of a different skin color, will no longer appear to us as a threat or an adversary but as a partner and friend. We will come to feel that as long as there are strangers— persons we do not know—we really do not know ourselves. "Once the assumption that the stranger is inferior is shattered, then he is experienced *as* a stranger. And once you admit that you do not understand *him*, you are gradually forced to admit that you do not understand yourself."[22] Gradually but with mounting urgency, we are realizing today that in order to answer the perennial question "Who am I?", we have to ask the question "Who are you?":

And this is a radically different question, for it not only cannot be answered without *you*, but it requires you as a fellow-questioner . . . and the "you" is the Pygmy, and the Muslim, and the woman, and the Communist, and the Christian, and the Democrat, and the wife, and the worker, and the poor. . . . How can we pretend to deal with the ultimate problem of Man if we insist on reducing the human being to only the American, or to only the Christian, or to the black, or the male, or the exclusively heterosexual, or the healthy and "normal," or the so-called civilized.[23]

Such realizations can be threatening. In experiencing the need and the unsettling complexity of learning from and living with strangers, many persons today are giving up the effort and are building even higher fences around their own backyards. There is a resurgent nationalism in many countries today. In a certain sense, this is not entirely unhealthy, for we need "roots," we need to know and appreciate our own culture as we try to learn from others. In attempting to understand the universality of cultures, we can find ourselves not really understanding any one of them. We need a clear grasp of who we are before we can expand and correct that grasp in learning about others. Becoming a world citizen does not and cannot mean giving up our original citizenship.

But the greater danger in the world of today seems to be that we will, in fear or pride, so cling to our own identities and our own nation that we will refuse to learn from the stranger. And a world of strangers is a world of enemies. If our divided world is not to go up in smoke, if it is truly to become a global village, then we must become world citizens. We must find our personal identities with others. The greatest threat to that need is nationalism and ethnocentrism. "The 100 percent American, or Russian, or what have you, is an enemy to all of us. We need an element of world citizenship in each person."[24]

What this newly recognized need for world citizenship implies for the religions of the world is evident: members of one religion must to some extent be members of other religions. Just as persons today are becoming aware that they cannot achieve an authentic personal identity unless they open themselves to free exchange and dialogue with others, so religious persons are sensing that they cannot really understand their own religious identities and their own religion unless they enter into communication with other religions. It is becoming clear how hidebound and naive and arrogant we can be when we never step out of our own temples or churches. To answer the question "Who is my God?", we must ask the question "Who is your God?"

This need to be open to others focuses a contemporary religious problem for many Christians. They feel that although so much of the rest of culture is struggling for a universalistic identity, their own religion is still dominated very much by a conventional religious identity. This introduces a certain schizophrenic tension in the self-awareness of many Christians; the contemporary world calls them to world citizenship, but their preachers or priests speak the language of "one and only" and of missionary conquest.

In face of the new experience of pluralism, especially religious pluralism, many churches are reacting with a kind of religious nationalism. In a world of so many differing opinions and of so many "gray areas," religion is becoming the one refuge of absolute certainty, of black and white, unchangeable truth. Such religious nationalism does provide a warm security blanket, but it does so, frequently, at the cost of a fanaticism that impedes any kind of personally appropriated faith and appears as an insult to human intelligence and integrity.

A religious world citizenship or a postconventional religious identity does not and must not rule out belonging to one's own religion. We need religious roots, too. A kind of "religious space trip" by which we try to cruise mystically above all religious traditions without belonging to any one of them does not permit serious religious commitment and living. To be religious and to be serious about it one must, generally, belong to a religion.

But a universalistic belonging to one religion is different from the traditional, conventional belonging. Charles Davis describes what it entails:

> A postconventional or universalistic religious identity is therefore realized when people, belonging to a religious tradition, but not tied to its fixed contents or forms, engage as free, autonomous persons in a process of unrestricted and unconstrained communication with others of the same tradition, of other traditions, or of no tradition on matters concerning religion with the aim of achieving agreement, not conformity.[25]

Universalistic religious identity, in other words, is another way of describing the unitive pluralism to which world religions today are being summoned. It is a new form of religious unity in which each religion maintains but discovers anew its own identity in and with other religions. Is the dream taking on greater substance?

Politics and Economics: The Need for a New International Order

In view of the present political and economic condition of our world, many are urging that this dream of a new unity among religions *must* take on greater substance. Anyone who reads the newspapers and follows the daily news cannot avoid, at least occasionally, the leaden feeling that somehow the world has gone amuck. There is a gnawing fear that the growing and ever more confusing tensions between nations and "isms" are suddenly going to blow up in a planetary conflagration. We know the problems too well: starvation and malnutrition, economic inequality, dwindling resources, exploitation and poverty, official flouting of human rights. And over all this tinder hovers the flame of nuclear weaponry.

In the opinion of many, the maladies afflicting our globe grow from a sick international system that cannot be remedied by Band-Aids and aspirin but only by radical surgery.[26] We are not indulging in doomsday prophecy when we find ourselves asking whether biological and human-cultural evolution has brought us to a critical juncture where the very survival of humankind and the planet are at stake. Something must be done. Important decisions must be made, decisions that will construct a new world order.

The central vision of this new order, as it is described by various prophets of hope, is captured in a children's story, *Dinosaurs and All that Rubbish*. The story deals with a man who devastated the earth so that he could build a rocket and travel to a better planet. After he departs, some dinosaurs, which had been asleep for ages under the ground, rebuild the earth into a planet flourishing in greenery and abundance. The man in his rocket, meanwhile, finds himself on a futile journey: all the other planets are barren.

He finally finds one that is green and beautiful and cared for by dinosaurs. In amazement, he realizes that this planet is the earth he left in devastation. Desperately he pleads with the dinosaurs for a small plot to live on, ". . . just a hill, or a tree, or a flower." Their answer summarizes the spirit of the new world order: "No," said the dinosaur.

> Not a part of it,
> but all of it.
> It is all yours,
> but it is also mine.
> Remember that.
> This time the earth belongs to everyone,
> not part of it to certain people
> but all of it to everyone
> to be enjoyed and cared for.[27]

The new world order envisions a world in which the earth does belong to all, a world in which the nations will assume values and structures that can change the economics of greed into the economics of community, a world in which each nation will finally realize that it can prosper only when it respects and promotes the prospering of other nations. It will be a world order in which the many communities of individual nations truly form a *community of communities*.[28] In this community, the word "we" will take on a new meaning; when persons say "we," they will no longer mean just their family, their neighborhood, their country. To say "we" will mean to speak in behalf of and to feel all humankind. Only if such a community of communities takes form out of our present fractured and feuding international order does our future seem possible.

World citizenship, described in the previous section, now is seen not only as a psychological need but as an economic and political imperative. But can such a new world order be fashioned? Has it not been the unfulfilled dream of humanity for the last few centuries?

Unrealized hopes do not mean unrealizeable hopes. Today the necessity of a new world order presses more than ever. It is the imposing task of politicians, philosophers, economists. Yet history seems to attest that the efforts of such specialists, although necessary, are not enough by themselves. W.C. Smith speaks for many:

> My own view is that the task of constructing even that minimum degree
> of world fellowship that will be necessary for man to survive at all is far
> too great to be accomplished on any other than a religious basis. From
> no other source than his faith, I believe, can man muster the energy,

devotion, vision, resolution, capacity to survive disappointment, that will be necessary—that *are* necessary—for this challenge.[29]

Certainly the hard work of social and economic analysis, the sagacity of political diplomacy, the charism of inspired leaders will all be absolutely necessary in struggling toward this community of communities. But what is equally and perhaps primarily necessary is that all these efforts be grounded in and inspired by religious symbols and myths that will ensure the value of the individual, the meaningfulness of justice and love, the vision of common fellowship in common origins, and especially the promise that our efforts to promote the unity of humanity will bear fruit, even if they cost us our lives.

A number of scientists and philosopher-theologians make use of the implications of biological evolution to argue the necessity of a religious basis for a new stage in the evolution of humanity. From the genes of our animal ancestors, we humans have inherited aggression toward outsiders and loyalties toward our own kin, both of which were essential for the survival and development of the most viable genotypes. In the earliest stages of animal-human evolution, a certain survival of the fittest through aggression was necessary if there was to be survival and advancement at all. Today, however, as biological evolution has given rise to cultural evolution and as cultural evolution has advanced from kinship interdependencies to the interdependence of nations, the conditions for survival have changed.

Now cultures and nations will survive not by aggression and dominance but by cooperation. Yet we are still burdened with our aggressive, selfish genes. This is where the world religions enter the process of evolution. They will provide not the "genotypes" but the "culturetypes"—not the new genes but the new social values—that will enable humans to overcome their natural selfishness and ethnocentrism. All the major world religions extol the value of self-sacrificing love for others; all contain symbols of the universal unity of humankind. The stage is now set for them to make their evolutionary contributions.[30]

To make their contributions they must work together. But here many will rightly object: this is precisely what the religions of the world have not done in the past nor are doing in the present. Former Secretary of State Cyrus Vance expressed the feelings of many when (in a talk at the Interreligious Peace Colloquium, 1975) he voiced his anger and dismay that "given the presumed strength of the religious community throughout the world, we should go from crisis to crisis, from conflagration to conflagration—that the religious community should have such apparently ineffective input into the management of our global village."[31] Efforts toward a new collaboration among religions must be preceded and inspired by a humble confession that, in the past and present, the world religions have contributed devastatingly to the division of humankind.

This egocentric, aggressive posture was perhaps unavoidable in the earlier stages of religious evolution when each religion had to establish its own identity and unity. Today, however, the need for a world community compels the religions to revive their inner visions of love and common fellowship. Whatever their divisions and aggressions of the past, world religions share something today that calls them and binds them together: "What the various religious traditions have in common is the fact that each is being carried today by persons who increasingly are involved in the same problems. Christians, Jews, Buddhists, Hindus, Muslims, and the others are all faced today, for the first time, by a joint challenge: to collaborate in building a common world."[32] Their common task is rendered all the more urgent by the consideration that their contribution may be the essential added ingredient or the catalyst necessary for the success of the politicians and the social engineers.

If this contribution is to be effective, it must be made together, by all the religions in collaboration. This means they must respect each other, learn from and dialogue with each other. Only if they form and then work out of a community of communities among themselves can they generate such a community among the nations. A unitive pluralism of religions, then, seems to be imperative.

THREATS AND OPPORTUNITIES FOR CHRISTIANS

The newly experienced multiplicity of religions has inserted itself into cultural awareness, and the vision of a unitive pluralism of religions excites the imaginations of many. Many Christians find themselves eagerly resonating with this new situation and vision. They spontaneously affirm the possibility—yes, the necessity—of a new form of unity among religions, and they want to add their efforts to the task of realizing it.

But such spontaneity is usually short-lived. When Christians step back from the glowing vision of a unitive pluralism of religions and more soberly relate its implications to their own Christian beliefs, they easily find themselves feeling uncomfortable, even threatened. The new vision of religious unity, they realize, does not seem to harmonize with what they believe about Christianity and Christ. Can they participate in efforts toward unitive pluralism and still honestly call themselves Christians? These new threats and new questions have to be faced squarely.

The Threats

The first barrage of threats comes from the newly experienced fact that there *are* so many other religions. Thinking Christians, aware of their beliefs, must ask the simple question: Why? Why are there so many religions? Why are they continuing with renewed life and identity? Why are so many millions of persons finding God outside Christ and Christianity—and doing a very good job of it?

Karl Rahner states boldly the Christian beliefs that give rise to these questions:

Because of Jesus Christ, Christianity understands itself as the absolute religion, intended for all men, which cannot recognize any other religion beside itself as of equal right. . . . This pluralism is a greater threat and a reason for greater unrest for Christianity than for any other religion. For no other religion—not even Islam—maintains so absolutely that it is *the* religion, the one and only valid revelation of the one living God as does the Christian religion. The fact of the pluralism of religions, which endures and still from time to time becomes virulent and even after a history of 2000 years, must therefore be the greatest scandal and the greatest vexation for Christianity.[33]

These threats become all the more insistent and painful in the light of the nature and demands of unitive pluralism. Can Christianity really take part in an interreligious dialogue that recognizes the possibility that other religions may be ways of salvation just as much as is Christianity? Can Christians admit that they may have just as much to learn from other religions as other religions do from Christianity? Can Christianity be open to the possibility that other religions are not meant to be converted to Christ and that they will continue to be just as valid and important as is Christianity? It seems that genuine efforts toward unitive pluralism demand a yes to all these questions. Yet Christians feel that they cannot give voice to this yes as much as they would like to.

The stumbling block seems to be the central Christian belief in the uniqueness of Christ. The fundamental premise of unitive pluralism is that all religions are, or can be, equally valid. This means that their founders, the religious figures behind them, are or can be equally valid. But that would open up the possibility that Jesus Christ is "one among many" in the world of saviors and revealers. Such a recognition, for the Christian, is simply not allowed. Or is it?

Unavoidable Questions and Opportunities

One of the most pressing tasks confronting Christian theology today is that of providing *an account of the existence and the renewed vitality of other religions*—in other words, a theology of world religions. If the role of theology is to focus the light of scripture and tradition on the unfolding history of human experience, then the new experience of religious pluralism demands some kind of Christian interpretation. This must be done not merely to satisfy the abstract requirements of theological methodology, but because many Christians, with increasing discomfort, are feeling and asking new questions about the meaning of other religions. W. C. Smith does not understate the task facing Christian theology:

How does one account, theologically, for the fact of man's religious diversity? This is really as big an issue, almost, as the question of how one accounts theologically for evil—but Christian theologians have been much more conscious of the fact of evil than that of religious pluralism. . . . From now on any serious intellectual statement of the Christian faith must include, if it is to serve its purpose among men, some sort of doctrine of other religions. We explain the fact that the Milky Way is there by the doctrine of creation, but how do we explain the fact that the Bhagavad Gita is there?[34]

A theology of other religions will have to be worked out primarily on the basis of Christian tradition—that is, in light of what the gospel reveals concerning the nature and value of other religions. But it will also require that the theologian have some knowledge of the other religions. As we shall see more clearly in subsequent chapters, the day when Christian theologians could go about their trade equipped only with a knowledge of Christianity, without any acquaintance with other religious traditions, is fast fading—if it has not faded away already.[35]

In the face of religious pluralism, Christian theology will not only have to elaborate an account of these other religions; it will also have to render a new account of *itself*. Herein lie the more difficult questions and therefore the greater opportunities. Most of these questions hover around the traditional self-understanding of Christianity as unique, exclusive, superior, definitive, normative, absolute. It is the old question posed by the pagan philosopher Symmachus to St. Ambrose in A.D. 384: If the Christian God is indeed a God of love who desires all to be saved, why did that God wait so long to send the savior? Why have human beings been allowed to seek God along so many different paths for such a long time? The question, in our age, is posed anew and with greater urgency. Perhaps, therefore, new answers can be hoped for.

As already implied, the question of the uniqueness of Christianity cannot be taken up seriously without facing the more delicate question of the uniqueness of Christ. Is he the only revealer, the definitive revelation of God? Is he the *only* Savior, the *only* Son of God, the *only* incarnation? These are questions that, for all their delicacy and "impropriety," are pressing on the consciousness of many Christians. Again, can we hope for new answers that will not violate the content of Christian tradition and identity?

A New Kairos *for Christianity*

Kairos, especially as used by Paul Tillich, signifies those special moments in time that are different from ordinary time (*chronos*). It is a point in history when, because of the particular constellation of events and personalities, genuinely new possibilities and advances are latent. A *kairos* is not just a situation; it is also an opportunity. If we miss a *kairos*, we miss something very important. A burden of responsibility is tied into the recognition of a *kairos*.

The genuinely new situation of religious pluralism, with its vision of a possible unitive pluralism of world religions, presents such a *kairos* for Christianity today. In assessing the new experience of many religions and in attempting to reassess itself in the light of a genuine dialogue with them, Christianity is offered the opportunity for genuine growth and evolution, and for understanding the gospel message anew, in a way in which the power of the gospel can shine forth in fresh and more understandable forms. To miss this opportunity would mean to put the light of the gospel under a bushel basket and to make the good news more difficult to believe.

To propose a *new* understanding of the gospel and of Christian tradition is not a novelty. Throughout its long life, Christianity has always been profoundly dependent on the ever changing contexts of history. It is not simply that Christianity affects the world; the world really affects Christianity as well. The church relates to and seeks to transform the world not merely by applying a well-defined deposit of truth to changing historical contexts; nor does the church simply utilize the concepts of a new situation or culture in order to give expression to an already possessed truth—as if the truth were already clear and merely needed a new medium. In a real sense, the medium *is*, or at least reveals, the content of the truth. The church learns from the world. Christianity and Christian truth are, therefore, evolving with the evolving world. As the church tries to speak to the world, it grows and changes with it. And just as the evolution of the world is one of "discontinuity within continuity," Christianity will find its vitality in *eternal* truths that are eternally *new*.

The history of the church shows how true this is. When the early community moved from its first cultural context, that of Judaism, into the Greco-Roman world, it underwent a far-reaching transformation. It was a transformation not only in the liturgical, sacramental life of the church and in the structures of its organization and legislation, but also in its *doctrine*—that is, in the *understanding* of the revelation that had given birth to it. The early Christians did not simply express in Greek thought what they already knew; rather, they discovered, through Greek religious and philosophical insights, what had been revealed to them. The doctrines of the trinity and of the divinity of Christ (the hypostatic union), for example, would not be what they are today if the church had not reassessed itself and its doctrines in the light of the new historical, cultural situations during the third through the sixth centuries. Similar if less radical transformations and reassessments took place as Christianity migrated into the Germanic cultures of northern Europe. Another reassessment occurred when Aquinas adapted Christian doctrine to the "pagan" philosophy and worldview of Aristotle.

Raimundo Panikkar's summarizing remarks on the history of Christianity are accurate: "History shows that precisely where the Christian message succeeded in transforming a society it was never because of 'utilization,' but because of a very deep assimilation—the Christian word for it being incarnation—into the particular religion and culture."[36]

So I am not out of step with history when I suggest that the Christian church, as it confronts a world of religious pluralism and interreligious dialogue, is perhaps experiencing a *kairos* with as great a promise of self-transformation as the *kairos* experienced in confronting the Greco-Roman world. A number of Christian theologians speak in precisely these tones. Geoffrey Parrinder views the dialogue with Eastern religions as a "third reformation," following upon the Reformation of the sixteenth century, when Luther challenged Christianity, and the second reformation in the nineteenth century, when science invaded Christian consciousness.[37] Canon Max Warren, former secretary general of the Church Missionary Society in London, argued that "the impact of agnostic science will turn out to be child's play compared to the challenge to Christian theology of the faiths of other men."[38] Missiologist Walbert Bühlmann entitled one of his recent books *The Coming of the Third Church*; in it he argues that the church must prepare itself for radical transformation as the bulk of its population and influence moves outside its traditional North Atlantic boundaries into the cultures and religions of the Third World.[39]

Karl Rahner harmonizes with Bühlmann when he suggests that what really began in the Second Vatican Council, even though most bishops and theologians did not fully realize it, was the first step toward the evolution of a truly "world church." This world church will make up what Rahner calls the "third stage" in the history of Christianity. The first stage was the church in its Judaic form, as found in the earliest period of the New Testament; the second stage was the church transformed into Greco-Roman, European (or Western) culture—a stage that, for the most part, has characterized Christianity for most of its history. The third stage, or world church, will be the church as it incarnates and reassesses itself within new cultures and enters into dialogue with Islam and Eastern religions. Rahner warns us that this will be a new church—not *totally* new, but *genuinely* new.[40]

As Christians face genuinely new and uncomfortable questions in their experience of and dialogue with other religions today, they can also expect new answers. The door is open to new understandings of the "uniqueness" of Christianity and of Jesus Christ. The rest of this book will try to illustrate how Christian theologians, over the past century, have struggled (or refused to struggle) with these new questions and answers.

PART I

POPULAR ATTITUDES TOWARD RELIGIOUS PLURALISM

As we have seen in the previous chapter, the recognition of many different religions has become part of general cultural awareness. This awareness has given rise to a variety of popular attitudes as to why there are so many different religions or what constitutes the differences. One encounters these attitudes throughout our culture—from the popular press to casual living room conversations. Naturally, Christians are influenced, perhaps more than they are aware, by such cultural attitudes. It is therefore not only helpful but necessary to take a critical look at these popular views before moving on, in Part 2, to the explicitly Christian responses to religious pluralism.

Popular attitudes toward religious diversity can be classified according to three different but allied camps: 1) all religions are relative; 2) all are essentially the same; 3) all have a common psychological origin. The following pages will study the historical, philosophical roots of each view. To give this study a concrete focus, each view will be presented through the eyes of a particular thinker who stands either as its "father" or its especially eloquent advocate. The three attitudes will be described as objectively and persuasively as possible. Some critical reflections will follow each description: how the three attitudes challenge Christian consciousness and how they themselves might be challenged by Christian belief or by deeper implications of religious pluralism.

Chapter II

All Are Relative

"You can't say that one is better than another." That is one of the most widespread and deeply engrained popular attitudes toward the diversity of religions in the world of today. All religions are relative—that is, limited, partial, incomplete, one way of looking at things. To hold that any religion is intrinsically better than another is felt to be somehow wrong, offensive, narrowminded. Or, if one holds that a particular religion is "better" than another, one must immediately add "for me" or "for them." "Christianity is the best religion for Christians. Hinduism is the best religion for Hindus." To make any kind of universal claims of validity or normativity for any one religion over another rubs against the grain of popular consciousness.

The many who share this view usually cannot say why they feel it so deeply. In this chapter, therefore, I shall try to study the roots of *Historical Relativism* so as to be better able to understand and evaluate it.

A philosopher-theologian named Ernst Troeltsch (1865-1923) will be our case study. As committed a critical thinker as he was a Christian believer, Troeltsch was among the first to recognize the reality of religious and historical pluralism and to feel painfully how it clashed with what he had learned about the nature of Christianity. He struggled resolutely with this problem throughout most of his life. The solution that he finally reached has come to be accepted, for the most part, by the Western world. In following him through these struggles, we not only grasp more fully the content of historical relativism; we can also better understand our own struggles. Much of what we feel concerning religious pluralism is mirrored in Ernst Troeltsch.

ERNST TROELTSCH: ADVOCATE FOR MANY

Ernst Troeltsch was certainly, in the terminology of Vatican II, in touch with "the signs of the times." Professor of theology and philosophy at the Universities of Bonn, Heidelberg, and Berlin, he did not limit his interests to his fields of specialization. His writings include a wide range of concerns: sociology, history, historiography, culture, social ethics. He also carried on an active political life and was once mentioned publicly as a candidate for the presidency of the Weimar Republic. Through it all, he was a deeply committed Christian. Yet he felt, like many today, that his Christian life and identity could not be detached from what was happening in the world. He felt that Christianity must listen and respond to the "signs of the times." If it did not, it would sink into the quicksand of irrelevance or of blind faith. The assessment of one of his critics poses him as a model for contemporary Christians: "His own personal history was a history of struggle, for a viable faith, as well as for an uncompromising intellectual honesty."[1]

In this struggle, Troeltsch found himself wrestling mainly with the clash between the historical consciousness of his age and the need, which he recognized in himself and in all persons, for solid religious commitment and values. On the one hand, there was historical consciousness, the intellectual revelation and revolution of the nineteenth century. Scholars in various disciplines were coming to realize with increasing clarity that the human being was not just a rational and a social being but also a *historical* being. This means that everything humans are and produce is limited by their historical context and is subject to the law of historical development. Historical contexts are many and they are always changing. Therefore everything in them—including the entirety of human culture and knowledge—is both limited and changing. What is so in one historical situation may be different in another; what is so today in a given historical context may be different in that same context tomorrow. The historical quality of all human achievements therefore excludes all absolutes, that is, all "one and only" or unchangeable truth-claims. Historical consciousness, in other words, seems to imply a radical relativity of all cultures. Troeltsch, in his intellectual honesty, felt he had no choice but to assent to this historical consciousness and the cultural relativity that it demanded.[2]

On the other hand, there is the natural human need for security, for reliable and certain truth, for a solid place on which to pitch one's tent, especially in matters of religious truth. This is precisely what Christianity, throughout its history, has claimed to offer! How can the certain, unchanging truth of the gospel be reconciled with historical consciousness and the relativity that it imposes? For if all is relative, then it seems that "anything goes." An anarchy of values results in which nothing can be asserted to be really right or wrong. This was the conflict that gripped Troelstch's mind and heart. It was a personal problem, for he realized that there must be values and truth for which he could live and die. It was also a theological problem, for he also felt how much all of this contradicted traditional Christian teaching. "It was largely out of this conflict," he wrote in one of the last lectures of his life, "which was no hypothetical one, but a fact of my own practical experience, that my entire theoretical standpoint took its rise."[3]

Troeltsch was not frightened by this conflict. He struggled boldly and creatively to resolve it. Part of his effort, as we shall see, stemmed from his conviction that if Christianity is truly to respond to historical consciousness and to the "signs of the times," it must undergo a pervasive overhauling. It would have to enter a new phase and give up many of its traditional forms. It would have to be open to new answers to new questions. He was convinced that this could be done without abandoning the spirit or the essential message of the gospel.

God, World, Religion

The starting point for Troeltsch's attempt to resolve the conflict between historical relativism and what, in the title of his best-known book he called "the absoluteness of Christianity," is to be found in his understanding of the relationship between God and the world. More precisely, he begins with a particular view of how divinity reveals itself within human history. (This is a starting point that reflects the views of many contemporary Christians, especially contemporary Roman Catholic theologians.)

Like many moderns, Troeltsch was dissatisfied with concepts of revelation that had God swooping down from heaven and intervening into history at particular spots. Such an image fashioned a much too transcendent deity, a deity that has its being unto itself and has to step across a great divide in order to make itself known to humanity. This view of deity also tended to picture God as a rather arbitrary parent who dispenses more parental love to some children than to others.

In place of such an intervening God, Troeltsch argued for what in technical terms can be called a metaphysics of *immanent transcendence*. Yes, God is transcendent, more than and not to be identified with the finite; yet the divine presence is to be found, and has its very life, within the unfolding of finite history. Divinity or the Absolute is, paradoxically, both beyond and within the world. There is a form of participation, of continuity, of sharing between the infinite and the finite. It can be said that for Troeltsch God is *coterminous with history;* history is the "march of God through the world" or the "mask of God," expressing the infinitely creative divine life. Or in the words of Ranke, "every epoch in history stands immediately to God."[4]

Troeltsch did not make such assertions arbitrarily. To use technical language again, he grounded his metaphysics of immanent transcendence in a psychology of *transcendental subjectivity*. Anticipating theologians like Karl Rahner and Bernard Lonergan, Troeltsch argued that the human spirit, or the human being's self-experience, gave imposing testimony to the immanence of God within our very being. Our own self-awareness, our restlessness, our constant searching for more, our innate need to trust and to love—all such experiences "seem to point to an active presence of the Absolute Spirit in finite things, to an activity of the universe, as Schleiermacher says, in individual souls."[5] Troeltsch calls this the *religious apriori* within the human spirit—the innate orientation toward and the experience of the divine built into human nature.[6]

But for Troeltsch this religious apriori, this inbuilt drive toward the divine, could not be perceived and become real merely in the inward experience of the individual—that is, only in the relation between the individual and the divine. As much as Troeltsch extolled the importance of the individual, he also realized that we are essentially *historical* beings, who can exist and experience ourselves only within history. Therefore the religious apriori can be lived and experienced only in and through historical process: dependent on and qualified by all the variety, constant change, and randomness of history.

This is where the religions enter the picture. They are the vehicles through which the human being's feeling for God takes concrete form within history. There is a mutual dependence between the religions and the religious apriori: all religions take their origin from the religious apriori built into human nature, and the religious apriori cannot exist concretely without the religions.

What Troeltsch offers us with this view of religion can be very helpful in our efforts to understand religious pluralism. In more theological language, the religions of the world are the concrete, varied, and independent manifestations of the universal revelation at work within all humankind. Troeltsch suggests to us that all religions share something in common: the divine presence or revelation. Yet he also accounts for their genuine differences, for each is a different, particular historical manifestation of that presence.[7]

Troeltsch added one more crucial element to his picture of how the Absolute manifests itself within the religions of the world. It stems from his pervasive historical consciousness and its demands for historical relativity. Although the Absolute is present to and manifest in all of history, no historical manifestation of the Absolute can be absolute! That would contradict the nature of the Absolute (which is always more than the finite) and the nature of the historical (which is always limited and changing).

This means that all religions, as bearers of the divine, are also relative, limited. Although each religion is a manifestation of the Absolute, there can be no absolute religion. This is of the very nature of historical process: it allows no absolutes; it admits only individual, concrete and therefore relative realities. No religion can affirm that it stands above this all-embracing relativity; no religion can claim to be the full and final realization of the divine presence. No religion can entirely step outside history! Even though Troeltsch admitted that the goal of all religions is the full realization of the Absolute, he held firmly that this goal cannot be realized within the course of history as we know it. If someday there is to be an absolute religion and a final, full manifestation of divinity, that will have to take place on a posthistorical, eternal stage. In the meantime, the road to that final goal is to be followed step by relative step.[8] No wonder that Ernst Troeltsch has been called "the father of historical relativism"!

This, then, is the platform on which Troeltsch begins his resolution of the problem of the many religions and their historical relativity. How does he move on to reconcile all this with the human need for certainty and the traditional claims of Christianity?

Christianity and Other Religions

Just how difficult and elusive this reconciliation was for Troeltsch can be seen from the tensions, even contradictions, that appear in his writings and especially from the fact that toward the end of his life he had to change his stance and admit that he had been wrong! Again he reflects the uncertain struggles of many Christians as they try to reconcile the pluralism of religions with their basic Christian beliefs.

The tensions in his struggle appear, first of all, in his conviction that although we must admit the radical relativity of all historical forms and all assertions of truth, this does not mean that we are therefore swept away in an "aimless" or "unconditional" relativism. Troeltsch felt that somehow he could—or that he *must*—judge some values or truths as superior to others; otherwise there would be no difference between right and wrong. He admitted that in such judgments a degree of personal choice or "confession" is involved. Yet these judgments need not be purely personal or subjective, for they can and must be based on an empirical study of history and on a comparison of various historical claims of truth.[9] Does all this sound a bit confusing? Yes. It seems that Troeltsch was seeking a platform outside the flux of historical relativities on which he could make such value judgments.

Troeltsh at first tried to follow this rather confusing procedure in his assessment of how Christianity relates to the other religions. This is especially evident in his book, *The Absoluteness of Christianity and the History of Religions*. On the one hand, he applied the demands of historical consciousness ruthlessly:

> Nowhere is Christianity the absolute religion, an utterly unique species free of the historical conditions that comprise its environment at any given time. Nowhere is it the changeless, exhaustive, and unconditioned realization of that which is conceived as the universal principle of religion. The Christian religion is in every moment of its history a purely historical phenomenon, subject to all the limitations to which any individual historical phenomenon is exposed, just like the other great religions.[10]

On the other hand, he felt he could (or did he feel he *must?*) argue for a superiority or normativity of Christianity over the other religions. He ended up attributing to Christianity a kind of "provisional" or "qualified" absoluteness. By this he did not mean simply a "naive absoluteness," which he described as the natural, spontaneous feeling persons have when they truly experience the reality of God; in all authentic religious experience a person will naturally feel that "this is it," "there is no other or better God." The absolute quality of this experience is naive because the person does not ask further questions concerning the plurality of religions, the immensity of God, and the historical quality of human life. Troeltsch admitted the propriety of such naive absoluteness. He saw it as a characteristic of the experience and message of Jesus.[11]

But this is not the kind of absoluteness he was affirming. The type of absoluteness that he thought he could attribute to Christianity was much more sophisticated and verifiable. Even though unable to be proven with absolute certainty and total objectivity, the superiority of Christianity, Troeltsch argued, can become evident to all those who truly open their eyes to the facts of religious history. For Troeltsch, these facts—or "criteria for religious superiority"—were two. The first was what he termed, simply, *success*. To judge the value of a religion or the quality of its expression of the Absolute, we must look to how well it has succeeded in holding human hearts. Has it withstood steadfastly the buffeting of history and cultural change? Has it held its ground in the encounter with other religions? On all these accounts, Troeltsch could give Christianity an "A," or perhaps an "A + ."[12]

The second criterion was the more determinative and, for Troeltsch, the more handy. It hinged on what he called the "spirituality" (*Geistigkeit*) of a religion. In applying this criterion, Troeltsch first sweepingly divided the entire history of religions into two main camps: the primitive religions, which he casually brushed aside as "irrelevant to the problem of highest religious values," and the "religions of ethical and spiritual greatness." This latter category he further broke down into religions that look upon the Ultimate as impersonal (Eastern religions, Hinduism and especially Buddhism) and those that view God as a person (Judaism, Christianity, Islam).[13] Although Troeltsch clearly admitted that the choice between the two is a matter of personal faith, he also ventured the assertion that there is sufficient evidence in the history of religions to indicate the superior values of the personalistic religions. He even went a step further: "The personalistic redemption religion of Christianity is the highest and most significantly developed world of religious life that we know."[14]

After having pressed the importance of historical consciousness with its incorrigible demands for the relativity of all historical claims of truth, Troeltsch ended up with the surprising statement:

> Thus Christianity must be understood not only as the culmination point but also the convergence point of all the developmental tendencies that can be discerned in religion. It may therefore be designated, in contrast to other religions, as the focal synthesis of all religious tendencies and the disclosure of what is in principle a new way of life.[15]

He added a number of qualifiers to this statement. The Christianity that serves as the point of convergence for all other religions is the *reformed* Christianity Troeltsch was proposing, a Christianity liberated from the superstition and uncritical thinking that characterized its past. And Troeltsch made his case only for the present state of affairs: "it cannot be proved with absolute certainty that Christianity will always remain the final culmination point, that it will never be surpassed."[16]

Still, Troelstch's case for the superiority of Christianity is clear and bold—and, for many readers, perplexing. It seems to be inconsistent with his position as "the father of historical relativism." Troeltsch, man of ruthless intellectual honesty that he was, was soon to experience this inconsistency.

The Radical Relativity of All Religions

In a lecture that he prepared for delivery at the University of Oxford in 1923 but that had to be published posthumously, Troeltsch admitted that he had been wrong in what he had said about the superiority of Christianity and its place as the point of convergence for all other religions. This lecture represents the final fruits of all his efforts to reconcile historical consciousness with "The Place of Christianity among the World Religions" (the title of the lecture). He drew the conclusion that earlier he had not seen or wished to face: the relativity of history means that "you cannot say one religion is better than another."

Troeltsch realized that all his "empirical" arguments for the superiority of Christianity had been influenced and determined by his own historical and therefore limited context and culture. To affirm that the highest religion will be the most personal religion may be true for a Western Christian, but it makes no sense to a Theravada Buddhist. Troeltsch confessed himself guilty of a form of cultural imperialism. His mistake was much like the one involved in developing intelligence tests on the basis of one's own cultural or ethnic background, applying them to others from a different background, and then "scientifically" declaring those others to be intellectually inferior. To declare Christianity higher than any other religion, Troeltsch realized, was really to declare Western culture superior to all others. Hardly an objective judgment, it is much more a grandiose act of self-flattery.[17]

Honestly and bravely, Troeltsch went on to draw further consequences from this realization—and here especially he speaks for many in the world of today: it is impossible to make any kind of judgment about the superiority of one religion over another. To make such a judgment properly, one would have to crawl into the cultural skin of that other religion; and this is impossible. Therefore the truth or the value of a religion depends only on two considerations: 1) how much the individual freely and critically has embraced that religion; 2) how much that religion fits the culture in which it was born and nurtured.

This means, more precisely, that Christianity may be the best or "absolute" religion for Westerners. "We cannot live without a religion, yet the only religion that we can endure is Christianity, for Christianity has grown up with us and has become a part of our very being."[18] Troeltsch realized, however, that Buddhism and Hinduism carry out the very same role for Easterners. "A study of the non-Christian religions convinced me more and more that their naive claims to absolute validity are also genuinely such. I found Buddhism and Brahminism especially to be really humane and spiritual religions, capable of appealing in precisely the same way to the inner certitude and devotion of their followers as Christianity."[19]

This can be called Troeltsch's view of "polymorphous truth"—truth will always have many cultural expressions, and it is impossible to judge one to be better than the other. Truths that are "universally valid" and can be accepted interculturally Troeltsch found to be "at bottom exceedingly little."[20] He foresaw the religions of the world developing on quite parallel tracks. He felt that it is probable that "the great revelations to the various civilizations will remain distinct" and "the question of their several relative values will never be capable of objective determination, since every proof thereof will presuppose the special characteristics of the civilization in which it arises."[21]

Implied in these final conclusions of Troeltsch is a certain cultural and religious isolation. He felt that we are so caught in our cultural skins that we really cannot understand and appreciate another culture. In another image, Troeltsch felt that we cannot be culturally or religiously "bilingual." We can learn the language of another culture sufficiently to make some historical study of it, but we can never learn to speak it well enough fully to understand and evaluate it. Really to understand and judge another culture or religion, we would have to join it—and leave our own behind.

In drawing these conclusions Troeltsch was not encouraging individual religions to go their own isolated ways without any concern for each other. "If each [religion] strives to fulfill its own highest potentialities and allows itself to be influenced therein by the similar striving of the rest, they may approach and find contact with each other." In this contact there can be "no conversion or transformation of one into the other, but only a measure of agreement and mutual understanding."[22] The contact, in other words, will be quite limited in its effects.

More and more, in the final period of his life, Troeltsch spoke about the unity of religions as a matter of the next world, the heavenly kingdom. He felt this to be entirely consistent with Jesus's own image of the kingdom of God: "Only the future would bring complete deliverance, perfect knowledge, and permanent victory. Jesus relegated the absolute religion to the world to come."[23]

For the meantime, Troeltsch advocated a tolerance built on love that offers an inspiring commentary on our problem of the one and the many: "In our earthly experience Divine Life is not One, but Many. But to apprehend the One in the Many constitutes the special character of love."[24]

But what about the natural human need for security, for certainty, for a solid place to stand? Troeltsch saw and accepted that this need can never fully be met—and that perhaps it would be dangerous if it were. To insist on certainty leads to the insistence that "my way" is the only way. And when I am convinced that my way is the only way, your way becomes fair game for my weapons of exploitation or dominance. So Troeltsch faces us with the question: Do we need absolute certainty about truth before we can be fully committed to it? "A truth which, in the first instance, is a *truth for us* does not cease, because of this, to be very Truth and Life."[25] Even though it is only "our truth," even though there may be many others, still we can live and die for it.

Is this a possibility? Does it lay the groundwork for a unitive pluralism of religions and for fruitful interreligious dialogue?

CONTEMPORARY THEOLOGIANS AND TROELTSCH

Troeltsch worked out his understanding of historical consciousness and its implications for religious pluralism at the turn of the last century. I have presented it as a mirror of contemporary popular attitudes and as a focus for the challenges facing contemporary Christians. That Troeltsch serves such a function is evident from the way representative contemporary theologians have endorsed the main content of Troeltsch's position. Theologians such as Bernard Lonergan, Langdon Gilkey, and David Tracy speak of a shift in cultural consciousness that has taken place within Western civilization over the past three to four centuries. The shift, which occurred gradually and is now complete, moved from what the theologians call "classicist culture" to (with a nod to Troeltsch) "historical culture."

Classicist culture was part of the prenatal environment in which Christianity was formed. A classicist consciousness held sway, with only a few dissenting voices, until the Enlightenment and the beginnings of modern science in the seventeenth and eighteenth centuries. Because it looked upon the world and all of reality as fixed and unchanging (as described in chap. 1, above),[26] it also had a well-honed image of what truth and culture had to be. Persons raised in a classicist culture took it for granted that truth was much the same as Aristotle's definition of scientific knowledge; it was "sure knowledge through causes." By knowing how things came about, one could unlock the intricacies of the given, unchanging order and come to truth. For anything to be true and reliable, then, it had to be certain and unchanging.

The understanding of culture followed suit. For the classicist it was, again, simply taken for granted that culture had to be *one, universal, normative*. There could really be only one culture to mediate and give expression to the one truth, the one order of reality. Of course this one culture was that of Europe. It was a universal culture, applicable to all. Anyone living outside it was a barbarian, who either was to be brought into the daylight of Western culture and religion or, if that was impossible, kept in a state of subjection fitting barbarians. Finally, this one culture was therefore seen as normative for all others. All other cultures had to be judged by and absorbed into it, for it alone supplied the norms by which persons were to understand their world, themselves, and their God. To question or reject this culture was to utter the cry of Lucifer, "I will not serve."

According to the theologians mentioned above, the Western world has undergone a cultural transformation. Classicist culture has evolved into historical culture. This new culture provides contemporary persons with a new consciousness, a new way of viewing themselves and their world. Historical culture understands all reality as ceaselessly changing in an infinite variety of ways. The contemporary understanding of the nature of truth differs from what obtained in classicist culture. Truth is no longer defined according to the Aristotelian notion of science: "certain knowledge through causes." Rather, "modern science is not true; it is only on the way towards truth. It is not certain; for its positive affirmations it claims no more than probability. It is not knowledge but hypothesis, theory, system, the best available scientific opinion of the day. Its object is not necessity but verified possibility."[27] On the personal level, truth is no longer seen as the pursuit of certainty but as the pursuit of understanding—ever greater understanding. This means that all "true understanding" will be open to change and revision.

The notion of culture has also been profoundly altered. Persons living in a historical culture know and feel that culture can never be one; there must be many cultures. Historical culture "is the culture that knows about other cultures, that relates them to one another genetically, that knows all of them to be man-made."[28] No one culture can be normative vis-à-vis others. All cultures and nations share together the common pursuit of truth—not as certainty but as further, ever developing understanding.

Although theologians who recognize historical culture would not agree with every plank in Troeltsch's general platform, they have accepted his insistence that the consciousness of the modern person is different from that of just a century ago. They underline, again, just how well Troeltsch speaks for popular attitudes of our day. These theologians also level the same demands at their churches that Troeltsch aimed at the Christianity of his time: unless Christianity adjusts to and takes on historical culture, its voice will fade more and more into the stratosphere of irrelevance. Jesuit Bernard Lonergan complains: "Only belatedly [in Vatican II] has the church come to acknowledge that the world of the classicist no longer exists and that the only world in which it can function is the modern world [of historical culture]." And he goes on to pose succinctly what the problem of contemporary Christianity really is: "In brief, the contemporary issue is not a new religion, not a new faith, not a substantially new theology, but a belated social and cultural transition."[29]

Troeltsch would certainly applaud such a statement. So would many other persons today, both inside and outside the Christian churches. The problem is that of a cultural lag. For the most part, Christians are still approaching the world and themselves with the mind-set of classicist culture. If Christians are going to speak intelligently to their contemporaries, and especially if they are going to be able to make sense out of the world of religious pluralism, they are going to have to become part of the historical culture of the world of today and recognize the reality of historical relativism. But is the problem or the solution that simple?

ALL ARE RELATIVE?

Relativism is part of the popular mind-set. But how much can it really be part of the Christian mind-set? In the following comments, I shall try to draw out what I think are the pressing questions that advocates of historical relativity force Christians to face. Such questions must be resolved, at least to some degree, by any Christian theology of religions. I shall also point out what seem to be the problems or excesses in the relativists' position, the areas where their approach can actually hinder a healthy encounter of religions or where they seem to discard traditional Christian beliefs too facilely.

Questions for Christians

First of all, can Christians agree with Troeltsch's foundational conviction that God's revelation is offered to all peoples and to all religions? As will be evident in the coming chapters on Christian attitudes toward other religions, this is a key question in any theology of religions. Unless it is answered affirmatively, there cannot be, it seems to me, any positive evaluation of other faiths or any basis for a dialogue with them. Although some Christians may have reservations about Troeltsch's image of God as coterminous with history, most of them do agree with Troeltsch's recognition of a universal divine revelation. (Some dissenters will be heard from in chap. 5.) Such a revelation is consistent with, even demanded by, Christian belief in a God who loves all human beings.

Troeltsch's central assertion that all historical forms are relative places Christians before a more difficult question. Many Christians, like their non-Christian contemporaries, feel in their hearts that Troeltsch is right. When they listen to his arguments, together with those of many contemporary theologians, their heads follows their hearts. Yes, everything in the world is historically conditioned, changing, and therefore limited. History will brook no absolutes within its confines, no "one and only," definitive expressions of truth. In simply and spontaneously accepting such historical relativity as a fact, Christians are finding that their toleration level for uncertainty and insecurity has increased. They are better able to live open-ended lives. They are realizing that there is no lifetime guarantee for the truths on which they attempt to build their lives. At the most, they can have only a temporary warranty. At any time, they must be ready to bring in their truths for a tune-up or possibly even for a trade-in. To demand that truth be certain and to pursue it as such is to condemn oneself to ultimate frustration. To view truth as a growth in understanding and to open oneself to that growth is to engage in a process that can be both peaceful and exciting.[30]

But can Christians integrate what they feel about historical relativity with their religious beliefs? Christians are gradually realizing that they can, that Christianity not only allows but even requires a recognition of the limitation of all historical revelation, of all human knowledge of God. After all, have not Christian mystics in general and theologians in their better moments insisted that God is "absolute Mystery," ever beyond the grasp of the human mind, never able to be captured once and for all in any doctrine, whether biblical or papal? And have not Christians been admonished by the Bible and most recently by the Second Vatican Council that they should look upon themselves as a "pilgrim people," on a journey of faith, and therefore always on their guard against trying to build a lasting city with final truths amid the flux and finitude of history?[31] In a sense, are not Christians required to be the most extreme of historical relativists?

In describing the prevalence of historical culture, and its assimilation into Christian consciousness, one must be careful not to paint a distorted picture of the real world. By no means have all peoples, certainly not all Christians, embraced the worldview of historical consciousness. As already indicated in chapter 1,[32] there is also evident throughout our contemporary world a rejection of historical relativity and of cultural pluralism; there is a resurgence of nationalism and fundamentalism. For the nationalists, it is "my country, right or wrong." For the fundamentalists, it is "my religion, one and only." They *do* affirm absolutes amid the swirl of history. And they are ready to fight and die for them. Their motives are not necessarily mean or ignoble. Perhaps because of their own historical conditioning, they simply cannot bear up under the uncertainty and challenge that come with the relativist claim that no truth can be absolute; perhaps they "cannot bear very much reality."[33]

This present-day backlash of nationalism and fundamentalism cannot be ignored or minimized. Yet neither should its virulence cloud the fact that for many persons, including Christians, historical culture has made its appearance and created the vision of a new world in which nations and religions can recognize their limitations and therefore their need of each other. Contemporary nationalism and fundamentalism can perhaps be understood as a cultural "last stand," as a final resistance to the death of the old world of divided nations, as a reluctance to give way to the difficult birth of a new world order, a global village. Every new stage in world history has been preceded by a last-ditch resurgence of the old.

Problems

Those who endorse Troeltsch and his position of historical relativism have to recognize a number of serious problems, both philosophical and theological, that their views entail. The first, perhaps the most evident and most crucial, is theological. Does not the assertion that all historical realities are relative unavoidably contradict one of the most central Christian beliefs: Jesus of Nazareth as the one incarnation of God in history and as the one and only savior of all humankind? The content of the doctrine of the incarnation and divinity of Jesus, theologians tell us, is that here, at this point in history, the "laws" of historical relativity do *not* apply. In this man Jesus, with all his historical conditionings, the Absolute, the fullness of divinity, *has* identified itself with a historical form. Here, Christians believe, they have the Absolute become history, divinity incarnated in humanity. And therefore in this man, in this historical form, there *is* present the full, final, normative revelation of God.

The incarnation is the one grand exception to Troeltsch's otherwise iron-clad law of historical relativity. Why or how this has taken place is precisely the *mystery* of the incarnation, the hypostatic union of divinity and humanity. Is this difficult for the person of historical consciousness to accept? Indeed it is, for it is the "scandal" of Christianity, the scandal of the mind and will of God.[34]

This same question about the compatability of historical relativity with the doctrine of the incarnation can be posed in a less "scandalous" form. One can grant that inasmuch as Jesus is a historical figure, the incarnation and revelation of God in him are also historically conditioned and therefore limited. One can concede, as well, that Jesus does not present the full or the absolute expression of divinity; like all historical expressions of the Absolute, he is relative. Yet even within the framework of Troeltsch's general position, is it not still *possible* that the revelation contained in Jesus is superior or more adequate than all other revelations? Amid all the relative, limited historical expressions of the divine life, is it not logically possible that one of them be more complete (less relative) than all the others? If this be the case, the religion founded under Jesus could still be relative and yet superior to, perhaps the culmination point for, all other religions. It seems to me that Troeltsch and those who embrace the view that no religion can be better than another have not sufficiently considered this possibility.

Such a possibility leads to a further question: How could we know whether what is possible has been realized? How could we verify that the revelation of Jesus and the religion that grew out of this revelation are *in fact* more adequate than, and therefore normative for, all other revelations and religions? Troelstch would hold that such a question could never be answered; it is a meaningless query. We can never know whether one religious figure is superior to another because each religious figure and each religion is confined to its own culture and historical context. Troeltsch told us that we cannot be culturally or religiously bilingual; we cannot sufficiently enter into another culture to decide whether our religion is superior to its.

But we must ask Troeltsch and those who follow him: Can one be sure of this? Perhaps in Troeltsch's world, less than a century ago, this may have been the case; cultures seemed so different and so distant from each other that there was an unbridgeable communication gap between them. But as James Luther Adams, a scholar of Troeltsch's thought, reminds us, since the turn of the century, "the world situation has changed rapidly. . . . We today have entered into an epoch different from that of Troeltsch, one in which universal history is becoming a reality."[35] As we saw in chapter 1, "universal communication'' and ''universalistic personal identity'' or world citizenship are becoming more of a possibility.[36] Perhaps this opens up the opportunity of knowing each other well enough to judge one religion to be the point of convergence for all others.

I say ''perhaps.'' In chapters 9 and 10, I shall explore further just what the doctrine of the incarnation means and how one might go about a dialogue among religions in an effort to see whether they might be able to ''converge'' around one religious figure or symbol.

Troeltch's historical relativism leads to another and more personal problem. It arises from his assertion that even though a truth is a truth only ''for us,'' it can still be ''very Truth and Life''—that is, it can still command our total commitment. If we look deeply into just what we feel when we come to claim something as true, vitally true for the way we want to live, can it really be a truth *only* for us? Do we not feel that it can also be a truth for others, that others will find fuller life in embracing it? This does not mean that our truth has to exclude the truths of others; but it does mean that we feel that their truth can be enhanced by ours. If something is true for us, we want to let others know about it. Stated philosophically, all truth is experienced as having *universal relevance*.[37] Truth drives us to dialogue with others, to overcome the cultural, historical walls that separate us. Historical relativism, as Troeltsch presented it and as many others today embrace it, is perhaps not sufficiently aware of this.

One final question: When Lonergan and fellow theologians explain that the main problem facing Christianity in its confrontation with historical consciousness is not one of ''a new religion'' or of a ''substantially new theology'' but rather one of a cultural adaptation to the modern world, are they not oversimplifying the problem? Are they not unduly softening the challenges that historical consciousness and religious pluralism are forcing Christians to confront? Even though Christians may have some questions about Troeltsch's understanding of relativism, they do affirm his central assertion that all historical forms are limited. To take this assertion seriously and to make the necessary cultural adjustments to historical consciousness, Christians may indeed need a different, a new, understanding of their religion, a substantially new kind of theology. Questions concerning the incarnation and the uniqueness of Jesus are cases in point. Chapters 8, 9, and 10 will suggest some genuinely (but not totally) new possibilities for Christian doctrine and practice.

Chapter III

All Are Essentially the Same

"Deep down, all religions are the same—different paths leading to the same goal." This is another of the deeply entrenched popular attitudes toward religious pluralism in our contemporary society—an attitude by which Christians, wittingly or unwittingly, are very much influenced. This viewpoint seems to make such eminent sense, especially for persons who believe in *one* God who is a God of love. Naturally this God wills to draw all peoples to salvation. Naturally God will have to do this according to the differing cultures and contexts of geography and time. So differences between the religions are merely accidental, cultural, time-conditioned. Behind all these cultural accidentals, there is the one God, the common essence. The familiar image of the different paths leading up to the sublime summit of Mt. Fuji represents for many today the world of differing religions all twisting their way to the same goal.

The view that "all religions are the same" is quite similar to and in basic agreement with that of "all are relative." In this chapter I shall indicate how those who claim the basic sameness of all religions certainly agree with the relativists but go beyond them. Members of "the school of common essence" attempt to describe *what* this common essence is and how it presents all religions with a common goal *within* history.

Again, my intent is to show the theoretical underpinnings for this popular attitude. The common essence school has many different champions from many different fields: philosophers, historians, mystics, specialists in comparative religions. My primary focus will be on a man who has been one of the strongest and most eloquent voices for the common core and goal behind all religions—a historian as famous as he was controversial: Arnold Toynbee (1889–1975)

TOYNBEE'S VISION OF THE ONENESS OF RELIGIONS

Toynbee was no theologian, but he clearly and unashamedly brought theological or religious concerns to his work as a historian. This merited him the criticism and even the ostracism of many of his colleagues. He offended the canons of "objectivity" imposed on all "scientific" historians. Worse still, the instrument of his offense was religion!

Toynbee shrugged off his critics' cavils and pursued his conviction, born of his scholarly research and also of his personal experience of two World Wars, that one cannot understand the dynamic of history without the ingredient of religion. A leitmotif behind all his historical investigations, seen especially in his monumental twelve-volume *The Study of History*, was that "religion is the heart of human life."[1] The quality of the twenty-six civilizations that he traces through the history of the world and the force that enabled them to respond to the political and moral challenges of historical process were decided by the quality of the religion that animated them.[2]

This mixing of religious and historical concerns not only merited Toynbee the scorn of many of his fellow historians; it also got him into trouble with church leaders and theologians. As popular as he was during the 1940s and early 50s, Toynbee was practically ignored in religious and theological journals from the end of the 50s. This was due especially to his increasing ecumenical concerns, his efforts to bring the religions of the world together. Perhaps he was simply ahead of his time. After all, Christians were then having enough trouble trying to get their own ecumenical act together; they had little surplus energy for a broader ecumenism with non-Christian religions.[3]

In any case, whatever may be the final verdict on his merits as a historian or on the orthodoxy of his theology, Arnold Toynbee speaks the mind and feelings of many persons today when they confront the reality of religious pluralism. He does this especially in the way he argues for the unity behind all religions and in his insistence that all religions must join ranks in order to improve the world.

Common Essence

Toynbee began his analysis of the nature of religion and its role in history by urging a distinction with which many today would agree. Within each religion, "there are essential counsels and truths, and there are nonessential practices and propositions."[4] If we can look behind the nonessentials of each religion, we will find that the inner core, the essential experience and insight of all of them, is essentially the same. Toynbee was attempting the difficult task of distilling the common *faith* experience from the amalgam of *beliefs* and practices. Using Western terminology, he called this essence or common experience a sense of the "spiritual presence" within all reality.

In urging this viewpoint, he was not speaking as a speculative philosopher. From his concrete historical studies of the seven major religions of the world he detected this spiritual presence, and he felt he could give it a relatively adequate description. The spiritual presence he found in Theravada Buddhism, Mahayana Buddhism, Hinduism, Judaism, Islam, Christianity, and

Zoroastrianism evinces the following common characteristics: 1) It flows from the experience that the universe is ultimately mysterious; the meaning of the world is not contained simply in itself or in humanity. 2) The meaning of the universe is to be found in an Absolute Reality or presence which, although "in" the universe, is not to be identified with it. 3) This presence contains not only the truth of which humans can be aware but also the good for which they thirst. Humanity therefore seeks not only to experience this reality but to be in harmony with it. 4) The way to live this harmony requires that human beings rid themselves of their innate self-centeredness: "In giving up self-centeredness he will have felt as if he were losing his life; but in achieving this act of self-sacrifice he will find that he has really saved his life, because he will have given his life a new center, and this new center will be the Absolute Reality that is the spiritual presence behind the phenomena."[5]

In tracing this one presence within all the major world religions, Toynbee did not shut his eyes to the significantly different forms it took in the various religions. He recognized, for instance, that six of the seven major religions looked upon the Absolute as personal; one of them, Theravada Buddhism, did not. Also, in trying to "harmonize" the self with the Absolute, a Theravada Buddhist strives for what looks like self-extinction, whereas followers of most other religions view this harmony as a communion between the self and God. Concerning the problem of evil, there are also telling differences, Hinduism locating evil *within* the Ultimate, most of the other religions trying to pin it on some kind of a devil figure. Such contrasts notwithstanding, Toynbee still felt that the inner essence or experience of all the religions was held in common.[6]

The most evident differences are found within the religions' nonessentials, which means that the differences are, really, nonessential. Toynbee listed examples of what he considered nonessentials: holy places, rituals, tabus (such as the burning of corpses), social conventions (such as celibacy for priests), and especially myths, dogmas, schools of theology. In other words, what Toynbee considered to be nonessential was the entire complex of *Creed* (symbols, doctrines, theology), *Code* (ethical systems), and *Cult* (ritual, liturgy) by which religions try to give expression to their experience of and efforts to be in harmony with the spiritual presence.

We must be careful not to misunderstand Toynbee. When he referred to these externals as nonessential, he did not mean that they are not necessary. They are. Without these externals of creed, code, and cult, which he also termed "accretions," a religion cannot communicate its message and its experience of the Absolute to persons in a particular society in a particular stage of its history. He put it neatly: "the price of redemption is incarnation." To communicate the redeeming experience of the Absolute, a religion must incarnate itself into a particular history and culture.[7]

Yet Toynbee's greater insistence fell on the need constantly to reevaluate, discard, replace, adjust these nonessentials, for only then can a religion continue to speak to a people implanted in an always changing history. More

importantly, only then can a religion constantly be on guard against identifying the nonessentials with the essential, for "we are always relapsing from
the worship of God into the worship of our tribe or of ourselves."⁸

This task of "winnowing the chaff away from the grain" is, Toynbee admitted, "as hazardous as it is indispensable."⁹ In discarding and replacing
the nonessentials, in revamping myths and doctrines and rituals, religious
persons run the danger of diluting or destroying the inner experience of the
spiritual presence. Toynbee compared the task and its risks to peeling an
onion or cleaning a picture:

> You might go on peeling an onion till you found that you had peeled
> away the heart as well as the skin; and you might go on cleaning a
> picture—stripping off successive coats of varnish and layers of paint—
> till, with a shock, you found yourself left with nothing but the bare
> canvas backing. In these two operations you are not likely to go to those
> disastrous lengths; yet, in every case at every stage, you clean and you
> peel at your peril. If, however, because of this risk, you refrain from
> trying to peel your onion, you will never have an onion to eat, and, if
> you refrain from trying to clean your picture, you will never reveal
> again, either to your own or to any other human eyes, the work of the
> old master who painted the now overlayed masterpiece.¹⁰

According to Toynbee, unless religious persons today make this distinction
between the essence and nonessentials of their religion—and hold to this
distinction—they will not be able to see through to what binds them all together. And, as we shall now see, they will not be able to respond to the
common task that today, more than ever before, confronts them.

Common Purpose

Toynbee's insistence on the common purpose of all religions is perhaps an
even stronger statement of current popular attitudes than is his claim for a
common essence. This common purpose is rooted in a conviction of his that,
again, most persons will find hard to deny: "to correct a self-centeredness
that is one of the intrinsic limitations and imperfections not merely of human
life, but of all life on the face of the earth."¹¹ It is what he called, using a
Christian symbol, original sin—the human heart turned in on itself (*cor curvatum in se*), seeking its own benefit over that of others.

Toynbee asserted that this struggle with selfishness, with what he called
"man worship," is the main incentive or catalyst stirring human beings to
faith in "something more." The origin of all religion lies in the recognition of
evil—that is, in facing the devastation that human self-interest can inflict
on the world. To offset such havoc, humans realize—or rather, they
"believe"—that they must recognize and be in harmony with some greater
reality. Toynbee was not at all surprised to find that all the higher religions

arose within a thousand years of each other, at a time when "Original Sin had shown its power by causing the downfall of one or two generations of secular civilization."[12] With such a perception, Toynbee is in fundamental agreement with the scientists and theologians considered in chapter 1 who proposed that only religious values can, at this point in evolution, enable humans to overcome their natural, genetically determined aggression.[13]

Toynbee again expressed the commonsense views of many today when he concluded that this common task facing all religions is *the* reason why they should recognize their common essence, the one spiritual reality that animates them all.

> In the unified world that has been called into existence by the worldwide expansion of the post-Christian modern Western civilization, all the living higher religions ought to subordinate their traditional rivalries and make a new approach toward one another in face of a fearful common adversary: a revival of the worship of collective human power, armed with new weapons, both material and spiritual.[14]

Claims of Superiority

In his resolute insistence on this last point, Toynbee gives further substance to popular attitudes: only if all religions abandon their own self-centeredness can they join hands to save the world from self-destruction. He admitted that there is a strain of egoism and pride within every religion, an egoism that is all the more insidious in that it camouflages itself under the cloak of the first person plural. The discomfort I might feel in placing myself before all others is much less noticeable when I rank not myself but my family, my people, my religion first.

All religions, indeed all groups, tend to do this. For Toynbee, however, the main offenders were the three Western religions: Judaism, Islam, and Christianity. Of the three, it seemed to him Christianity had the worst record of intolerance and arrogance. His words were hard; his demands were uncompromising: "We ought . . . to try to purge our Christianity of the traditional Christian belief that Christianity is unique."[15] He admitted that this "exclusive mindedness" is congenital to Christianity, inherited from its parent religion, Judaism, and that it has become intrinsic to Christian beliefs. Yet he was also convinced that it belongs to the nonessentials of Christianity, for it can be discarded without maiming the essence of the gospel.

The essence of Christianity consists in the experience of and belief in a God whose name is love, who therefore "is not self-centered, but just the opposite: self-sacrificing." Therefore Christians not only can, they *must* sacrifice themselves and give up their self-centered claims of superiority and exclusiveness. That is a theological argument. Toynbee also advanced a very practical reason for discarding absolute claims that, again, many today would endorse. As a historian, he felt he could show that this arrogant spirit was precisely the reason why Christianity was rejected by the Japanese and the Chinese in the seventeenth century and by so many intellectual leaders of the West during these last centuries. In his assessment, the prospects for Christianity were not bright:

> If Christianity is presented to people in that traditional arrogant spirit it will be rejected in the name of the sacredness of human personalities—a truth to which the whole human race is now awakening under the influence of modern Western civilization, which originally learned that truth from Christianity that modern Man has been rejecting.[16]

In agreement with Troeltsch, Toynbee urged that such an abandoning of the claim of religious uniqueness need not undermine the strength of religious faith. According to the psychology of religious commitment, persons can be convinced that their revelation is truly from God and worthy of total trust and at the same time believe that it is not the unique or sole revelation. Why does religious truth have to be "one and only" or "the best" in order to be true? We can, Toynbee suggested, be fully committed to our own religion and at the same time fully open to the truth of other religions. Again, his suggestion resonates with the sensitivities of many today as they face the world of religious pluralism.

The Oneness of Religions

But how did Toynbee actually envision a relationship among the religions in which none of them meets the others with claims of superiority? Surprisingly, and yet perhaps understandably, we note the same ambivalence, struggle, and change of mind that marked Troeltsch's efforts to reconcile historical relativism with the traditional claims of Christianity for absoluteness. In his earlier days, during the 1940s, Toynbee had little doubt that in our new age, in which the world religions are encountering each other as never before, Christianity would emerge as the complete victor; it would absorb all the others. In the 50s, his certainty softened. In a "peaceful competition" among the religions, one religion, he felt, would win out. It would be the one with the "fullest vision of God and the greatest means of grace." He contended that in this competition, "Christians can face the future with confidence."[17]

But by the 60s, Toynbee, like Troeltsch, had changed his mind. Perhaps because he became better acquainted with the content and depth of experience in other religions, perhaps because he saw more clearly how cultural convergence was leading to a new unity among nations rather than to a victory of one over the others, he came to endorse a radical *sameness* or *commonality* of all religions. No one religion had a privileged perception of the spiritual presence within them all. In making this claim for a radical relativity and sameness of all religions, Toynbee went beyond Troeltsch. He did not envision each religion going its own way, culturally cut off from genuine communication with the others. Rather, he pictured the various world religions as "so many worldwide diasporas, none of which will be in a majority at any point, because all will be intermingled with each other everywhere."[18] The different cultural and spiritual heritages will become, increasingly, "the common possession of all mankind." "I think one can foresee a time when the heritages of Islam and Buddhism will also have become part of the Christian society's background."[19] Because we will be neighbors to each other culturally, we will also be so spiritually. And no neighbor will be better than another. All will learn from and change with each other.

In his earlier work, *A Study of History*, when he still numbered four major world religions (rather than seven), he previewed this vision of the oneness, this new interrelating unity of all religions:

> The writer of this study will venture to express his personal belief that the four higher religions that were alive in the age in which he was living were four variations on a single theme, and that, if all the four components of this heavenly music of the spheres would be audible on Earth simultaneously, and with equal clarity, to one pair of human ears, the happy hearer would find himself listening, not to a discord, but to a harmony.[20]

While Toynbee also argued that in this new cultural context persons will be more ready to change religions, even abandoning the one in which they had been brought up, he felt that personal adherence to one religion rather than to another would not be determined by the intrinsic superiority of that religion over all others. Rather, it would be a matter of psychological need and preference. He made a perhaps extravagant use of Jung's personality types to make clear what he meant. He contended that Hinduism and Buddhism, with their propensity toward a more impersonal deity within all reality, were *introverted* religions. Judaism, Christianity, Islam, worshiping a more transcendent, personal God, would qualify as *extroverted* religions.

Making an even more bold use of Jung's subtypes, Toynbee identified Hinduism with *thinking* and its opposite, Christianity, with *feeling*; Buddhism was characterized mainly by *intuition*, and its opposite, Islam, by *sensation*. Naturally, Toynbee recognized that each religion, like every individual, is never exclusively any one type; other types are and must be included, even though in subordinated form, in order to have a balanced religious personality. And yet certain psychological types do seem to dominate in the various religions. Persons will naturally feel more at home and fulfilled in a religion that corresponds to their own personality type.[21]

Even though Jung's personality types, and especially Toynbee's application of them to world religions, are controversial, many today would feel that Toynbee does have a point. Human beings do differ in basic personality structure and the way they encounter and experience the world around them. Naturally, then, there will be an abiding need for different religions, for different ways of experiencing and being in harmony with the universal spiritual presence.

Toynbee, with his historically validated claims for the common essence within all religions, and with his vision of how all religions can and must work together for a better world, articulates widely held popular attitudes within contemporary Western society.

OTHER VIEWS OF THE COMMON ESSENCE

There are many notable names on the roster of what we are calling the school of common essence. Among those who would agree with Toynbee's recognition of a common core within all religions are Immanuel Kant, Friedrich Schleiermacher, Rudolf Otto, Friedrich Heiler, Ernest Hocking, Sri Radhakrishnan.[22] To round off this chapter, I shall focus on two other contemporary proponents of this view: Wilfred Cantwell Smith and Frithjof Schuon.

Although both of them are in basic agreement with Toynbee, they each approach the issue of religious pluralism from a different perspective. Smith is a historian of comparative religions, with specialization in Islam; Schuon is a philosopher-mystic who has devoted himself to a study of religions. Both these thinkers clarify and sometimes correct certain contentions made by Toynbee; and both of them go beyond Toynbee in trying to state just what the common spirit within all religions is. They will aid us in better understanding the school of common essence and in evaluating how much it promotes religious dialogue as well as how much it conforms or clashes with traditional Christian doctrine.

Wilfred Cantwell Smith

We have already heard a good deal from W.C. Smith in chapter 1. As professor of the comparative history of religion at Harvard (for nine years he directed the Harvard Center for the Study of World Religions) and as a world-renowned specialist in Islamic studies, Smith has serious reservations about any approach that sees all religions as "really the same." He is a very critical pupil in the school of common essence and perhaps would not even want to be on its roster. Precisely for this reason, he can help us understand how this approach to religious pluralism has moved beyond earlier simplifications. Smith especially makes clear that what is *common* to all religions in no way excludes what is genuinely *different* among them.

Smith is best known for his strenuous efforts—which some would say have been admirable but futile—to expunge the word "religion" from the vocabulary of those who study it and of those who try to live it. "Religion," he contends, is a Western concept, not to be found in other, especially Eastern, religions. Conceived in the womb of the insistence of the West that we can know reality only with our heads, the word "religion" has led to "making religion into a thing," into an "objective systematic entity." It has "reified," packaged, and then neatly studied a reality that, by its very nature, is beyond the structured categories of the mind. Once packaged and systematized, the religions are then compared and ranked, usually with mine on top of yours. The word "religion" has prostituted the very reality it pretends to embody.[23]

But what *is* the living reality that the word "religion" fumblingly tries to convey? Smith suggests that what is meant by "religion" can be better respected and grasped if understood from an entirely different approach. Instead of looking for this abstract "thing" called religion, scholars as well as ordinary believers should set their sights on two living phenomena that Smith terms *faith* and *cumulative tradition*.

"By 'cumulative tradition' I mean the entire mass of overt objective data that constitute the historical deposit, as it were, of the past religious life of the community in question."[24] These are the external expressions—the creeds, codes, cults—that have nourished and continue to nourish the faith of individuals. Cumulative tradition corresponds to what Toynbee meant by historical accretions or nonessentials, although Smith most likely would be uncomfortable with those terms. The traditions are in constant change and are varied within themselves; this is what Smith implies by calling them cumulative. The principle that determines how they change or even whether they persist is simply the degree to which adherents find in them nourishment and expression for their faith. A tradition that does not speak forth the faith of a community eventually dries up and dies.[25]

But what is faith? This is the hinge pin for Smith's view of religious reality and his distinctive contribution to the common essence approach to religions. He describes faith in almost exclusively personal terms. Faith stands for "an inner religious experience or involvement of a particular person; the impingement on him of the transcendent, putative or real." "Faith . . . is not an entity. It is, rather, the adjectival quality of a person's living in terms of transcendence." "It is not a fixed something, but the throbbing actuality of a myriad of someones."[26] Faith is what one feels and the way one lives when one encounters what Smith calls "transcendence."

This, basically, is all he says about faith. And he thinks this is all that should be said. He then moves on to assert that such *faith* is what is common to all religions: the essence of them all (although he would hesitate to use that overladen word). Faith is something as real as it is impossible to pin down. The common element binding persons within the same religion and in different religions is not even to be located in personal faith itself but in the object of that faith: "what they have in common lies not in the tradition that introduces them to transcendence, not in their faith by which they personally respond, but in that to which they respond, the transcendent itself."[27] Smith reminds followers of the school of common essence that they should constantly be wary of trying to define, objectify, "reify" what it is that is common to all religions.

Smith goes on to argue that on the basis of this universalist faith a *new relationship* among all the religions can be constructed. As we saw in chapter 1, Smith is among the most vocal and learned of those modern prophets who announce that now, more than ever before, a new, cooperative unity of religions is both possible and necessary. Whatever form this unity will take, the starting point in working toward it will be to recognize and to act out of the *faith* that is common to and stirs within every religious community.

When members of different religions meet, therefore, they can find a common bond not primarily in their doctrines and rituals but in the depths of their own hearts and in the encounter with the hearts of others. This sounds somewhat airy and mystical—unavoidably so, for Smith is calling for a *personal* meeting of religions and a *personal* perception of their common bond. One cannot codify or simply follow directions for personal relationships.[28]

The exchange between religions should not remain on the mystical level of personal, shared faith. From this level, and only from this level, it must attempt to bring together the cumulative traditions. First of all, Smith maintains, if persons of different religions meet each other on the basis of their faith, they can recognize that the criteria of religious truth or falsehood are beyond objective determination. A particular doctrine or practice is not true or false because it conforms with some given, already known, norm. Rather, a tradition is true insofar as persons participate in it and find through it a genuine contact with transcendence. Therefore the tradition of Christianity or Hinduism is not true in itself; rather it *becomes* true. And "it can *become* true, if and as you or I appropriate it to ourselves and interiorize it, insofar as we live it out from day to day."[29]

Granting this subjective basis for religious truth, we can speak about and compare our doctrines, rituals, ethics. In fact, Smith contends that on the basis of our shared universalist faith, we can understand and see through the differences between our doctrines. Universalist faith becomes the determinative ingredient in what he calls a "critical, corporate" search for religious truth and reality.[30] Together, drawing on the richness of a plurality of traditions, we can enter more deeply into the mystery of transcendence and discover how it enables us to fashion our world into a community of communities. Smith even proposes that in the future all theology, whether Christian or Hindu or whatever, will have to be *global*: we will have to articulate and verify what we hold true and sacred not only before our own community but before other communities. Only if, to some degree, others are able to say yes to our Christian beliefs will we ourselves be able fully to affirm them. We shall hear more about this bold appeal for a "global theology" in chapter 10.[31]

Understanding a universalist faith as the common essence of all religions, what does Smith, a devout Christian himself, have to say about Christianity and its traditional claims for uniqueness and finality? More consistently but also more delicately than Toynbee, he urges that such claims be quietly stored away on the shelves of history. Yes, claims of exclusivity have been made in the past, and perhaps for understandable reasons. Today, however, if we take seriously a universalist faith and the need for a new unity among religions, a certain "theological surrender" will be required of Christians; they will have to be willing to let go of their traditional beliefs that their religion or even their Christ is superior to and normative for all others.[32]

Smith makes a suggestion that renders this call for theological surrender less threatening: instead of arguing that God has been revealed "fully" or "normatively" in Christ, let Christians assert that God has "really" been revealed in Christ and that this revelation is "potentially fuller than it is actually." This assertion still allows for total commitment to Christ, but it also leaves room for a deeper understanding of Christ through recognition of other revealers.

Such a christology will also bring about something that Smith feels is urgently needed in Christian attitudes: a theology that is more *theo*centric than *christo*centric; a theology that is not limited only to what God has done in Christ but is more open to what God is doing universally in all religions.[33] We shall hear more of such suggestions in chapter 9.

Frithjof Schuon

Another expression of the school of common essence comes from what has been called the "perennial philosophy." It offers a vision of the core of all religions quite different from what we have heard from Toynbee and W.C. Smith. Among the most recent advocates of a perennial philosophy are the philosopher Aldous Huxley, the orientalist Ananda Coomaraswamy, the Hindu scholar René Guenon, the Islamist Seyyed Hossein Nasr, and a more recent convert, the popular scholar of world religions, Huston Smith.[34] What makes this philosophy "perennial" and what especially recommends it for inclusion in this chapter is that it traces its roots back to the origins of Eastern religious experience. Its fundamental view of reality and its understanding of the unity of religions reflects that of Hinduism, especially Vedantic, and of Buddhism, especially in its Mahayana and Zen forms. What it offers therefore is an Eastern slant on the common essence view of religions.

Metaphysician-mystic Frithjof Schuon applies the perspective of perennial philosophy to the question of how to understand religious pluralism. Although Schuon is relatively little known in theological and Christian circles, T.S. Eliot could say of him: "I have met with no more impressive work in the comparative study of Oriental and Occidental religions."[35] For ordinary persons who hold to the popular attitude that all religions are the same, Schuon's view may appear bizarre. But it may offer them a tantalizing insight into what they have felt all along but have never been able to say.

To lay hold of Schuon's main point, we first must understand that he sees the dividing lines among religions running not *vertically* between the different religions but *horizontally* across them all. It is not that all Christians are different from all Hindus. Rather, there is something that makes for a definite difference between one Christian and the next; this same something makes for the same difference between one Hindu and the next. And what makes for common differences among Christians as among Hindus also constitutes a fundamental unity between certain Christians and certain Hindus. These dividing lines are what he calls, with a philosopher's delight in bending the language, "esotericism" and "exotericism." The real divisions in the religious world are not the many religions but these two very different types of religious persons: esoteric believers and exoteric believers. Both types are found among all religions. To anticipate Schuon's argument: among the esoteric believers there is a common essence or unity, no matter to which religion they belong.

What Schuon means by "esoteric believers" is both simple and profound. It is not based primarily on metaphysical speculation but on mystical experience, especially as described by Hindus and Buddhists. His main contention is that the esoteric religious person has grasped or been grasped by the underlying unity between God and creation, or better, by the *nonduality* between the Absolute and the finite. It is the same unity, the same oneness embracing difference, that Eckhart experienced between God and the soul, which the Upanishadic seer sensed between Brahma and atman or between the "That" and the "Thou," which the Buddhist sees between nirvana and the finite world of samsara.[36]

Such nonduality should not be simplistically equated with pantheism. It does not urge a substantial identity between God and the world, in which divinity is reduced to finite reality. Rather, nonduality tries to express, always inadequately, the experience of Ultimate Being as it manifests, actualizes, expresses itself in and through everything that is finite. So one can say, with the mystics, that the soul *is* God, but at the same time one must also say that it is not. God and the world are not one, but neither are they two. This is the esoteric mystery of nonduality.[37] It is a reality that is beyond visual imagination, beyond reason. The human mind cannot grasp it "any more than it can visualize light that is simultaneously wave and particle, electrons that jump orbit without traversing the intervening space, or a particle that travels alternate paths simultaneously without dividing."[38] Such nondual unity can be known, truly known, only through direct experience, through intuition, through that part of the human being that *is* the Absolute expressing itself within him or her.

Schuon also insists that although this experience of nonduality is direct, it is never unmediated. It will always take place within, or at least start from, some particular form, some finite symbol, practice, doctrine, ritual. Esoteric believers therefore will never abandon their religion to take off on a naked flight to the Absolute. Schuon states this unequivocally: "there is no possible spiritual way outside of the great orthodox traditional ways. A meditation or concentration practiced at random and outside of tradition will be inoperative, and even dangerous."[39]

Esoteric believers make use of religious symbols and beliefs, but their grip on them is always somewhat loose, ready to let go if need be. "The esoteric finds the Absolute within the traditions as poets find poetry in poems."[40] Although esoterics see and use symbols and doctrines, they also see through them—just as we see light only in a particular color and yet we can also be conscious of "the colorless essence of light," which can never be confined to any one color.[41] Esoterics realize profoundly that God and the nonduality of God/world can never be fully expressed. Even more adamantly than Troeltsch and Toynbee, they proclaim that there can never be an absolute, final expression of what God is. There can only be many such expressions, each true but inadequate. In fact, there *must* be many.

Here we can locate the distinct differences between esoteric believers and what Schuon calls exoteric religious persons. The principal distinguishing mark of exoterics, who Schuon feels constitute the bulk of the world religious population, is an "irreducible dualism."[42] The faith of exoterics is real—that is, they do sense and respond to the reality of God—yet they still perceive this God as some kind of Superperson distinct from the world. They miss the deeper and more satisfying oneness between divinity and humanity. The unspeakable mystery of it all is too much for them. They need to cling to some concrete form, some definition of God.

This need to externalize God makes for the practical and, Schuon would say, harmful difference between exoterics and esoterics. Because the mystery of nonduality eludes them, exoterics tend to identify the external form of their religion with the Ultimate. They have to. For them to recognize that their revelation or their way to God is limited, inadequate, not the one and only, is to be thrown into the insecurity of relativism. For the exoteric, Jesus cannot be only a reliable way to God, a Son of God, he must *be* God, the *only* Son of God. For exoterics, therefore, religion cannot be anything but absolute, exclusive, nonnegotiable.[43] "Absolutize the relative or fall into relativism—these, for the exoteric, are the only options."[44] Because they cannot cope with mystery, they must pin it down in some particular form.

On the platform of this "horizontal" difference between esoteric and exoteric believers, Schuon states what the common essence of all religions is and what the relationship between religions should be. The common essence is to be found only among esoteric believers, no matter what their religion. The experience of the nonduality of God and world—this sublime mystery itself—is what binds religions together. This experience is similar to W.C. Smith's "universalist faith" within all religions. But Schuon tells us more about the content of this faith experience: the oneness of the Absolute with the finite. Schuon would agree with Smith, as well as with Toynbee. But he is saying much more.

To promote the unity of religions, therefore, we should promote esoteric faith. The more religious persons can penetrate the esoteric depths of religious experience and intuit the nonduality of themselves and God, the more they will realize that all religions are basically the same. Schuon warns the promoters of the common essence school that they should not try to locate the sameness of religions in creeds, codes, and cults. The unity is ineffable, never really to be grasped with finality. The forms of religion are many, and they are to remain many, all equally true.

Schuon's final view of the many religions is perhaps the most extreme assertion we have yet encountered that all religions are both "deep down the same" and "relative":

> To come to the main subject of this book, it must be emphasized that the unity of the different religions is not only unrealizable on the external level, that of the forms themselves, but ought not to be realized at that level. . . . If the expression "transcendent unity" is used, it means that the unity of the religious forms must be realized in a purely inward and spiritual way and without prejudice to any particular form. The antagonisms between these forms no more affect the one universal Truth than the antagonisms between opposing colors affect the transmission of the one uncolored light.[45]

For Schuon this means that Christianity must give up its exoteric claims to be the one and only or the best among the religions of the world. He further argues, in somewhat strained detail, that it can do so, for Christianity as it issued from the experience of its founder, Jesus of Nazareth, was basically an esoteric religion. Jesus was one of the most notable mystics in human history. He was an esoteric believer.[46]

ALL THE SAME?

In order to determine what can be learned, positively and negatively, from the school of common essence, I shall, once again, first pose what I think are the questions that this position raises for Christians, and then the problems or dangers entailed in the assertion that all religions are fundamentally the same. I hope these critical comments will help focus the central issues in any Christian attempt to understand and dialogue with other religions.

Questions for Christians

1) Is there really *something common* to all world religions, something shared by all the religious traditions that have endured through the centuries? If Christians must respond negatively to this question, not only are they in brittle opposition to what seems to be a growing contemporary consensus; they are also removing what appears to be a necessary common basis for a positive dialogue among world religions. But cannot Christians agree with the main point of the common essence school? In fact, do they not *have to recognize,* on the basis of their own beliefs, that there is something common to all the religions of the world? As already stated in chapter 2 and as will be clear in the coming chapters on Christian approaches to other religions, most

Christians today recognize a universal divine revelation. This, from the Christian perspective, might be the something common within all religions. Because all the Christian churches believe in a God of love, a God who "wants all to be saved and come to know the truth" (1 Tim. 2:4), it seems that they not only can but must agree with the popular attitude that all religions have something in common.

2) But can this something common, this revelation, be called a "common essence"? To clarify their own attitude toward religious pluralism and their own contribution to interreligious dialogue, Christians today must face this more complex question. If by common "essence" they understand common "experience," can Christians agree that the content, or the object, of *experience* behind all the religions is essentially the same? If God is one, and if this one God is being revealed in all the religions, then what is being experienced in the religions would seem to be basically the same.

Differences will appear in *how* it is experienced. And these differences will be important, very important. After all, to relate to God as Father and to relate to God as Cosmic Process represent very different ways of encountering the Ultimate. Such dissimilarities cannot be glossed over; yet it seems that Christians can admit that despite the differences, the same divine reality is being experienced. They might recognize, with W.C. Smith, a universalist faith within all religious traditions. On the basis of this recognition, should not Christians be disposed to see the evident differences among the religions (differences in "how" the common object of religion is experienced) as more *complementary* than *contradictory*? If these differences are complementary, then there is much that can and *must* be learned from a dialogue with other faiths. In chapters 8 and 10, more will be said about the possibility of a common content of experience through differing religious mediations.

Problems

1) All the advocates of the common essence approach invoke the distinction between essence and nonessentials, or between faith and cumulative tradition, or between the inner heart of a religion and its external expressions in creed, code, and cult. The distinction is valid, in fact indispensable; yet it is as *dangerous* as it is necessary. Almost all the authors we studied seemed to be aware of this. Yet they, or those who listen to them, do not always seem to hold consistently to this awareness.

In the way they stress the distinction between essence and nonessentials, followers of the common essence school give the impression that the more one enters into and becomes one with the inner core or essence of religious experience, the less one needs the nonessentials of religion. It seems, in fact, that in order to hold to the essence, one is better off discarding the nonessentials. Toynbee in particular seems to suggest this. To follow his suggestion, however, conflicts with a psychologico-anthropological fact of religious experience: one cannot encounter and become truly aware of the *universal* common reality in all religion except through the mediation of some *particular* form or symbol. The universal is not simply there for the taking; it always makes itself present through some particular manifestation—even though the universal always breaks the bonds of any particular expression.

Not to realize this bond between the universal and the particular is to expose oneself to dangerous illusions. As the sociologists of knowledge insist, we are influenced by our social context more profoundly than we can ever realize. Every time we attempt to talk about the essence of our own religion or of all religions, we are doing so through the concepts, mythic structures, and especially the social needs of our culture. To think we are stating the heart of our religion in its pure essence, without any cultural accretions, is to fool ourselves. All too often we thereby fall into the trap of idolatry or ideology; instead of communicating what we think is the undiluted core of religion, we are passing on our own pet notions or cultural prejudices. Every experience and statement of the common essence of religions is bound up with some nonessentials.

Another pitfall in this same area is the way many followers of the common essence approach subtly suggest that what Toynbee calls the nonessentials of religion are incidental, or completely arbitrary. This impression is strongly present in Schuon's arguments, more moderately so in those of Toynbee and W.C. Smith. It seems that anything goes; any creed, code, or cult can express the mystery of the Ultimate as long as it is personally appropriated, as long as it fits the needs of many. The doctrines, the rituals, the ethical practices of all the religions are valid; they are all equally true. Although most of our authors would not state it that baldly, that is the popular conclusion many draw.

What is too naively forgotten is that the external forms of religion *do* affect the way the Ultimate is experienced and the way that experience is lived out in daily life. It is possible that some nonessentials can distort the reality of God and lead to practices that are not in harmony with the truth and goodness of the Ultimate. Also, certain "accretions," certain beliefs and ethical norms, may provide a more adequate image of deity or a more relevant morality than other beliefs and norms. Of two religious attitudes, for instance, one advocating the burning of widows and the other, the equality of all men and women, most persons would venture the judgment that one is a more adequate and relevant articulation of religious experience than the other. Religions differ and the differences can and often should make for a certain ranking. Many who hold to the common essence view miss this point. Put simply, "many" does not mean "any." There will always be many different voices for the one common essence within all religions, but this does not mean that any voice will do the job or that one voice is necessarily just as good as another.

Just how to determine which expressions are "better" is a whole different and thorny question. It opens up an array of problems concerning how religions are to dialogue with each other. These questions will be with us again in the final chapters of this book.

2) Another problem in the common essence school is related to the one just described. Among the authors we studied, and more so among their popular interpreters, there is the danger that one ends up in a kind of conciliatory and tolerant attitude that hamstrings genuine dialogue. An exaggerated stress on what is common to all religions does not leave much to discuss. Differences are too easily minimized. If we already agree on all the essentials, what are we really discussing in religious dialogue?

This tendency to gloss over differences and present the religions as one happy family appears, to a certain extent, in Toynbee's version of the common essence within the seven major world religions. When he admits that religions differ in their images of the Ultimate as personal or impersonal, or in their understanding of evil as part of or distinct from deity, but then goes on to state that such differences do not impair their essential unity, he may be right. (Personally, I believe he is.) But it is too easy. More must be said before that conclusion can be so serenely reached. Such differences do matter. They can make for a dialogue that will expand and reconceive, perhaps painfully, the present self-understanding of the religions involved. These differences should not be lost in the solvent of a common essence.

Another related obstacle to dialogue among religions arises from the extreme version of the common essence school presented by Schuon and the perennial philosophers. If the common essence of all religions is to be found in a "transcendent unity" rooted in the mystery of God's nonduality with the world, if this unity is beyond all words and religious forms, and cannot be spoken of or realized here below—then why talk about it at all? This leads to a total emptying of all real content for interreligious dialogue. It also gives free vent to a lazy tolerance that makes provision not only for *many* expressions of the essence of religion, but also for *any*. The common experience or essence of religions can never be put into words, Schuon insists; each religion can stammer as it will.

This criticism of Schuon's vision, it should be noted, does not necessarily negate his proposal that the depth of every authentic religion arises from an experience of a nondual unity between God and the world—a unity that most Western Christians miss. Yet if dialogue among religions is going to be possible, there will have to be a unity that, although it is ever beyond all our thoughts and words, still can be spoken of and symbolized with some relative adequacy. This means that some expressions may be more adequate than others. Such possible differences would be revealed in dialogue.

3) What has just been said leads to another difficulty or question for the followers of the common essence school. All the authors we studied ended up with the absolute denial that there can be an absolute or final or "best" expression of this common essence within the world of religions. Admitting that there is a definite element of truth in this denial, one has to ask whether it might be too absolute. It is basically the same question posed to Troeltsch and the relativists. Does not such a staunch denial of any absolute religion run contrary to the nature of authentic religious experience? Does not any genu-

inely personal experience of the Ultimate contain a degree of absoluteness in leading one to assert that not only is this true for me but it can also
be true for others? The experience of the Ultimate brings one to the natural
contention, not that other religious experiences are false, but that one's own
can also be true for them. Again, devotees of the common essence approach
often fail to recognize this "absolute" quality of religious experience.

A more difficult and more serious problem, already raised for Troeltsch
and his followers, is even more fitting for Toynbee, Smith, and Schuon:
granting that the common essence of all religions can never be captured by
any one of them, is it not still possible that one religion may offer a fuller
expression of that essence than all others? This is asked as a possibility, not a
necessity. But the possibility appears more likely when we hear Toynbee and
Smith urging the necessary role to be played by religion in the forming of a
new world unity, a "community of communities." Does it not seem logical
that if there is going to be one united world built on a common religious
ground, there will be one religious symbol or expression that would include
and unify all the others? It would be a case not of religious exclusiveness but
of "first among equals." We are talking about a possibility. Do the advocates of the common essence school sufficiently recognize and allow for this
possibility?

4) Finally, we are faced with a question for Toynbee and company, which
has, and will, come up frequently throughout this book. Does the common
essence approach too easily throw out the traditional Christian belief in the
uniqueness, the normativity, and finality of the revelation given in Jesus the
Christ? When Toynbee calls for an abandoning of Christian intolerance,
when W.C. Smith urges a "theological surrender," are they too readily sur-
rendering something that makes up part of the essence of Christianity, and
perhaps does so for good reason? Maybe, just maybe, Jesus of Nazareth
offers a symbol and a message that will prove to be the central focus of all
religious experience and expression. When I say "maybe," I mean it seriously. "Maybe not" is also a real possibility. But both possibilities have to
be seriously explored. It seems that many within the ranks of the common
essence view are not disposed to do so.

Chapter IV

Common Psychic Origin

The attitudes we are going to survey in this chapter may not be as well known as those represented by Troeltsch and Toynbee. Although somewhat more sophisticated, they are growing in popular awareness. They all have to do with the assertion that religious faith has its genesis in the human psyche: all religions arise from (or as part of) a common psychological process within the individual, which can be examined and interpreted by the scientists of the psyche—modern psychologists and psychiatrists.

We shall first try to understand precisely what such views on the psychic origin of religion contain and how they are being used to urge a greater dialogue and "unitive pluralism" among all the world religions. Some critical questions will follow: What might Christians learn from this psychological approach to religious pluralism? Does it really promote interreligious dialogue?

Our guide through the various versions of the psychic origin of religion will be the man who stands today as one of the founding fathers of modern psychology of religion: Carl Gustav Jung.

JUNG: THE COMMON SOURCE AND FUNCTION OF RELIGIONS

Born in Switzerland in 1875, the son of a minister of the Swiss Reformed Church, Jung soon broke with his father's devotion to Christianity. His attitudes toward religion were to follow a circular path that many persons today have experienced: from naive possession to radical disenchantment to repossession through a "second naiveté." He was nurtured in the stern embrace of Calvin's reformation theology, only to reject it at an early age as so much "fancy drivel" and oppressive "mumbo-jumbo."[1] Armed with the tools of science, he moved on to the study of medicine, associated himself with Freud from 1907 to 1913, and accepted Freud's view of religion as a projection of our childhood fancies and fears.

Another break soon ensued, this time with his mentor, Freud. From 1921 on, and especially in the final period of his life (1952–1961), Jung came to see

55

the image of God as an ingredient necessary for psychological health. Although he spoke off the record of his personal belief in God, he insisted that his psychology of religion was anchored not in personal faith but in the data he amassed from his patients and from his extensive studies of the archaic cultures of Central Africa and North America.[2]

However questionable Jung's research methods may have been,[3] his conclusions have enabled many today to affirm all the more coherently the "common essence," the "relativity," and the need for dialogue among world religions. We shall examine Jung's views on religion under four headings: 1) the unconscious; 2) the archetypes and symbolism; 3) the "divine content" of the unconscious; and 4) the role of world religions, especially of Christianity.

The Reality of the Unconscious

Jung was heir to a surprising discovery made at the end of the last century. For our understanding of what we human beings are, it was as momentous as the discovery of biological evolution or of DNA. It revealed, in the words of William James, "an entirely unsuspected peculiarity of human nature."[4] We humans are not simply what we *think* we are! We are animated by more than what we are expressly aware of. Below and in vital connection with our "consciousness" there is what has come to be called the "unconscious" or "subconscious." This unknown part of us is as much what we are as is our self-consciousness. In fact, as Jung argues, it contains our true selves. He compared the conscious part of us to an island surrounded and sustained by the ocean of the unconscious. Unless we recognize and progressively become aware of this unconscious, we shall never fully be or become what we really are.

Freud was one of the best known early explorers of this new domain, and Jung learned much from him. Yet for Freud, at least in his early writings, the unconscious was a kind of refuse bin of our past lives, both individual and communal. It contained the repressions of our infancy, the primal and erotic urges of the id, the destructive instincts of what he called the death wish. Jung could agree with much of this. But his studies led him to see other, more important and more positive contents of the unconscious, contents that were much more mysterious than Freud's earthy and primarily sexual libido.

Jung admitted that he could never fully and clearly say just what the unconscious was and what it contained. He called it a *Grenzbegriff*, a limit concept, a pointer to something that is as real to our experience as it is impervious to our full comprehension. (Interestingly, the same term *Grenzbegriff* was used by Kant to designate the concept of God.) The unconscious was an "undifferentiated energy" stirring within us, an "élan vital" that seemed to behave and call us as if it had its own intelligence and purposeful volition.[5] Not to be confused with a "ghost within the machine," it was as much part of us as it was more than what we think we are. One of the clearest and most provocative descriptions Jung gave of our unconscious selves was "the whole man, who is at once the greater and the future man."⁶ Somehow, the unconscious contains both the present and the future; in its unknown content it is presently active within us, but we have yet to realize and actualize that content.

The Archetypes: The Silent Voice of the Unconscious

If there be such an undifferentiated energy, such a future self within us, how can we know it? How can we come into contact with it? How can we respond to it? Jung's first answer to such questions was a warning: not through our purely rational processes. Our intellect, our powers of logical reason, will not do the job. According to Jung, the reality of the unconscious represents the mysterious, the suprarational, element within us and all the world. Before it, the human being is humbled into recognizing that the real is ever beyond our mind's grasp and technological control.

One of the most reliable, though still mysterious, pathways into the suprarational yet creative darkness of the unconscious is what Jung came to term the archetypes. They can be called the "silent voice of the unconscious." They are a voice; they speak forcefully. Yet to hear them we must use more than our ears. The archetypes are not innate ideas or prepackaged messages. Rather, they are predispositions toward the formation of images, *a priori* powers of representation, inbuilt stirrings or lures that, if we can feel and follow them, will lead us into the depths of what we are and where we are going. They might be called messages-in-code, which we must decode and bring to our conscious awareness.

It is difficult to speak about what these messages contain. Their general contents, Jung tells us, have to do with light and darkness, death and rebirth, wholeness, sacrifice, and redemption. He saw such archetypes as the common seedbed of all religions.⁷

Jung discovered a mechanism by which the archetypes could be decoded: symbol and myth. If the archetypes are the silent voice of the unconscious, symbols and myths are for Jung the means with which we can hear them. The archetypes are common to all religions, but symbols and myths will be different, dependent on the varying cultural, historical contexts. So we have the divine mother, the wise old man, the dying god, the young virgin, the hero-savior, the cunning evil one, the hidden treasure—all of them clothed in their varied cultural garbs, having different faces and names.

Symbols and myths have the power to affect our minds and at the same time launch us beyond our powers of reason. They touch the whole person at once, Jung tells us, our thoughts and feelings, our senses and intuitions. This is the mysterious but so evident power of symbolism, proving that the human being must be defined not only as a rational animal but as a symbol-needing and symbol-creating animal. It is through symbols that we are put into contact with our unconscious; through symbols the suprarational darkness within us can become, increasingly, a guiding light.

Common archetypes, similar symbol patterns within diverse cultures—

what brought about these similarities? Jung felt there was enough evidence to posit a fundamental, hidden unity animating all humanity. He came to grasp an even more mysterious facet of the unconscious: it is not only personal and individual; it is also collective. If the unconscious can be looked upon as a deeper well or source within each of us, then all the individual wells lead down to a common underground stream.

As to what constituted or gave rise to this common stream, Jung seemed to view it both as a given and as the result of a long evolutionary process. "The collective unconscious contains the whole spiritual heritage of mankind's evolution, born anew in the brain structure of every individual."[8] If everything else about us is the product of evolution, then certainly our unconscious should be also. Jung could wax poetic in describing the reality and implications of the collective unconscious: "In some way or other we are part of a single, all-embracing psyche, a single 'greatest man,' the *homo maximus*."[9] "The greater and future man," by which Jung had described the unconscious, turns out to be all of humanity. What this means for the commonality and future unity of the religions is already evident.

God: The Content of the Unconscious

One of the archetypes that Jung discovered within the unconscious was what he called the "self." It represents the goal of the process of "individuation," the process that is really what life is all about: "the systematic confrontation, step by step, between the ego and the contents of the unconscious."[10] Individuation, or the formation of the self, then, is the gradual coming together of our consciousness and our unconscious, the explicit realization and appropriation of what we are, that "greater and future man." But to his own amazement, Jung also discovered that he could not really distinguish, psychologically, the realization of the self from the *imago Dei,* the image of God. To realize what we are is to realize God, our basic oneness with deity. "Strictly speaking, the God-image does not coincide with the unconscious as such, but with a special content of it, namely the Self. It is this archetype from which we can no longer distinguish the God-image empirically."[11] As Aniela Jaffe, one of Jung's closest associates, comments, "The encounter with the mystery of the psyche cannot be distinguished from an experience of God."[12]

How could Jung dare raise such a claim among his sophisticated, skeptical fellow scientists? It was because the self, the deepest treasure of our unconscious, bears all the characteristics that religious persons and theologians have given to the reality they call God: 1) The self, hidden and beckoning within us, is *ineffable,* beyond all our reasoning powers and concepts; it is radical mystery, which, however, is radically real in the effects it has upon us. 2) It is also a reality both *transcendent* and *immanent*—truly with us and part of us, yet ever more than what we now know ourselves to be.[13] 3) In Rudolf Otto's well-known description of God, it is a *mysterium tremendum et fascinosum*—a mysterious power that both frightens us in its darkness and fascinates us in its promise.[14] 4) Finally, the self cannot be distinguished from the God-image in that it seems to fit what Aquinas called the human being's *desiderium naturale Dei*—the heart's natural desire for God. The "undifferentiated energy" within us has the same power to draw and call us as has been attributed to God by many world religions.

So Jung, as a scientist of the psyche, could conclude that the human being is "an entity endowed with the consciousness of a relationship to Deity. . . . As the eye to the sun, so the soul corresponds to God."[15] If to some religious persons this sounded like hubris, if to his colleagues it looked like a theological interpolation, Jung responded: "I have been accused of 'deifying the soul.' Not I but God himself has deified it! I did not attribute a religious function to the soul, I merely produced the facts which prove that the soul is *naturaliter religiosa* [naturally religious], i.e. possesses a religious function."[16]

Both theologians and scientists pressed further questions. Does this prove the existence of God? Is God thereby reduced to a psychological function? To both queries he staunchly responded no. To the religious persons who tried to elevate him to some kind of modern defender of the faith who had finally proven the reality of God, Jung answered that he had done no such thing. As a psychologist-scientist, all he had done was provide the data that there is an "imprint" of God within the unconscious; where this imprint came from, whether there was an "Imprinter," Jung as a scientist could not say.[17] "The human intellect can never answer this question, still less give any proof of God."[18] The answer to this question is a matter of faith. Jung goes on to chide theologians who are always looking for rational proofs of God's reality. "It is quite clear that God exists but why are people always asking me to prove this psychologically?"[19]

The idea of God is a psychological fact, and belief in God seems to Jung to be a psychological necessity. Look at the fruits of such a faith: it provides a person with a "great treasure," with a "source of life, meaning, and history." "Where is the criterium by which you could say that such a life is not legitimate? Is there, as a matter of fact, any better truth about ultimate things than the one that helps you to live?"[20] For many today this makes practical sense; it establishes the validity of all world religions.

To those who tried to pin the badge of an atheist on him by announcing that he had reduced the reality of God to an archetype or to a feeling within the psyche, Jung's rather impassioned comment in a personal letter to one of his critics speaks clearly:

> I was astonished to find that even you, too, did not understand the concept of the "Self." How on earth did you get the idea that I could replace God—and with a concept at that? I can establish the existence of a psychological wholeness to which our consciousness is subordinate and which is, in itself, beyond precise description. But this "Self" can

never take the place of God, although it may, perhaps, be a receptacle for divine grace. Such regrettable misunderstandings are due to the assumption that I am an irreligious man who does not believe in God, and should be shown the road to faith.[21]

Jung's response is based on simple logic: to say that God can be identified with a psychological experience or process does not mean that God is *only* that. The difficulty, Jung points out, that religious persons or theologians have with locating God *within* the human psyche is that theirs is a "God all out there"—a deity whose being is outside the person and the world, having therefore to speak *to* rather than *within* the human being.[22]

The Religions: Their Common Origin and Function

From his discoveries of the unconscious and the presence of the God-image within it, Jung drew conclusions concerning the nature of the established religions, their differences and their similarities. His conclusions aid many today in making sense of the reality of religious pluralism.

First, Jung's psychological rendition of the theological notion of revelation lays a common foundation for all religions on which they can appreciate and speak to each other. All revelation has its origin, or at least part of its origin, in the individual and collective unconscious. "Revelation is an unveiling of the depths of the human soul first and foremost, a 'laying bare,' hence it is an essentially psychological event, though this does not of course tell us what else it could be."[23] It is the experience of God speaking from within— essentially the same *within* for all human beings. The differing dogmas and doctrines are attempts to give symbolic expression to this essentially ineffable experience. They do differ, and yet they are rooted in the same archetypes.[24]

Religions therefore play a valuable, a necessary, role in mediating between the "divine content" of the unconscious and a person's conscious awareness; without them, the process of individuation is hamstrung. So Jung could call the world religions the great psychotherapeutic symbol systems of the world; they provide the symbols by which the archetypes can be touched and called forth. They tune us to the mystery within so that we can feel its call and not be frightened by its unknown demands. They assure us that this mystery is real and at work within us. Jung's well-known comment on the value of religious faith is not limited to Christianity or to any one religion:

Among all my patients in the second half of life . . . there has not been one whose problem in the last resort was not that of finding a religious outlook on life. It is safe to say that every one of them fell ill because he had lost that which the living religions of every age had given to their followers, and none of them has really been healed who did not regain his religious outlook.[25]

We should not understand this bold statement as a blanket endorsement of all religions. To the end of his life Jung held to many of the criticisms he had leveled as a youth against his father's brand of Christianity. They all converged into one complaint, which is still strongly felt by many contemporaries: Christianity had become too externalized, formalized, institutionalized, and thus lost its bond with the God of the unconscious. So much of Christian creed, code, and cult had become something professed or performed, not something that stirred inner feelings of the divine presence within the human psyche. The powerful symbols of Christianity had become effete signs. Such religion, Jung had to conclude, whether it was Christianity or Buddhism, was not a religion at all. "So long as religion is only . . . outward form, and the religious function is not experienced in our own souls, nothing of any importance has happened. It has yet to be understood that the *mysterium magnum* [the great mystery] is not only an actuality but first and foremost rooted in the human psyche."[26]

Jung's convictions about the necessary role of the religions as mediators between individuals and their "divinity within" led him to further conclusions. No religion, no symbol can claim to be absolute, the one and only. We have heard such statements in previous chapters; this time they rest on psychological supports. "It is altogether inconceivable that there could be any definite figure capable of expressing archetypal indefiniteness."[27] In other words, the God-image is utter mystery, ever beyond our realization; it cannot be captured in any one form. Expressed somewhat differently, the process of individuation is a never-ending journey of integration between the self and the divine; an absolute, final religion would mean trying to bring the journey to an end.

Does such a condemnation of religious absolutes lead to a stultifying religious relativism? Jung had to face this question, too. His response was simple and direct: the denial of a final, definitive religion does not necessarily lead to relativism (the impossibility of making any truth claims) but it does lead to pluralism. "Is it not thinkable," Jung gently suggests, "that . . . God has expressed himself in many languages and appeared in divers forms and that all these statements are true?"[28]

Jung was aware of what theologians would call the christological implications of such a question. He had much to say about Jesus as the Christ: "The Christ symbol is of the greatest importance for psychology insofar as it is perhaps the most highly developed and differentiated symbol of the self, apart from the figure of the Buddha."[29] Jesus is called Christ because he represents the completion of the process of individuation, the realization of the self, the integration between the individual person and the universal God. In the later period of his life, Jung came to see the theological concept of incarnation as another model for what he meant by individuation.[30] And he saw the passion as a further symbol of the pain and trust involved in the process of individuation, in leaving the ego in order to abandon and integrate it into the mystery of the self-in-God.[31]

As is evident, Jesus is for Jung one of the best symbols of the Christ, but he is not the only one. Jung had a psychological explanation for the traditional Christian claim for the exclusive uniqueness of Jesus: from the early history of the church, Christians have held that Jesus is "one and only" precisely because he is such an effective symbol; having been grasped and transformed by this symbol, they naturally attribute to it "a universally binding truth— not of course by an act of judgment, but by the irrational fact of possession, which is far more effective."[32] In other words, "one and only" means "the symbol really works, take it seriously." Yet there are for Jung other symbols that work as effectively for others. "In the West the archetype [of the self] is filled out with the dogmatic figure of Christ; in the East, with Purusha, the Atman, Hiranyagarbha, the Buddha, and so on."[33] As suggested above, were Jung to rank these figures, he would most likely put both Jesus *and* Buddha on top.

Granting such an understanding of similarities and differences among religions, Jung went on to advocate a dialogue among them. Especially in the encounter of Christianity with Eastern religions he felt there was much to be learned. The East, in Jung's estimation, had long been aware of the reality of the unconscious and the necessity of penetrating its depths. "It is a well known fact that this problem [of the unconscious] has been seriously occupying the most venturesome minds of the East for more than 2,000 years, and that in this respect methods and philosophical doctrines have been developed which simply put all Western attempts in the same line into the shade."[34]

Jung recognized that just as the West had lost touch with the inner life and the God within, the East tended to ignore the reality of the material world.[35] There is much to be learned on both sides. Yet he felt that "the East is at the bottom of the spiritual change we are passing through today. . . . this East . . . lies essentially within us."[36] "We must get at the Eastern values from within and not from without, seeking them in ourselves, in the unconscious."[37] Eastern religions can provide us with the challenge and the means of discovering the divine within us. Here Jung gave special credit to Zen; it offers us techniques for getting beyond our conscious selves to an energizing, peace-giving experience of ourselves as "nonegos" within the "universal mind" or consciousness.[38]

Yet Jung warned Westerners against trying to become Buddhists or Hindus. We are limited by our cultural experiences. The differences between East and West are stark; they dare not be brought together into a simplistic unity. "It is much better to accept the conflict [between East and West], for it admits only of an irrational solution, if any."[39] Jung seemed to believe that a solution can and must be found. It will be a paradoxical unity of opposites, beyond reason, in which East and West will balance and enrich each other. Only a paradoxical unity of opposites can express the unity of differences between the conscious and the unconscious, between the human person and God. "Since there is only *one* earth and *one* mankind, East and West cannot rend humanity into two different halves."[40]

Jung's very complex psychological framework for understanding religious experience and the religions ends with a very practical payoff. It convinces many contemporaries of the essential sameness of all religions and the contemporary need for interreligious dialogue.

OTHER PSYCHOLOGICAL VIEWS HARMONIZING WITH JUNG'S

Jung's case for the psychological value and even necessity of religion was, originally, the revolt of a lone individual against the mighty master, Freud. He was and still is today scorned by many of his colleagues for his philosophical and theological "flights of fancy." Yet his revolt caught on. During his lifetime there were many who followed his lead. Today Jung can be seen as the main voice in a chorus of psychologists for whom religion is much more than a meaningless crutch. What follows is a brief overview of reputable figures in modern psychology who, sometimes in express dependence on Jung, have joined him in trying to understand the common psychic origin of all religions. They all lend further support to what is a growing popular attitude toward religion and religious pluralism.

William James

William James, whose *Varieties of Religious Experience* is the first thought of many when the psychology of religion is mentioned, constructed his view of the psychological structures of religion at the same time as Jung (1902) but quite independently. It is remarkable how, starting from opposite sides of the ocean, they both arrived at similar discoveries. James harmonizes with Jung in his "scientific" recognition that all religion flows from a kind of sixth sense, an intuitive perception or feeling of a greater reality that pervades us and all creation.[41]

James, like Jung, also asked just where this sixth sense, this power of feeling the divine, is to be located. Throughout *The Varieties of Religious Experience* he hints that this religious perceptivity is in "our mental machinery," part of "the human ontological imagination," in the "non-rational," having to do with "the subconscious."[42] In the final chapter, these hints become a hypothesis that for James is quite amply verified: the sense, even the reality, of the divine is part of the human subconscious:

> Let me then propose, as an hypothesis, that whatever it [deity] may be on its *further* side, the "more" with which in religious experience we feel ourselves connected is on its *hither* side the subconscious continuation of our conscious life. . . . The further limits of our being plunge, it seems to me, into an altogether other dimension of existence from the sensible and merely "understandable" world.[43]

We seem to be hearing a more eloquent version of Jung's description of the divine qualities of the unconscious. With Jung, James draws his scientific conclusions about the existence of God. It is a simple, pragmatic argument: "God is real since he produces real effects."[44] It is something like Jung's "if there's an imprint, there must be an Imprinter." We have this sense of a greater whole; it enables us to live more fully. "But that which produces effects within another reality must be termed a reality itself, so I feel as if we had no philosophical excuse for calling the unseen or mystical world unreal."[45]

Like Jung, James did not spell out in detail the implications of his understanding of religious experience for religious pluralism and dialogue. Yet his hints blend with Jung's: there is a wide and necessary variety of religions, but underlying them all is an essential sameness: "When we survey the whole field of religion, we find a great variety in the thoughts that have prevailed there; but the feelings on the one hand and the conduct on the other are almost always the same, for Stoic, Christian, and Buddhist saints are practically indistinguishable in their lives."[46] The differences are important, and some religions will offer a more coherent expression of this greater reality than others. Yet James, like Jung, affirms the need for all religions to respect each other and learn from each other. "Each attitude being a syllable in human nature's total message, it takes the whole of us to spell the meaning out completely."[47]

James was a contemporary of Jung. Today Jung's basic approach to the positive contents of the unconscious has been affirmed and made all the more popular by what has been called "the Third Force" in modern psychology.[48] The movement is broad and includes the varied perspectives of such respected scholars as Rollo May, Adrian Van Kaam, Carl Rogers, Eric Fromm, Gordon Allport, Karen Horney, Abraham Maslow, Victor Frankl, James Hillman, Roberto Assagioli. The focus of their agreement is on the unconscious not as a reservoir of impulses and repressions but as a storehouse of potentialities awaiting actualization; for them the human being is not a bundle of mechanisms but a self-actualizing, creative creature. Not all of these psychologists treat explicitly of religion or give it an important role in human actualization. But all of them recognize the "spiritual dimension" of the human being's quest for wholeness and the "God-likeness" of the most fulfilling human aspirations: love, creativity, beauty, selflessness.[49]

Abraham Maslow

One of the prime movers within the Third Force who has much to say about religious experience is Abraham Maslow. Best known for his notion of "peak experiences" or "core-religious experiences," Maslow provides both an affirmation and a "de-esotericization" of Jung's views.[50] Peak experiences bear all the characteristics of what theologians have called religious experience: they bring about a sense of peace and of the value of life, of oneness with the universe and with others, of self-worth and yet selflessness.[51] Such religious or peak experiences are for Maslow natural and can be examined by the psychologist-scientist. Although he does not speak about their origins within the unconscious, he holds that they can be triggered for every human being by the most ordinary occasions: natural beauty, art, childbirth, philosophical insight, athletic success, friendship, sexual love. With Jung, Maslow argues that not only can all persons have such experiences, but need to; such experiences are "instinctoid" —integral needs of the human organism. To lack them is like having a deficiency of vitamin B12; it leads to neurosis.[52]

Peak experiences, arising from within the human being, are for Maslow "the very beginning, the intrinsic core, the essence, the universal nucleus of every known high religion."[53] Thus he ventures the "very plausible hypothesis" that "all religions are the same in their essence and always have been the same."[54] Maslow urges his contemporaries to penetrate behind the organizational, social forms of religions and touch this common experience within them all.[55] He goes on to suggest, with Jung, Troeltsch, and Toynbee, that this inner essence rooted in the human psyche should be the "meeting ground" for a new dialogue among all the religions of the world.[56]

Roberto Assagioli

One more member of the Third Force of psychology merits mention: Roberto Assagioli, who presents one of the most creative elaborations of Jung's basic approach. A pioneer of psychoanalysis in Italy around 1910, Assagioli soon developed a theoretical framework and practical method for exploring the positive forces of the unconscious; he called it "psychosynthesis." His portrait of the conscious and the unconscious is essentially that of Jung, although he recognizes a realm of the unconscious that he termed the "superconscious"; it is the fount of what is most noble in humanity: artistic inspiration, ethical insight, scientific intuition. It is both personal and collective.

He steps beyond Jung when he describes the greater self—that is, what a person can become by penetrating and appropriating the contents of the Superconscious. Assagioli calls this greater self "the transpersonal self." He expressly states that this transpersonal self participates in or is potentially at one with what can be called "the Universal Self." It is this Universal Self, both immanent and transcendent, to which all the religions of the world have pointed with their various symbols of divinity. Assagioli, therefore, affirms where Jung only suggests: at the apex of the individual, personal self one finds the universal divine self. Among the various symbols he uses in his technique of psychosynthesis, the figure of the "Inner Christ"—an image of the unity of particular and universal, human and divine, within each person—holds a prominent position. Here again he agrees with Jung in exalting Christ as one of the most effective symbols of the self.

Assagioli also affirms the common psychic origin of all religions. He is in fundamental agreement with Jung when, on the basis of this common origin, he suggests a " 'psychosynthesis of the religions'; which does not mean creating a unique religion and abolishing the existing ones; it means that understanding and appreciation between the different religious confessions can be developed, and some fields of cooperation can be established."[57]

There is, then, a shared belief among many modern psychologists and psychiatrists that all the world religions are offspring of a common parent: the human psyche. For many persons today the implications of their views seem to corroborate what Troeltsch and Toynbee had to say about the relativity and the commonality of all religions. Can Christians concur with these widespread views?

COMMON PSYCHIC ORIGIN?

Jung and his followers raise for Christians a number of pressing questions that open new opportunities for understanding both Christian tradition and that of other religions. Christians cannot hide from these questions if they want to live and understand their faith within the world as it is. Yet the popular attitude that all religions have a common psychological source can also be pushed to extreme conclusions that harm more than help interreligious dialogue. To conclude this chapter, I should like to comment on what I think are the challenges and the extremes in the psychological approach to religious pluralism.

Questions for Christians

Religious and Psychological Experience

Whatever is real religiously or theologically must also be real psychologically. If God is actual, if God has entered one's life with grace, revelation, redemption, then there must be some evident psychological traces of all this in one's own experience. That was what Jung was telling theologians and religious persons in his attempts, sometimes obscure and sometimes audacious, to spell out the implications of his psychological discoveries for religion.

Can Christians agree with him? It seems they must, for if religious experience is not a psychological experience, if it does not register and have its effects in a person's psyche, it is no longer his or her experience. In this case, religious experience will be based purely on something outside one's own self, on someone else's experience or someone else's authority. It will give rise, as Gregory Baum warns, to a religion of extrinsicism, grounded mainly in "what the Bible says" or "what the pope declares."[58]

Christians must also admit the general accuracy of many of Jung's and Maslow's indictments of Western Christianity. Its symbols and sacraments have for many become effete signs; its dogmas and morals have lost their rooting in the psyche and thus have become propositions or laws that persons accept without knowing or feeling why they do so. The "great mystery," the

God of Jesus, has been lost, for many, behind the clouds of doctrinalism and legalism.

God and the Unconscious

Can Christians affirm what Jung, James, Assagioli and others have said about God and the unconscious? This is one of the most delicate issues in the exchange between theology and psychology, the point where cries of "reductionism" are loudest.

Martin Buber and many other theologians have severely criticized Jung for containing the transcendent God within the confines of the human psyche. In Buber's view, Jung reduces religion to psychology; "God" becomes nothing more than a powerful feeling and consciousness of deity, only self-consciousness.[59] Buber's concerns are legitimate. Such reductionism would destroy the distinction between God and the human and would thus eviscerate the central beliefs of most religions that the human being is not alone in the universe, that there is a "more" that pervades reality and grounds the efforts of humanity to find meaning and to better the world.

Jung's defense against such accusations is simple and direct: to say that God must be a mighty movement within the soul is not to say that God is nothing more! Jung counters with a sobering question: Why are so many Christians afraid of granting God a place within human psychology? These fears seem to flow from a determination, especially on the part of theologians, to preserve a turf that is exclusively religious in order to maintain a clear distinction between God and the human being. God must remain God (out there) and humans must remain human (down here). To insinuate, as Jung, James, and Assagioli do, that God and humanity are intimately involved and have their being in each other is seen by many Christians as a violation of the divine dignity.

In this delicate area of the relationship between God and the psyche, Jung and his school of religious psychology offer, I believe, an important challenge to Christians: to recognize and overcome the *dualism* between God and the world that has burdened Christian thought and piety for much of its history. Such a dualism sees God as totally other, unchangeable and impassable, and unable to be affected by human events. Opposed to the foundational Christian symbols of incarnation, resurrection of the body, and a God of history, this dualism entered Christian attitudes on the back of Greek philosophy by which Christian thinkers made their first attempts at theologizing. The results are that many Christians today are "anonymous" or unconscious dualists.[60]

Can Christians, then, learn from religious psychologists such as Jung and Assagioli (and from the East) and recognize a God who, although distinct, is not separate from the world? Jung and his followers have offered Christians "evidence" that God is a reality within and part of humanity. As mystics in all the religions have asserted (in varying terminology), we are divine! Can

Christians affirm (and experience!) a *nondualism* between God and the world? For the nondualist, God and the finite are not *one* (that would be pantheism or monism); nor are they *two* (that would lead to supernaturalism). God and the finite are bonded in a mystical, inexpressible unity beyond "one" and "two"; this unity can really be known only in experience. God and the finite have their being in each other (of course in different proportions). Distinct, they cannot, however, really exist without each other. Can such a view of the God-world relationship be called Christian?

Within the framework of his nondualistic view of the relationship between God and humanity, Jung formulated his understanding of how Jesus is the Christ and what it means to call him divine. Again, can Christians endorse the main lines of Jung's christology? Might the content of the traditional language about Jesus' hypostatic union, about two natures and one person, be faithfully retained and yet meaningfully interpreted if Jesus is understood to have realized divinity *within* his humanity? Might Jesus have discovered his divine self within his human unconscious? He would be divine because he achieved the fullness of "individuation." There are complex implications within such a interpretation of Jesus' divinity; it implies that what was accomplished in him can and *should* be realized in others. We shall return to Jung's christological suggestions in chapter 9.

A further question for Christian theology: Might this nondualistic view of divinity and humanity aid Christians to grasp more coherently what "universal revelation" really means and how it works? From Jung's perspective, if deity has its being within our unconscious, it is not dependent on extraordinary events to reveal itself; it does not have to "step down" and enter history here and there, through "mighty deeds" (although mighty deeds need not be excluded). Rather, the divine is *already there*, constantly revealing itself from within. Historical events of revelation remain important, very important. But they are not simply messages from above, messages that come to us entirely from outside. Rather, they come from within each one of us and serve as expressions and further clarifications of a grace and divine presence that is already there, constantly available. As theologians such as Karl Rahner assert, this process of universal revelation within all history is what one should expect to find in all the religions of the world. Such universal revelation, Jung would say, is not only a theological conclusion; it is a psychological fact.

The Criteria of Religious Truth

Jung's psychological approach to religions might also provide Christians with a valuable tool for interreligious dialogue. Can Christians make use of Jung's simple and pragmatic criterion for judging whether a religion is true: the truth of any religious belief or practice can be assessed in light of the psychological wholeness it promotes? If a religion furthers the health of the individual, if it enables the person to engage in healthy relations with others, if it offers a sense of peace and enables a more intense, productive engagement in the world—can one deny that God, the one God of all creation, is acting and revealing through that religion? In view of such positive psychological effects, cannot the basic truth of a religion be accepted before and during all the theological efforts to work out doctrinal or ethical differences?

Jung's criterion for religious truth also works in reverse. If a religion does not promote psychological health, something is wrong; its claims of truth should be questioned. Can (must not) Christians acknowledge and make use of the "hermeneutics of suspicion" of contemporary psychology in approaching religions? If religion is a crutch, if it does not allow us to assume responsibility for our own lives, if it leads us to be manipulated by others, then its truth must be seriously doubted. In other words, good religion should always make for good psychology.[61] In chapters 9 and 10 we shall examine further the validity of judging religious truth by its practical fruits and of basing interreligious dialogue on praxis before theory.

Problems

Too Individualistic/Subjective

A fundamental problem with the Jungian approach to religion is raised by theologians, philosophers, and anthropologists: it is too individualistic, subjective, ahistorical. Jung and his followers do not sufficiently recognize the role that society, culture, and the general historical context play in determining which symbols stir the unconscious. The impression is easily given by Jung that the archetypes are preformed entities swarming within the ocean of the unconscious, waiting for the appropriate symbols that will lure them to the surface of consciousness.

Cultural anthropologists such as Emile Durkheim, Mary Douglas, and Victor Turner have made it clear how much culture determines and limits religious symbols.[62] For instance, if the human psyche has an archetypal need for a God with feminine qualities, this need will not find ready symbols within a patriarchal society. Or, the archetype of the hero-savior might have a difficult time finding symbols of this-worldly redemption in a feudalistically structured society in which the poor cannot feel their own worth and power. Society therefore not only provides the symbolic expressions for the archetypes; it also determines the contents of the archetypes and muffles their voice. To release the power of religious symbol, one may also have to reform society.

An overly individualistic-subjective tone is also evident in Jung's understanding of how symbols work and what determines their truth. One must be careful, as Jung often was not, to avoid viewing the truth of a symbol or of a religion *only* in its ability to stir the heart and resonate in the psyche. True, unless one feels moved by a symbol, it is impossible to even begin to speak about its truth; yet merely to be moved is not enough. One can also be moved to an apparent wholeness that not only harms oneself but also others. The Marxist critique would apply. The criterion for the truth of any symbol or religion must also be its ability to lead to redemptive or positive praxis, to social betterment. To be true, religion must foster not only individual but societal wholeness.

The followers of Jim Jones were powerfully moved by the symbols he presented to them; many of them were moved to suicide. The devotees of Reverend Moon are also deeply stirred; but it must also be asked whether they are being liberated or manipulated. The poor of Latin America, for generations, were consoled by the symbol of heaven and the rewards awaiting them after they passed through this vale of tears; yet their deep religious feelings also allowed the landowners to take even greater advantage of them, assuring them through Christian symbols that the degree of their suffering here below was in direct proportion to the consolation awaiting them in the next life.

Another expression of Jung's overly subjective understanding of myth and symbol is the ambiguity that clouds his view on the relationship of myth and history. He and other contemporary psychologists of religion seem to imply that a myth is powerful only in its mythical content. They do not seem to be aware of such questions as: Is there any difference between nonhistorical myths and myths that are rooted in history? Does a historical myth have any added potency to stir and convince the heart? Even more important, does Jung's view of myth allow for what a particular historical event can add to the truth and power of a myth? More precisely, can history —for instance, the historical event of Jesus—bring forth something that never has entered the mythic imagination of the human being? Can a historical event or person create new archetypes not yet found in the unconscious? Such questions, not easily answered by either psychologists or theologians, must be taken up in any encounter between Christianity and other religions. Such questions lead us to further christological difficulties inherent in Jung's psychology of religion.

Jesus

In evaluating Jung's understanding of Christ as a symbol of the Self, theologians aim a series of criticisms at Jung—only to find many of them ricocheting back onto themselves. A first difficulty flows out of what has just been said about the relationship of myth and history. Jung locates the saving power of Jesus mainly, even exclusively, in his ability to function as an effective symbol of the self. Theologians immediately ask: How important then is the historical Jesus? How essential was it that Jesus actually realized in his own life the process of individuation? And further: How necessary for Christian faith is certainty about who Jesus actually was, what he thought of himself, whether he fully "practiced what he preached"? Jung's view of Christ opens anew the well-worn and complex question about the relationship between "the historical Jesus and the Christ of faith." Jung would probably insist that the Christ of faith or the symbolic Christ *is* more important than the historical Jesus.[63] He would chide theologians such as Hans Küng and even Edward Schillebeeckx for spending too much time trying to establish the risk of faith on scientifically reliable knowledge of the historical Jesus. In so doing, they easily miss the power of myth. Other theologians— David Tracy, Norman Perrin, John Shea—are taking Jung's admonitions seriously; for them the story of Jesus is more important than the history of Jesus.[64]

For Christian theologians, however, to understand the saving power of Jesus mainly as the power of myth triggers even more tangled soteriological questions: What does salvation mean? How did Jesus effect redemption? To follow Jung means to run counter to the popular and traditional image of Jesus' dying for our sins, satisfying the Father's justice, and thus opening the gates of heaven. In Jung's view, Jesus saves not primarily by *doing* something (e.g., paying a divine debt) but by *revealing* something—by showing an image of God and a vision of life that moves persons deeply and empowers them to liberating action; in living this life they know it to be the reality of salvation. Modern theology seems to be moving in a Jungian direction by viewing Jesus more as a "final cause" of salvation (through revelation) rather than as an "efficient cause" (through working a change in divine-human relationships).[65]

Jung's views of Christ, finally, provoke the same questions concerning the uniqueness of Jesus that prodded us in the previous chapters. Can it be said that Jesus and Buddha are both equally effective mediators of God—that is, of the divine unconscious within us? Jung at least offers us a tool for answering this question. He tells Christians to look at Buddhists and their way of life. If Christians witness in Buddhists the same fruits of peace, liberation, harmony as in Christianity, there must be an equal cause. Jung's method seems to be valid: compare the two religions, or let them compare themselves in dialogue. The real question is whether this method has so far been sufficiently applied to warrant Jung's certain conclusion that Jesus is no more effective a savior than Buddha or many other religious figures. We shall take up this question in chapters 9 and 10.

In any case, the arguments Jung advances against the uniqueness of Christ are another example of the multiplying questions that Christians must face as they make their traditional statements about Jesus as the one and only savior and incarnation of God. Such questions, as we have seen, are coming from various quarters. Troeltsch and Toynbee expressed some of them, and Jung strengthens them with his arguments from psychology. Christians are being bombarded from this arsenal of arguments. Theology cannot bury its head in the sands of tradition and simply keep repeating the same assertions in the same language.

PART II

CHRISTIAN ATTITUDES TOWARD RELIGIOUS PLURALISM

The preceding chapters have attempted to show that for Christians who take their faith seriously, who want to understand and live it honestly, religious pluralism poses no small problem. The overview, in chapter 1, of how religious pluralism is being experienced today, and the analysis, in chapters 2–4, of the different popular attitudes toward the many religions, raised a barrage of critical questions about the traditional self-understanding of Christianity. To summarize the most explosive of these questions: In our contemporary world of many religions, encountering each other as never before, can Christianity continue to be the same Christianity it has been for the past nineteen centuries? Can Christians continue to understand and present their religion as bearing the fullness and the normative expression of God's revelation? More specifically and more painfully: Can they continue to proclaim Jesus of Nazareth as the only savior and incarnation of God in human history?

The following four chapters will look at the differing, frequently contradictory, answers that Christians have been giving to these questions, especially since the beginning of this century. In an effort to order and clarify their contradictory variety, these answers will be presented as different Christian models for understanding religious pluralism. Each model will be named and examined according to its roots in a particular Christian confession. These confessions represent different traditions, different styles, in which the gospel has been understood and lived, and which are readily identified by both sociologists and theologians. The confessional models to be examined are the conservative Evangelical, the mainline Protestant, and the Roman Catholic. There will also be a chapter on a new or "theocentric" model, which reflects quite different and what can be called "liberal" approaches to religious pluralism; these new approaches are taking shape across denominational boundaries.

The use of models presents both advantages and dangers. The dangers arise from the way a model can easily blur the differing opinions within each confessional type as well as the overlapping areas of agreement between different confessions. Each model is rooted, historically and theologically, in a particular confession, but it is not necessarily limited to that confession. For instance, the conservative Evangelical model is also followed in part by some mainline Protestants and Roman Catholics. Even more clearly, many mainline Protestants endorse the Roman Catholic model—and vice versa. In our age of ecumenism, "purebred" or 100 percent Lutherans or Catholics or Evangelicals are becoming more and more rare. So a model is not to be taken absolutely, as offering an exact replica of a particular Christian confession. Each model, often enough, crisscrosses various confessions. Where such crisscrossings are frequent, they will be pointed out.

The advantages of studying Christian attitudes toward other religions according to these models outweigh the drawbacks. The models do reflect differences that have existed and still do exist among Christians. These differing attitudes toward other religions are rooted in the various confessions that have grown up in the history of Christianity. By clearly marking these differences and understanding their roots, Christians can better understand each other—and therefore, one hopes, dialogue and learn from each other. The result, one hopes further, will be a more coherent and dialogical Christian theology of religions.

The following chapters are intended to offer both an overview of the origins of each model, as well as a description of how the model is being used today. Each chapter will contain a general description of the model in question and a focus on one or more of its representative theologians. The purpose of the focus is to grasp as best as possible the theological principles behind the understanding both of the other religions and of Christianity in the given model. Respecting the convictions and commitments which stand behind each of these views, I will try to present them as objectively and sympathetically as possible. But respect allows criticism; I will also give my own assessment as to how well each model reflects both Christian tradition and contemporary experience.

Chapter V

The Conservative Evangelical Model: One True Religion

"To look at American religion and to overlook Evangelicalism and Fundamentalism would be comparable to scanning the American physical landscape and missing the Rocky Mountains."[1] To offer a survey of contemporary Christian attitudes toward other religions and not to include the Evangelicals would entail the same drastic oversight. As extreme and outdated as the Evangelical model for understanding other religions might seem to those who have felt a basic sympathy with the "popular attitudes" traced in chapters 2 to 4, the Evangelical voice must be heard.

What might appear as extreme in this voice flows from a deep concern for what Evangelicals deem to be the heart of Christianity—especially as that heart beats in the churches of the Reformation. To dismiss Evangelical attitudes as outdated is simply to ignore the fact that these attitudes *do* represent a strong, and an increasingly louder, voice within the Christian population.

EVANGELICAL CHRISTIANITY

But who are we talking about? It is not easy neatly to define or especially to locate followers of this model in any one Christian denomination. Fundamentalist or Evangelical attitudes and lifestyles can be found in all the churches, including mainline Protestant and Roman Catholic. A quick review of the history of the Evangelical movement will bring it into clearer focus.

Although the term "Evangelical revival" includes a widespread movement in eighteenth-century Europe and America, represented by Pietism in Germany, Methodism in England, and the Great Awakening in North America, the name today refers to a new style of Christianity that took shape at the turn of this century in the form of Fundamentalism. Many Protestant Christians in the United States then decided it was time to do something about the way current liberal notions were eroding the heart of Jesus' message. Among the most destructive of such liberal views they identified the following: the new belief in evolution that questioned the veracity of the biblical accounts of creation; the recently born study of comparative religions and psychology that seemed to place Christianity on a par with other religions; and the emergence of the "Social Gospel" within Protestant churches that seemed to imply that God's kingdom could be brought about by social action rather than by spiritual transformation.

As is evident, many of these new views are clearly reflected in what we heard from Troeltsch, Toynbee, and Jung. For many Christians at the turn of the century, to admit such "modern discoveries" into Christian thought was to build a Trojan horse within the camp of Christianity.

It was time to get back to the fundamentals. A series of twelve booklets entitled *The Fundamentals* were decisive in launching the Christian counterattack on liberalism. Authored by a number of prominent theological conservatives and financed by two wealthy Los Angeles businessmen, some three million copies were sent out free of charge to ministers, evangelists, and Sunday school superintendents between 1910 and 1915. With prophetic vehemence, the books castigated all the evils mentioned above. The times were ready; the spark caught and became a conflagration. Fundamentalism was born.

But divisions were soon to develop in the ranks of the Fundamentalists. During the 1940s and 50s a growing number of theologians and evangelists who shared the theological convictions of the Fundamentalists reacted against their polemical spirit, their anti-intellectualism, and social unconcern. In 1941 these protesters formed the National Association of Evangelicals. Although they reaffirmed the Fundamentalists' basic doctrines and concerns about the erosion of the Christian message, they "wanted no dog-in-the-manger, reactionary, negative, or destructive type of organization."[2] The new movement grew under the able leadership of such notables as Harold Ockenga, Carl F.H. Henry, and especially Billy Graham. Graham founded his Evangelistic Association in 1950; it became, for all practical purposes, the embodiment of the new Evangelical Christian movement and solidified the distinction between Fundamentalists and Evangelicals.[3]

The distinction was really more in style than in theology. The Evangelicals shared basic theological viewpoints with the Fundamentalists: 1) an affirmation of verbal inspiration, inerrancy, and absolute authority of the Bible; 2) a stress on the necessity of a personal faith experience of Jesus as the only savior and Lord; 3) a resolute commitment to the urgency of converting the world to Christ; 4) a mistrust of modern theology, especially the historico-critical method of interpreting the Bible.[4] Yet in their way of pursuing these doctrinal concerns, Evangelicals showed a greater regard for demonstrating the intellectual content and coherence of their views. They also wanted to be more open to and cooperative with other Christian denominations and more conscious of the social implications of the gospel.

Further divisions, however, developed among the Evangelicals. Since the

1960s and especially the 70s many Evangelicals have been pressing for further adjustments to the modern world. This liberal swing has given shape to what can be called the "New Evangelical" movement. Their concerns are concentrated in three areas: 1) They are open to even more extensive ecumenical cooperation with other Christians and participate in the World Council of Churches and in national ecumenical movements. For this reason, they are often called "Ecumenical Evangelicals." 2) They are moving away from insistence on the absolute inerrancy of the Bible and affirm, rather, "a limited inerrancy," or the "infallibility" of the Bible in matters of faith and practice but not necessarily in questions of history or science.[5] 3) They claim that Evangelicals in the past have been socially and politically naive and have aligned themselves with the oppressive status quo. They insist that political involvement and efforts for liberation of all the oppressed is part of living the gospel. Many of the New Evangelicals make up what has been called the "New Evangelical Left."[6]

To put some clarifying order into the developments within Evangelicalism since the beginning of this century, we can follow the classifications given by David Barrett in his *World Christian Encyclopedia*.[7] He lists three types of Evangelicals: 1) Fundamentalists, who still carry on the founding spirit of *The Fundamentals* and insist on the seven fundamental doctrines of authentic Christianity: inerrant verbal inspiration of the Bible, virgin birth, miracles of Christ, physical resurrection, total depravity of the human being, substitutionary atonement, premillennial second coming; 2) *Conservative Evangelicals,* who, as explained, want to carry on the intent of Fundamentalism but in a more open, critical style; most of them belong to the World Evangelical Fellowship; 3) the *Ecumenical* or *New Evangelicals,* described in the previous paragraph.

Although the differences between these three groups are clear and although they signify a very important evolution within Evangelicalism, one must also recognize that all three still make up one Evangelical family. There are family ties that hold them together and allow them to stand as a distinct presence within the panorama of contemporary Christianity. Fundamentalists, Conservative Evangelicals, Ecumenical Evangelicals—all three groups hold to the primary authority of the Bible as the one absolute source of knowledge about God and the human condition, whether the Bible be regarded as "inerrant" or as "infallible." All three groups also proclaim the universal lordship of Jesus as the only savior of the world and the necessity of personal experience of his saving power. Finally, all three groups stress the necessity of mission, of witnessing the Lord Jesus to all peoples, so that all can come to salvation.[8]

United by these common bonds, admitting their differences, Evangelical Christians (primarily Protestant) have, over the past few decades, stepped prominently before the eyes of the American public. If we use belief in biblical inerrancy as a criterion for membership in the Evangelical camp, then some 42 percent of American adults qualify.[9] *Christianity Today,* the best known of Evangelical journals, is more reserved but still claimed that in 1979 Evangelicals numbered some 20 percent of the North American population.[10] George Gallup put the figure at 30 percent and in 1978 predicted that the 80s would be "the decade of the evangelicals."[11] From sheer numbers, then, it can be argued that especially in its conservative and ecumenical form, "Evangelical Christianity has finally emerged from its anticultural ghetto into the mainstream of American life. It is now a force to be reckoned with." Evangelicals "today seem to wield the most powerful sword of any religious group."[12]

This sword is a definite force in influencing Christian attitudes and approaches to other religions. For this reason, I begin my analysis of the way Christianity views religious pluralism with the conservative Evangelical model. As the title of this chapter indicates, the views we shall be studying are mainly those of the conservative or nonecumenical Evangelicals (which views, for the most part, reflect those of the Fundamentalists). Ecumenical Evangelicals would balk at many of the claims of this model and would rather rank themselves within what, in the next two chapters, will be called the mainline Protestant or Roman Catholic models. Still, in view of the common bonds among all Evangelicals, we must also recognize that the central concerns of the model we are examining are shared also by Ecumenical or New Evangelicals, especially in the affimation of Jesus' unique lordship and the necessity of evangelization. When it comes to the question of Jesus' uniqueness and centrality, the bonds among Evangelicals are tight.

A general picture of the conservative Evangelical model for understanding other religions is painted clearly and forcefully in the well-known and influential "Frankfurt Declaration." Formulated by the Tübingen Evangelical theologian Peter Beyerhaus, it was approved by a theological convention of Evangelicals in Frankfurt on March 4, 1970, and soon gathered enthusiastic support throughout conservative ranks in Germany. After *Christianity Today* presented it to North Americans as "a most heartening missionary document," it won widespread applause throughout conservative Evangelical churches.[13]

The declaration was formulated as a counterposition to a "fundamental crisis" and "an insidious falsification of their [the Christian churches'] motives and goals" within the World Council of Churches. The crisis, according to the Evangelicals, was caused by the new attitudes toward other religions and by the humanizing tendencies sweeping through many ecumenical Protestant churches.

The position of the Frankfurt Declaration was spelled out with steel-hard clarity. Methodologically, it stated that the "primary frame of reference" for understanding Christianity and evaluating other religions is and can only be the Bible. The verdict of the Bible on other religions is then put forth. Inasmuch as "salvation is due to the sacrificial crucifixion of Jesus Christ, which occurred once and for all and for all mankind," and inasmuch as this salvation can be gained "only through participation in faith . . . we therefore reject the false teaching that the nonchristian religions and worldviews are also ways of salvation similar to belief in Christ." This means that there is "an essential difference in nature" between the Christian church and other religions. To substitute a "give-and-take dialogue" with other religions "for a proclamation of the gospel that aims at conversion" is absolutely rejected as a prostitution of the gospel. The bottom line of the declaration is an urgent appeal to all Christians to take up their missionary obligation to all non-Christians.[14]

The implicit reason for the obligation to evangelize is spelled out explicitly by Harold Lindsell, a conservative Evangelical theologian who heartily endorsed the Frankfurt Declaration: "If they [non-Christians] die without knowledge of Jesus Christ, they perish."[15] Not all Evangelicals would be that prompt to consign to eternal damnation anyone who has not heard of Jesus. Many voice a bold but veiled trust that somehow God will give every good-willed pagan the chance to hear of Jesus, "even if this be not in this life."[16] All conservative Evangelicals, however, would agree that without an encounter with Christ, eternal life is not possible.

The harsh, uncompromising tones of the Frankfurt Declaration were softened but its basic message was reaffirmed by an even larger and more significant gathering of Evangelicals in Lausanne, Switzerland, July 16–25, 1974—the International Congress on World Evangelization. "Certainly the most important evangelical meeting to be held this century,"[17] it was the brainchild of Billy Graham and gathered some 2,470 participants from 150 countries and 135 Protestant denominations (with about 1,200 representatives from Third World countries). Like the Frankfurt meeting, it was organized as a reaction against the liberalizing trends within the World Council of Churches, "in particular, a dominant trend toward syncretism, universalism, and a de-emphasis of evangelism."[18] Like the Frankfurt statement, it strongly reaffirmed the absolute authority of the Bible, the uniqueness of Christ, and therefore the pressing need for evangelism. Because Jesus is "the only God-man," because he is the "only mediator between God and man," the congress rejected "any kind of syncretism and dialogue that implies that Christ speaks equally through all religions and ideologies." Expressly denied was any possibility of salvation through other religions.[19]

But the Lausanne Congress also shifted certain emphases in the Frankfurt Declaration and so signaled an adjustment in the conservative Evangelical approach to other religions. Besides clearly affirming the necessity of "Christian social responsibility," it recognized the need for "that kind of dialogue whose purpose is to listen sensitively in order to understand." The statement in itself seems to indicate a new openness to the value of other religions. But such is not really the case, for dialogue is qualified as "indispensable to evangelism."[20]

More recent Evangelical statements clarify what this qualification means: dialogue with other religions is necessary because you cannot convert persons without first understanding them. Dialogue, then, is valid only as a means for proclamation and conversion. As the well-known Evangelical theologian John Stott explains, dialogue must always be understood as "elenctics"— from the Greek verb, *elengchein*: to convince, to rebuke, to call to repentance. One of the central purposes of dialogue is "to show the absurdity of heathendom."[21]

These are the broad lines of the conservative Evangelical Christian appraisal of other religions. For many they may sound intolerant and narrow-minded. To understand more clearly and perhaps more sympathetically the theological foundations, as well as the deep faith and sincerity, that undergird Evangelical claims, we turn to one of the theological giants of this century: Karl Barth (1886–1968). Certainly Barth cannot be proposed as a classical Evangelical; in fact, many in the older vanguard of Evangelicalism have rejected Barth and his "neoorthodox theology" as being too soft on liberalism.[22] Today, however, Barth is being "reinstated" among Evangelicals. "Evangelicals now find their theological insights in those neoorthodox theologians (Karl Barth, Emil Brunner, Dietrich Bonhoeffer) condemned so vehemently by their predecessors in the 1950s and 1960s."[23] Evangelicals, both conservative and ecumenical, are "finding real potency and balance in the neoorthodox approach to critical issues."[24]

As the following analysis of Barth's evaluation of religion will make clear, his strong affirmation of the central Evangelical principles of the authority of scripture, the centrality and uniqueness of Jesus Christ, and the necessity of Christian witness to the world make Karl Barth an eloquent and sophisticated advocate for the Evangelical attitude toward religious pluralism.

KARL BARTH: ADVOCATE OF THE CONSERVATIVE EVANGELICAL MODEL

From his historical niche as the founder and most influential representative of "neoorthodox theology," Barth enables us to grasp the context, the concerns, and the Christian convictions of present-day conservative Evangelicals. As contemporary scholars point out, the usual liberal dismissal of neoorthodoxy as a blind, *deus-ex-machina* affirmation of the authority of the Bible and the saving power of Jesus is a gross misreading of Barth (and of Evangelicals).[25] Such an accusation implies that Barth had no real concern for speaking to human experience and intelligence. On the contrary, the new orthodox theology, which exploded and spread across Europe with the publication of Barth's *Römerbrief* ("The Epistle to the Romans") in 1922 (second edition), had much in common with the "liberal theology" of such thinkers as Ernst Troeltsch: it very much wanted to respect and speak to what persons were experiencing. But it read that experience very differently!

In this different reading of the human condition, we can perhaps appreciate what Barth and contemporary Evangelicals are saying. What Barth saw in the world around him during the 1920s and 30s is much the same as what the Evangelicals perceive in the 70s and 80s. That perception can be summarized under three central insights.

1) For Barth, the state of affairs in Europe during the early part of this century was an incapacitating *time of confusion*. Christians were inundated with a flood of new, "liberal" ideas, and were awash in a sea of pluralism and relativity. No one, Barth himself included, really knew what they were talking about. Christians were not able to choose, to make a genuine commitment. Much, if not most of this deplorable situation was engendered by the liberal theology that Barth had eagerly learned from his teachers, Wilhelm Herrmann and Adolf Harnack. Something is wrong, Barth realized; a resolute about-face was needed—a return to the core and clarity of the gospel. What is particularly significant is that Barth came to this realization and penned his first prophetic call to a neoorthodoxy not from the shelter of a professor's podium but from his pastor's pulpit in the little Swiss town of Safenwil. Here he realized that his trendy, liberal sermons did not speak to the deepest spiritual needs of his people.

2) Part of this problem, Barth's analysis went on, was that theologians of the time did not face up to the *reality of evil*. The evolutionary optimism and the affirmation of the autonomous human being's limitless possibilities, which liberal theology inherited from the Enlightenment, did not take into account the fact of human limitation, selfishness, and ideological illusion. Such givens in the human condition generate a seeming incapacity in humans really to love each other and achieve a world of unity and peace. Again, Barth came to these convictions not from philosophical musings, but from the specter of horror and slaughter that was World War I. For Barth, "the heady wine of nineteenth century optimism, evolutionary progress and universal brotherhood went perceptibly flat on the fields of Flanders and Verdun."[26] What was needed, then, was a reaffirmation of the basic gospel message: the "bad news" that we are indeed sinners—answered by the "good news" that sin can be confronted and overcome in the power of Jesus Christ.

3) Facing the confusion and evil in the world around him, Barth came to a further insight: human beings cannot figure things out by themselves! Expressed theologically, humans cannot, by their own powers, really understand the full content of the human condition and, more importantly, *they cannot really know who God is*. Here Barth agreed with Troeltsch—all human knowledge is limited and historically conditioned. But he radicalized the claims of historical relativism by acknowledging what persons of his time were sensing: human knowledge, by itself, is so limited that it cannot determine who we are or what we are to do. Again, the solution is a return to the heart of the gospel, especially as proclaimed by Paul and the Reformers: salvation comes through faith, not works—by ourselves we cannot know God or find salvation. Therefore, "let God be God"—this is the theme that thundered through the theology of Karl Barth, from his *Commentary on Romans* to the twelfth and last volume of his *Church Dogmatics*. We must recognize the infinitely qualitative distinction between God and humanity. This means admitting our own inadequacies, accepting God's self-revelation, and letting God save us. And this is precisely what God has done in—and only in—Jesus of Nazareth.

From the foundation of this Evangelical reading of the human condition, Barth elaborated his assessment of the world religions. The following review of this assessment will focus on the famous "paragraph 17" of volume 1/2 of his *Church Dogmatics*. (This is quite a paragraph—it numbers 81 pages!)[27] Here is Barth's clearest and most stirring statement on what Christian revelation has to say about religion.

It was written at the end of the 1930s, when Barth's attack on the excesses of liberal theology was at the height of its prophetic intensity. Even though in later years (toward the end of the 1940s) the prophet assumed milder tones and had more positive things to say about the condition of those who do not know Christ, his verdict on the religions remained intact.[28] It was this verdict, especially as championed and propagated by Hendrick Kraemer, that became *the* Protestant attitude toward other religions during the 40s and 50s.[29] In studying Barth's theology of religions, we are examining a piece of history that, in the Evangelicals, is still with us.

Barth's Verdict: "Religion Is Unbelief"

Barth first declares the one starting point and the one measure for all he has to say about religion in general and the religions in particular: God's revelation in Jesus Christ, as contained in the New Testament. Only here can we start; only here can we finish. This is so, not only because of Barth's existential analysis of human beings' incapacity to truly know themselves or God, but also, and especially, because this is what revelation tells us we must do. He insists therefore that a Christian view of the religions cannot make any use of comparative religious studies or of philosophical notions about the nature of religion. Only God's word can tell Christians what the religions really are.

According to Barth, what this word tells us rests on two foundation pieces of the New Testament message. The first is that *only God can make God known*.

> Revelation is God's self-offering and self-manifestation. Revelation encounters man on the presupposition and in confirmation of the fact that man's attempts to know God from his own standpoint are wholly and entirely futile; not because of any necessity in principle, but because of a practical necessity of fact. In revelation God tells man that he is God, and that as such he is his Lord. In telling him this, revelation tells him something utterly new, something which apart from revelation he does not know and cannot tell either himself or others.[30]

Barth both affirms and negates the human being's ability to know God. He tells us that the truth that only God makes God known is a truth that humans are able to know; but they can know it only if God tells them. So Barth concludes: "We need to see that in view of God all our activity is in vain even in the best life; i.e., that of ourselves we are not in a position to apprehend the truth, to let God be God and our Lord."[31]

But what about those New Testament passages that have traditionally been understood to teach a "general revelation" beyond Christ? The sermon of Acts 14:15ff., speaking about the gentiles, tells us that "in bestowing his benefits, he [God] has not hidden himself completely, without a clue" (v. 17). According to the account of Paul's sermon in the Areopagus in Athens (Acts 17:22ff.), Paul speaks favorably of the Athenians' statue to the Unknown God and tells them that "they were to seek God, yes to grope for him and perhaps eventually to find him" (v. 27). And in the classic text of Romans 1:18ff., Paul states clearly that from the works of creation, "what can be known about God is plain to them, because God has shown it to them" (v. 19).

On all these passages, Barth totally turns the tables. He argues that these texts are speaking about a potential, an ability to know God; but what revelation in Christ makes known, if we read on in each of these passages, is that this potential is never realized. Indeed, it is abused! What did the Athenians do with this knowledge of God? They built temples and made "statues of gold or silver or stone" (Acts 17:29)—which for Barth means that they rejected this revelation "in favor of a capricious and arbitrary attempt to storm heaven!"[32] And Paul in Romans 1:21 continues: "They certainly had knowledge of God, yet they did not glorify him as God or give him thanks." What they did with this knowledge was to sink even deeper into idolatry and moral decadence (Rom.1:22–32). This describes, for Barth, the state of all persons—Jews and gentiles—who do not know Christ. In no way was Paul trying to "link up pedagogically" with a "primal revelation" among the gentiles.[33] He was rejecting it entirely!

The second foundational truth of the New Testament is related to the first and can be stated more briefly. Just as only God can reveal God, so also *only God can save humankind*. We are saved "*sola gratia*"—"only by grace," without any works of our own. Barth spells this out even more clearly: "the affirmation which revelation makes and presupposes of man is that he is unable to help himself either in whole or even in part."[34] This means that every time persons try to do anything to find salvation, they automatically fall into sinful rebellion against God. Barth presses his case even further: only from God's revelation can we truly know that we are in such a sorry state. Only through revelation can we *know* that of ourselves we cannot and therefore should not do anything to save ourselves!

What these two basic truths of Christianity mean for the religions of the world may sound harsh, but Christians must, Barth urges, accept it honestly. This verdict is not meant to be "in any sense a negative value-judgment" based on a scientific or philosophical study of the religions. Indeed Barth recognizes "the true and the good and the beautiful which a closer inspection will reveal in almost all religions." What Barth has to say about all these "human values" in the religions is nothing else but "the judgment of divine revelation upon all religion."[35] Because revelation tells us clearly that only God can reveal God and save humanity and that God has done this only in

Jesus Christ, religion must be seen as the human being's attempt to do what only God-in-Christ can do and has done. Therefore, Barth's verdict on all religions:

> Religion is unbelief. It is a concern, indeed, we must say that it is the one great concern, of godless man. . . . From the standpoint of revelation religion is clearly seen to be a human attempt to anticipate what God in His revelation wills to do and does do. It is the attempted replacement of the divine work by a human manufacture. The divine reality offered and manifested to us in revelation is replaced by a concept of God arbitrarily and willfully evolved by man.[36]

Having announced God's judgment on the religions as "unbelief," Barth draws his practical conclusions concerning the relationship between the gospel and other traditions. In no way may theologians or missionaries seek a relationship between Christian revelation and the religions; in no way may they look for questions in the religions for which revelation supplies the answers; in no way may they seek "points of contact" (*Anknüpfungspunkte)*. The relationship between the Christian message and the religions is an "either-or." The "slightest deviation [from], the slightest concession" to the religions violates the gospel. "We have here an exclusive contradiction."[37]

In view of the biblico-theological evidence, such a verdict on religion is for Barth unavoidable. But one further element is crucial and must be added. This harsh judgment, Barth proclaims, applies not only to the "other" religions but to Christianity as well! What he means by this both softens and sharpens his overall verdict.

Christianity as the True Religion

Barth insists that any talk about "the truth" of Christianity must be prefaced by "the recognition that this religion, too, stands under the judgment that religion is unbelief."[38] In fact, "it is our business as Christians to apply this judgment first and most acutely to ourselves."[39] From this confession Barth draws a conclusion that exemplifies the complexity of many conservative Evangelical attitudes toward other religions: it is impossible to make any kind of comparison between Christianity and other religions—not because the Christian religion is so superior and in "a different class," but because there are no differences at all! It is impossible, Barth tells us, to offer any kind of empirical evidence that Christianity is any better than any other religion. If one looks at all the elements that make up Christianity as a religion—its conceptions of God, its theology, worship, church structure, morality, art, social praxis—there is the same "unbelief, i.e., opposition to the divine revelation," the same "active idolatry and self-righteousness" that is rampant in other religions.[40] In the encounter with other believers, therefore, Christians have absolutely no grounds for a "better-than-thou" attitude.

How, then, can it be said that Christianity is "true" and different from all other religions? The answer is simple and yet profound, and it comes from the heart of Reformation theology: "We can speak of 'true religion' only in the sense in which we speak of a 'justified sinner.' "[41] Just as human beings, despite and *with* all their natural sinfulness, can be accepted and saved by God, so a religion, in all its corruption, can be "exalted" by God. How? "Not of its own nature and being but only in virtue of a reckoning and adopting and separating which are foreign to its own nature and being, which are quite inconceivable from its own standpoint, which come to it quite apart from any qualification or merits."[42] The religion offers nothing; God does everything. It is saved *sola gratia,* only by grace.

If all this is understood, "we need have no hesitation in saying that the Christian religion is the true religion." What "differentiates our religion, the Christian, from all others as the true religion" is not that Christianity can sport "any inward worthiness," "any immanent rightness or holiness."[43] It is just as ostensibly corrupt as all other religions. What makes the difference is that, thanks to revelation, Christianity *knows* all this! It knows that it was and remains sinful but that despite such sinfulness (Luther's *troztdem*) God, because of the "infinite satisfaction for our sin" made in Christ, accepts this religion.[44]

This is a very complex, "dialectical" affirmation of the truth of Christianity. If we unpack its content, we see that it rests on two central claims: 1) The *reason* there can be *only* one true religion is that *revelation and salvation are offered only in Jesus Christ.* 2) This one religion is justified in such a way that *nothing is really affirmed or answered in the world of religions.*

1) In the first claim we see how tightly Barth's evaluation of other religions is tied to his christology. If Barth can say that "in his revelation God is present in the world of human religion," he immediately adds that this can be so only within the framework of the incarnation as the *assumptio carnis*— "the assuming of flesh." Religion is related to revelation as Christ's human nature to the divine person; the unity between the two is limited to a "determined event."[45] Only "as an annex to the human nature of Jesus Christ" can religion be called true.[46] This means: just as only *one* human nature was assumed by God, so only *one* religion has been justified and made true by God. "The divine fact of the name of Jesus Christ confirms what no other fact does or can confirm: the creation and election of this religion [Christianity] to be the one and only true religion."[47]

2) Barth's christology also determines his understanding of *how* revelation renders religion true. If Christianity is justified in Christ, this does not depend on or have anything to do with its quality as "religion"—just as the assumption by God of one particular human nature (Jesus') had nothing to do with any positive qualities or dispositions in that nature. It was simply God's free choice—grace! This helps us understand why Barth could insist that as a religion, in its contents and external appearance, Christianity is in no way different from other religions. This seems to imply that nothing of

religion—nothing we can find in the achievements of world religions—is answered or affirmed by God's justification; also, nothing of religion is really affected or changed by this justification.

That nothing of religion really is justified or made true is astoundingly clear in Barth's well known analogy of the sun: just as the light of the sun falls on one part of the earth and not on another, enlightening one part and leaving the other in darkness, without really changing anything on the earth, so Christ's light falls on the world of religions; it makes *one* of these religions luminous and true, leaving the rest in darkness and falsehood—but without bringing any essential change to the true religion.[48] Christianity is the one true religion only because God decided so, only because the light of Christ falls on it—you might say, only because it can bear the name "Christian." No matter how good and true any other religion might seem, it is false, useless—because the light of Christ has not fallen on it.

How absolutely Barth means this is evident in one of his infrequent concrete references to another religion. He compares the teachings of Christianity with the doctrines of the Pure Land Schools of Amida Buddhism. There is an astounding similarity. Amida Buddhism seems to teach the essence of St. Paul's and the Reformers' insistence that we can find salvation "only by faith," and "only by grace." (Barth admits that the same could also be recognized in Bhakti forms of Hinduism.) Devotees of Amida are told that of themselves they can do nothing and must place their full trust in the saving love and power of Amida. Can we therefore talk about "truth" in these religions? Barth's answer is a resounding no. His reason: "Only one thing is really decisive for the distinction of truth and error. . . . That one thing is the name of Jesus Christ . . . which alone constitutes the truth of our religion."[49] There is a difference between the religious doctrine about grace and "the reality of grace itself." Only the reality of grace makes a religion true and valuable. And only Christianity, standing in the light of Christ, has this reality.[50]

This, then, is Karl Barth's Evangelical evaluation of other religions. Contemporary conservative Evangelicals, in general, qualify or move beyond some of its more radical elements. For instance, many Evangelicals today admit a form of knowledge of God, even revelation, beyond God's self-manifestation in Christ. But they add that such non-Christian revelation is profoundly limited and cannot lead to an authentic, saving knowledge of God; it barely qualifies as revelation in the true sense of the word.[51] And although contemporary Evangelicals may not be as adamant as Barth in forbidding any "points of contact" between the religions and the gospel, they reflect Barth's views by insisting that these contact points are much more negative than positive. As Donald Bloesch states it in his *Essentials of Evangelical Theology,* "In our view, the Gospel is not added to what man already knows but instead overturns man's knowledge and calls him to break with his past orientaton."[52]

Finally, most contemporary conservative Evangelicals would not hold to the opposition that Barth sees between revelation and religion. They do recognize, however, a real distinction between revelation and religion, maintaining that revelation always transcends religion, that the works of religion can never merit or fully express revelation, and that there is only one true religion sanctified by God's grace.

Despite these differences between Barth's views and those of contemporary Evangelicals, there is an evident basic agreement between them. In his insistence on God's revelation in Christ as the only criterion for judging religion and in his analysis of the human condition and of the transcendence of God over the human, Barth provides the deeper theological foundations for the conservative Evangelical model for a theology of religions. Barth enables us to grasp how profoundly this model is rooted in a christology that holds Jesus Christ to be the only savior (*solo Christo)* and in a soteriology that sees salvation occurring "without works" and "only through faith" (*sola fide).* Barth and the Evangelicals are loyal sons and daughters of the Reformers—and, we must add, of St. Paul. This chapter and the one following (on the mainline Protestant model) forces the question whether adherence to this traditional Reformational understanding of Christ and salvation can allow for any kind of a genuinely positive approach to other religions.

THE EVANGELICAL MODEL: INSIGHTS AND INADEQUACIES

Perhaps more than any other Reformational confession, the Evangelicals keep alive one of the central traits of the Reformers: they are Protest-ants. With all the conviction and vivacity of a Luther, they are today still protesting whenever they feel their fellow Christians, in dialogue with other religions, are violating the word of God. In the following evaluation, I shall indicate the Evangelical protests that must be taken seriously. I shall also point out areas where, it seems to me, they "do protest too much"—areas in which they themselves run the risk of misrepresenting or abusing God's word.

Insights

"Faith Alone" and the Human Condition

In their reading of the human condition and in their interpretation of Paul's and the Reformers' "by faith alone," the Evangelicals are telling us something about humanity that we can forget only at our peril—something that, because it is so uncomfortable, many Christians and humanists sweep under the rug of consciousness: as things stand presently, there is something wrong with us and the world. With the religions of the world, we may call it "original sin," or *dukkha* ("suffering"), or *avidya* ("ignorance"). Philosophers prefer more sophisticated language: evil, finitude, radical limitation, illusion, *angst.* Wherever it came from, however it works, whether and how it can be removed (important questions with importantly different answers from the world religions and philosophies), it is there.

For many contemporaries, the language of the Evangelicals may be foreign and in need of qualification and toning down. Still, when they tell us that we are "sinners," that there are limits to the human condition, that sound reason and good will of themselves do not automatically insure progress, they are telling us something very real. To ignore this reality of evil and of essential limitation, to pretend it is not there as we carry on our individual lives and our socio-political projects, is only to compound the problem. Psychologically, it leads to reality-avoidance and to a false image of a limitless self. Politically, it is the fertile soil of ideology or, to use a religious term, idolatry; it leads groups or nations to think that theirs is the flawless, the perfect political or economic system, which all too eagerly they then impose on others.

From this recognition of evil, the Evangelicals move on to make a further assertion that should claim our attention. It too is firmly anchored in the Christian message and adequately attested to by common experience: that by ourselves we can neither figure out nor resolve this "something wrong" in the human condition. Troeltsch and the relativists were right—there are limits to human knowing and achieving. All the religions of the world (even Buddhism) seem to recognize this. But the Evangelicals add something more. With particular urgency, they voice the almost universal religious message: we must, and we can, recognize the possibility of being helped, perhaps even rescued, by a Reality that is more than what we are. By ourselves, by our own "works," we cannot grasp why Humpty Dumpty keeps falling off the wall, nor can we put him back together again. Rather, we must open ourselves, we must trust—by faith alone—that there is a power, a reality, available to enlighten our minds and empower our efforts. To recognize the reality of such revelation or grace does not require us to endorse magic and to expect that it has to knock us off our horse or come as a voice from heaven. The Evangelicals do not always make clear, however, that the power that is beyond us can be experienced as part of us.

With their understanding of "by faith alone" and their insistence on the human need for revelation, Barth and the Evangelicals are reminding Christians that there is a real—they would say "qualitative"—*distinction* between God and humanity. ("Distinction," we should immediately add, does not necessarily require "separation.") Insofar as Christians forget this, insofar as they give in to a humanistic or Pelagian merging of the human and divine, they lose hold of "an element of radical mystery, which anyone hoping to understand the Christian God should at some point recognize."[53] To forget this radical mystery is to violate the Christian message and impoverish the human condition.

Radical mystery implies radical surprise. Perhaps the reality of the "more," of the God of Jesus, holds surprises for us and our confused condition of which we have never dreamed. This brings us to the second central lesson the Evangelicals have to offer us.

"By Christ Alone" and the Uniqueness of Christianity

The Evangelical model presses even more insistently a question raised in the concluding comments on the views of Troeltsch, Toynbee, and Jung. Is it not possible that Jesus of Nazareth might represent something thoroughly surprising, thoroughly exceptional and unique in the history of humanity? For the Evangelicals, there is no doubt about it. This is precisely the heart, the point of power, of the Christian message. We may have serious difficulties with the *way* the Evangelicals arrive at and make this claim—the hermeneutical naivety with which they find it in the New Testament, the uncritical rigor with which they brook no questioning of it. Yet, both critical Christians and skeptical humanists must be open to the *possibility* that *what* they are saying may be true.

Not to admit this possibility is intellectually dishonest. The Evangelicals add that historically and theologically it is a manhandling of Christian tradition. For this is precisely what Christianity, for most of its long life, has claimed. This has been its particular contribution to the efforts of humanity to find a way through the maze of history. Christianity challenges us to say and embrace what otherwise we would not dare to think. In Christ, humans face a "surprising possibility," or an "impossible possibility."[54] In Christ, God has turned the tables on human reason and expectations.

This is the "scandal of particularity." In one particular person and event, God has overcome the relativizing conditions of history; in one event God has offered a truth and a grace found nowhere else, on which the salvation of the world hinges. If God be God, this is possible. And if only we would allow ourselves to accept this possibility, the Evangelicals tell us, we would realize the peace and empowerment it brings.

Evangelicals fittingly warn liberal Christians that by shying away from the scandal of particularity or the element of surprise, they comfortably accommodate Jesus to what they want him to be, instead of accepting what he wants them to be. As Barth correctly saw, by reducing Christ to an "archetype" of what is already contained in our unconscious or to a cipher for what is already going on in history, liberal theology reduced him to "little more than an eminent Victorian with quaintly democratic instincts, or a German paterfamilias given to highmindedness and sweet talk."[55] Jesus becomes the divine seal of approval for the secure middle-class ideologies of Christianity.

Furthermore, the Evangelical insistence on the scandal and the surprise of Christ's uniqueness might not be as incredible and arrogant as it sounds. One of the chief lessons of comparative historical sociology seems to be that critical breakthroughs to new levels of consciousness have occurred in society by an insistence on a particular truth or figure that runs against the grain of what is generally accepted. Through such particular bravery, new breakthroughs are made to a new universal vision.[56] To be more precise, humanists today argue that humanity must achieve forms of unity never before realized and nations must make up a "community of communities." Religious humanists add that world religions must make a vital contribution to this new world unity.

But can such a unity, international and religious, be achieved by the kind of religious pluralism advocated by humanists and liberal Christians? Much of the popular understanding of pluralism so stresses the common essence and the relativity of all religions that the religions end up forming a kind of religious soup in which the ingredients differ only in the different sizes and colors of the boxes they are packed in. As the soup boils, it may seem to change as new and different boxes of ingredients are added; but it remains basically the same soup. If the soup is really to change, if religions are to make a real contribution to a new world order, then what may be required is that one of the revelations, one of the religious figures, be genuinely different from all the others—yes, superior to and normative for all the others. This revelation, this religious figure, could serve as a *symbol of unification* for all the others. By affirming the truth of the others, such a symbol would also elevate them to a new level of consciousness and integration. You cannot have a new level of unity without some unifying agent. And this, Evangelicals suggest, is precisely God's gift to humanity in Christ.

In this line of reasoning, the Evangelical model just might make sense. At any rate, it cannot be dismissed lightly.

It seems, then, that with David Tracy we must admit the "permanent achievements" of the Reformation as they are preserved in neoorthodoxy and Evangelicalism. Christianity (and humanity) have an abiding need of what Tracy terms "proclamation models" for understanding religion in general and Christianity in particular. These models continue to insist that there is available to us a power and a grace and a revelation that come not only to manifest and fulfill what is already given in our experience (that is what "manifestation models" do) but also to surprise, overwhelm, correct us—and to offer us possibilities we never thought of or attempted.[57] I shall try to incorporate these achievements in the suggestions to be made in chapters 9 and 10.

Inadequacies

Admitting its permanent achievements, we must also point out the inadequacies of the Evangelical model. I shall focus on three of them; they all signal key issues that must be faced by any Christian theology of other religions.

1) A first problem with the Evangelical model is a question of method. It is triggered by Barth's and the Evangelicals' insistence on the absolute authority of the word of God contained in the Bible. As was pointed out, Barth in no way wanted to bypass human experience in his neoorthodox approach. He wanted to speak to the needs of all his contemporaries. But he felt he could best do this by starting and ending with the revelation given in Christ as recorded in the New Testament documents. In a sense, Barth and many Evan-

gelicals hold that they can best relate to human experience by showing that there is nothing to which to relate. What an analysis of human experience reveals is that experience tells us nothing—nothing that can get us anywhere. Therefore, when there is a conflict between what our experience or reason tells us and what we find in revelation, there is no question as to who has the last word. We must stand corrected by the word of God.

We have seen how consistently Barth applied this theological method in his evaluation of religions. Like the cherubim guarding the gates of paradise with their fiery swords, he would admit into his theology of religions absolutely no data from the phenomenology or philosophy of religion. It is precisely this concrete application of his method that lays bare its weaknesses. To state the problem somewhat simplistically, it leads Barth and the Evangelicals to the attitude of: "My mind's made up. Don't confuse me with facts." A case in point is his verdict on Amida Buddhism. What both the scholar of religious history and the Christian theologian see in this form of Buddhism is, as Barth admits, the very same belief and practice of "salvation through faith alone." But our eyes and mind deceive us, Barth tells us. Why? Because the Bible tells us that salvation through faith is possible only in Jesus Christ.

This is a problem we shall face in other Christian models for an understanding of world religions. Any method for a theological understanding of religions that insists on Christian tradition (the Bible for Protestants, the magisterium for Catholics) as the only or the final criterion of religious truth seems to blind or at least blur the Christian's vision of what the other religions are saying. It prevents a real listening, without which authentic dialogue collapses.

How, then, is the Bible to be understood? What is its place in theological method in general and in a method for a theology of religions in particular? This pushes us into the bramble of contemporary questions concerning biblical hermeneutics and theological methodology. For the moment, only a few general comments are possible.

The word of God cannot be understood in itself—that is, merely by asking what it *meant* (its "sense"). Rather, we must ask what it *means* (its "referent"). This can be done only by relating it to our present-day experience and knowledge and living. In Hans Georg Gadamer's terminology, the horizon of meaning in the Bible, as in any classic, can be understood only insofar as it is "melted" into our own contemporary horizons of meaning (*Horizontverschmelzung*).[58]

To state this in more general terms, any viable method of theology will have to make use of *two* sources—Christian tradition (scripture and its living interpretation through history) and human experience (which includes both thought and praxis). Both these sources must be listened to openly and honestly; both must be brought into a mutually clarifying and mutually criticizing correlation.[59]

Applying the two-source approach to a method for a theology of religions, we must recognize that a Christian understanding of and approach to other religions cannot be fashioned only from the fabric of Christian beliefs. We will want to start with what the Bible or the official statements of councils have to say about other religions. And what we find must be taken seriously. But no final conclusions as to the value or the truth of other traditions can be reached until our Christian "data" is brought into relationship with a concrete knowledge (theory) and experience (praxis) of other religions. Yes, this will place heavy demands on any theologian working in this area; perhaps it cannot be a one-person task and can be handled only collaboratively. As we shall see in chapter 10, more and more Christian theologians are admitting this and rolling up their sleeves for such a "global method of theology."[60]

2) A second weak point in the Evangelical position—an issue that has already pained us in past chapters—resides in the claim that revelation—authentic revelation that enables someone to know the true God and truly respond to God—can be found *only* in Jesus Christ. We have heard how absolutely Barth and the Evangelicals voice this assertion. My question is: Can it be made so assuredly? Its ironclad certainty is softened on three fronts: contemporary New Testament scholarship, the profound experience of historical relativity by our culture, and our broader knowledge of other religions. At the moment, we can but state the questions. Answers will be attempted in chapters 8 and 9 on the uniqueness of Christ.

As stated above, we may want to admit that the Evangelicals are preserving one of "the permanent achievements" of the Reformation in their insistence that our human knowledge is limited, that by our own efforts we cannot unravel the mystery of ourselves or of God, and that therefore we have to be open to receiving "help" and "an answer" from God. Still, the question remains whether God has provided this answer only in Christ. This is a pivotal question in any theology of religions. As we shall see in the next two chapters, the Evangelical understanding of "only in Christ" is not accepted by other Christians. The mainline Protestant model and the Roman Catholic model, in different ways, will claim that God does offer answers, that there is authentic revelation, apart from Christ.

In light of New Testament exegesis, Barth's argument that the word of God does not allow for any such revelation beyond the Christ event is not airtight. Barth's reading of the "classical texts" dealing with general revelation (Rom. 1:18ff.; Acts 14:15ff.; 17:22ff.) is open to serious criticism. He argued, as we heard, that although these texts admit of God's revelation to the gentiles, they also affirm that this revelation never bears fruit and is always abused. But can Barth be so certain that Paul was so certain? Was Paul making absolute, ontological statements as to the human condition in general, or was he describing what was his experience of the gentile world at that time, in those places?

More importantly, how are we to understand, in its personal and sociological context, the nature of all the evident New Testament language about "only in Christ Jesus," "no other name," "only begotten Son of God"? Is such language part of the *essential message* of the New Testament or does it belong to the *medium* used to get that message across? Further, is it *philosophical* language about the structures of the relationship between the infinite and the finite, meant to *negate* all relationships to the divine apart from Christ? Or is it *confessional* language, meant to *affirm* the importance of what God had done in Jesus? Again, we shall take up a more detailed answer to these questions later.

Furthermore, Evangelicals do not seem to realize that their commendable concern to preserve the "scandal of particularity"—that is, the *particular* importance of Christ for all human beings, is undermined for many by the Evangelical understanding of *only* in Christ. The problem Evangelicals ignore is that many honest persons, as we saw in chapters 1 and 2, are convinced of the historical relativity and nonfinality of all human knowledge and truth claims. Tom Driver may overstate the case somewhat, but he speaks for many:

> I am gradually becoming convinced that the gap between Christianity and modern theories of relativity is widening so much that the churches' teaching about Christ is in danger of losing both its intellectual and its moral credibility. . . . We have reached a stage in history, characterized by awareness of relativity, in which the more we make absolute claims about Christ, the more we empty Christ of all meaning. Ideas that do not make sense *within* relational fields make no sense at all, deceptively attractive as they may be. We are in danger of losing Christ utterly through our attempts to make Him (*sic*) a fixed and eternal point for all time.[61]

The Evangelical model must confront the possibility that an embrace of the *relativity* of all truth-claims does not necessarily force one into a universal *relativism*. One can still announce and commit oneself to a particular statement of truth, even though one realizes that that statement is not the whole truth. This means that the Evangelicals should face the further possibility that Christians can maintain and proclaim the particular importance of Christ—even, *perhaps,* scandalously, as a universal truth for all religions—without having to negate the importance of universal truth in other religions.

The possibility that Christ's truth may not be the only truth also confronts Evangelicals through the knowledge and experience that Christians today have of other religions. The conservative Evangelical declaration that there can be authentic, reliable revelation only in Christ simply does not hold up in light of the faith, dedication, love, and peace that Christians find in the teachings and especially in the followers of other religions. If, as many Evangelicals insist, the Bible tells us that such religious faith is only "groping" for God without any genuine "discovery," then many of our contemporaries will find themselves forced to abandon the Bible.

3) A third general question takes up Barth's and the Evangelical interpretation of "only by faith" and its implications for the way in which a religion is

"justified" and rendered true. We have seen how Barth, invoking the Reformational insistence that we are saved only by grace accepted in faith, absolutely ruled out any possibility that the "good works" of a religion could either prepare for grace or give reliable evidence that grace had been granted. We heard, also, how Barth grounded this assertion in his understanding of incarnation as the "assuming of flesh."

We must ask whether such a weighted insistence on salvation only through faith mirrors the entire New Testament witness. Does it not allow Paul's voice to shout down all other voices in the New Testament? Although Paul seems to exclude "good works" (but did he really?), the Epistle of James and the synoptic Gospels see them as intrinsic to the experience of salvation (James 2:14–26; Matt. 7:15–21; Luke 6:43–49) Also, does Paul's extolling of "by grace alone" exclude, as Barth seems to insist, the possibility that we are truly transformed by that grace? Paul allows us to be the *adopted* children of God, but the Johannine author omits any legal qualifications and simply states that we *really* are "children of God," "born of God" (John 1:12–13; 1 John 2:29, 3:1–3); and the author of 2 Peter can even announce that we share in the divine nature (1:4).

It can even be asked whether Barth's interpretation is faithful to the Reformers themselves. Although Luther insisted that our good works cannot force God's hand and are not needed to merit God's love, he also taught that good works must follow from the experience of grace as a "*constitutive* sign." In other words, one cannot really experience grace without being transformed into an agent of good works.[62] Today ecumenical dialogue between Protestant and Roman Catholic theologians has recognized that the encounter with God is a paradoxical union of both "faith alone" *and* "good works."[63]

Today, too, the neoorthodox absolute disjunction between revelation and religion is being severely criticized. To argue with Barth that revelation and grace are constantly at odds with religion and that revelation makes use of religion only as a "necessary evil," is to do theological violence to the nature of grace, to the capacities of human nature, and to the meaning of the incarnation. The Chalcedon proclamation that in Jesus divine nature and human nature were truly united in one means that divinity "assumed flesh" not as one puts on a coat but as wine mixed with water becomes one liquid—God *becomes* human. Therefore, all revelation and grace can be considered incarnational. Therefore, revelation not only can but must take on flesh in religion. Grace and revelation cannot be what they are without the mediation of—without becoming—religion. Therefore, if religion is made true by God, it is transformed, not merely pronounced true.[64]

Furthermore, if, as much Roman Catholic and process theology contends (as we shall see in chap. 9),[65] the divine assumption of human nature in Jesus does not stand as one grand exception in the historical process, if rather it is the (or a) full expression of what God is up to in history, then it follows that grace is given as a constitutive part of nature. It also follows that this grace is operative and comes to expression within all the world religions. Once again we see how vitally a Christian theology of religions is tied to christology.

These have been theological arguments against Barth's extrinsicist understanding of how revelation justifies religion. There are also very practical reasons for us to question it (although these reasons may not be so compelling for many Evangelicals). Simply put, such a view of religion hamstrings dialogue before it can even get started. In Barth's view of revelation as assuming religion without working any real empirical change in it, Christianity and the other religions really have nothing they can talk about.

As we saw, for Barth no religion, including Christianity, can offer any empirical data, any "immanent rightness or holiness," any "inherent advantages," for its value and truth.[66] This would exclude any doctrinal comparison, even any evaluation and contrasting of experience. The only thing Christians could tell the other religions would be that "the sun of God's grace fell on us, not you. Even though there may be no evident differences between our religion and yours, we have the truth and you do not." No wonder interreligious dialogue never got off the ground during the decades of neoorthodox dominance over Protestant thought. No wonder Christians were considered by adherents of other religions as the most arrogant of humans.

I have already pointed out that more recently Evangelicals have toned down, even set aside, the neoorthodox refusal to allow revelation to assume and transform religion. (Even Barth, in his later years, moved in this direction.)[67] In the Lausanne statement, it is evident that they see revelation taking shape, becoming incarnate, within the Christian church. They have followed Luther's recognition that grace, although it cannot be merited, must express itself and "become" good works. This is laudable. But conservative Evangelicals must also recognize that this admission harbors implications for the way they should approach other religions. If they say that wherever you have revelation given by God you will also have religion used and transformed by God, the reverse would also apply: where Christians encounter religions that, from all appearances, are full of good works—followers recognizing the reality of a Transcendent Being and living lives of love and justice—there Christians should also expect to find God's revelation and grace. From their fruits you will know them. From their fruits other religions will attest to the presence of the Reality Christians call God.

Let me summarize my overall evaluation of the conservative Evangelical model for understanding religious pluralism. The conservative Evangelicals make claims that cannot be abandoned or slighted in the Christian approach to other religions. Yet in the crucial areas just discussed, they lose touch with the full content of Christian tradition and with contemporary experience. Most importantly, they raise serious roadblocks to the kind of interreligious dialogue that many Christians feel called to if they, as well as adherents of other faiths, are to make their religious contribution to the welfare of our divided world.

Many mainline Protestants recognize these deficiencies in the conservative Evangelical model. The next chapter will show how they try to resolve these deficiencies and still remain faithful to the spirit of the Reformation.

Chapter VI

The Mainline Protestant Model: Salvation Only in Christ

The central difference between the mainline Protestant model and that of the conservative Evangelicals can be stated succinctly: the mainline Protestants seek a more positive, a more dialogical, Christian approach to other faiths. To understand the more positive intent of this model, as well as its early history, I shall give special attention to Paul Althaus (1888–1966) and Emil Brunner (1889–1966).[1] Already in the 1930s and 40s they raised their voices (then minority voices) against what they felt was the narrowness and extreme exclusivity of Barth's and the neoorthodox view of the world religions. In their early protest, we find the foundation and basic structure of a Protestant approach to the religions of the world.

We shall also hear from other systematic theologians (Paul Tillich, Wolfhart Pannenberg, Carl Heinz Ratschow, Carl Braaten) and from mission theologians (Lesslie Newbigin, Stephen Neill, Paul Devanandan, M.M. Thomas). These theologians build on the foundation laid by Althaus and Brunner, but, more attuned to our contemporary context, they move beyond Althaus and Brunner. What marks all these Protestant thinkers is the desire to fashion a more open attitude toward other religions on the basis of their Reformational understanding of the Christian message. This chapter will examine how well they succeed.

Throughout this examination, it should be remembered that we are working with a *model,* and that models are not to be taken absolutely. They do not cover the field perfectly. As we shall see, there is a school of Roman Catholic thought that is in basic agreement with this mainline Protestant model. There are also many contemporary Protestant theologians (especially within the World Council of Churches and the camp of process theology) who seem much more at home within the Roman Catholic model; we shall hear more about them in the next chapter. We are again reminded that ecumenism has made it impossible to build neat fences between neighbors.

REVELATION—YES!

Against Barth and many contemporary conservative Evangelicals, mainline Protestants argue that Christians not only can but must recognize that the God revealed in Jesus is truly speaking through voices other than that of Jesus. Their argument arises from what they see in both the New Testament and in the human condition.

Arguments for a General Revelation

Mainline Protestants invite Barth and his followers to go back and redo their exegetical homework on the traditional New Testament passages that point to a revelation among the gentiles (Rom. 1:18ff., 2:12–16; Acts 14:15ff., 17:27ff.; John l). It is an abuse of the texts, they say, to claim that this revelation never really "works," that it bears no real fruits. What these texts are really announcing is what Althaus calls "original revelation" (*Uroffenbargung)*; Brunner, "creation revelation" (*Schöpfungsoffenbarung)*; Tillich, "general revelation."[2] They insist that such an interpretation is sound Reformational doctrine. Calvin, in basic agreement with Luther, spoke of a "sense of God" instilled into human nature so that "the knowledge of God and of oneself is connected by a mutual bond."[3]

Such a general revelation, these mainline theologians point out, is not to be confused with a "natural revelation" or a "natural theology," as if it were something that humans were discovering or contriving on their own. Rather, it is the work of God, due to "the stirrings of the divine Spirit," another way in which the Father is drawing all things to himself.[4] Althaus even explicitly and, for his time, boldly states that this revelation has a validity and efficacy independent of revelation in Christ: "It is valid through itself; it shines on its own light; it is not essentially bound to faith in Jesus Christ and to his Gospel."[5]

Besides the New Testament, Protestant theologians also call on the evident data of human experience to support their case for universal revelation. Here they anticipate many of the same arguments we shall find among Roman Catholics in the next chapter. Althaus hears the clear voice of an original revelation in our experience of existence as "given" and yet incomplete, the proddings of conscience, the "call of history" and the responsibility we feel for our neighbor's welfare, the beauty and order of nature, the hidden depth of interpersonal relationships.[6] Such experiences, available to all, attest to a divine revelation given in the very stuff of human existence. According to Althaus and Brunner, this original revelation is the originating and sustaining force behind all world religions. "Religion and religions are misunderstood, they are grasped only phenomenologically or anthropologically, when they are not seen against the background of God's general revelation."[7]

Paul Tillich's case for a general revelation within all religions is widely known. It pivots on his contention that every human being seeks and can be "grasped" by an Ultimate Concern. Whenever one is so grasped, religion is born: "Religion is the state of being grasped by an ultimate concern, a concern which qualifies all other concerns as preliminary and which itself contains the answer to the question of the meaning of life." The content of the ultimate concern of a particular individual or religion may not provide a final answer; indeed, it may obscure the final answer. But wherever such a "being grasped" takes place, there is authentic revelation and religion.[8]

On the contemporary scene, Carl Heinz Ratschow, who has been called one of the chief advocates of the German Lutheran attitude toward religions,[9] agrees with Althaus, Brunner, and Tillich: "The first mover in all religions is the irresistibility of God." From his study of other religions he can be more specific. This revelation takes place through what he terms God's *Heilshandeln* ("God's saving action"), some specific event in which the divine reality is originally experienced, and through the divine *Welthandeln* ("God's action in the world")—the divine mystery shining through nature.[10]

One of the more recent and influential proposals for a Protestant theology of religions comes from Wolfhart Pannenberg. (His basic approach reflects that of Carl Braaten who has been so instrumental in making Pannenberg's thought available to the North American theological public.) Pannenberg's argument for a general revelation is distinguished from those we have just reviewed by its emphasis on human experience as essentially *historical*. For him, revelation is a given in the process of history. It results from an interplay between, on the one hand, a person's natural "openness" and "quest for more" (*Weltoffenheit* and *Fraglichkeit*) and, on the other, the concrete events of history. This interplay provides humanity with a revelation of the divine—a revelation, however, that is constantly called into question by the movement of history and that, therefore, is always in process. Pannenberg insists on what he feels is evident to human experience: that real or full revelation can occur only at the end of history.[11] Nevertheless, this revelation, always in process, is precisely what can be seen within the history of religions: "the history of religions is the history of the appearing of the divine mystery which is presupposed in the structure of human existence."[12] Pannenberg can even maintain that this ongoing search for the fullness of revelation through the maze of history provides the history of religions with both a basic "unity" and a certain "competition."[13]

To these arguments for a general revelation from the New Testament and human experience, mainline Protestants add a theological consideration. If Christians are going to announce, as they must, that Jesus Christ brings a full and final revelation, this revelation cannot drop "perpendicularly from above" (as Barth claimed) on barren terrain. The soil must have been made ready; there must be "something to plug into" (*Anknüpfungspunkte*). Althaus expresses a mainline consensus when he affirms an "indissoluble" connection between general revelation and the revelation brought by Jesus. He insists that faith in Christ is possible *only* if it is the response to and fulfillment of a person's previous knowledge of God in general revelation. To encounter the God of Jesus Christ is not to meet a stranger.[14]

Pannenberg urges the same argument from a more scientific slant. He states that any claim for superiority or normativity in Christian revelation cannot stand until it is verified through a dialogue with the revelation found in other world religions. Christian theology, therefore, by its very nature, is obliged to make use of data from other religions.[15]

What General Revelation Reveals

What has been said so far about general revelation hovers in the realm of the abstract. If we grant that such a revelation exists, what, according to the mainline Protestant model, does it say? Different theologians offer different descriptions of its contents. It would be impossible and perhaps confusing to list them all. The varying perspectives, however, seem to focus on certain common themes. At the risk of generalization, they can be summarized under two headings:

1) Most of the theologians who use the mainline Protestant model recognize that general revelation not only makes known the existence of an ultimate reality but that it can also reveal that this reality is somehow *personal* and *benevolent*. The knowledge born of this revelation is not simply the product of theoretical reasoning; it is not only a "demonstration" proving a "first mover." It also provides a "call" that can elicit in a person a "confession," a response. God can be experienced in other religions as a "thou," even though there may not be full clarity about divine personhood.[16] Pannenberg can even argue that it is only from this original religious experience of divinity as personal that humanity arrives at an idea of human personhood.[17]

2) The mainline Protestant model takes another clear step beyond Barth and the conservative Evangelicals: general revelation within the religions can also offer definite insights into the insufficiency of the human condition and into the human *need for redemption*. Expressed in familiar Reformational terminology, followers of other religions can experience their own sinfulness, acquire a sense of divine justice, and thus come to the realization that there must be a "mortification" before there can be a "vivification." This can even lead to the recognition that there must be some kind of divine intervention, that God must step in before one can fully live: "the need for human and world redemption is the theme of all religions." Many of the authors point out that such insights are undeniably portrayed in the so-called religions of grace—Amida Buddhism and Bhakti Hinduism.[18]

In clear opposition to Barth and much of the conservative Evangelical model, mainline Protestants conclude that all the religions of the world play a part in salvation history. God's will to save is not confined to the Christian drama: "all that happens in the world, in nature and history, is a whole which in its individual moments serves as God's means for realizing the goal of his love."[19] The religions therefore are *willed* by God; their gods are "representatives'' of the Almighty; they are God's ''tools'' (*Werkzeuge*).[20] This would seem to imply that, according to the mainline Protestant model, the religions are ''ways of salvation.'' But does it?

SALVATION—NO!

When the question of salvation through other religions is broached, the Protestant model swings in a direction quite different from the one it followed regarding revelation. The change is both clear and, for many, confusing. Not all the representatives of this model explicitly take up the question whether God is actually using other religions to offer salvation. (As we shall see, this is much more of a Catholic question.) Those who do (they are primarily the ''old-timers,'' Althaus and Brunner) offer an unambiguously negative response. Tillich, Pannenberg, Braaten, and Ratschow handle the question of salvation obliquely. When they do admit to a salvific value in the religions, they seem to load this admission with qualifiers that make it difficult to grasp clearly just what they mean; or, one might wonder whether they can mean what they say. The following analysis will present both the clear and the opaque answers.

Before taking up this analysis, a brief word on what is meant by ''salvation'' is necessary. We are not talking about ''what no eye has seen, nor ear heard . . . regarding what God has prepared for those who love him'' (1 Cor. 2:9). Our concern is the beginnings of *salvation in this life*: what Christians mean when they talk about ''being in Christ Jesus,'' knowing the Father, the experience or awareness of God that brings both meaning and freedom, and thus promotes human welfare. According to the mainline Protestant model, can such religious experience occur in and through other religions?

In formulating their responses to this question, the theologians we are studying base their answers on two main sources of information: what is evident in the history of religions and what is evident in Christian belief and practice.

What the History of Religions Tells Us

Almost all the followers of the Protestant model would agree that any Christian judgment concerning salvation in other religions rests ultimately on the ''knowledge born of faith.'' Theirs is truly a *theology* of religions; and for them theology is faith seeking understanding. In formulating this understanding, however, they all make judgments on the factual state of affairs in other religions. The implication, at least, is that these judgments can be borne out through a study of other religions. Pannenberg, with his constant concern for scientific theological method, turns this implication into a methodological principle. For him, any assessment of the salvific potential of other religions cannot rest solely on the presuppositions of Christian faith; rather, all Christian evaluations of other religions must be verified by ''an unprejudiced understanding of the total process of the universal history of religions''—that is, by ''the facts of the sciences of religion.''[21]

What the Protestant model does see in ''the facts of the sciences of religion'' are two tendencies that make salvation in other religions either totally impossible or profoundly inadequate.

1) First, there is in all followers of other religions an ineluctable tendency to *effect their own salvation*—that is, to try to force God's hand, to establish their own worthiness. It amounts to this: other religions do not really accept salvation ''by faith alone.'' This overall verdict on the state of world religions is expressed most graphically by Althaus and Brunner.

The distinction Althaus had earlier made between ''original revelation'' and ''revelation in Christ'' now becomes that between original revelation and ''salvific revelation'' (*Heilsoffenbarung*). He speaks clearly: ''Outside of Christ there is indeed a self-manifestation of God, therefore knowledge of God, but it does not lead to salvation, to union between God and man.''[22] Thus, all the positive elements that Althaus had listed in original revelation seem to go nowhere. Although non-Christians experience God's personhood and offer of love, they cannot escape despair. Although they realize their own insufficiency, they still try to win salvation themselves. Although there is truth in the religions, there is also so much error that finally truth is swallowed in error and darkness. The *Deus revelatus* (''revealed God'') in original revelation turns out to be much more of a *Deus absconditus* (''hidden God''). So although Althaus could previously speak about an ''indissoluble'' connection between original revelation and the gospel, this connection is now seen to be one of ''total antithesis'' and ''unconditional opposition.''[23]

Brunner agrees with Althaus. Creation revelation is just not able to break out of the human being's ''heart turned in on itself'' (*cor curvatum in se*), which is expressed in ''egocentricity'' and the ''inveterate tendency to be absorbed in self.'' In all ''non-Biblical religions,'' no matter how deeply mystical or highly ethical, ''. . . man seeks himself, his own salvation; even in his surrender to the Deity he wants to find his own security.''[24]

Carl Heinz Ratschow offers a succinct statement of the central problem that Althaus and Brunner find in all religions. Even though he could speak of ''God's salvific activity'' throughout the world, even though he stated that all religions are ''religions of salvation'' (*Erlösungsreligionen*), he also claims a ''total and central difference'' between Christianity and other religions when it comes to the matter of justification; stated simply, in other religions the human role in salvation is *constitutive;* in Christianity, it is *consecutive*. The religions, therefore, are bound within the confines of the Reformational understanding of ''the law'': they try to work out their own salvation, and to do so puts it out of reach.[25] Thus, if other faiths are called religions of salvation, the term must apply only to their search, not to their discovery.

2) A second tendency that corrupts any genuine realization of salvation in the religions is identified by both the earlier and the contemporary representatives of the mainline Protestant model. It is closely related to the first cor-

rupting tendency: in trying to achieve their own salvation, all religions, in one way or another, end up attempting to *capture* God. They try to contain divinity in their doctrines or manipulate it with their "good works." Some form of idolatry rears its head in all religions.

Both Althaus and Brunner find Paul's judgment in Romans 1:21–32 confirmed by what they see in the religious world; the authentic knowledge granted in general revelation becomes material for constructing idols. Such idols need not be in the form of images; they can be very sophisticated efforts to reduce God to human size and reach. Brunner explains his claim that "the God of the 'other religions' is always an idol": the religions either *personalize* God into a divine fellow (or fellows) whose action they can then predict or dictate; or they *depersonalize* God into some kind of abstract principle that they can grasp with their reason. In either case, the essential mystery and transcendence of God is stuffed into the container of human thought or desire.[26]

Paul Tillich's case for the way all religions try to capture God is more nuanced and perhaps more perplexing. On the one hand, he states that inasmuch as there is genuine revelation in all religions, there is also salvation. The two cannot be separated. All human beings can be grasped by the Ultimate; what he calls "New Being" or "Spiritual Presence" is operative throughout history.[27] Yet because of the estrangement of human existence, all persons and all religions are bound to misuse this revelation and offer of salvation. Therefore they are in need of and are searching for a "religion of paradox" or of "the concrete Spirit." This means they are searching for a "symbol of a divine mediator" that would be a "concrete symbol of grace"—that is, a symbol that would consistently point beyond itself and not allow itself to be identified with the transcendent reality it is symbolizing. But according to Tillich, they never find such a symbol. The religions do not have the means in themselves to correct their constant, idolatrous misuse of general revelation; they are bound to wander between what Tillich calls their "sacramental" and "theocratic" aberrations—that is, they either absolutize their mediating symbols or they try to do away with them.[28] When Tillich allows for salvation in the religions, therefore, it apparently can be only in a corrupted, fragmentary form.

From a different starting point, Pannenberg makes the same case as Tillich for the way revelation in the religions always moves toward an idolatrous attempt to pin God down. (Once again, Carl Braaten would be in fundamental agreement with Pannenberg's position.)[29] As was already pointed out, he held that the fullness of God's revelation will come only in the future, at the end of history. God is essentially a "God of the future." The problem within all religions, however, is that they do not really know this! Pannenberg finds that all religions end up with a "finitization of the divine mystery." They either concretize God in some particular medium or idol, or they believe that the fullness of divine manifestation took place in some primordial time and must now be merely repeated through history. In either case, they do not recognize that God is ever beyond all their images and myths and that all their concepts must be constantly transformed toward a fuller revelation in the future.[30]

In the final analysis, therefore, the religions of the world for Pannenberg express only the *Fraglichkeit* of human nature—its constant questioning. Never can they attain any real answers. With Barth, Pannenberg interprets Romans 1:18ff. universally: *all* religions try to contain and therefore misuse the revelation God offers them. "The non-Christian religions perceived the appearance of the divine mystery only in a fragmentary way."[31] And this would seem to imply that salvation, a true experience of the true God, is at best only partial and inadequate.

What Christian Tradition Tells Us

For the followers of the mainline Protestant model, this inability to admit true salvation outside Christianity is based upon more than the empirical data of the history of religions; it results primarily from what Christians have come to experience and know in Jesus Christ. The contention that other religions cannot really mediate a truly saving encounter with God rests upon the Reformational insight into salvation "by faith alone," which in turn rests on the more fundamental belief in salvation "by Christ alone." The final mainline Protestant verdict on the religions is rooted, as was the case with Barth and the Evangelicals, in christology.

Mainline Protestants staunchly oppose Barth's denial of revelation in other religions, but they find themselves agreeing with him on the question of salvation. For here they are dealing with the *articulus stantis et cadentis ecclesiae,* the article (of faith) on which the church stands or falls. To jeopardize belief in the salvific centrality of Christ is to tear the heart out of Christianity.

In an effort to grasp just what this christocentric understanding of salvation means, we can distinguish two ways in which adherents of the mainline Protestant model insist on the necessity of Christ for salvation; one is ontological, the other epistemological.

1) The ontological necessity of Christ is more evident among the earlier proponents of the Protestant model—Althaus and Brunner. Without understanding the fall literally, as a historical event, they see it as representing a real rupture in the relationship between God and humanity. Humankind is caught in a pervasive rebellion, an offense against God. This is the *human condition.* Something must be done to remedy this situation. Divine justice—yes, divine wrath—must be satisfied.

Jesus Christ, in his life, death, and resurrection, is the event that works this change in the ontological structures of the God-humanity relationship. In him, especially in his death, both divine justice *and* love are expressed. Althaus points out that this is not the simplistic, "pagan" understanding of the satisfaction theory in which Jesus' death is assessed as the *price to be paid* before God could love. Yet in expressing divine love, God also had to satisfy the intrinsic demands of divine justice. All therefore hinges on Jesus. He is not to be understood, as much Roman Catholic theology implies, as a symbol, a "new idea," a clearer expression of what God is doing universally. Rather, Jesus as the Christ is a *historical* fact that, as an *event* found nowhere else, works an ontological change in "the order of things" between God and humankind.[32]

From this insistence on the historicity of the Christ event, followers of the Protestant model either state explicitly or imply that in order to experience salvation, one must enter into a historical or physical *contact* with Christ. The salvation brought by him is not universally or cosmically available. To experience the effects of the event one must, as it were, be connected with the event itself; and the connection, according to traditional Reformational theology, is the word. Christ, the gospel, must be proclaimed in order for salvation to be possible. Paralleling the former Catholic insistence on "outside the church, no salvation," much of the Protestant model adheres to "outside the word, no salvation."

All this language rings with the fervor and the vocabulary of the Reformers. We can take a contemporary spokesman for the mainline Protestant model, Carl Braaten, as an example of how the language and tone may change, but the same affirmation of the ontological necessity of Christ for salvation shines through. Braaten forcefully announces what he holds to be the clear message of the New Testament—that if salvation is available to humans, its one source is Jesus Christ: "He is depicted not as *a* son of God, but as *the* only begotten Son of God, not as *a* savior, but as *the* Savior. . . . He is the one and only Savior or he is no Savior at all."[33]

Braaten goes on to emphasize that this salvation is not meant to be an exclusive possession of only some persons; it is intended to be universal. He clearly tries to distance himself from what he calls the Evangelical view that would result in "a heaven sparsely filled with only card-carrying Christians."[34] Yet he also excludes any other way of encountering and experiencing this salvation than Jesus: "New Testament universalism . . . is always a predicate of the uniqueness of Jesus Christ, not a metaphysical attribute of the world in process, . . . or of a saving potential inherent in the world religions, or of an existential possibility universally available to every person in a moment of decision."[35] The offer of God's love is always "a predicate of the only gospel of salvation we know"—the preached word.[36]

So Braaten and mainline Protestants *must* exclude any "saving potential" in the religions. Attempts by some theologians to allow the religions to be ways of salvation constitute a "whittling away at the foundations of the Christian conviction that Christ and his church are God's links of salvation to the world he loves."[37] Evidently, these are the *only* links God has provided.

But would not such a reality result in a heaven of only card-carrying Christians? Braaten answers with an appeal to mystery: "Christianity must accept and hold resolutely to the paradox that God will attain the universal goal of salvation through the particular means he has chosen [i.e., Christ and the church], though it appears to reason that an unbridgeable gulf exists between means and end."[38] He does, however, offer a faint appeal to reason: "It is because Jesus Christ is the only Savior of mankind that we can hope for a universal restitution (*anakephalaiosis ton panton*) inclusive of people who worship at shrines where the name of Jesus is not yet known. As Lord of history Jesus Christ is also Lord of the world's religions."[39] The implication, stated explicitly by other followers of the Protestant model, is that what cannot be done during the course of history will be taken care of at its end: at the end of time, all will know Jesus and thus have the chance to enter salvation. In the meantime, though, in history as we know it, there can be no other vehicle of salvation than the gospel.[40]

2) The argument for the ontological necessity of Christ for salvation is bolstered and perhaps made more coherent by the Protestant claim for what can be called the *epistemological* necessity of Christ. A direct contact with Christ via the word is the only way salvation can be mediated because it is the only way salvation can be properly *understood*. Outside Christ one simply does not know how salvation works, and thus one lacks the necessary psychologico-cognitive conditions to accept it.

This means primarily that *only in Christ* can one realize that one is saved *only by faith*. This line of reasoning is evident in the more traditional theologians we have been studying—Althaus, Brunner, Ratschow (also Barth!). Without Christ humans cannot fully grasp the depth of human sinfulness or the seriousness of God's holiness and wrath. The *fact* that redemption is a combination of both God's love *and* justice, that love is expressed *through* the satisfaction of God's justice and wrath, is "contrary to all evident reality," "unseen, unheard of, impossible," a "pure miracle." Even if, by some "miracle," humans could speculate that God might act in this way, it would be impossible to believe, to trust, that God actually did.[41] The incredible possibility can be real only in the historical fact of Jesus. Brunner summarizes: "The only power that in principle unconditionally excludes self-redemption is the message of the mediation of Jesus Christ."[42]

This is why Althaus and Brunner, after marveling at the insights of "the religions of grace"—Bhakti Hinduism and Amida Buddhism—end up rejecting them as possible ways of salvation. Yes, these religions speak eloquently of God's love and of the need for humans to abandon themselves to that love. But they do not speak of "the divine wrath"; they talk of "divine mercy but not of atonement." Not grasping the full reality of human sin and divine justice, not realizing that "grace" must also and first of all be "forgiveness of sin," they announce a cheap grace. So these religions are ultimately branded "ways of self-redemption."[43] The reason, again, is clear: they do not know Christ: "Bhakti has everything the New Testament has, except Jesus Christ; and that means they have nothing of the New Testament."[44]

The more contemporary figures using the Protestant model also hold to an epistemological necessity of Christ; but they do so via an indirect route, without explicit talk of "by faith alone." We heard Paul Tillich, for example, describing the entire history of religions as an unsuccessful search for a "con-crete symbol of grace"—that is, a symbol or form of revelation that would truly mediate the mystery of the Ultimate without identifying itself with that Ultimate. He implies the reason why this search is unsuccessful:

> The break-through and the perfect self-surrender must happen in a per-sonal life, or it cannot happen at all. Christianity claims that it has happened and that the moment in which it happened is the center of the history of revelation and indirectly the center of all history.[45]

This center, of course, is Jesus the Christ. Jesus is the Christ precisely because he "shows no break in his relation to God and no claim for himself in his particularity. What is particular in him is that he crucified the particular in himself for the sake of the universal."[46] Tillich, with all the other followers of the mainline Protestant model, emphasizes that he does not wish to extol Christianity as a religion over other religions; however, he *does* extol the revelation of Jesus the Christ over all other revelations. Only Jesus is the true realization of the concrete symbol of grace. Only here can other religions *know* and therefore achieve true salvation—a salvation that can defend itself against the constant temptation of idolatry.[47]

Pannenberg makes much the same case as Tillich. The reason why the religions of the world cannot really grasp God as "the power of the future," the reason why they keep "finitizing" God in their concepts and symbols is that only in Jesus is God really revealed as a future God. Only Jesus is the "prolepsis," the anticipation of God's final revelation at the end of time. In him the future appears, and so humans are enabled to allow the fullness of God to remain in the future. Pannenberg explains this as Tillich did: "Jesus is the *revealer* of the infinite God only because he in his own person pointed the way to the coming reign of God. He did not bind the infinite God to his own person, but sacrificed himself in obedience to his mission."[48]

Pannenberg sometimes hints that it might be theoretically possible that other religions have truly grasped the essential futurity of God, but he more often states that it is revealed uniquely and exclusively in Jesus: "If God is revealed through Jesus Christ, then who or what God is becomes defined only by the Christ event. . . . The essence of God is not accessible at all without Jesus Christ."[49]

Carl Braaten, faithful follower of Pannenberg, even more clearly pro-claims that the end of history, the "enigma" and the "goal" of history, is made known to humanity only in the revelation of Jesus: "apart from Jesus Christ we would not be able to affirm that history has a final and a fulfilling meaning."[50] All of this means that without Christ, humans simply cannot *know* or *understand* what salvation means or how it is being offered in the present. The "by Christ alone" again turns out to be the final test for the final failure of other religions.

The overall assessment of the religions by the mainline Protestant model, therefore, is that they are bearers of authentic, divine revelation, but barren of authentic salvation. What then is or should be the relationship between Christianity and the other religions of the world? Although there are many heart-warming calls for openness, respect, dialogue, although it is even said that Christians can learn from other faiths and through them find "new expressions" for "the true identity of Jesus,"[51] still the basic category for the relationship between Christianity and the religions is that of "the law and the gospel," as understood by the Reformers.

The law has been given not only to the Jews but to all peoples as a "preparatory revelation" for the full and saving revelation of the gospel of Jesus Christ.[52] For all its positive content, it remains basically a *negative* preparation. It prepares for Christ in that its truth ultimately breaks down and proves inadequate. Carl Braaten states it succinctly: "Religions are not systems of salvation in themselves, but God can use even them to point beyond themselves and toward their own crisis and future redemption in the crucified and risen Lord of history."[53]

MISSION THEOLOGIANS
AND THE MAINLINE PROTESTANT MODEL

My analysis of the mainline Protestant model for understanding other religions has so far been drawn from well-known Protestant systematic theologians: the traditional formulations of Althaus and Brunner, and the more contemporary reformulations of Tillich, Pannenberg, Ratschow, and Braaten. For the most part, they speak out of the German-Lutheran tradition. (Brunner is the exception.)

In order to see how well this model fits and clarifies other strains of Protestantism, we will now take a brief look at the thought of four representative Protestant mission theologians: Lesslie Newbigin, Stephen Neill, Paul Devanandan, and M.M. Thomas. They all reflect traditions other than that of Lutheranism and, more importantly, they all have formulated their theologies of religion in the context of actually dealing and dialoguing with followers of other faiths.[54]

Newbigin and Neill

Lesslie Newbigin, a Scottish Presbyterian, and Stephen Neill, a British Anglican, have much in common. Both are bishops; both spent many years of missionary service in India where they were instrumental in forming the Church of South India (a union of Anglican, Methodist, and Reformed churches); both served as associate general secretaries of the World Council of Churches; and both have become authoritative voices in Protestant mission theology. They illustrate how the mainline Protestant model is being applied on the practical level.

Both Newbigin and Neill have witnessed the futility and impropriety of a totally negative, Barthian approach to other faiths: "There is something deeply wrong when Christians imagine that loyalty to Jesus requires them to belittle the manifest presence of the light in the lives of men and women who do not ackowledge him [Christ]."[55] Both Newbigin and Neill call for an open dialogue, in which Christians must be prepared not just to teach but to learn.[56] Such a "bright picture" of other religions stems from the recognition that there is "a real self-communication of God in the wider experience of mankind."[57] So for Newbigin and Neill, the first piece of the Protestant model—universal revelation—is in place.

Yet both these theologians hasten to add: "there is a dark side to this bright picture."[58] The darkness emanates from something else found in all religions—the innate tendency to take the gifts given in revelation "and make them into an instrument to cut ourselves off from God, to establish our independence from God."[59] In other words, human beings, in religion, try to justify themselves; they do not accept the gift of salvation *by faith alone*.

For both Newbigin and Neill, the reason why other religions cannot come to accept salvation by faith alone has to do with their Protestant understanding of salvation "by Christ alone." The "scandal of particularity," Newbigin insists, belongs to the heart of Christianity and determines its relationship to other religions.[60] This scandal is understood ontologically:

> In Jesus the one thing needed to happen has happened in such a way that it need never happen again in the same way. The universe has been reconciled to its God. Through the perfect obedience of one man a new and permanent relationship has been established between God and the whole human race. The bridge has been built.[61]

Both Newbigin and Neill imply that only if one knows and walks this bridge is salvation really possible. Christians are not allowed to recognize that God's saving purpose "is to be accomplished in any way which ignores or bypasses the historic event by which it was in fact revealed and effected."[62]

The necessity of Christ is also understood epistemologically. Unless one knows Christ, one cannot know the one, true God:

> Who is God? We usually assume that we know. But the Chritian answer is that we do not know until we have seen Jesus Christ. . . . The greater part of Christian theology has been unwilling to take this tremendous affirmation as seriously as it is taken in the New Testament. If, when we see Jesus Christ, we see God, then any previous ideas we may have had of God must undergo a reconstruction which amounts to rebuilding from the basement to the coping-stone.[63]

Without Christ it is also impossible to know what it means to be human; without him, humans cannot grasp that life is to be led "in a state of total dependence upon God."[64]

Newbigin reflects Pannenberg and Tillich in spelling out what this episte-mological necessity of Christ means: "The general religious experience of mankind, if no event in history is allowed decisive place, does not and cannot furnish clues as to the meaning of history as a whole."[65] Christ is this decisive, unique event. Without knowing and accepting this event, humanity cannot know where history is going or how it is to get there. On this basis, Newbigin points out what he thinks is the radical difference between Christianity and Eastern religions. Eastern faiths hold that "salvation is only of 'the soul,' " whereas Christianity, because of Christ, affirms a salvation of "the whole history of man and of nature," a salvation that embraces the human commu-nity, not just individuals.[66]

Newbigin's and Neill's final verdict on the religions is consonant with the Protestant model: because *only* "the cross of Jesus" can expose and remedy the innate tendency of humankind to save itself, no religion, including Chris-tianity, can be considered a "means of salvation." Newbigin expressly rejects the Roman Catholic view of other religions as ways of salvation. Although he immediately adds that this does not mean that therefore followers of other faiths are automatically lost, he still insists that the cross of Jesus shows that religion actually "takes us further away from the place where he [God] ac-tually meets us." The cross exposes "us as the beloved of God who are, in our highest religion, the enemies of God."[67]

What is, then, the final relationship between Christianity and other reli-gions? Newbigin does not endorse a "total discontinuity" (that would be the conservative Evangelical model), but a "radical discontinuity." Christianity and other religions are much more at odds than they are at one: "This is, I submit, a case in which there can only be 'either-or' and not 'both-and.' "[68] It is, in other words, what we described above as the traditional Protestant understanding of how the law relates to the gospel: in "fulfilling" other reli-gions, Christianity *replaces* them. The religions can be seen only as negative preparations for the gospel.

Devanandan and Thomas

Paul Devanandan (d. 1962) and M.M. Thomas are recognized as "two fig-ures who . . . have contributed most profoundly to the development of Indian theology."[69] They developed their theologies concomitantly with Newbigin and Neill; but they have done so as Indians. Perhaps this is what makes them strikingly different from their European colleagues. Like Newbigin and Neill, Devanandan and Thomas assess the religions from the perspective of God's universal revelation, but they ground this revelation in a "cosmic christology." For them, Christ is the *one* savior, without whom the world would be devoid of any possibility of knowing and responding to God (onto-logical necessity!). Yet they do not limit the effects of the Christ event to actual knowledge and acceptance of that event: "The ferment of the Kingdom of Christ and of Salvation-history is not confined to the Church."

Christians are therefore called upon to discern "the work of Christ and the ferment of the Kingdom in all histories." All of creation is imbued with the cosmic power of Christ that renders creation a continuous process of redemption.[70] With such assertions about the cosmic Christ and the universal possibility of salvation, Devanandan and Thomas are out of harmony with Newbigin and Neill, and with much of the Protestant model.

Both these Indian theologians point their fellow Christians to Hinduism and other religions to discern the workings of the cosmic Christ. More resolutely than most representatives of the Protestant model, Devanandan and Thomas call for Christian participation in interreligious dialogue. Both of them have set an example of how this requires Christians not only to meet and talk with Hindus and Buddhists but thoroughly to study their histories and sacred scriptures.[71]

To urge Christian dialogue with other religions, Thomas uses the dialectical theology of Karl Barth and Hendrik Kraemer—but with a determinative twist. He holds up Barth's "christocentric relativization of all religions" as "the most fruitful theological starting point to interpret religions." But here is the twist: Barth should have recognized that because Christ transcends the Christian religion while affirming it, he is free to do the same with other religions. Because Christ relativizes all religions, he cannot be confined to any one religion.[72]

For Thomas and Devanandan, one of the clearest contemporary signs that Christ is working in other religions is the growing awareness of these religions, especially neo-Hinduism, that they must be involved in "nation building." Because of the presence of Christ, religions are awakening to their need to remove injustice and promote a "new humanity."[73]

Thomas admonishes his fellow Protestant Christians that, because of the influence of Barth and Kraemer, they have been too afraid of "syncretism." This fear has prevented them from a genuine encounter with other faiths. Thomas proposes a "Christ-centered syncretism": "This approach would enable Christians to be open to interpenetration at cultural and religious levels, but with Jesus Christ as the principle of discrimination and coherence." Christ remains final, normative, "the universal ultimate truth."[74] But it is an ultimate truth that recognizes and affirms the existence of truth outside Christianity. Because the Christian church explicitly recognizes this ultimate truth, it "is the foretaste and sign in the world that God has always been and is contemporaneously doing what it takes to make and to keep human life human."[75]

Because of their affirmation of the cosmic Christ, their recognition that salvation history transcends Christianity, their acceptance of Rahner's theory of "anonymous Christianity" and Tillich's notion of "the latent church,"[76] it seems that Thomas and Devanandan have broken the boundaries of the Protestant model and belong to what I shall describe in the next chapter as the Catholic model. No doubt, they move in this direction. Yet when they come to integrate their positive view of other religions with their

Reformational understanding of salvation "by faith alone through Christ alone," they return, ambiguously, to their Protestant home.

Thomas and Devanandan insist that one of the essential contents of Christian belief and one of the crucial elements in interpreting other religions is the recognition of "the reality of the human person as a fallen creature." Devanandan explains what this means: "Man individually and collectively chooses to direct his affairs in accordance with his own will. . . . The root cause of all this disorder is the individual and collective selfishness of man."[77] Thomas adds that "the innate tendency of individals and groups for self-love and self-centeredness leading to search for power over others" is the product of "a total alienation from God, neighbor, nature, and oneself." This leads one "to create means of self-justification, that is, idolatrous religions to justify himself before God . . . the endless and frustrating struggle of man for self-justification."[78] It comes down to the inability of humankind to understand and accept "justification by grace through faith not by works."[79] Such an inability pervades all religions.

Thomas and Devanandan continue with their understanding of "by Christ alone": the propensity of humankind toward self-centeredness and self-justification can be recognized, confronted, and gradually overcome only through:

> [acknowledgment of] the reality of the crucified and risen Jesus Christ as the true man and as the source of renewal of human nature. . . . The cross of Jesus is also the answer to the human problem of justification of human existence. Responding in faith to the free divine forgiveness and acceptance offered by the Crucified, man is released from the necessity to seek security and justificaton by his own spirituality and moral and social idealism.[80]

The implication of such a claim is that without the response of faith in Christ, no one can find a release from the urge toward self-justification. A further implication, so it seems, is that the salvation that Thomas and Devanandan say can be present in other religions is profoundly inadequate, if it can be said to be present at all.

So their final statement on how Christianity is to relate to other religions turns out to be very much in line with the Protestant model. Devanandan concludes that insofar as Christ, "the radical renewer," represents a new beginning in human history, the encounter of Christianity with Hinduism may not mean "total destruction," but it does mean "radical renewal."[81] Thomas recognizes that because Christianity contains in Christ the "universal ultimate truth," it "is bound to see other religions and ideologies . . . as partial or distorted manifestations of that truth."[82] Despite his extolling of "the positive responses of faith" to the cosmic Christ within other religions, Thomas seems to see their manifestations of truth as more distorted than partial when he asserts: "To decide for Christ and the World he stands for implies a break with one's religious past."[83] It sounds, again, like the law-gospel relationship—more replacement than fulfillment.

My overview of the theology of religions offered by Newbigin and Neill, and especially by Devanandan and Thomas, confirms the same question that resulted from my review of the systematic theologians: How much does the traditional Protestant understanding of salvation "by faith alone through Christ alone" allow for a really positive attitude toward other faiths and for a genuine dialogue with them?

Before moving to some comments on the mainline Protestant model, I should point out that there is a significant school of Roman Catholic theology that stands behind the same podium as do the Protestants. Two of its principal teachers are Jean Daniélou and Hans Urs von Balthasar. Although this "Protestant Catholic model" clearly recognizes a "cosmic revelation" at work within the religions, it is very reluctant to admit that other religions can be channels of genuine salvation. To move in this direction, they argue, is to flirt with Pelagianism (salvation by works) and to forget that God's self-communication does not come through religious systems but through radical trust. The concepts of deity found in other religions fail to grasp the absolute transcendence of God and the unqualified character ("without works"!) of God's love. Religions are better called "attempts at" rather than "ways of" salvation (*Heilsentwürfe* rather than *Heilswege*). Emphases may differ but the substance of such Roman Catholic approaches is that of the mainline Protestant model.[84]

THE MAINLINE PROTESTANT MODEL: INSIGHTS AND INADEQUACIES

There are insights within the mainline Protestant model that mirror, perhaps with greater precision, the same "permanent achievements of the Reformation" expressed by the conservative Evangelicals. With their continued insistence on "by faith through grace alone" and on "by Christ alone," mainline Protestants remind all Christian theologians that any assessment of Christianity and other religions should recognize the *reality* of evil, sin, limitation, and the *possibility* that the Christ event may contain a "surprise," something uniquely different from anything found elsewhere in human history. The contents of these reminders were spelled out in my concluding comments to the previous chapter. The mainline Protestants, however, clearly move beyond the conservative Evangelical model and, in doing so, they bring into sharper focus some of the most crucial and controversial issues in any Christian theology of religions.

Insights

1) Where the advocates of the mainline Protestant model clearly break rank with the Evangelicals is in their affirmation of a *universal revelation*. When Althaus and Brunner launched their offensive against Barth at precisely this point, they were constructing the basis for their more positive theology of religions. What can and should be learned from this model is a theological confirmation of what was already urged in chapters 2–4, above: that some recognition of universal revelation is the keystone for any Christian approach to other religions. Without it, Christian conversation with adherents of other faiths can never really begin. Tillich was correct when he insisted that the first "presupposition" for interreligious dialogue must be "that both partners acknowledge the value of the other's religious conviction (as based ultimately on a revelatory experience)."[85]

Without this keystone, a theology of other religions cannot really call itself Christian. The mainline authors we have studied show convincingly that the doctrine of a universal revelation is firmly grounded in Christian scripture and tradition. The "classic texts" to which they refer are individual rays of a central light that glows within the entire Judeo-Christian Bible: that Jahweh or Abba is a God of love who "wants all people to be saved and come to know the truth" (1 Tim. 2:4) or who, as Edward Schillebeeckx concludes in his massive study of the New Testament, desires "man's truth, well-being and happiness."[86] How could God be such a God without offering revelation to all peoples?

The further argument adduced by mainline Protestants for the necessity of a general revelation is also convincing: the belief that Christ bears a special and a final revelation is neither logical nor verifiable unless it is received and evaluated within a common human history alive with the revelatory presence of God. To claim that there is authentic revelation only in Jesus would make the God of Jesus a *deus ex machina*.

2) Another insight offered by the mainline Protestant model is found in the way it attributes a positive value to the religions as part of "God's means for realizing the goal of his love."[87] Here it clearly corrects Barth's assessment that religion, the artifact of godless humanity, is opposed to revelation and is never really used or sanctified by God. Yet the mainline Protestants tell us that this affirmation of religion must always be a *qualified approval*. We have heard their affirmation that within every religion of the world, Christianity included, there is the innate tendency to domesticate God, to capture deity in the certainty and security of human knowledge. Paul Tillich defines this tendency as "the demonic element" within all religion, the element by which a religion seeks to make itself and its creeds, codes, and cults more important than the revelation and experience it is meant to serve.[88] Only the blind or the "too well established" will miss this demonic element in the history of every religious tradition. We can thank Freud and Marx for laying bear its subtle presence in the way religions tend to provide too much security

and thus end up becoming "crutches" or "opiums"— or "secure jobs."

Every theology of religions, especially the more liberal Roman Catholic views, should hold firmly to this Protestant reminder—what Tillich calls "the Protestant principle." As true, as good, as necessary as religion is, it is always "ambiguous," always a "mixed blessing," always in danger of being its own worst enemy. So every religion needs this Protestant reminder that it is corruptible and corrupt and in *constant need of reformation*. Without the Protestant principle, dialogue among religions cannot be a realistic, hard-nosed encounter; all too easily, it becomes a sugary irenicism in which the religions of the world come together to tell each other how good they are.

Although accepting the Protestant principle, we must question the manner or degree in which the Protestant model applies it to the question of the salvific value of other religions. Does the Protestant principle exclude an authentic experience of salvation outside Christianity? I turn to the inadequacies of the Protestant model.

Inadequacies

1) In my evaluation of the Evangelical model, the issue of a method for a theology of religions was raised. Advocates of the Protestant model, especially Pannenberg, would endorse our criticism of Barth's categorical refusal to admit any data from the science of religions into a theology of religions; such data, they would urge, must be weighed in any Christian evaluation of other religions. The mainline Protestants, however, reveal the problems contained in such a method in that, although endorsing it, they do not (or cannot) really apply it. As we shall see in more detail below, their theological verdicts concerning other religions are open to serious criticism by both those who have studied and those who believe in these religions. Is it true that all religions are ways of self-redemption, that all of them end up trying to pin down divine transcendence, that all of them miss the divine "power of the future," that none of them ever finds a "concrete symbol of grace"?

So we must press the question again: is the mainline Protestant perception of other religions perhaps blurred or even blinded? More precisely, are their own Christian beliefs, especially their affirmation of "Christ alone," a filter that permits them to see only what they want to see? If this is so, a more thorny question arises: What must Christians do to be able to see and understand another faith? How can the data of the science of religion be honestly and openly used in a Christian theology of religions? In order to be objective about other religions, must Christians suspend their own beliefs, especially in the uniqueness of Jesus? Is such an effort possible? Is it proper? The mainline Protestant model helps us confront such questions. Answers will be suggested in chapter 10.

2) The mainline Protestant doctrine of universal revelation was recognized as the keystone for any theology of other religions. This recognition, however, brings up a question: Given the way these theologians position that

keystone in their theology, can it remain in place? The problem arises from the way they distinguish general revelation from Christian revelation. Certainly, some kind of distinction between the two is necessary; otherwise all differences are discarded and the religions of the world become but different bowls of the same religious soup! But is the difference to be defined as *general* revelation in other religions and *salvific* revelation in Christianity?

Not only does such a distinction appear arbitrary, artificial, and blind to what is evident in the lives of non-Christians; it also leads to a concept of God that would make many Christians very uncomfortable. The Protestant theologians we have studied insisted that general revelation is not just "natural revelation"; rather, it is the work of God, of God's Spirit illuminating the minds and hearts of all. But what kind of a God is this who offers a revelation that can never lead to salvation, to an authentic experience of the divine? Is it not a rather capricious, teasing God, who offers just enough knowledge of divinity to frustrate persons, or to confirm them in their sinfulness? To keep the concept of general revelation locked within the confines of "the law" and never to allow it to become "the gospel" seems, therefore, seriously to jeopardize belief in a God of love, willing the welfare of *all* human beings.

It seems that both human logic and Christian theology require that if one admits the *fact* of divine revelation apart from Christ, one must also admit at least the *possibility* of salvation apart from Christ. Such a conclusion brings us to the central difficulty of the mainline Protestant model (really, of all the Christian models we are studying): their understanding of the necessity of Jesus Christ for salvation.

3) The mainline Protestant view of how Jesus is unique aids us in defining further contours of a question that has already become central to this book (and which I shall try to answer in chapters 8 and 9). I tried to pinpoint the reason why the mainliners could allow revelation, but not salvation, outside Christ: it was because of their adherence to the *ontological necessity* of Christ for salvation. Whether in the traditional language of "divine justice and love" or in the more existential image of the sole "prolepsis" of the future kingdom, the theologians we have studied seem to hold that the Christ event is *constitutive* of whatever salvation is available to humankind. If redemption is real, if divine grace is offered, it is only because of what happened in Jesus Christ. Carl Braaten set up the mainline Protestant *ne plus ultra,* the sign bearing the legend "no trespassing beyond this point," for all Christian theology: Jesus "is the one and only Savior or he is no Savior at all."[89] Either we hold on to this or we stop calling ourselves Christians.

Such deep conviction and radical insistence call forth equally serious and honest difficulties. The first is as straightforward as Braaten's claim. It does not seem possible to maintain this traditional insistence on the ontological necessity of Christ for salvation and at the same time coherently profess belief in the universal salvific will of the Christian God. This is especially so when the necessity of Christ is further tied to some kind of direct contact with Christ through the preached word. How can we really take seriously God's love and desire to save all persons when that saving love is tied so exclusively to one channel?

Theologians have devised (the word is used deliberately) various ways out of this dilemma. We heard Braaten's appeal to "mystery" and his suggestion that at the end of history all will know Jesus and have a chance. Althaus speaks of a "relative salvation" through the religions and implies, like other theologians, that salvation is available in other religions "in smaller dosages."[90] In the next chapter we shall see how Roman Catholics try to devise a way out of this dilemma through some form of the "anonymous Christianity" theory. All such suggestions seem to be rather arbitrary devices, theological speculations for a dilemma that, perhaps, is more a problem for theologians than for God. Through the haze of theological speculation, a simple question takes shape: Why can there not be other saviors besides Jesus? Must this suggestion be so audacious, even blasphemous for Christian ears?

We are now brought to a second problem with the mainline Protestant understanding of the ontological necessity of Christ. It is a question I raised in the preceding chapter. Carl Braaten helps formulate it more sharply when he asserts that "at the core of this revelation [the New Testament witness] is the exclusive uniqueness of Jesus." I must ask, Is this so? Again, one faces the necessity of questioning the nature of such "one and only" statements about Jesus—whether perhaps we are abusing this language when we read it as clear-cut declarations about the ontological relationship between God and humanity.

For the moment, we can add some further difficulties with the way mainline Protestants read the exclusive uniqueness of Jesus in (or "into"?) the heart of the New Testament. Besides the numerous texts that seem to tie salvation to some kind of "contact" with Jesus, what about another strand of New Testament thought that goes in the opposite direction? The last judgment scene in Matthew 25:31–46 seems to number among the elect those who loved their neighbor without knowing anything about Jesus. More significantly, what about the wisdom (*sophia*) or word (*logos*) christology, rooted in the Johannine and Deutero-Pauline writings and developed by the Fathers, which sees a universal presence of the word within all of history? If it truly be the word of God, it would have the potential not only to reveal but to save.[91] Have proponents of the mainline Protestant model given sufficient recognition to these elements of Christian revelation? (We saw that M.M. Thomas and Paul Devanandan have tried to.)

The vigor of the mainline Protestant insistence on the ontological necessity of Christ finally elicits an "opposite force" and prompts the simple but fundamental question: Is it true that all salvation is *constituted* by the Christ event? Is there an ontological rift between God and humanity—whether that rift be understood as a sinful fall or as the inability of humanity to find the "concrete symbol of grace"? And has this rift been repaired at only one bridge point?

The Protestant response to these questions needs balancing and correcting by some of the suggestions we already heard in chapter 4, on Jung and contemporary psychology of religion. These suggestions will be strengthened in the next chapter, on the Catholic model. Perhaps there is no ontological rift at all between God and humanity. Perhaps human nature, as its "unconscious" seems to witness, is in its very constitution at-oned with God, even though this awareness is covered over by ignorance and a history of selfishness. Or as Rahner will put it, perhaps "nature" in its very makeup is graced (the supernatural existential). This leads to a further "perhaps": that Jesus saves not by "doing" or "repairing" anything, but by showing, revealing what is already there but so often unfortunately missed. We shall be investigating such possibilities more carefully in coming chapters.

4) Representatives of the mainline Protestant model argue that the ontological necessity of Christ for salvation is corroborated by his epistemological necessity. The "evident" fact that nowhere in the world of religions is the meaning of salvation properly understood is further proof that Jesus is the one, true agent of salvation. Again, I ask the direct question: Is this really so? A full argument that it is not would require a detailed study of other religions, which would be another book. For the moment, I offer a few suggestions, drawn from authors who have written such books.

If an explicit recognition of "sin" and divine "justice and wrath" are defined as prerequisites for admission into the circle of the elect, then admittedly few Hindus and Buddhists would qualify. But are Althaus and Brunner themselves limiting God by laying down such prerequisites? It appears that the reality behind the symbol of sin is caught by the Hindu symbol of *avidya* ("ignorance") or the Buddhist experience of *tanha* ("selfish craving"). Even though the Buddha did not speak about an infinite offense against divine justice, he perhaps has another angle on what is wrong with the human condition when he announced that *dukkha* ("suffering") is universal and is caused by craving.

Another perspective on the futility of "good works" may be offered in the Zen Buddhist warning that we miss the really Real by trying to lay hold of it with our intellects—or in the insistence of the Bhagavad Gita that we shall never know peace if we keep seeking the fruits of our actions. As the Lutheran World Assembly in Helsinki (1963) admitted, the Reformational categories of "sin" and "guilt" and "wrath" may have to be translated before they can speak to the contemporary person's need of salvation. Many mainline Protestant theologians are missing the help that other religions offer for that translation.[92]

Similar questions can be asked of the way Pannenberg, Tillich, and Braaten, as well as Newbigin, Neill, Thomas, and Devanandan, exclude an authentic understanding of salvation in other religions. They hold that the religions "finitize" God by not being truly open to "the power of the future," by missing the eschatological character of salvation, by never being able to lay hold of a "concrete symbol of grace," by refusing to accept total dependence on God. But what about the evident "negative theology" that pervades so much of Eastern religious thought—the Hindu *neti, neti* (Brahma is "not this, not that"), Buddha's "noble silence," the Zen insistence that there is an ineffable mystery behind all concepts and symbols? Might not the fascination of Western Christianity for doctrine and dogma profit from such warnings against "finitization"? Concerning the lack of eschatology in other religions, perhaps with Thomas Merton we can find in the Eastern insistence on "the eternal now" a necessary reminder that the kingdom preached by Jesus was, paradoxically, a *future* fullness to be realized *in the present*.[93] Perhaps the Christian understanding of salvation has much more to *understand* from other religions.

This chapter ends with a conclusion similar to that of the preceding chapter: there are insights in the mainline Protestant model, especially dealing with general revelation, that must be preserved in any theology of religions. But the inadequacies of the model, especially the way it ties salvation to the Christ event, call for modification, perhaps radical revision. The Catholic model may provide some help.

Chapter VII

The Catholic Model:
Many Ways, One Norm

It might come as a surprise to many that of all the confessional attempts at a Christian response to contemporary religious pluralism, the Roman Catholic effort seems the most open and ready to come up with new models. Gerald Anderson, one of the most noted North American Protestant missiologists, surveys the past and predicts the future of Roman Catholic mission theology and its attitude toward other religions:

> Roman Catholic mission theology has undergone more radical change in these fifteen years than in the previous century. And there is obviously a great deal more ferment to come in the last fifth of the twentieth century. What we see so far, in my judgment, is but a foretaste or the first fruits of a radical realignment of Catholic mission theology that by A.D. 2000 will be as far from our thinking today as our thinking today is from where Catholic mission theology was twenty years ago.[1]

This chapter will examine this "radical change" in Catholic attitudes toward other religions. The analysis of the Catholic model will be somewhat more extensive than that of the previous two models, mainly because the "radical change" promoted by Catholic theologians is also taking shape, as we shall see, in other confessions. Also, the Catholic model represents, as it were, the "end point" in confessional Christian efforts to come to a more positive theology of other religions. Even so-called liberal theologians, Catholic and Protestant, do not venture beyond it.

Our examination begins with a bird's-eye survey of Roman Catholic attitudes toward other religions previous to the Second Vatican Council. This historical background will make clear why the council signaled such a radical change in these attitudes. To unpack the contents of this new Catholic model, our focus will be on its chief author and eminent spokesman, Karl Rahner.

The majority of contemporary Catholic theologians reflect Rahner's approach, although some of them, more recently, are attempting to move beyond it.

VATICAN II: A WATERSHED

To understand how Vatican II and contemporary Roman Catholic thought form a watershed in Christian relationships with other religions, we must have some idea of what went before. Risking the dangers of generalization, one might describe the attitudes of the Roman Church toward other faiths, from the patristic age to the twentieth century, as a teeter-tottering between two fundamental beliefs: God's universal love and desire to save, and the necessity of the church for salvation. As early as 473 the Council of Arles condemned anyone who held that "Christ, our Lord and Savior, did not undergo death for the salvation of all peoples"; more positively, it affirmed that Christ "does not wish anyone to perish."[2] This had to be balanced, however, against the dictum, formulated by Origen (d. 254) and applied by Cyprian (d. 258), that "outside the church, there is no salvation."[3] Throughout the ensuing centuries, balancing both these beliefs was not easy. Indeed, most of the time the teeter-totter was tipped to the side of the importance of the church rather than of God's universal love.

Such an imbalance does not seem to have been the case during the first three centuries of the life of the church. Although the early fathers of the church clearly held to the uniqueness and finality of Christ, they also endorsed a fairly "common opinion" that an authentic revelation and possibility of salvation was offered to all peoples. Justin Martyr, Clement of Alexandria, Origen, Theophilus of Antioch, Athenagoras spoke of "the seminal word" (*logos spermatikos*), "the word of whom all humankind partakes." All who live by this word are, for Justin, already Christian even though they have not heard of Jesus.[4] Tertullian makes the same point with his notion of "the naturally Christian soul."[5] Even Augustine could hold that the one true religion existed "from the very beginning of mankind" and that "the saving grace of this religion . . . has never been refused to anyone who was worthy of it."[6]

It is with Augustine, however, that the balance begins to shift toward an exclusivity of revelation and grace within the church. A number of historical and social factors prompted the change. Under Emperor Theodosius (379–395) Christianity became the official state religion; no longer did Christians have to argue the reasonableness of their beliefs before pagan believers and philosophers. Christianity became Christendom; the church became more secure, and security breeds ideology—that is, the intent to maintain one's privileged position. Also, as the popes became political leaders, the security of the empire was linked with the security of the church. So the enemies of the empire became the enemies of the church. These enemies,

Alaric and the Visigoths, captured Rome in 410; while Augustine lay dying, in 430, the Vandals were besieging his beloved Hippo. The "pagans" and their religions were naturally seen as barbarous opponents to church and state.

To such political factors was added the theological controversy with Pelagianism. Augustine spearheaded the opposition to this heresy that held salvation to be possible through human effort alone, without grace. The counterattack on Pelagius seemed to go to the opposite extreme; to stress the necessity and gratuity of grace, Augustine tended to limit it. A limited commodity is always more precious. So "humanity lost without grace" came to be equated with the pagans and their religions. Augustine arrived at his theory of "double predestination": God, from all eternity, predestines some to salvation, others to perdition.[7] One of his pupils, Fulgentius of Ruspe (533), drew further conclusions that were eventually to be incorporated into the Council of Florence: "There is no doubt that not only all heathens, but also all Jews and all heretics and schismatics who die outside the church will go into that everlasting fire prepared for the devil and his angels."[8]

Augustine's influence was to weigh heavily on Christian attitudes toward other religions throughout church history. It is well illustrated in the Middle Ages. While the scholastic dictum, "God does not withhold grace from those who do what they can" (*facienti quod est in se Deus non denegat gratiam suam*), was generally accepted, it seemed that "those who do what they can" were found only among Christians.

Once again, politico-historical factors colored theological vision. Islam, the first world religion (after Judaism) that Christianity was to encounter, turned out to be a political foe that was not only mighty but highly successful. The Islamic threat to Europe during the eighth and ninth centuries and the Crusades during the eleventh to the thirteenth centuries did not, to say the least, encourage an attitude of interreligious dialogue. In fact, the Christian conflict with Islam was to solidify the negative attitudes of the church toward other faiths for centuries to come.[9] How much the Crusades influenced Aquinas's views of those outside the church is difficult to say. He admitted the possibility of salvation for the gentiles of classical antiquity through implicit faith in divine providence, but he also held to the current belief that outside the church and its sacraments there was no salvation. If God withholds saving grace from non-Christians, it is "out of justice, in punishment for sin, at least original sin, as St. Augustine affirms."[10]

Official pronouncements during the Middle Ages on the situation of those outside the church are not lacking in clarity. The Fourth Lateran Council (1215) repeated Cyprian's formula "outside the church, no salvation" and added "at all" (*omnino*).[11] Pope Boniface VIII, in his bull *Unam Sanctam* (1302), clarified further that to belong to this church and find salvation, one had to accept papal authority.[12] The Council of Florence (1442) repeated almost verbatim the declaration of Fulgentius mentioned above and added: "no persons, whatever almsgiving they have practiced, even if they have shed blood for the name of Christ, can be saved, unless they have remained in the bosom and unity of the Catholic Church."[13] Clearly, God's universal salvific will was outweighed by the necessity of the church.

Such exclusivistic statements were easier to make in an age when it was believed that the gospel had been preached throughout the world. A better balance between belief in the universality of God's love and the necessity of the church, however, was demanded when "the age of discovery" broke upon Europe in the sixteenth and seventeenth centuries. The explorations of Henry the Navigator, Christopher Columbus, Vasco da Gama, Ferdinand Magellan, Francis Drake revealed millions of persons who had never heard of Christ or the church. Were they automatically designated for hell, through no fault of their own? The Council of Trent, with the help of theologians such as Bellarmine and Suarez, came up with a formula by which it tried to balance the teeter-totter horizontally between God's universal love and the necessity of the church. If pagans could not be baptized with water (*in re*), they could "through desire" (*in voto*). If they followed their conscience and lived morally, they were implicitly expressing a desire to join the church and could thus get through the doorway of salvation.[14]

This more positive attitude toward the "pagans," using the notion of "implicit desire" to affirm both God's universal love and the necessary channel of the church, has characterized Roman Catholic attitudes into the twentieth century.[15] What took place was a development in Roman Catholic theology from an *exclusive* to an *inclusive* understanding of the church as the sole channel of grace. To state it differently, Catholic belief moved from holding "*outside* the church, no salvation," to "*without* the church, no salvation." The universal possibility of salvation was clearly recognized, but especially during the first half of the twentieth century Catholic theologians came up with ingenious concepts to include *within* the church all traces of salvation *outside* it: saved non-Christians belonged to the "soul" of the church; they were "attached," "linked," "related to" the church; they were members "imperfectly," "tendentially," "potentially."[16]

What is often forgotten in the praise of this more inclusive, "catholic" picture of universal grace is that, as it took shape from the sixteenth to the twentieth century, it did *not* include a more positive view of other religions. Theologians, even quite recently, spoke of the universal offer of grace as if it were some free-floating agent that touched individuals privately, through some form of mystical communication. No one ventured the suggestion that such grace might be operating through pagan religions. Piet Schoonenberg describes his exposure to such a theology: "When I was studying theology in the thirties everyone was quite happy with this solution [a private, implicit desire for baptism], and hardly anyone asked whether the whole embodied-ness, socialness, and historicity of mankind played any role there at all; whether 'faith without a preacher' is indeed possible."[17]

From this historical overview of Catholic tradition, the Second Vatican Council, especially in its "Declaration on the Relationship of the Church to

Non-Christian Religions,'' stands as a watershed. It carries on the tradition, but it does so in clearly new directions. More resolutely than ever before, the council affirms the universality of grace and salvation, stating that even express atheists who follow their conscience are moved by grace and can partake in eternal life.[18]

A new direction is taken when, for the first time in the history of official church statements, the religions of the world are singled out and praised for the way they have answered "those profound mysteries of the human condition." The council summarizes the beliefs and practices of Hinduism, Buddhism, and Islam, and recognizes that they contain what is "true and holy" and reflect "the truth that enlightens every human being." Further, the council "exhorts" Christians "prudently and lovingly, through dialogue and collaboration with the followers of other religions, and in witness of Christian faith and life, [to] acknowledge, preserve, and promote the spiritual and moral goods found among these persons."[19]

It is true that the council does not explicitly state that the religions are ways of salvation. Some Catholic interpreters find the mainline Protestant model in the declaration on other religions; they argue that it affirms revelation in the religions but reneges on salvation.[20]

As we shall see, the majority of contemporary Catholic theologians offer a very different interpretation. For them Vatican II clearly teaches—or at least clearly implies—that authentic "religious experience" takes place in and through the religions.[21] Pietro Rossano, former secretary of the Vatican Secretariat for Non-Christians, reads the council documents to hold "that gifts of 'grace and truth' do reach or may reach the hearts of men and women through the visible, experiential signs of the various religions."[22]

Yet, as much as Vatican II forms a watershed in Roman Catholic attitudes toward other faiths, we cannot deny a residual ambiguity in its understanding of just how effective the truth and grace within the religions are and, especially, how far Christian dialogue with them can go. The ambiguity stems from the same tension between God's salvific will and the necessity of the church that is evident throughout the history of Catholic thought. Although the council has said some very new and positive things about the religions, it still maintains that "the church is necessary for salvation," and that "it is through Christ's Catholic Church alone, which is the all-embracing means of salvation, that the fullness of the means of salvation can be found."[23]

Does this mean that the religions are "included" in and already "embraced" by the Catholic church? Also, what is the purpose of dialogue? The declaration on the religions sees dialogue as a means to mutual understanding, but the decree on the missions seems to view it as an avenue toward conversion.[24] Whether and how the theologians who are elaborating a Catholic model for a theology of religions answer these questions will be a major concern in the following analysis.

RELIGIONS: WAYS OF SALVATION

If Vatican II is a watershed in Christian attitudes toward other religions, Karl Rahner is its chief engineer. His 1961 study on Christianity and the non-Christian religions broke new ground; so did his earlier and more foundational investigations into the relation between nature and grace and between universal and special salvation history. With these bold explorations into unfamiliar theological territory, Rahner not only prepared the way for Vatican II but indirectly contributed to much of its substance.[25] Subsequently, he attempted to show how the council opened doors to a genuinely new stage in the history of the church—an opening, he suggests, of which many of the conciliar fathers were not fully aware.[26]

The Starting Point: God's Universal Salvific Will

Rahner's starting point for a more positive theology of religions is a belief that, as we have seen, is part of the fabric of Christian doctrine: God's desire to save all humankind. Rahner applies what he thinks is simple logic: if God really has this desire, God will act on it. This means that grace, without which salvation is impossible, must be offered to all. Rahner concludes that Christians should be animated by a *Heilsoptimismus;* they should "think optimistically" about the possibilities of salvation outside Christianity, no matter how much error and evil they seem to find in the world. To think "pessimistically of men" is to underestimate God's love and grace.[27]

With such an optimistic understanding of the divine salvific will, Rahner constructs his well-known teaching on the supernatural existential. It might be called a Catholic version of the mainline Protestant affirmation of general revelation. Grace, offered to all, is given not as an extrinsic addition to human nature; we do not receive grace as we put on a new coat. Rather, grace infuses and becomes part of human nature—that is, part of the psychological structures of human consciousness. This is evident in what we experience ourselves to be: "spirit," or infinite openness to infinite mystery. In all our human acts of knowing and loving finite objects, we are reaching out to (*Vorgriff*) an Infinite that gives these objects their meaning and attractiveness. Grace, then, infuses or energizes this natural openness and gives it a new dynamism. We receive a "supernatural horizon." Therefore, for Rahner and for most contemporary Catholic theologians, there is no such thing as "only nature" (*natura pura*). With images similar to Jung's view of divinity within the unconscious, Rahner sees our very "existence" as "supernatural": nature is more than just human nature.

This means that there is a "transcendental revelation" built into our very nature. Every time we reach out beyond ourselves, to what is true and good, we are experiencing and responding to grace; we are experiencing and truly knowing God even though this knowledge may be "unreflexive" or "unthematic," not yet objectified. Such an encounter with revealing grace can be experienced in a variety of real-life situations. It is contained in the "fundamental option" by which we choose to live our lives not only for ourselves but for others. It is implicit in every act of freedom by which we take on responsibility for others, or trust in the face of death or meaninglessness, or experience the deep beauty or wrenching demands of commitment to another human being or to a humanitarian cause. To know God in these different ways is for Rahner not just revelation. It includes salvation: a communion with the one true God, an experience of purpose, peace, and growth for the individual and society.[28]

Grace built into nature, universal revelation that not only reveals but saves—this is the starting point for most contemporary Roman Catholic theologians as they confront the question of other religions. Lonergan takes the same transcendental, personalist approach as Rahner and traces the power of grace within the cognitive structures of human nature; our pure, unrestricted desire to know is fulfilled and transformed when, through grace, we find ourselves "loving unrestrictedly."[29] Heinz Robert Schlette, Piet Schoonenberg, and Walbert Bühlmann show the workings of revealing grace not so much in the psychological structures of the person as in the ongoing process of history and society. Salvation history is universally present within the events of profane history.[30] Hans Küng proposes this same universalist starting point for a theology of religions when he urges Christians to abandon their ecclesiocentrism (funneling all grace through the church) and to take on a more theocentric approach to other faiths. Such an approach recognizes the mysterious activity of God, not the church, within the world outside Christianity.[31]

The Conclusion: Religions Are Ways of Salvation

The next step in Rahner's evaluation of other faiths hinges on what can be called the "sociological link" in the Catholic model for a theology of religions. Catholic tradition understands the human being to be not just spirit but flesh, not just a rational but a social animal; humans live and move and have their being in history and society. Therefore for grace truly to be universally available, for there really to be a universal salvation history, for the human transcendental openness to be activated, God's universal will to save must take on historico-social flesh. It must become word, body, event, symbol. And where else should one expect to find this socio-historical mediation of grace than in the religions of the world? There can be many social channels of grace, but certainly the religions are among the most available and effective.

Rahner criticizes theologians who try to exclude grace from other religions. "Arbitrary and improbable postulates" is the way he defines their arguments that grace is offered non-Christians solely through interior inspiration, or as special guidance at one's first moral choice, or as a special illumination at the moment of death. If we deny that persons can experience salvation in and through their religions, "we would be understanding this event of salvation in a completely ahistorical and asocial way. But this contradicts in a fundamental way the historical and social character of Christianity itself, that is, its ecclesial character." According to Rahner, if Christian theology holds that Christians must work out their salvation in a religion, the same applies for Hindus and Buddhists.[32]

Rahner cautiously draws his conclusions, well aware that what he was saying, in 1961, was "offensive to many pious Christian ears." He contends that non-Christian religions can be considered "lawful," that they contain "supernatural grace-filled elements." Then he goes on to explain what this means: the non-Christian religions can be "a positive means of gaining the right relationship to God and thus for the attaining of salvation, a means which is therefore *positively included in God's plan of salvation.*"[33]

Rahner realizes that he has to face an objection: Does not the evident error and corruption within the religions vitiate their ability to serve as channels of grace? He responds with an appeal to the Old Testament. Certainly all Christian theologians would recognize the Jewish religion as a vehicle of salvation. Its weaknesses and corruption, however, are well attested to in the Bible. For all the guidance provided by the prophets, individual Jews, like individual Hindus or Buddhists, were left to their own intelligence and conscience to sift out truth from error. One never has to buy the whole religious package of truth *and* error in order to belong to a particular religion.[34] As is all too evident in the history of Christianity, that a religion gives growth to weeds does not mean it cannot produce wheat (Matt. 13:29–30).

Since 1961, Rahner's cautiously structured case for the salvific value of other religions has been accepted and expanded into a common opinion among Catholic theologians. Two recent efforts, by Walbert Bühlmann and Arnulf Camps, to develop a more open theology of religions restate Rahner's basic argument.[35] Lonergan, adopting the terminology of Wilfred Cantwell Smith, recognizes a universalist, saving faith behind the various beliefs of all religions.[36] Writing not long after Rahner's seminal article, H.R. Schlette is less cautious than Rahner and affirms that "it is God's will that the religions should be ways of salvation, *independent* of the special way of salvation of Israel and the Church." With Hans Küng he goes on to describe the world religions as the "ordinary," the common, way to salvation, whereas Christianity makes up the "extraordinary," the special way.[37] In his comprehensive study, *Catholicism,* Richard McBrien reviews the different Roman Catholic approaches to religious pluralism and finds that they all agree in recognizing the "validity" of the other religions as possible "instruments of salvation."[38]

The Limits: Anonymous Christianity

Roman Catholic views of other religions are often associated with the well-known and controversial theory of anonymous Christianity. Originally proposed by Rahner, this theory demonstrates both the breadth and the limits of the understanding of other faiths by the Roman Catholic model. Since he first advanced the theory in the early 60s, Rahner has repeatedly tried to clarify its primary intent. First of all, it is meant only for Christian consumption—that is, it is to be used within Christian theology and not as a tool for dialogue with other religions. More importantly, its main purpose is to broaden and engender more "optimistic" Christian attitudes toward other believers. In showing that other believers can be called "Christians without a name," Rahner tries to break through Christian exclusivism.

He attempts to make Christian consciousness aware that the grace of Christ cannot be confined, "that God is greater than human nature and the church." Further, to call believers in other religions anonymous Christians disposes Christians to approach them with the realization that, most likely, they are not simply "pagans," total strangers, and that the gospel does not necessarily bring them anything essentially new or "absolutely unknown." As anonymous Christians, "pagans" already know the one God of love who is active in their midst, already bringing about the kingdom. Rahner feels that his theory, therefore, promotes a more open, authentic dialogue with other religions.[39]

In broadening the Christian view of other religions, however, the image of anonymous Christianity also has clear limits. It states not only that there is saving grace within other religions but also that this grace is Christ's. There is no such thing as "pure grace"; it is always grace won by Christ and essentially oriented toward him. Therefore—here the limits are defined—the religions, for all the "supernatural elements" they may contain, are incomplete until they come to know and embrace Christ. Only in him can they find their true identity and the fullness of salvation.

Especially in his earlier writings, Rahner clearly sets a time limit for the validity of the religions. Once a religion really confronts the gospel—once the gospel is translated into the new culture and embodied in community—then that religion loses its validity. It must make way for him who is greater.[40]

The theological foundations for the theory of anonymous Christianity and for the limits it sets to the validity of other religions are found in two beliefs, concerning Christ and the church, that Rahner feels must be affirmed by all Christians. First, Christ is the *constitutive cause* of salvation (this term is not Rahner's). Whatever saving grace is present in the world has been constituted and caused by the event of Jesus Christ. Rahner, however, does not consider Christ an *efficient* cause of grace, as if Jesus had to *do* something to bring about God's universal love. Rather, Christ is the *final* cause of God's universal salvific will, what God, from the beginning of time, had in mind in calling and offering grace to all humankind. Jesus of Nazareth, then, is the final goal, the end product of the entire process of universal revelation and grace. For Rahner, that final goal is a necessary cause of salvation. Without that goal, realized in one historical individual, the entire process would not take place: "God desires the salvation of everyone; and this salvation is the salvation won by Christ. . . . *This* relationship of God to man [the supernatural existential] . . . rests on the Incarnation, death, and resurrection of the one Word of God become flesh."[41]

For Rahner, this makes eminent sense, both from the standpoint of God and humanity. God makes clear what creation is all about; Christ is the "final, unsurpassable, irreversible" historical realization and manifestation of what God is doing in history. This satisfies what Rahner argues is the teleology of human freedom. Confronted with a multiplicity of possible truths and choices, humans search for the ability to make a final and definitive commitment. In Christ they are enabled to do so. He is the "absolute perfection and guarantee" of God's love and grace, "the greatest support and source of confidence" for committing oneself to this God. In other words, Jesus Christ, as the final, constitutive case of salvation, tells humanity what it is, where it is going, what it can hope to achieve.[42]

The second theological support for the theory of anonymous Christianity is an extension of the first: what has been realized in Christ is carried on in the church. The church is "the continuation of the mystery of Christ, his permanent visible presence in our history . . . his continuing historical presence in the world."[43] Again, for Rahner this is common Christian belief. It does not identify Christ with the church, but it finds an essential, integral relationship between the two. The church plays an essential part in the whole process of salvation, not so much because all grace must be channeled through it, but because every experience of grace, every anonymous Christian, has a real, even if unconscious, orientation toward the church as the continuation of Christ.

This orientation is as natural as it is necessary. As every seed seeks to become the full-grown plant, as every idea presses toward expression in word or symbol, so every experience of God seeks its full identity and self-awareness in Christ, and that means in Christ's Body, the church.[44] With his theory of anonymous Christianity, Rahner tries to provide a contemporary solution to an age-old tension; with it he attempts to affirm and balance both the universal salvific will of God and the necessity of the church.

Even though Rahner continues to affirm the necessity of the church, he insists that his theory of anonymous Christianity demands a thoroughly different understanding of the mission of the church and of its relationship to other religions than was current in Catholic ecclesiology prior to the Second Vatican Council. No longer should Christians consider the church an island of salvation surrounded by a sea of perdition. And no longer should missionaries find their motivation in the belief that they must preach to "pagans" who otherwise would have little chance for salvation: "the Church will not so much regard herself today as the exclusive community of those who have a claim to salvation but rather as the historically tangible *vanguard* and the historically and socially constituted explicit expression of what the Christian hopes is present as a hidden reality even outside the visible Church."[45]

Despite a chorus of protests that his theory undermines the élan of missionary work, Rahner insists that the need to preach the gospel is as urgent as ever before. He proposes what he feels is a more theologically correct and personally mature motivation for missionaries: the desire to "serve the incarnational dynamic of grace" —that is, to aid others to become more fully aware of and thus more committed to what they already are: children of the one God. In his earlier writings Rahner stated that such full awareness in the church made for "a still greater chance for salvation." More recently, he has emphasized Christians' greater responsibility for the welfare of others rather than their greater personal privilege.[46]

As we shall see, many theologians have serious problems with the term "anonymous Christians." Still, the majority of Catholic theologians who are trying to work out a theology of religions endorse the substance of Rahner's theory. They adhere to an understanding of Christ as constitutive cause of a universal salvation aimed at achieving its finality in the historical community of Christ's Body, the church. In a 1979 lecture, Pietro Rossano summarized the church's teaching on other religions and echoed Rahner's understanding of Christ as final cause of salvation. Christ is "the center of the universe and of history . . . the key to decipher all the religious traditions of humankind . . . the future of humanity, the image of the perfect human on whom we are modeled (1 Cor. 15:48–49).[47] Pope John Paul II, who in his encyclical *Redemptor Hominis* has high praise for other religions, shows even clearer reflections of Rahner's theory of anonymous Christianity: "The human person—every person without exception—has been redeemed by Christ; because Christ is in a way united to the human person—every person without exception—even if the individual *may not realize this fact*."[48]

The content, though not the terminology, of Rahner's theory of anonymous Christians is even more clearly affirmed in the ecclesiology that has become general Catholic teaching since Vatican II. The church, its nature and mission, is understood as "the *sacrament* of salvation for the entire world." No longer an exclusive "sanctuary" of the saved, the church is a "sign raised up among the nations," a "symbol," a *pars pro toto* ("part for the whole"), a "representative," a "prototype" of the kingdom of God at work throughout all history. As with any sacrament, the church is the full, concrete expression of the reality of grace (the *res sacramenti*) that is always broader than the sacrament but always intrinsically oriented toward it.[49]

RECENT DEVELOPMENTS—BEYOND RAHNER

Although most Catholic theologians accept the basic building blocks of Rahner's model for a theology of religions, many, especially in recent years, have felt the need to refashion some of his arguments and to expand his model. Most of their problems have to do with the last part of his argument, with the limits he sets to it by his theory of anonymous Christianity. Theologians, reflecting the uncertainty within the Christian community, are asking whether and how Christ plays a unique role in the history of salvation, whether, as Rahner maintains, "the salvation willed by God is the salvation won by Christ"[50]—that is, whether Christ is the constitutive cause of salvation. Such uncertainty extends to questioning whether God really wills that all persons and all religions become Christian.

Hans Küng is a representative critic of the notion of anonymous Christianity. For him the theory is simply the most recent "theological fabrication" that sweeps "the whole of good-willed humanity . . . into the back door of the 'holy Roman Church' and thus tries to save the 'infallible formula' of 'outside the church, no salvation.' "

Küng points out the wobbly foundations of this fabrication. Empirically, he can detect no "dynamic orientation" among Buddhists or Hindus toward the church; they are happy to remain what they are. Personally, he finds the idea of anonymous Christianity presumptuous, offensive, and a block to dialogue. Even without being told, if Hindus or Buddhists know that Christians already count them on the Christian side, they are bound to feel that Christians are not really listening. Theologically, Küng argues that the theory vaporizes the church into a universal presence that, because it is everywhere, is really nowhere; Christianity thus loses its essentially social nature and its distinctiveness. Küng therefore urges that the theory of anonymous Christians be dropped, which means dropping the dogma of the necessity of the church for salvation. He argues for a theocentrism to take the place of ecclesiocentrism in the Christian understanding of salvation.[51]

Other efforts to move beyond Rahner's understanding of the unique and constitutive role of Christ and the church are found in those theologians who are questioning the "time limit" that Rahner placed on the validity of other religions. What some theologians—Gregory Baum, Rosemary Ruether, John Pawlikowski—are proposing for Judaism is being extended to all religions. As we shall see in chapter 8, these theologians claim that the Jewish religion was not meant to be "superseded" by Christianity; Judaism preserves its own value and role in God's plan, alongside Christianity.[52] Might not the same thing apply, other theologians ask, to Hinduism, Buddhism, and Islam, especially in view of their continued growth and success?

To admit this permanent validity of other religions, alongside Christianity, is perhaps what it means to take Christian eschatology seriously; the fullness of the kingdom, in which all will truly be one, is something that will be realized only when this earth is transformed. "There is a good deal of evidence that the actual religious pluralism is the will of God for humanity."[53] Perhaps the "desire for the church" (*votum ecclesiae*) that Rahner and others try to find hiding within the religions is better understood as a "desire for the kingdom of God" (*votum regni coelestis*).[54]

Because of this recognition of the possible permanent validity of other religions, alongside (outside) Christianity, theologians are urging Christians to pursue interreligious dialogue not only, as Vatican II stated, "prudently and lovingly," but eagerly and adventurously. If other faiths have their own validity, Christians must reform their traditional view that there is no *new* revelation after the death of the last apostle. There is much that can and must be learned from other faiths. Not only can other religions enable Christians to understand more profoundly what they already have in Christ; not only can new treasures be drawn from the ones already owned; but brand new treasures might be discovered in other religions, treasures not found in the salvific revelation constituted by Christ. Christians who are engaged in such a dialogue (e.g., Panikkar and Griffin with Hinduism; Dumoulin, Johnston, Lassalle with Buddhism) seem to be substantiating the speculations of Rahner and Walbert Bühlmann that the needed renewal of Christianity will come out of the churches of the southern hemisphere, the churches engaged in conversing with and learning from new religions and cultures.[55]

Further questioning of Rahner's traditional argument that all salvation is constituted by Christ and must be completed in him is drawn from the new image of the church as "sacrament of salvation." Theologians argue that if the church is to be understood not as an exclusive sanctuary but as a universal symbol of salvation, then the real mission of Christ and his church is not redemption but "epiphany"; the church finds its raison d'être not in "saving from sin" but in showing "the complete epiphany of God"—that is, in re-presenting more clearly, bringing to fuller consciousness and engagement, the presence of grace and truth that has already been "constituted" in the religions (but not only in the religions), independently of Christ and the church.[56]

These are not merely subtle distinctions for theologians to play with; they have a very practical payoff in determining how Christians understand themselves and how they deal with other religions. Theologians who see the church as a symbol rather than a sanctuary of salvation affirm Rahner's suggestion that the meaning of being a Christian is not to have a better chance of being saved; rather one chooses to be a Christian because one accepts the responsibility of serving, clarifying, promoting the presence of God wherever and however it is found.

In other words, the church exists not to promote the church but the kingdom of God. This means that the foremost concern of the church is not to seek conversions and augment its membership. Rather it is to foster the love and justice, the truth and peace, that make up God's kingdom on earth. Conversion to Christ and the church is a means to this end, never an end in itself. The first concern of Christians should be to cooperate with, not necessarily to convert, anyone who is already promoting this kingdom. Mission theologians are specifying even more concretely what this means in regard to other religions: "The Church has the duty to be a sign and sacrament of salvation to the whole of mankind; it should help Buddhism progress along its own course of the history of salvation, and in a way work to make the Buddhist a better Buddhist."[57]

These efforts to move beyond Rahner and beyond traditional understandings of Christ and the church are no doubt significant. One must, however, ask how far they really go. In the end, they seem to amount to more of a remodeling than a radical change in Rahner's basic approach. All (or most) of the Catholic theologians who criticize Rahner still adhere to the decisive ingredient of his theology of religions. Even though they no longer wish to assert that Christ is the constitutive cause of all salvation, even though they do not try to claim for the church any example of saving grace outside the church, they still continue to hold up Christ and the church as *normative* for whatever revelation and grace are found throughout history.

In an excellent review of contemporary understandings of the necessity of Christ and the church, Peter Schineller explains what "normativity" means in these new, more liberal views: "It indicates . . . a measurer, a superior or ideal type, which can function to measure, correct, and judge others by its own standard. . . . It does not imply that he [Christ] is the constitutive, unique . . . mediator of salvation for all mankind."[58] So there is a shift in the Catholic model from a *constitutive* to a *normative* understanding of the role of Christ and the church in salvation. But we ask: What difference does that really make?

Again, Hans Küng helps us pursue that question. After his resounding call for a recognition of the salvific value of other religions and for a move from an ecclesiocentric to a theocentric understanding of salvation, he insists with equal vigor that to be a Christian means to recognize and proclaim Christ as "normative" (*massgebend*) not only for Christians but for all peoples. Jesus of Nazareth is "ultimately decisive, definitive, archetypal for man's relations with God, with his fellow man, with society." Jesus cannot be listed as one of the "archetypal men" that Karl Jaspers had identified throughout history. He is uniquely different, normative for all others.[59]

In applying this normativity of Christ to other religions, Küng asserts that Christianity therefore is the necessary *critical catalyst* for all other faiths. The word "critical" is of the essence. Without Christ's revelation, the religions, according to Küng, cannot really understand and appropriate the salvation at work within them. He attempts to give this assertion some empirical verification. Without Christ, he tells us, the religions cannot really adapt their spiritualities to "modernity," to the demands of our world-affirming, technological age; without the gospel, they are caught in their "unhistoricity, circular thinking, fatalism, unworldliness, pessimism, passivity, caste spirit, social disinterestedness."[60]

With his understanding of Christ as normative, Küng seems to end up with much the same ambiguity that he criticized in Rahner's theory of anonymous Christianity. On the one hand, he extols other religions as the "ordinary way of salvation," denounces Christians' "arrogant domination . . . [and] absolutism,'' and points out areas where Christianity has much to learn from other believers.[61] But he also implies that unless the other religions are ''critically catalyzed'' by the normative revelation in Christ, they are lacking something essential. The revelation they possess finds *''full realization* in Christianity.'' Or more explicitly: ''that God may not remain for them the unknown God, there is needed the Christian proclamation and mission announcing Jesus.''[62] Evidently, in dialogue, other religions are ''more open to question than Christianity'' and have much more to learn.

Küng makes a paradoxical statement (or is it a contradiction?): Christianity must be ''ready to revise its own standpoint . . . while claiming *absolute validity.''*[63] For Küng, Christians can go only so far in recognizing the value of other religions and in learning from them, for in Christ they hold the normative, the final, word. How different, then, is ''normative'' from ''constitutive''?

Küng's efforts to move the Catholic model from ecclesiocentrism to theocentrism really turn out to be a *move to christocentrism*. This assessment applies to most of the Catholic theologians who are trying to work out a more coherent theology of religions. They still hold to Christ as the *norma normans non normata* (''the norm above all other norms''). Lonergan recognizes an ''inner word of grace'' within all religions; however, ''the historical Word'' of God, God's definitive manifestation of salvation, is found only in the historical Jesus and his church.[64] Schlette, for all his praise of the religions as the general way of salvation, insists that Christ and the church bear ''an absolute quality, clarity, and binding character which essentially transcends the level of general sacred history.''[65]

In a recent attempt at a more liberal, positive attitude toward other religions, Bühlmann summarizes the christocentrism prevailing in Catholic thought: ''Surely in Jesus Christ, God's self-communication has reached a point that it is unthinkable for other revelations ever to surpass or even equal. There cannot be a more-than-Christ. In him the last age, the final time, has already begun.''[66] Not as constitutive cause but as final norm, Christ and Christ's presence in the church remain for the Catholic model the center, the decisive focal point for God's relationship with humanity. Once again, christology turns out to be the final touchstone and limit for Christian attempts to understand religious pluralism.

Because of their christological foundations, followers of the Catholic model will enter the dialogue with other religions with the expectation of finding an abundance of grace and truth—but also with the presupposition (anonymous or explicit) that other religions are inferior to Christianity. Those who hold to Christ as constitutive of salvation and endorse some form of the anonymous Christianity theory will see the other religions as ''advent forms,'' ''previews'' (*Vorentwürfe*), ''pathfinders'' (*Wegbereiter*) for Christianity. The religions will be, as Vatican II and tradition phrase it, a *praeparatio evangelica*—a preparation for the gospel.[67]

Others, who question the anonymous Christian approach but still endorse Christ as the norm for all religious experience, will admit that the religions have a validity of their own and need not be converted to Christianity. Still, even though they may not wish to admit it, these theologians must maintain that without conversion to Christ and the church, the religions remain incomplete. Adherents of other faiths are not called anonymous Christians; to be honest, however, they are considered *potential* Christians. Of course, that potential need not be realized for salvation to be experienced; until it is, though, something is missing. As exemplified in a recent study of Arnulf Camps, even for the more liberal wing of the Catholic model, the religions still remain a preparation for Christianity.[68]

There is, then, a fundamental point of agreement between the Catholic and the mainline Protestant models. Whereas mainline Protestants, for the most part, view the religions as a negative preparation for the gospel, Catholics see them as a positive preparation. We shall have to ask whether even such an attitude, for all its positive content, can still provide the necessary condition for authentic interreligious dialogue.

THE CATHOLIC MODEL: A MAINLINE CHRISTIAN MODEL

As is the case with the other Christian models for a theology of religions, the Catholic model is not the exclusive property of one church or confession. Although it has been elaborated extensively by Roman Catholic theologians and although it has firm roots in the Catholic tradition of natural theology and the goodness of human nature, this model is being proposed by Christian thinkers from a variety of traditions. In fact, the approach to other religions we have been studying in this chapter can well be termed the "mainline Christian model" that has been evolving since the 1960s across confessional lines. What follows is but a brief sketch of this growing ecumenical consensus.

Anglican Views

Both Catholic confessions, the Anglican and the Roman, hold in common a natural theology that assumes the presence of a universal revelation in a variety of sacramental forms. The Anglican version of what this means for other religions has been stated extensively by M.A.C. Warren, Kenneth Cragg, and John V. Taylor. Typical of the Anglican tradition, these theologians speak with admirable respect for the spiritual values of other religions. They advocate a method of dialogue called "Christian presence"; it requires a long, respectful listening before trying to converse with members of other faiths.

When these theologians take up that conversation, however, they restate much of Rahner's theory of anonymous Christianity. Warren speaks of "the unknown Christ" who saves even when "unrecognized as the Savior." Through his method of Christian presence, Cragg seeks to "unveil" the hidden Christ—that is, "the elements that are already 'in Christ' " within the other religions. Taylor points out that every religion has its "jealousies," its tenets that carry a "universal significance and finality" for all humankind. For Christians this jealousy is the assertion "that Jesus is central to God's purpose for mankind . . . that from the beginning the world was held in existence by the Redeemer who was to die." This Christ is "the invisible magnetic pole" that draws all peoples in their quest for the Ultimate.[69] Christ is clearly both the constitutive cause and the final norm for salvation within all religions.

Eastern Orthodoxy

Here again we see a clear reflection of the constitutive-normative christology that supports the Catholic model. Georges Khodr, metropolitan of Mount Lebanon in Lebanon (a diocese of the Greek Orthodox Patriarchate of Antioch), speaks for his tradition when he insists that "the economy of Christ cannot be reduced to its historical manifestation." Rather, the economy of Christ is carried on universally in all religions through the activity of the Spirit. Through the Spirit, Christ is actively but clandestinely present in all religions: "Any reading of religions is a reading of Christ."

Khodr will brook "no blurring of the centrality and ontological uniqueness of Christ Jesus." Like Rahner and the Roman Catholics, he attests to "a secret form of communion with all men in the economy of the Mystery whereby we are being gradually led towards the final consummation, the recapitulation of all things in Christ." Christ in his church remains normative.[70]

Third World Protestant Theologians

I indicated, in chapter 6, that not all Third World Protestant theologians make use of the mainline Protestant model in their efforts to understand and meet other faiths.[71] Choan-Seng Song, Kosuke Koyama, and D. Preman Niles are examples of the younger generation of Third World Protestant Christians who seem more comfortable with the Catholic or mainline Christian model. All of them insist that missionary efforts and Christian dialogue with other believers must begin with a theology of creation.

According to Koyama, the Holy pervades the created order, like the *tapas,* the Hindu symbol of divine heat-energy within the cosmos.[72] C.S. Song can even speak of creation as incarnation; divinity, as "a creative force," animates the evolutionary process, supplying history with ever greater promise. Therefore, human history is full of what Song calls "a redemptive quality," "redemptive moments and events."[73] Niles bases his recognition of God's saving presence within history on a cosmic christology; Jesus Christ is "not simply a parochial savior but a cosmic presence" that enables "other faith traditions and histories to bear witness to him."[74]

Such a view of creation, these theologians insist, demands a more engaging Christian encounter with other faiths. They argue forcefully that Christianity has too long borne the trappings of Western culture; through dialogue with non-Western cultures and religions the Christian church *must* now assume an Asian (and an African) face.[75] All these theologians, however, maintain that in the incarnational dialogue of Christianity with other religions, Christ remains "decisive," the final norm of truth, for he, and only he, is the "second Adam," the "culmination" of all God's saving activity in history: "The ultimate meaning of all 'goings out' in God's election is found in Jesus Christ.''[76] Song sees the dialogue between Christianity and other religions as "the meeting of the Truth and truths.''[77] He calls for a shift "from Israel to Asia," which would place the religions of the East in the role of Israel—preparing the way for Christ.[78]

With Roman Catholics, therefore, this new generation of Asian theologians recognizes the universal possibility of salvation within other religions, but it is a salvation whose constitutive cause and final norm is Jesus Christ.

Process Theology

Working out of a Whiteheadian framework, process theologians John B. Cobb, Jr., Schubert Ogden, and Norman Pittenger speak a language different from that of most Roman Catholic theologians. In their approach to other faiths, however, they endorse a model essentially the same as that of more recent Roman statements. They avoid any shadow of the anonymous Christian theory and any talk of salvation constituted by Christ; still, Christ remains the ultimate norm for the way God is trying to draw the entire process of history toward ever greater beauty and unity.

John Cobb affirms the universal presence of revelation and redemptive grace with his understanding of the *Logos* as "the principle of creative transformation" pervading the world. "Christ" is the designation for this Logos insofar as it actually incarnates itself in historical forms, wherever that may be.[79] Schubert Ogden's entire theology starts with the claim that God's pure unbounded love so saturates history that all human beings have the possibility of achieving authentic human existence; an "original possibility of existence *coram Deo* (before God) . . . belongs to man as such.''[80] Pittenger sees the "divine lure" toward ever greater love and fulfillment incarnating itself in the world from the beginning of time.[81] Such a universalist perspective is used to overcome the sorry exclusivism that has so long characterized Christian attitudes toward other faiths. Christ, understood as the realization of the universal incarnation of the Logos, "is the Way that excludes no Ways." Faintly echoing Rahner, Cobb finds Christ (not Jesus) within all religions. Christians therefore must recognize and learn from the truth—the Christ—present in other religions.[82]

But in calling for such an open attitude, process theologians are not willing to let go of the unique normativity of Jesus. Arguing from exegetical evidence in the New Testament and from a process-ontological explanation of how the "very selfhood [of Jesus] was constituted by the Logos," Cobb concludes that the Logos was "distinctively embodied in Jesus." Jesus is "the full incarnation of the Logos," "a paradigm case of incarnation." This means: "This perfect incarnation of the Logos is at the same time the highest embodiment of humanity."[83]

Cobb honestly admits that there is no *a priori* reason for denying that what happened in Jesus did not happen elsewhere: "There might be someone of whom history has left no record who was constituted much as Jesus was, but that is an idle speculation. So far as we know, Jesus is unique."[84] The implications of such an understanding of Jesus, which Cobb does not state, are that the Christ incarnate in Christianity is normative for the Christ within other religions.

Ogden agrees with Cobb, even though he builds his understanding of the normativity of Jesus more on the existential relevance of "the Christ" than on knowledge about "the historical Jesus." He states his case succinctly:

> The claim "only in Jesus Christ" must be interpreted to mean, not that God acts to redeem only in the history of Jesus and in no other history, but that the only God who redeems any history—*although he in fact redeems every history*—is the God whose redemptive action is decisively re-presented in the word that Jesus speaks and is. [In Jesus, God's redemptive activity is] transparently [present] with all the force of final revelation.[85]

The World Council of Churches

Especially since its Third Assembly in New Delhi (1961), the World Council of Churches has clearly broken with the previous negative, exclusivistic attitude toward other religions that, under the influence of Barth and Kraemer, had prevailed since the Tambaram Missionary Conference in 1928. Since New Delhi, in numerous consultations with representatives of other religions, the WCC has endorsed a "Dialogue with Men of Other Faiths and Ideologies" (the name of the subunit founded in 1971), based on what can be called a "cosmic christology." It rests on much the same foundation as does the Roman Catholic theory of anonymous Christianity: the effects of redemption are not limited to the Christian communities; Christ, cosmically through the Spirit, "illumines" all peoples and "is at work in every man's heart."[86]

During this past decade, the WCC pursuit of dialogue has continued unabated. The theological foundations for such dialogue, however, have become more controversial and blurred. This is due, to a great extent, to the added numbers of Evangelical churches within the WCC. Thus the statement at the Fifth Assembly at Nairobi (1975) on "Seeking Community: The Common Search of People of Various Faiths, Cultures, and Ideologies,'' turned out to be ''unsatisfactory and inconclusive.'' Many Evangelicals felt that it tended to ''blunt the cutting edge of mission'' and of the uniqueness of Christ.[87]

In the dust of such theological controversy, the WCC issued in 1979 its *Guidelines on Dialogue*. It was heralded as ''a historic turn,'' a ''landmark in the development of the dialogue debate in the ecumenical context.''[88] Indeed, it vigorously insists that interreligious dialogue is not a pleasant luxury for Christians but a necessary ''means of living out our faith in Christ in service of community with our neighbor.'' It warns that dialogue should not be a ''secret weapon in the armory of an aggressive Christian militancy.'' It even urges that Christians avoid the ''position of superiority'' lurking in such notions as ''anonymous Christians,'' ''the Christian presence,'' ''the unknown Christ.''[89]

Still, clarity and enthusiasm fade when it comes to recognizing the theological implications for such an understanding of dialogue. After a rousing call to dialogue, the *Guidelines* list a number of unresolved questions; among them is the issue of the uniqueness and normativity of Jesus: ''What is the relation between the universal creative/redemptive activity of God towards all humankind and the particular creative/redemptive activity of God in the history of Israel and in the person and work of Jesus Christ?'' The document goes on even to question whether this ''universal creative/redemptive activity'' provides authentic revelation and salvation in other religions: ''Are Christians to speak of God's work in the lives of all men and women only in tentative terms of hope that they may experience something of Him, or more positively in terms of God's self-disclosure to people of living faith and ideologies and in the struggle of human life?''[90]

Such unresolved questions concerning whether salvation or revelation can be present in other religions would seem to place Christian participation in interreligious dialogue on a rather insecure basis. S.J. Samartha warns us not to expect too much from WCC statements. Their aim is to work for consensus, not impose it: ''Given the tremendous differences in the background of the churches affiliated to the WCC,'' the *Guidelines* try to offer ''suggestions, recommendations meant to change attitudes rather than to provide *a* theology of religions.''[91]

One can acknowledge the admonitions of Samartha and still point out that if theological questions concerning whether God is really active in other religions are unresolved, the whole possibility and purpose of dialogue remains blurred. As John Cobb admits, ''despite the strong emphasis [of the WCC] on listening in dialogue, it is not clear just what Christians are expected to learn. . . . The World Council of Churches promotes dialogue, but it has not yet suceeded in clarifying its purpose.''[92] Given the ''landmark'' clarity of the *Guidelines* on the importance of dialogue, together with its unclarity on theological issues, one might place the WCC approach to other faiths somewhere between the mainline Protestant and the Catholic models.

THE CATHOLIC MODEL: INSIGHTS AND INADEQUACIES

As the most open and liberal of the Christian models we have studied, the Catholic model represents an approach to other religions that many Christians would say is "as far as we can go." The following remarks will indicate how the Catholic model (as articulated by both Catholics and Protestants) both summarizes the achievements and focuses the main stumbling block in Christian efforts to understand and dialogue with persons of other faiths.

Insights

1) The main achievement of the Catholic model is its argument, based on central Christian beliefs, that Christians not only can but must look on other religions as possible *ways of salvation*. This model takes seriously and consistently a conviction common to all Christian confessions: that the God of Jesus Christ is a God of universal love. Representatives of the Catholic model do not tie that love to an encounter with Jesus, as both the conservative Evangelical and mainline Protestant models, in different ways, tend to do. For the Catholic model, both revelation *and* salvation are alive and well beyond the borders of Christianity.

The "sociological link" by which the Catholic model argues from God's universal salvific will to the salvific potential of all religions is, for the most part, sound. It fills a serious lack in the other two Christian models. The Reformational tradition is, admittedly, less "sacramental" than the Catholic (both Roman and Anglican) and places less stress on the need for a historico-social incarnation of God's grace. Still, Protestant theology has moved beyond Barth's and Bonhoeffer's image of Christianity as a "religionless religion"; it recognizes that revelation, though always distinct from religion, cannot do without religion. Here Rahner's simple conclusion takes hold: if this is true for the Christian, it must be true for the Hindu. Grace can never be naked; it must be dressed in some historical form.

At this point, however, the Catholic sociological argument needs a word of caution from the Protestants. The qualification that Rahner usually adds to his conclusion concerning the religions as ways of salvation is frequently omitted by his followers: the religions *can* be vehicles of saving grace; it is not certain or necessary that they *are*. There can be much in other religions, as in Christianity, that is a definite obstacle to truly knowing and responding to the one God. One must be careful of applying Rahner's "salvific optimism" too facilely.

Also, it must be added that although we should expect the religions to be the most likely candidates for providing a social mediation of grace, they are not the sole candidates. As the World Council of Churches has been emphasizing, other social and political "ideologies" can also do the job, frequently a more effective job.

2) Another achievement of the Catholic approach, which addresses central difficulties noted in the Evangelical and mainline Protestant models, is its understanding of Christ and the church as a *sign or sacrament of salvation*. Christ, in his historical ministry and still through the church, is savior not as an efficient cause of saving grace, which a person has explicitly to know or somehow contact in order to be saved. Rather, Christ, still present in the church, is the final cause of salvation, which cause clearly expresses and incarnates a divine presence given and operative in all religions.

Such a view seems entirely consistent with Christian tradition, especially with the wisdom or Logos christology of the early church. It corroborates the understanding of human nature and of the role of Christ that is suggested (chapter 4) by modern psychology of religion. Serious questions are still to be raised whether such a sacramental understanding of Christ's salvific role requires him to be "normative" for all religions. Still, this seems to be the only view of Christ and of the church that coherently allows Christians to enter the dialogue with other religions with the expectation that also other believers have experienced the one God and therefore have something important to contribute to the dialogue.

3) A further achievement of the Catholic model is its resolute and sincere insistence that Christians today not only can but must engage in a *dialogue with other religions*. This call to dialogue was sounded with official clarity in the Second Vatican Council and backed up with the establishment of a Vatican secretariate for other religions in 1964. Statements and actions, since 1961, of the World Council of Churches are an even more resolute effort to speak and listen to other faiths. The theological reasons given for this call to dialogue make it clear that the main intent of encounter with persons of other faiths is no longer the desire to convert them (although, clearly, conversion is not ruled out). Rather, the primary goals of dialogue are twofold: to cooperate with other religions in providing a unified religious contribution to the social-economic-political crisis facing the international community of nations, and to enable Christians to learn from other religious traditions and thus to become better Christians. If such an understanding of interreligious dialogue truly becomes the common conviction of all the churches, it will certainly represent a "new age" for the way Christians understand themselves and live in the world.

But it is at this point—that is, in the concrete practice of dialogue—that a stumbling block appears not only within the Catholic but within all Christian models for a theology of religions.

Inadequacies

As will be argued in greater detail in chapter 10, one of the first prerequisites for interreligious dialogue is that the partners speak out of personal convictions and are not afraid to take clear positions. More technically, they must be able to make claims of "universal relevance"—that is, be able to state why the truths they affirm are true not only for themselves but for all peoples. Without such clarity and conviction, dialogue becomes chit-chat and will never attain its integral goal: growth in knowledge and commitment.

But there is a difference between religious truth presented as *universally* relevant and truth presented as *definitively* and *normatively* relevant. All the representatives of the Catholic model, even those who reject any form of the anonymous Christian theory as offensive to their partners in dialogue, still adhere to Christ as the full and final expression of divine revelation, the *norma normans non normata,* the norm above all other norms. In other words, they bring to the dialogue religious claims that are not only universally, but definitively and normatively, relevant.

Are not such claims an even more subtle co-opting of dialogue? A missionary theologian, veteran of dialogue with African religions, who abandoned the ecclesiocentrism of the anonymous Christian approach but still held to the christocentrism of present-day christology, states the difficulties he encountered:

> A dialogue in which one of the partners reserved the right (but not the mutual right, apparently) to judge the other solely according to his own criteria would be a strange one indeed!

> . . . by positing the absoluteness of Jesus Christ and of God's Revelation in him, . . . we are still envisaging the other religions from within the absoluteness of Christianity; fundamentally the other religion is none the less disqualified. And, in every fibre of its being, it refuses to be disqualified.

> If Christianity (because of Christ) is the definitive truth, the absoluteness of God's revelation to mankind, it only remains for the other religions to convert to Christianity. . . . What we have, in fact, is dialogue between the elephant and the mouse.[93]

The Catholic model thus provides us with a final focus on a question, a recurring stumbling block, that we have encountered throughout this study. The Catholic approach recognizes both revelation and salvation outside Christ and Christianity; it admits that Christ need not be considered the constitutive cause, the sole vehicle of God's saving love in the world. It continues to affirm, however, that Christ must be proclaimed as the fullest revelation, the definitive savior, the norm above all other norms for all religions. This, they say, is as far as Christians can go. To move beyond this point is to jeopardize the distinctiveness, the essence, of Christianity.

But in the light of contemporary religious pluralism and the demands of interreligious dialogue, we must ask: Is this true? Must Christians proclaim a final normativity for Christ? Can they? To express it more precisely, what are the conditions for the possibility of making such an affirmation? This is a question I shall try to answer in the last two chapters. For the moment, it will help to sharpen the import of the question.

Some will argue that Christians must insist on the normativity and finality of Christ for all religions because this is what their *personal experience of Christ* tells them. But is this really so? What is "felt" by those who experience and commit themselves to the power and truth of Christ? Certainly they experience that Christ is an utterly reliable and demanding expression of who God is. This includes the conviction that Christ has something crucially important to say to all peoples (universal relevance). But such a Christian faith-experience does not seem to imply that Christ is the *one and only* utterly reliable and demanding expression of God's reality. When a Christian experiences Jesus Christ to be "my savior" and "savior for all," that does not necessarily mean "only savior."

Others will hold that Christians must attest the normativity and finality of Christ because that is the clear content, the unifying thread of the New Testament witness and Christian tradition. To this, two questions immediately arise:

1) Can such a claim be made on the authority of tradition when tradition seems to contradict our present experience? The voice of such experience has been heard throughout these pages: the relativity of all revelations and religious truth-claims, the truth and goodness of other religions, the encounter with other believers who also state that their experience and revelation is a message for all times and all peoples, the demands of dialogue that require that no one enter the conversation with a prepackaged final word. As such theologians as David Tracy and Paul Tillich tell us, such a contradiction between traditional belief and common human experience sounds the call for some form of "revision."

2) This need for revision prompts the other question: Is it true that belief in the normativity, finality, unsurpassability of Christ forms an essential part of the Christian message? We shall see that a careful analysis of the language and socio-cultural world of early Christianity suggests that it does not.

Such questions, however, do not necessarily imply that Jesus Christ is not the "norm above all other norms." As was said in earlier chapters, this may well be the case. The distinctiveness of Christianity may be that it contains a "surprise," an unimagined possibility. This cannot be automatically excluded. Yet we must ask again: What would be the grounds for recognizing such a possibility? What is it that would make Jesus Christ the fullest, the definitive, the normative revelation of God? Because such claims are universal, the reasons for them would have to be universally available—to all peoples. Our review of the Catholic model has not offered such evidence. Besides Hans Küng's very debatable argument that only Christianity can adapt to "modernity," all the reasons given have been Christian faith statements: Jesus is normative because he is the unique, perfect incarnation of God; his selfhood was the only one "constituted" by the Logos (Cobb). A further faith-claim could be added: only Jesus was raised from the dead. Yet how do these statements, made in Christian faith, stand up universally? How intelligible are they to open, honest believers of other faiths? How can Christians be sure that all this took place *only* in Jesus of Nazareth? A suggested reply, to be developed in chapter 10, is that such questions can be answered only in the dialogue with other religions.

Before moving on to our own final comments and conclusions, one more Christian model for a theology of religions must be examined. It is a minority position that is attempting to move beyond all that we have heard so far.

Chapter VIII

The Theocentric Model: Many Ways to the Center

Should Christians move beyond the Roman Catholic model in their attitude and approach to other religions? Can they? In the previous chapter, we saw that the Catholic model might be called a "mainline Christian model." Liberal theologians, representing both Catholic and Protestant confessions, endorse the positive assessment of other religions by the Catholic model and its insistence on the need for authentic dialogue. But they also affirm its traditional claim that Jesus Christ represents God's final and full revelation; in the encounter with other religions, Jesus remains the norm that must judge all other norms.

As has been indicated, even this "liberal" position bears a number of inadequacies, especially in the way it seems to throw up obstacles to the honest and open dialogue everyone is advocating. Still, for most Christians, the Catholic model contains a warning sign: "no trespassing beyond this point."

Are there any Christian theologians who are venturing beyond it? Tom Driver, who, as we shall see, is exploring such a venture, feels that he is alone; he finds that even well-known liberal theologians (such as Langdon Gilkey, Van Harvey, John Cobb, David Tracy), who are eloquently sensitive to cultural and religious pluralism, still put "Christ at the *center* of things."[1] Ignace Puthiadam, caught in the daily pressures of interreligious dialogue in India, announces with a note of frustration: "at present no Christian seems ready to question the universality and uniqueness of Christianity, since this community is the sacrament of that primordial and definitive encounter of God and men, Jesus Christ."[2] Peter Schineller, in his comprehensive review of contemporary understandings of the uniqueness of Christ and the church, suggests that any attempt to move beyond the "normative christology" of the Catholic model "seems somewhat ineffective in an age of pluralism, since it affirms that we cannot make decisions among religions and religious savior figures."[3]

This chapter will try to show that these judgments are not accurate. There

145

are Christian theologians who, in their efforts to understand and dialogue with other religions, are clearly and seriously questioning the finality or definitive normativity of Christ and Christianity. They are still a minority voice within the Christian churches. Yet their voice is growing stronger. A new consciousness within Christianity seems to be forming.

To assess the contents of this "minority position" we shall first hear from three of its main proponents, each with his roots in the models we have studied: John Hick, originally an Evangelical Christian; Raimundo Panikkar, a Roman Catholic priest; Stanley Samartha of the Church of South India. Two other sources critical of the normativity of Christ and Christianity will then be studied: theologians involved in the Jewish-Christian dialogue and certain political and liberation theologians.

All these minority voices have much in common. They all raise their criticisms out of the practical encounter with religious pluralism. They all suggest a revision of Christian attitudes that will preserve the distinctiveness of Christ and at the same time allow for a more open and authentic interreligious dialogue. In other words, they all feel that they have a solution to what Langdon Gilkey calls the "theological trick" of admitting the relativity of Christ without lessening his universal relevance.[4]

Although there is an underlying agreement among these different theologians, each of them uses a particular perspective in attempting to revise the traditional understanding of Christ's normativity and finality. I shall try to bring these individual perspectives into clear focus and indicate, at the end of each section, other contemporary theologians who are using the same perspective. My intent is to show that there is a growing number of theologians, from various confessions, who are trying to establish a dialogue with other religions on the basis of a nonnormative christology.

JOHN HICK: THE MYTH OF THE INCARNATION

John Hick describes his "spiritual pilgrimage" as a stumbling but steady progression in personal commitment and intellectual clarity. His frustration with "the infinite boredom" of much of institutional Christianity in England was resolved by "a spiritual conversion" that turned him into "a Christian of a strongly evangelical and indeed fundamentalist kind." Jesus became his "living lord and savior," Jesus as "God the Son Incarnate," the one savior of all humankind. Hick became a minister in the Presbyterian Church of England.

As he pursued his studies in philosophy and theology, however, he could not escape persistent questions that assailed the clarity of his evangelical beliefs. Among the most annoying of such questions were those stirred up by "the diversity of apparent revelations." The fact and the challenge of religious pluralism, especially as Hick experienced it personally in the large Muslim, Sikh, Hindu, and Jewish communities surrounding him in Birmingham, soon forced him into another conversion. Through this conversion, he retained his personal commitment to Jesus as his Lord, but thoroughly re-modeled his theology. He experienced a "Copernican revolution" in his Christian self-understanding, a revolution that, since 1973, he has been urging for all of Christianity.[5]

Hick is the most radical, the best-known, and therefore the most controversial of the proponents of a theocentric model for Christian approaches to other religions. We shall examine his arguments in some detail, in order to grasp clearly what he is saying and what he is not saying.

A New Map of Religions

Hick applauds the efforts of Roman Catholics to free Christianity from the exclusivism and elitism of most Evangelical and Protestant attitudes. He considers the Catholic theories of implicit faith, baptism by desire, anonymous Christianity, the ordinary and extraordinary ways of salvation, and Christianity as a "critical catalyst" to be attempts at a "charitable extension of the sphere of grace to people who had formerly been regarded as beyond the pale." Still, in the final analysis, he finds them much like the "epicycles" that scientists added to the Ptolemaic view of the universe to protect it from the data being amassed by the Copernicans—"circles revolving on circles to complicate the theory and bring it closer to the facts." More benignly, he considers the Roman Catholic model "a psychological bridge between the no longer acceptable older view and the new view which is emerging." But Hick adds: "sooner or later we have to get off the bridge on to the other side."[6]

So he proposes his "Copernican revolution in theology." It parallels Copernicus' model of the universe:

[It] involves an equally radical transformation in our conception of the universe of faiths and the place of our own religion within it . . . [It demands] a paradigm shift from a Christianity-centered or Jesus-centered to a God-centered model of the universe of faiths. One then sees the great world religions as different human responses to the one divine Reality, embodying different perceptions which have been formed in different historical and cultural circumstances.[7]

Hick would heartily endorse the description given in chapter 1 of the modern experience of religious pluralism. He locates the birth of the major world religions in a "Golden Age of Religious Activity," roughly 900 B.C. to A.D. 200.[8] Conceived in isolation (but by "one Divine Spirit"), the religions, for the most part, have grown up in isolation from each other. Distance, language, fear were the separating walls. Today, however, as never before, the religions are coming out of their historico-cultural ghettos and are getting to know each other. Today they can and must develop in unison.

Hick proposes a "new map for the universe of faiths." In describing this map, he speaks repeatedly about the one Spirit, the one Divine Reality or

Absolute, the one Logos behind all the religions. Although religions may conceive this one Reality either theistically (as personal) or nontheistically (nonpersonal), Hick implies that such differences are only historical, cultural, or psychological adaptations.[9] Many have accused him of an ahistorical idealism or a naive relativism that presses all the religions into a common dough.[10]

But when Hick explains his new map more technically, he makes it clear that for him the differences between the religions are not incidental or insignificant. In affirming the one "ultimate reality" behind all the religions, he concludes not that every religious expression is therefore true, but that every religious expression is therefore relative. He appeals to a distinction that he argues is "both ancient and widespread"—namely, "between, on the one hand, the Godhead in its own infinite depths beyond human experience and comprehension and, on the other hand, the Godhead as finitely experienced by humanity."[11] To explain this one reality within a diversity of interpretations, Hick makes use of both modern cybernetics and Kantian epistemology. The Godhead is the "one divine noumenon," the "external reality" that provides the "cognitive" or "informational input" behind all the religions. This "input" is "interpreted by the mind in terms of its own categorial system" and is "expressed in different modes . . . which can be transformed from one mode to another." These different expressions of the divine input are "not necessarily competitive, in the sense that the validity of one entails the spuriousness of the other." But neither are all interpretations "equally adequate"; "some mediate God to mankind better than others."[12]

Showing clearly that he wishes to avoid the pitfalls of relativism, Hick admits that "if we think for a moment of the entire range of religious phenomena, no one is going to maintain that they are all on the same level of value or validity."[13] Relativity does not mean equality. The problem, then, is how to judge whether a particular religion actually does mediate the ultimate reality or whether one religion does the job better than another.

In his more recent publications, Hick suggests that in trying to evaluate a religious tradition (one's own or another), one should ask: "Is this complex of religious experience, belief, and behavior soteriologically effective? Does it make possible the transformation of human experience from self-centeredness to Reality-centeredness?"[14]

From his study of the major world religions, Hick believes that all of them share a "common ethical ideal" or a common "soteriological structure";[15] this common ideal arises from the fact that all of them are animated by and in search of the same ultimate reality. All the major religions seek to transform the human situation that they judge to be in need of salvation/liberation— that is, full of suffering (*dukkha*). They urge this transformation by calling their followers to transcend self-interest and to become alive to broader dimensions of reality. Through "a voluntary renunciation of ego-centeredness and a self-giving to, or self-losing in, the Real," religious persons will live lives of "acceptance, compassion, love for all humankind, or even for all life." To judge the value or truth of a religion, therefore, one must examine whether or how much it promotes "that limitlessly better quality of human existence which comes about in the transition from self-centeredness to Reality-centeredness."[16]

Hick concludes, however, that such criteria, though they can and must be applied to particular religious practices or beliefs, cannot be used to rank "the great world religions as totalities." The major religions are too diverse and complex; an individual's knowledge of other religions is too limited. Whether the vision of ultimate reality held by one religion surpasses all others can be known, according to Hick, only eschatologically, only at the end of history as we know it.[17]

In the meantime, Hick urges an exchange, a dialogue, among all religions that will enable them to contribute more effectively to the transformation of human existence, a dialogue that will also aid religions to clarify and expand their individual interpretations of the reality that stands beyond them all. He suggests that ultimately even the apparently contradictory differences between the world religions—God as personal or impersonal, religious experience as individual or communal, world-affirming or world-denying—will turn out to be much more complementary than contradictory. He appeals to Sri Aurobindo's "logic of the Infinite": all we can say about the ultimate reality is much more a matter of "both-and" than "either-or."[18]

How does Hick think the future map of the universe of faiths will look? Clearly, he does not envision a single world religion that will absorb all the present diversity. Cultural and psychological differences will remain with us, and he feels it is good that they will. As the "growing world ecumenism" spreads, however, "the common commitment of faith in a higher reality which demands brotherhood on earth" will become more important than differences in doctrine and ritual. As these differences become less significant, there will be a transformation of the individual religions. Perhaps "one day such names as 'Christianity,' 'Buddhism,' 'Islam,' 'Hinduism' will no longer describe the then current configurations of men's religious experience and belief." Certainly "the sense of belonging to rival ideological communities" will diminish.[19]

A New Christology

Hick does not evade the implications of his Copernican revolution: "This paradigm shift involves a reopening of the Christological question."[20] Admitting that "this must be the most difficult of all issues for a Christian theology of religions,"[21] he works out a solution that allows Christians to continue to adhere to Christ as their unique savior without having to insist that he is necessarily unique or normative for others. Hick's main device for doing this, and his main contribution to the theocentric model to be studied in this chapter, is his view that Christian belief in the incarnation and the divinity of Jesus is mythic and therefore not only allows but demands reinterpretation.

Talk about Jesus as the incarnation of the Word and as the Son of God was, Hick tells us, one of the many symbolic-mythic models used by the early followers of Jesus to try to express what he meant for them.[22] This mythic interpretation turned out to be "*the* essential Christian belief," the hallmark of Christian identity. Hick insists, however, that it was not so in the very beginning. He makes much of the "all but certain" consensus of biblical scholars that Jesus did not designate himself Messiah or Son of God, or accept any such confession about himself from others.[23] Tracing the development of the myth of incarnation, Hick finds its embryonic form in the Jewish image of "son of God," a title often used for the Messiah, which, however, could be applied to any extraordinary religious person; it indicated uniqueness, but not exclusivity.

As the early community moved into the Greco-Roman culture, the image of the son of God was tightened into the notion of incarnation and unique deification: "ideas of divinity embodied in human life [were] . . . widespread in the ancient world . . . so that there is nothing in the least surprising in the deification of Jesus in that cultural environment."[24] This deification process is evident already in the Gospel of John, but it was especially in the conciliar debates of the ensuing centuries, which drew heavily on Greek philosophical concepts and worldview, that the mythical images of "son of God" and "incarnation" were ontologized into absolute and exclusive categories. Thus took place "the very significant transition from 'Son of God' to 'God the Son,' the Second Person of the Trinity." The mythic, poetic language of incarnation "hardened into prose and escalated from a metaphorical son of God to a metaphysical God the Son, of the same substance as the Father, within the triune Godhead."

Hick does not at all consider this process to be erroneous or a falsification of the Christian experience. It was natural that the early community should try to express its experience of Jesus "in the language of absolutes." Jesus as the Son of God consubstantial with the Father was "an effective way, within that cultural milieu, of expressing Jesus' significance as the one through whom men had transformingly encountered God."[25]

But the myth of the incarnation is not so effective today. One of the chief problems with it is that, when taken literally, it leads to all the uncomfortable "onlys" in Christian self-consciousness: Christ is the "only Savior" or the "only final norm" for all other religions.[26] So Hick urges not that the myth of the incarnation be done away with (as some of his critics have accused), but that it be taken as a myth—that is, not literally but seriously. He finds precedent for his hope that this will take place: "Christianity will . . . outgrow its theological fundamentalism, its literal interpretation of the idea of the incarnation as it has largely outgrown its biblical fundamentalism."[27]

In the way Hick explains his interpretation of the meaning of the myth of the incarnation, he often exposes himself to ready misunderstanding and criticism. He states that language about Jesus as the incarnate Son of God is not meant to be a "factual statment" about "empirical, metaphysical" realities. The imagery of incarnation "lacks any non-metaphorical meaning. . . . The real point and value of the incarnational doctrine is not indicative but expressive, not to assert a metaphysical fact but to express a valuation and evoke an attitude."[28] Hick's point is that when Christians call Jesus the Son of God, they are announcing that he has saved them, that he is the means by which they have known God, the revelation to which they are totally committed and that has transformed their lives. The emphasis is on attitudes, emotional response.

Hick does not mean, however, that the myth of the incarnation expresses *only* emotions, only a personal response, as if there were no reality apart from the emotions. In more technical jargon, he is not denying that there are any "cognitive claims" or assertions of truth to the myth of the incarnation. He is not reducing the traditional ontological christology to a functional christology. For him, there are *facts* that constitute the content and the cause of the myth. If Christians came to talk about God incarnate in Jesus, it was because they experienced him to be "so powerfully God-conscious that his life vibrated, as it were, to the divine life; and as a result his hands could heal the sick, and the 'poor in spirit' were kindled to new life in his presence. . . . He was so totally conscious of God that . . . [others] could catch something of the consciousness by spiritual contagion. . . . He was a soul liberated from selfhood and fully open to the divine Spirit."

Although Hick believes that Jesus grew into this consciousness, that it was not given him prepackaged from above, still Hick is making the "factual statement" that this is what Jesus *was*.[29] Incarnational language refers not just to something that happens in us, but to something that happened in Jesus.

Even though Hick holds that "metaphysical facts" are not the "main point" of the incarnation, he does offer his own metaphysical commentary on what the myth means. He wants to shake off the Greek metaphysics of substance, nature, hypostasis that has colored christology since the Council of Chalcedon. Such a thought world is not biblical, nor can it speak to modern experience.

Embracing more of a process metaphysics, Hick tries to explain the content of the myth of incarnation in terms of "purpose" and "action" and "operation." The divine nature is not a quantity of substantial stuff, but an activity carrying out a purpose. If, as Christianity has always held, this activity is *agape*—love ("God is love," 1 John 4:8)—and if this love is at work in history "from the inside," then someone described as the incarnation of God would be a clear case of the "inhistorization" of the divine *agape*. There would be a "numerical identity" between God's *agape* and Jesus'. "Jesus' *agape* is not a representation of God's *agape;* it *is* that *agape* operating in a finite mode; it is the eternal divine *agape* made flesh, inhistorized.''[30]

With such a metaphysics of the incarnation, Hick feels, room is left for other religions and other saviors. He explains that if we understand the incarnation "as a temporal cross-section of God's Agapeing," it is "not the entirety of that of which it is a cross-section." Or, more clearly:

> We want to say of Jesus that he was *totus Deus,* 'wholly God,' in the sense that his *agape* was genuinely the *agape* of God at work on earth, but not that he was *totum Dei,* 'the whole of God,' in the sense that the divine *agape* was expressed without remainder in each or even in some of his actions.[31]

So, according to Hick, by understanding the incarnation as a myth, Christians can declare that God is *truly* to be encountered in Jesus, but not *only* in Jesus. Furthermore, they can announce that Jesus is the center and norm for their lives, without having to insist that he be so for all other human beings. Such a christology lays the foundation not only for the possibility but the necessity of interreligious dialogue.

Examples of other theologians who make use of Hick's perspective—the mythic language of the incarnation—as a means for working toward an interreligious dialogue based on a nonnormative christology are Monika Hellwig (we shall hear from her in a following section) and John A.T. Robinson who, like Hick, interprets the "word pictures" of the incarnation to mean that Jesus was "*totus Deus,* the one who is utterly expressive of Godhead," not "*totum Dei,* the exhaustive revelation" of God.[32] Alan Race, in his book *Christians and Religious Pluralism,* also follows but goes beyond Hick by proposing an "action christology" that would drop all metaphysical claims of preexistence and of divine-human union in Jesus as "frankly mythological" and sees Jesus as the "decisive focus" of God's activity "not for all the light everywhere in the world, but for the vision he has brought to one cultural setting.''[33]

RAIMUNDO PANIKKAR: THE UNIVERSAL CHRIST AND THE PARTICULAR JESUS

We have already heard much from Raimundo Panikkar in chapter 1. He is one of the most profound and eloquent, as well as one of the most experienced, advocates of what Hick would call a new map of world religions. As the son of a Spanish Roman Catholic mother and an Indian Hindu father, he grew up in two religious traditions. His life of faith and scholarship has continued to be nurtured by both traditions.

A Roman Catholic priest (of the Diocese of Varanasi, India), holding doctorates in science (chemistry), philosophy, and theology, Panikkar is a recognized Catholic theologian and an accredited scholar of Hinduism. Because of what he has learned from his cross-cultural, interreligious experience, Panikkar has been called a "mutational man" —that is, "one in whom the global mutation has already occurred and in whom the new forms of consciousness have been concretized."[34]

A Worldwide Ecumenism

Since the early 1960s Panikkar has been urging what he calls "an ecumenical ecumenism." It is an ecumenism among world religions following the same spirit and ground rules as the ecumenism among Christian churches. Like the Christian ecumenism that has been developing since the beginning of this century, this ecumenical ecumenism strives for "unity without harming diversity." And like Christian ecumenism, it presupposes and works out of a common origin and goal, a "transcendent principle" or mystery, a basis for shared experience that is active within all the myriad diversity of the world religions. Panikkar calls this shared mystery "the fundamental religious fact" that "does not lie in the realm of doctrine or even of individual self-consciousness," but that "well may be present everywhere and in every religion." This fundamental religious fact is the mystery known in every authentic religious experience but always more than that experience can feel and say.[35]

All this sounds like an echo of the "school of common essence" described in chapter 3. It is not. Panikkar firmly rejects "the naive and uncritical notion that 'there is' one 'thing' that Men call by many names—as if the naming of the mystery were simply a matter of attaching such tags as culture or language puts at our disposal." More than most proponents of the theocentric model for interreligious dialogue, Panikkar insists on the importance of diversity among religions. Differences, for him, make a vital difference. Each interpretation, each name for the "fundamental religious fact," both "enriches and qualifies that Mystery which is neither purely transcendent nor purely immanent."[36] Panikkar is affirming, on the basis of his knowledge of religions and his own religious experience, that the mystery within all religions is both *more than* and yet *has its being* within the diverse experiences and beliefs of the religions. He uses a familiar image to try to explain what he means:

> It is not simply that there are different ways leading to the peak, but that the summit itself would collapse if all the paths disappeared. The peak is in a certain sense the result of the slopes leading to it. . . . It is not that this reality [the ultimate mystery] *has* many names as if there were a reality outside the name. This reality *is* the many names and each name is a new aspect.[37]

The purpose of the new ecumenical ecumenism is to deepen one's grasp and living of this mystery. But for this to happen—and here Panikkar moves beyond the current Roman Catholic model—he insists that the traditional religions must "give up any pretense to monopoly of what *religion* stands for."[38] In other words, no religion can enter the dialogue claiming final or absolute normativity for all other religions. Panikkar is challenging the traditional understanding of the definitive normativity of Christ. It took him a decade of interreligious experience and reflection to come to this point. In the first edition of his *The Unknown Christ of Hinduism* (1964), he still asserted that in the historical Jesus the fullness of revelation had occurred. But in his more recent writings and in the "completely revised and enlarged edition" of this same book (1981) he has revised his notion of the normativity of Christianity and Jesus. He now rejects all models of encounter between Christianity and other religions that presume, from the outset, the superiority or fulfillment of other religions in Christianity.[39]

Panikkar's main hermeneutical argument for this revision is that, because of the reality of pluralism and historical consciousness, "the *world,* that is to say, the range of human experience, subjective and objective, has radically changed since the time in which Christian doctrine was formulated."[40] And when the "world"—that is, the horizon of meaning—changes, so must understanding. Therefore, Christians can and must reinterpret their traditional understanding of the uniqueness and universality of Christ. Panikkar's proposal for a new interpretation, which will be both different from and continuous with past tradition, is founded on his distinction between the universal Christ and the particular Jesus. This is his distinctive contribution to the theocentric model.

An "Authentically Universal Christology"

Panikkar is convinced that the new age of religious pluralism demands "an authentically universal Christology."[41] His own proposal for such a new christology begins with an "authentically universal" understanding of the Christ. Panikkar's notion of what "Christ" really means preserves, he feels, the substance of the traditional logos or wisdom theology and illumines it by the cross-cultural religious experience of today.[42]

"Christ is . . . a living symbol for the totality of reality: human, divine, cosmic."[43] This totality of reality is what he calls the "primordial theandric fact," or more recently, the "cosmotheandric reality." These terms try to express "that intimate and complete unity . . . between the divine and the human." Panikkar explicitly calls this unity a "non-dualist vision." It is essentially the same vision expressed by Schuon (in chap. 3) and implied by Jung (in chap. 4). God and the finite world make up a unity neither monistic nor dualistic:[44]

> Man and God are neither two nor one. . . . There are not two realities: God *and* man (plus world); but neither is there one: God *or* man. . . . Reality itself is theandric. . . . God and man are, so to speak, in close

constitutive collaboration for the building up of reality, the unfolding of history, and the continuation of creation. . . . God, man, and the world are engaged in a unique adventure and this engagement constitutes true reality. . . . Theandrism is in a paradoxical fashion (for one can speak in no other way) the infinitude of man . . . and the finitude of God.[45]

Christ, for Panikkar, is both symbol and substance of this dynamic non-dualistic unity between God, humanity, and world. Christ, therefore, is synonymous with "God the Son, the Logos." This leads us into Panikkar's trinitarian theology. The Father is the apophatic dimension of the godhead—beyond knowing or saying: the creative silence, the "invisible origin" of God. The Christ or the Logos is the external expression, the creative communication of the Ultimate, "whatever God does *ad extra* ['outside']."[46] Panikkar piles up traditional images to try to express the breadth and the intimacy of this divine activity. Christ is "that from which the World comes forth, the Alpha and Omega . . . the historical action of divine providence that inspires Mankind in different ways according to time and place, and directs human life . . . toward its fullness." There is, then, only one Christ, "only one link, one mediator between God and the rest, between the one and the many. . . . Between these two poles everything that functions as mediator, link, 'conveyer' is Christ, the sole priest of the cosmic priesthood, the Lord par excellence." This Christ is both divine and human, "really 'human,' or rather worldly without ceasing to be divine . . . a reality which not only connects the two poles, but which 'is' the two poles without permitting them to coalesce." The Christ, therefore, is the ground of divinity within all humanity; "the 'vocation' that summoned man into being destined him from the very beginning to be the Son of God, one with the only Son."[47]

Panikkar's notion of the universal Christ forces questions about the historical Jesus. What is the relationship between the two? At this point Panikkar reveals where he agrees with and where he steps beyond the current christology of the Roman Catholic model. With such theologians as Rahner and Cobb, he affirms that the Logos or Christ, eternal and universal, has been incarnated in Jesus of Nazareth. But he parts company with them in refusing to maintain that such an incarnation has taken place solely, finally, definitively, normatively, in Jesus. As we saw, in the first edition of his *Unknown Christ* (1964) Panikkar still held that "a full Christian faith is required to accept . . . identity" between Christ and "Jesus the Son of Mary." This made Christianity "the place where Christ is fully revealed, the end and plenitude of every religion."[48] Since the early 70s, however, he has been silent about "identity" and "plenitude," and has moved in new directions.[49]

Following these new directions, Panikkar clearly states that no historical name or form can be the full, final expression of the Christ. Christ, "as the universal symbol for salvation cannot be objectified and thus reified as a merely historical personage." This means: "Christ the Savior is . . . not to be

restricted to the merely historical figure of Jesus of Nazareth.'' More generally, Panikkar tells Christians that they should recognize that ''Christ will
never be totally known on earth, because that would amount to seeing the
Father whom nobody can see.'' Therefore it is good that Jesus ''disappeared
and went away; otherwise Men would have made him a king or a God.''[50]

Panikkar warns against an idolatrous form of historicism in Christianity.
The saving power of Jesus is not to be found only in his historical concreteness and actions; the primary reason the historical Jesus saves is that he em-
bodies a reality, the Christ, which is beyond every historical form. To
overstress the historicity of Christianity is to turn historical facts or events
into idols. It is also to turn them into tools of conquest rather than liberation:
''When the myth of history begins to take hold of Western Christianity, Jesus
Christ becomes the embodiment of the supreme Imperium.''[51]

In admitting the limitations of the historical Jesus, Panikkar in no way
intends to downplay his necessity. He warns against diluting the Christian
claim that the universal Christ has become concrete in Jesus: ''This concreteness has in the past been the stumbling stone for Christian dialogue with other
religions, but nobody for the sake of dialogue has a right to blur the issue by
minimizing Jesus or overlooking the central Christian affirmation of the
Lordship of Jesus.''[52] The reason for this warning is Panikkar's recognition
of the necessary role played by particular, concrete mediators in all religions.
The universal Christ, the cosmotheandric fact, can become real only through
some particular, historical form; it must take on a concrete name. For himself, as for all Christians, he recognizes that Jesus is the ultimate form of
Christ: ''this Lord [Christ] whose Lordship can appear in innumerable forms
has taken for me an ultimate form which is indissolubly connected with Jesus
of Nazareth.''[53]

He is convinced, however, that a Christian can make such a personal confession and at the same time admit that ''when I call this link between the
finite and the infinite by the name of Christ, I am not presupposing its identification with Jesus of Nazareth. . . . Though a Christian believes that 'Jesus is
the Christ' . . . this sentence is not identical to 'the Christ is Jesus.' '' Jesus,
therefore, is a concrete historical name for the ''Supername''—that is, the
Christ, which is always ''the name above every name'' (Phil. 2:9).[54]

Therefore Christians can and should acknowledge that ''all religions recognize in one way or another'' this Christ. The name above all names—the
Christ—can go by many historical names: Rama, Krishna, Isvara, Purusha,
Tathagata.[55] The reality of the universal Christ does not destroy the necessity
and universal relevance of the particular Jesus. Panikkar can say, on the one
hand, that ''this Lord [Christ] is exercising his *sui-generis* ['unique'] Lordship in and through all possible agencies, including the religions of the
world.'' On the other hand, he can also announce that ''Jesus . . . would be
one of the names of the cosmotheandric principle, which has received practically as many names as there are authentic forms of religiousness and which
at the same time finds a historically *sui-generis* epiphany in Jesus of Nazareth.''[56]

A number of other contemporary theologians, in their efforts to elaborate a nonnormative christology, make distinctions similar to the one Panikkar draws between the universal Logos or Christ and the historical Jesus: Wilfred Cantwell Smith urges Christians to use the adverb "really" rather than "fully" when they speak of God being revealed in Jesus. Don Cupitt explicitly holds that although there surely is only "one Jesus," there can be "many Christs". John Macquarrie proposes a model for interreligious dialogue based on "commitment and openness"—total commitment to Jesus and radical openness to other revelations beyond Jesus. Thor Hall calls upon Christians to relativize the particularity of the incarnation (Jesus) and to universalize the principle of incarnation (Christ), and therefore to "consider the Christ-principle capable of self-realization in a plurality of Christ-events."[57]

STANLEY SAMARTHA: THE RELATIVITY OF ALL REVELATIONS

Stanley J. Samartha speaks out of a long history of ecumenism, both Christian and interreligious. An Indian by birth, presbyter of the Church of South India, he served, from 1968 to 1980, as director of the WCC Program on Dialogue with People of Living Faiths and Ideologies.

Throughout his life, Samartha has advocated dialogue among world religions as the demand of our age. In his earlier writings, he heard this demand mainly from the new world of pluralism and cross-cultural communication: never before have the religions had such an opportunity to work together to discover new dimensions of divine truth. Since 1970 the demand for dialogue has become for Samartha even more imperative, for the religions have found themselves "caught up in a worldwide struggle against injustice." Interreligious dialogue has received new motivation. Together religions must seek after truth in order that together they might promote justice, for there can be no lasting justice unless rooted in divine truth and no authentic divine truth that does not give forth the fruit of social justice.[58]

Concerning the theological grounds for interreligious dialogue, it is often difficult to pinpoint Samartha's own opinions, especially in his earlier writings, most of which report the views of the WCC. He finds the "theological reasons why dialogue is and ought to be a continuing Christian concern" in the Christian belief in the God of Jesus Christ; this God calls Christians to enter into relationship with all peoples, to seek after truth together with persons "of other faiths and ideologies," and to establish a "truly universal community" that will "cut across boundaries" of nation and religion.[59] In laying out his theological foundations for dialogue, Samartha seems to have accepted the theological framework of the WCC approach to other faiths during the 50s and 60s. This was a "cosmic christology," which saw the saving light of Christ shining within all religions but emanating, fully and normatively, from the historical Jesus.[60]

In his more recent statements, during the second half of the 1970s, Samartha has changed his tone. It is much the same change of tone we noted in

Panikkar. Samartha is now suspicious of all Christian approaches to other religions based on a theory of anonymous Christianity or cosmic christology: "One may enlarge the boundaries of the church to accommodate 'anonymous' Christians. . . . One may emphasize the 'cosmic' Christ to include principalities and powers, even nature, in his domain. But this kind of 'co-option' may be regarded as patronizing by our neighbors of other faiths."[61]

Like Panikkar, Samartha has come to question the absolute finality and universal normativity of Christ. His guiding argument for doing so, and his distinctive contribution to the theocentric model, is his insistence that before the total mystery of God, no religious figure or religion can call itself the final and full word. It is basically the same assertion of "historical relativity" that we examined in chapter 2. But instead of building this assertion on the essential limitation of all historical, cultural expressions, as Troeltsch did, Samartha makes it a theological argument rooted in the nature of God as Mysterious Other: "The Other relativizes everything else. In fact, the willingness to accept such relativization is probably the only real guarantee that one has encountered the Other as ultimately real." So he urges a model for interreligious encounter that will "recognize God alone as Absolute and . . . [will] consider all religions to be relative."[62]

In relativizing all particular religious figures and revelations, Samartha, again like Panikkar, does not intend to deny their necessity or to reduce them to a common denominator. The Mysterious Other must confront us through particular mediations. Samartha clearly rejects any model for dialogue that argues that "all particularities [are] equally valid" and demands "that no particularity should claim universality."[63] Still, although each particular revelation is genuinely different, although each may claim a relevance for other religions, each religion and each divine revealer remains limited: "a particular religion can claim to be decisive for some people, and some people can claim that a particular religion is decisive for them, but no religion is justified in claiming that it is decisive for all." Samartha insists that this truth applies also to Christ and Christianity: "All religions, including Christianity, have an 'interim' character. . . . At depth the essential feature of all religious life is its pilgrim nature. . . . Finality should not be claimed to [*sic*] the oases on the way."[64]

Samartha warns against a "christomonism" that has infected Christian doctrine and so absolutizes Jesus that it turns him into "a kind of cult figure over against other religious figures." Christians must never forget that "in the incarnation God relativizes himself." Instead of a christomonistic approach to other religions, Samartha advocates a theocentric approach, which, he holds, will be more faithful to the original message of Jesus himself: "although the witness of the New Testament writers is christocentric, Jesus Christ himself is theocentric."[65]

With such a theocentric model for understanding and encountering other religions, based on a nonnormative christology, Christians, Samartha concludes, will still be able to hold to their personal commitment to Christ and to their belief in his universal meaning. They will still be able to tell other religions that *for them,* for Christians, "nowhere else is the victory over suffering and death manifested so decisively as in the death and resurrection of Jesus Christ." But such an announcement will be an enthusiastic *witness* to their own revealer, *not* a denigrating *judgment* about other revealers. Although Christians continue to carry out what they feel is their universal mission of witnessing to Christ, they will be able to "recognize that their neighbors too have their 'missions' in the same pluralistic world."[66] There may be other "universally relevant" revelations, other "norms," other saviors. To recognize this is not necessarily to jeopardize what Christians have experienced in Jesus Christ.

Samartha's recognition of the necessary relativity of all religions and religious figures before the mystery of God is a perspective that can be found in most contemporary theologians who are working toward a less christocentric approach to other religions. Among those who make particular use of this perspective are Howard Burkle, who insists that we must approach other religions well aware of "the inescapable relativity of *all* human consciousness" and the inescapable relativization of the Absolute in the incarnation, and Donald Dawe and Langdon Gilkey, who find an essential relativity or limitation in all of God's covenants with humankind.[67]

JEWISH-CHRISTIAN DIALOGUE: JESUS IS NOT THE FINAL MESSIAH

The previous proposals for a theocentric model of encounter with other religions and for a universal but nonnormative christology have all been fashioned under the strain of actual dialogue with followers of other faiths. This section will concentrate on one corner of that dialogue, a corner that is experiencing particular strains and is frequently neglected in general studies of Christian encounter with other religions. The contemporary dialogue between Christianity and its parent religion, Judaism, contains some of the boldest proposals for a theocentric model of interreligious dialogue and some of the most severe criticisms of the traditional normative christology. Christian-Jewish dialogue is growing, and so is its literature. What follows is only a selective review, with a focus on the christological question.

Christian participants in the dialogue with Judaism are stirred by the same problem that bothers their colleagues in the dialogue with Hinduism, Buddhism, Islam: the fact that the traditional self-understanding of Christianity either writes off or subordinates the value of Judaism. From their own experience of dialogue with Jews as well as from their own experience of what faith in Christ means, the theologians we shall now study feel there is definitely something wrong with the "supersessionist" approach to Judaism. This is the traditional belief that the New Testament makes the Jewish Bible the "Old" Testament, that the new Israel must supersede the old Israel.[68] All these theologians are convinced that such a model of Christian-Jewish encounter must be discarded. And with equal clarity, all of them point out that this cannot be done "unless the church is ready to significantly rethink its traditional interpretations of christology." More explicitly, they have come to "the conclusion that part of our traditional christology is severely inadequate and should be perhaps discarded."[69]

It is impossible to analyze the details of the different ways Christian theologians are going about such a "profound reevaluation" of traditional christology. John Pawlikowski offers a useful outline for summarizing the most notable differences. He lists the new Christian approaches to Judaism under either a "single covenant" or a "double covenant" perspective.[70] Those who maintain a single covenant embracing both Judaism and Christianity tend to view the Christ event as a means of extending the one and original covenant with Judaism to the non-Jewish world. Even after this extension, Judaism preserves its own value and purpose within the one covenant. This view is proposed, again with significantly different emphases, by such theologians as Monika Hellwig, Paul Van Buren, A. Roy Eckardt, J. Coos Schoneveld.[71] From all of them, especially Van Buren, it is difficult to determine whether there is any other real difference between Christianity and Judaism besides the "extension" that Christ brought.

The double covenant perspective stresses that there are real differences, two distinctly different covenantal religions. The differences, however, are not ultimately contradictory but complementary; both religions provide each other with needed balance. This perspective is followed by Rosemary Ruether, Gregory Baum, James Parkes, J. Coert Rylaarsdam, E.P. Sanders, and John Pawlikowski.[72]

Although it would be interesting to unravel the differences between these two perspectives, it is their points of agreement that command our attention. There is almost unanimous agreement that it is difficult, if not impossible, for Christians to continue talking about Jesus as the final Messiah—that is, as he who has brought about the messianic kingdom and who therefore has realized God's final, definitive salvation for all history.

Chastened by the dialogue with their Jewish brothers and sisters, these Christian theologians have come to recognize that according to the messianic promises, which Jesus is supposed to have fulfilled, the true Messiah cannot be considered only as a perfected individual; he must also bring about a kingdom. And here is where the "facts of history" do not seem to sustain the Christian claim: "Our two thousand years of human experience" do not allow Christians to maintain that Jesus is the Messiah, the final savior, who has brought about the kingdom. Christians "can no longer simply claim that the Jewish notion of the Messianic age was realized in the Death-Resurrection of Christ."[73] Honest dialogue with Jews has forced Hellwig and Ruether to admit that in a real sense, Jesus is *not yet* the Messiah or the Christ. To proclaim that "Jesus is Lord" designates not a *fait accompli* but a task yet to be accomplished.[74] This rules out any finality or absolute normativity for Jesus.

Most of the authors we have mentioned would follow Ruether's reading of how Christians came to fashion Jesus into an absolute and exclusive savior. In the very beginning, the first Jesus followers (most of them Jews) understood Jesus as he, most likely, understood himself—in a very Jewish, a very eschatological sense. He was a prophet who played a crucial role in proclaiming and bringing about God's future kingdom in the world. But the kingdom did not come. And so the early Christians set about trying to understand what this meant for them and for their understanding of Jesus.

Ruether uncovers two main trends in this search for new understanding. The first, found clearly in Luke's writings, involved a "historicizing" of the eschatological; the future kingdom was claimed to have been already realized in the history of Jesus, and this historical realization was carried on in the church. But because there was not an overabundance of empirical evidence for such a realization of the kingdom, a second trend accompanied the first. It is found especially in Paul and John who "spiritualized" or "interiorized" the kingdom into a reality within the heart of the individual. In both aspects of this interpretation, an exclusive finality is attributed to Jesus and, by extension, to the church. Christ and Christ's church were seen as the only way to God. This, according to Ruether, paved the way for the anti-Semitism, as well as the anti-Buddhism, and so forth, which was to infect the Christian churches through the centuries.[75]

None of the Christian theologians involved in the dialogue with Jews has worked out a fully developed christology that would avoid the exclusivism of making Jesus the final Messiah but that would maintain his saving role in preparing for the eschatological future. Some of them, however, offer suggestions and guidelines for such a christology. Ruether summarizes her own suggestions: "the messianic meaning of Jesus' life . . . is paradigmatic and proleptic in nature, not final and fulfilled.'"[76] Jesus, in what he was and in what he symbolizes, is the "paradigm of hope" for Christians. Keeping alive the memory of his resurrection from the dead, his followers have a basis for their refusal to take evil as the last word and for their hope that God will win in the end. Jesus therefore does not attain a finality that can be captured within history; rather, he points to a finality that is still ahead and toward which we must still work.

Ruether allows for other paradigms that carry out the same function. Specifically, she compares the paradigm of the resurrection and the Jewish paradigm of the exodus. They are complementary or parallel, rather than contradictory or subordinate:

> In each case, the experience of salvation in the past is recounted as the paradigm for continued hope experienced in the present and pointing to that final hope which is still ahead of both Jews and Christians. When

Easter is seen, not as superseding and fulfilling the Exodus, but as redu-
plicating it, then the Christian can affirm his faith through Jesus in a
way that no longer threatens to rob the Jew of his past, eliminate his
future, and surround his present existence with rivalrous animosity.

She feels that the same might be said of other paradigms of hope within other
religions.[77]

Monika Hellwig, reflecting the approach of John Hick, suggests that a
reinterpretation of traditional christology might well begin with a recognition
of the nature of the language used by the early Christians to speak about the
divinity and the uniqueness of Jesus. It is "religious language," mythic,
poetic, used to express "the unknowns in Christian experience of divine intervention." Such language will always remain "elusive" and should not be
pinned down to absolute, ontological statements. Hellwig suggests that such
language be interpreted phenomenologically—that is, as expressing how
Jesus was for Christians their place of radical encounter with God.[78]

John Pawlikowski agrees with the general direction of Ruether's and
Hellwig's suggestions; he is concerned, however, about maintaining some
form of uniqueness for Jesus. The perspective he uses for holding to uniqueness, without falling into exclusivism or absolute finality, is quite similar to
what we heard from Panikkar. Pawlikowski uses the model of incarnation
and understands it as a "manifestation of the divine-human nexus":

> Put somewhat simply, what ultimately came to be recognized with clar-
> ity for the first time through the ministry and person of Jesus was how
> profoundly integral humanity was to the self-definition of God. This in
> turn implied that each human person is somehow divine, that he or she
> somehow shares in the constitutive nature of God. Christ is the theo-
> logical symbol that the Church selected to try to express this real-
> ity . . . Thus in a very real sense one can say that God did not become
> man in Jesus. God always was man; humanity was an integral part of
> the Godhead from the beginning. The Christ event was crucial, how-
> ever, for the manifestation of this reality to the world.[79]

It is not always clear just what Pawlikowski means by "crucial." On the
one hand, he states that this intimate union between deity and humanity
could not have come to "full awareness" without the revelation of Christ and
that no other human being "will ever share the same intimacy with the divine
nature that existed in the person of Jesus." Yet he also shows, at great length,
how belief in the incarnational unity between God and humanity was
seminally but truly contained in the Pharisaical revolution that was transforming Judaism at the time of Jesus; in many ways, Jesus was part of and
continued this revolution.[80] Pawlikowski goes on to conclude that the
"unique" revelation of God in Jesus "is in principle no greater than the

sacred acts through which Israel was originally elected."[81] "The revelation at Sinai stands on equal footing with the revelation in Jesus."[82]

What Pawlikowski is saying reflects the general view of most of the authors we have mentioned: if there is something unique or "normative" in Christ that Judaism needs, there is also something unique and normative in Judaism needed by Christianity: "Christians are not in a position to simply offer Christ as the means to salvation. They must also acknowledge their own salvific nakedness and stand ready to learn from the Jewish tradition."[83] Areas in which Christians need to learn from Jews include: the Jewish insistence on salvation as communal and as demanding historical transformation, the goodness of creation, and the danger of making anything final before the kingdom of God has come.[84]

Christ/Christianity and Judaism are really different, but they are also really complementary. Neither is superior or final. As Gerald Anderson has pointed out, if Christians are able to say this about Judaism, then, by a "domino theory," the same can apply to other religions.[85]

LIBERATION/POLITICAL THEOLOGIES:
ABSOLUTE NORMS ARE UNETHICAL

Another clear, even shrill, call for a thorough revision of the traditional understanding of Christ as normative and final comes from the perspective of liberation and political theology, as that perspective is being employed by First World theologians such as Dorothee Sölle, Rosemary Ruether, and especially Tom Driver.[86] Their contribution to the theocentric model for a theology of religions is mainly methodological. In a sense they uncover the method, or an essential element in the method, that is operative in all the proposed revisions of christology that have been studied in this chapter.

As is well known, liberation theologians insist on *praxis* as an essential ingredient in all theological method. Their hermeneutical approach (or way of understanding) argues that we cannot begin to understand, criticize, or verify the meaning of scripture or tradition unless we are doing so from an actual practice of liberation—from some concrete involvement in trying to make our world better.[87] Latin American liberation theologians have not applied this method to the traditional doctrines of Christ's uniqueness and finality. Tom Driver and Rosemary Ruether have. It amounts to what might be called an "*ethical hermeneutics*." It means, simply, that we must judge the truth of any christological statement by its ethical fruits. Stated negatively, if a particular belief in Christ either causes *or* sanctions a Christian practice that, judged by basic Christian standards, would be unethical, something is wrong with that belief. More positively, "the church should teach nothing about God or Jesus which does not make a positive contribution to social justice." Again, if such teaching is not doing this, it must be thoroughly reevaluated.[88]

Driver states clearly, "my methodological proposal [is] to locate christology within ethics and not prior to it."[89] This demands a radical rebalancing of the norms for what Christians believe about Jesus. The witness of scripture, the official statements of tradition, are indispensable for knowing who Jesus is and what he means, but for Driver they are no longer the "norm above all other norms": "The Jesus we know from scripture, insofar as scripture is ancient, is not the decisive authority for teaching about Jesus. . . . No historical documents are normative, and neither is the fruit of any research concerning them."[90] The scriptural witness from the past must be criticized and understood in light of the present moment—that is, in light of the actions, decisions, attitudes to which this witness now leads us.

On the basis of such a method, the ethical report card of traditional christology is not something one would want to bring home to a God of love and justice. Driver and Ruether maintain that the image of Jesus Christ as "central norm," as "the center of history," as the "one and only" incarnation of God in history, has, consciously or unconsciously, caused or condoned a long trail of what must be called sinful attitudes or actions. The most glaring of such sins are the superiority, intolerance, and rash judgments that have marked Christians' attitudes toward other religions:

> The immoral factor in the "scandal of particularity" today is its insistence upon a once-and-for-all Christ in a relativistic world. . . . It precludes Christianity's ability to affirm that all people have a right to their place in the sun. . . . If the incarnation of God in finite humanity can occur but once, the religious value of all other human history is nil.[91]

If not nil, certainly inferior.

Ruether asks theologians who proclaim that authentic humanity was achieved only in Jesus (e.g., Hans Küng) whether they realize how much such a belief feeds the attitude "that all other peoples have an inauthentic humanity." For Ruether the most convincing piece of evidence for the immorality of traditional normative christology is the sordid Christian history of anti-Semitism: "Theologically, anti-Judaism developed as the left hand of christology. Anti-Judaism was the negative side of the Christian affirmation that Jesus was the Christ."[92] Dorothee Sölle can even describe much of christology as "christofacism" in the way it has disposed of or allowed Christians to impose themselves upon not only other religions but other cultures and political parties that do not march under the banner of the final, normative, victorious Christ.[93]

Finally, Driver and Ruether would place at least part of the blame for the racism and sexism infecting Christian behavior at the doorstep of a christology that holds that the perfection of humanity, the full and normative presence of God, has been realized only, definitively, in a white male. If the medium is the message, the whiteness and maleness of the medium share in the normativity of the message: "Nonmales and nonwhites therefore were in peril of being regarded as nonpersons by virtue of their generic difference from the Son of God.''[94]

Even if only a portion of such charges are accurate, even if a normative christology has only indirectly sanctioned, not caused, such unethical conduct, still, these theologians hold, such a christology must be, at the least, highly suspect. So they call for a "paradigm-shift" in christology and in Christian attitudes toward other faiths and ideologies. Their suggestions for how such a shift might begin reflect proposals we have already heard in this chapter. Driver endorses Ruether's call to move Christ from the "*center* of history," where he is "the embodiment of a humanity already made perfect in God," to "the *lead edge* of history," where he will serve as "a herald of the future."[95] Driver also reflects Panikkar's notion of the incarnate Christ as the expression of a general cosmotheandric reality, as well as Pawlikowski's view of Christ as "the manifestation of the divine human nexus." Jesus, for Driver, is someone who realized and expressed the given, ontological non-dualism between God and the world, the "dialectical reciprocity of finite and infinite":

> Infinity is not a state nor a substance of any kind. It is a quality *of* the finite, the quality of its reach beyond itself toward a completion it does not possess but of which it speaks by its very existence. Without the finite, infinity makes no sense. [But he adds a nonexclusive, nonnormative qualifier:] To see Jesus as a conjunction of the finite and the infinite is to see him neither as unique in all time nor as changeless. . . . The infinite commitment of God to finitude in Jesus does not indicate something done once and once only for all time.[96]

As already pointed out, an "ethical hermeneutics" colors the method of most theologians who are trying to reinterpret the uniqueness of Jesus in the light of interreligious dialogue. Such a hermeneutics is especially evident among such missionary theologians as Aloysius Pieris, Ignace Puthiadam, Henri Maurier, Eugene Hillman, Burlan Sizemore, all of whom have been engaged in the actual praxis of dialogue with persons of other faiths. They have painfully witnessed how an absolutist or normative christology has fostered the "cultural imperialism" of the West, how it has roadblocked dialogue and actually been "one of the principal reasons for the disappointing results of missionary work." In view of such unethical effects, these scholars, like the liberation theologians, are calling for a revision of traditional christology.[97]

CONCLUSION: AN EVOLUTIONARY SHIFT IN CHRISTIAN CONSCIOUSNESS?

This chapter has documented what has been called a "Copernican revolution" or a "paradigm-shift" in Christian understanding of other religions and of Christ. Such terms bear the connotation of abrupt change, radical turning about. Perhaps the insistence and urgency with which many of the theologians we have studied pressed their case may have increased this sense of revolution. If, however, we step back from our analysis of these different thinkers, if we try to describe the forest from above the treetops, what we see is not an abrupt change but a gradual evolution. What these different theologians are part of, what they are promoting, is an evolution that has been taking place within Christian consciousness from the early part of this century, an evolution from ecclesiocentrism to christocentrism to theocentrism.

The evolution from ecclesiocentrism to christocentrism began to take place when the different Christian churches started adapting to the environment of Christian ecumenism. For Protestants, it took shape in the formation and growth of the World Council of Churches. For Catholics, it was expressed in the Second Vatican Council. The churches realized that no one church can capture the full reality of Jesus Christ and the gospel. Each church carried on his presence and message, but that presence and message were larger and more important than any one of the churches. A consensus grew that the church is not to be identified with the kingdom of God and that the church is not really necessary for salvation. These insights were applied to other religions. Jesus Christ was seen working mystically, cosmically, anonymously within all religions. He, and not the Christian church, was the center of the salvific universe.

But as this wider ecumenism with other religions intensifies, a new evolutionary awareness is emerging. Just as, within Christian ecumenism, Christians admitted that their narrow understanding of church was an obstacle to dialogue, so within ecumenical ecumenism they are beginning to realize that their narrow understanding of Christ is a similar obstacle. Traditional christology, with its insistence on finality and normativity, just does not fit what is being experienced in the arena of religious pluralism. We are in the midst of an evolution from christocentrism to theocentrism.

What the various theologians we have studied are proposing is theocentrism. From their various perspectives—the myth of incarnation, logos christology, the relativity of all religions and religious figures, ethical hermeneutics—they are placing God, not the church or Jesus Christ, at the center of things. And as with all evolutionary change, they feel they are not negating or abandoning what went before. As the evolution from ecclesiocentrism to christocentrism both reevaluated and reaffirmed the importance of the church, so this new stage of evolution, as the next chapter will try to show, both revises and reaffirms the universal importance of Jesus.

The "Copernican revolution," therefore, has brought about a theocentric model for a theology of religions. I believe that this model both addresses the inadequacies and preserves the values of all the other models we have studied. Although I have reservations about some of the individual arguments used by its various proponents, I feel that this model holds the greatest promise for the future of interreligious dialogue and for the continued evolution of the meaning of Jesus Christ for the world.

Many, however, would argue that the theocentric model does not represent an evolutionary advance but an evolutionary dead-end. Their arguments are chiefly christological—that a move to theocentrism violates the understanding of Christ maintained by the New Testament and by tradition, and debilitates both personal commitment to Jesus Christ and a distinctly Christian contribution to the needs of the world. The next two chapters will try to show that this is not the case. They will argue for the validity of a theocentric christology and a theocentric method for interreligious dialogue.

PART III

A MORE AUTHENTIC DIALOGUE

A brief review of where we have been will help define where we hope to move in these two concluding chapters. We began with an introductory description of the reality of religious pluralism, the prospect of a new "unitive pluralism" of religions, and the problems such a prospect poses for Christians (chap. 1). Part 1 reviewed popular attitudes toward religious pluralism (chap. 2–4), and Part 2 did the same for the contemporary Christian models for understanding other religions (chap. 5–8). Both the insights and inadequacies of these popular attitudes and Christian models were pointed out.

These last two chapters will try to pull things together—to confirm the various insights, to resolve the inadequacies, and so to lay the foundation for a more authentic dialogue between Christianity and other world religions. Parts 1 and 2 tried to offer an objective analysis of the views of others (recognizing, however, that no one is ever purely objective), but these concluding chapters are admittedly more subjective; they attempt a personal synthesis. So I feel more comfortable—and honest—using the first person singular even more frequently in these final chapters than I have in previous chapters.

Really, though, the personal synthesis began already in chapter 8. The theocentric model provides, I believe, the most promising path toward a valid reinterpretation of Christian doctrine and toward a more authentic interreligious dialogue. But it is a controversial path. Much more needs to be said about why it is a valid Christian model and how it can be applied in the actual process of dialogue.

So these final chapters offer both a defense and a proposal. Chapter 9 will defend and elaborate the christology of the theocentric model as a valid reinterpretation of Christian tradition and experience. Chapter 10 will propose a method of applying this model in the actual conversation with followers of other faiths. Although this defense and proposal are personal and subjective, I hope to show that they are also rooted in the scholarship of reputable contemporary Christian theologians.

Chapter IX

How Is Jesus Unique?
Toward a Theocentric Christology

The gadfly-question that has pursued us throughout this study has been that of the uniqueness of Jesus Christ. No Christian theology of other religions, no Christian attempt to dialogue with them, can avoid a serious confrontation with this issue. Is Jesus unique among the religious figures of history? If so, how?

We have seen that many of the popular attitudes toward religious pluralism (esp. those of Troeltsch and Toynbee) tend to dismiss the question too facilely; denying any uniqueness for the Nazarene, they boil all revelations down to a common "something" and fail to face the possibility that some revealers, maybe one, may be "better" than others. But neither do most of the Christian models for a theology of religions confront the problem of the uniqueness of Jesus seriously enough.

All the Christian models insist on some form of uniqueness. The conservative Evangelical and mainline Protestant models hold to an *exclusive uniqueness,* affirming that only in Jesus can true revelation or salvation be found. In such an understanding, the Christ event is *constitutive* of any true encounter with God, anywhere in history. The Catholic model, dissatisfied with such exclusivity, proposes an *inclusive uniqueness* for Jesus; God's revealing-saving action in Jesus includes all other religions, either as an anonymous, cosmic presence within them or as their final fulfillment. In this view, Jesus remains, if not constitutive of, at least *normative* for, all religious experience, for all times. All these traditional Christian claims are insufficiently sensitive to the way they contradict contemporary awareness of historical relativity and to the way they impede authentic dialogue with believers of other faiths.

The theocentric model proposes what can be called a *relational uniqueness* for Jesus. A fuller explanation of what this means will come in the next chapter. It affirms that Jesus *is* unique, but with a uniqueness defined by its ability to relate to—that is, to include and be included by—other unique religious figures. Such an understanding of Jesus views him not as exclusive or even as normative but as *theocentric,* as a universally relevant manifestation (sacrament, incarnation) of divine revelation and salvation.

In what follows, I shall try to show that such a nonnormative, theocentric christology does not contradict the New Testament proclamation of Jesus and therefore is a valid interpretation of that proclamation. Also, I shall indicate how such a nonnormative understanding of Christ is consistent with contemporary methods of christology: the interpretations of Jesus advanced by Karl Rahner, by process thought, by liberation theologians. I shall then explore whether such a new interpretation of Jesus is consistent with faith in his resurrection. Finally I shall try to illustrate how a nonnormative, theocentric view of Jesus still allows, even demands, a total personal commitment to him. Such a commitment calls for a distinctive Christian praxis within society and a distinctive Christian contribution to the new dialogue among religions.

A NEW *KAIROS,* A NEW CHRISTOLOGY

The christology that undergirds the theocentric model for understanding other religions and that is being defended in this chapter is, admittedly, new—so new that many Christians will want to reject its very idea. Before arguing for the validity of a nonnormative christology, therefore, something needs to be said, briefly, about its possibility. Let me recall what was proposed at the end of chapter 1: that new ideas, new doctrines, in the history of Christianity are nothing new. There has been a genuine evolution of self-understanding, of doctrine and morals, throughout the history of Christianity. "Evolution" means that such new ideas are both continuous *and* discontinuous with what went before; they are not *totally* new, but they are *genuinely* new. We noted how such evolutionary advances seem to occur according to particular *kairoi* within history, particular moments when the environment of experience and ideas is such that breakthroughs in understanding the gospel can take place.[1]

To apply this general understanding of doctrinal evolution specifically to the interpretation of New Testament or dogmatic texts about Jesus means that to fully understand a particular text about him, it is *not* sufficient to locate and interpret that text within its historical context. Rather, as Hans Georg Gadamer explains (chap. 5, above),[2] the text and the context can be understood only within the "horizon" of experience and meaning as that horizon expands through history. Raimundo Panikkar calls this the "universal context" or the "texture" of the text—the constantly expanding human universe of new experiences, allowing new insights and calling forth new judgments and decisions. Unless the text and its context are continually being reheard in the ever new texture, one is really not hearing what the text means. And when there are real shifts or changes within the texture, especially when human experience evolves from the tribal to the global, there *must* be new interpretations of the text. Otherwise, we are not being faithful to the New Testament; we are not hearing what it really means.[3]

One of the principal concerns of this book has been to show that there has been a genuinely new evolution in the "texture" of human experience, very different from the "context" of the New Testament and past dogmatic statements about Jesus. This texture includes a new "historical consciousness" of the relativity of all cultures and historical achievements, a new awareness of pluralism, and especially a clearer realization of the need to fashion a new form of unity among peoples. Not to understand Jesus anew in this new texture, not to open oneself to the possibility of a new christology, is to run the risk of confining the past in an idolatrous "deposit of faith." Secure in such a deposit, one can comfortably avoid the call of the past to conversion and action in the present.

UNIQUENESS AND NEW TESTAMENT CHRISTOLOGY

To expect to find a unified response among New Testament scholars on the question of Jesus' uniqueness would be about as naive as to look for a consensus on economic theory among Washington politicians. If we attempt even a general survey of contemporary works on New Testament christology we find ourselves in a thicket of divergent opinions and academic disputes. Yet beneath the thicket is a fertile field of expanding knowledge and increasing areas of consensus.

In what follows, I shall try to avoid the soft spots of extreme controversy and uncertainty. My intent is to work with the firmer areas of scholarly consensus (rarely total consensus) and to try to form a picture of what was going on during the first decades of Christianity. How did the early disciples come to understand Jesus, and what can we learn from them in our own efforts to comprehend this Jesus and his uniqueness?

Jesus Was Theocentric

One of the few issues on which New Testament experts are in full agreement is that the focus and core content of Jesus' original message was the "kingdom of God."[4] Jesus' main task was to announce this kingdom, a kingdom soon to come, yet already mysteriously present and at work (Luke 11:20, 17:21). The present moment was heavy with urgency and responsibility; persons must turn their lives around, convert, in order to be part of this kingdom. Jesus' mission and person, therefore, were profoundly kingdom-centered, which means God-centered. All his powers were to serve this God and this kingdom; all else took second place. "Thy kingdom come; thy will be done," was the content of his prayer and his work.[5]

But if the original message of Jesus was theocentric, the pervasive message of the New Testament is undeniably christocentric. After his death and resurrection, the proclaimer became the proclaimed. The focus shifted. As we shall see, there is a logic, even a necessity, in this shift. In it, the original message of Jesus was transformed, not lost. The christocentrism of the New Testament does not lose hold of Jesus' original theocentrism. Jesus never takes the place of God. Even in the three texts in which Jesus is proclaimed as God or as divine (John 1:1, 20:28; Heb. 1:8–9), an evident subordination is preserved.[6] Even Paul, in urging his radical christocentrism, reminds his communities that "You belong to Christ, and Christ belongs to God" (1 Cor. 3:23). His final vision is "that God may be everything to everyone" (1 Cor. 15:28). The New Testament maintains a delicate, sometimes difficult, balance between christocentrism and theocentrism.[7]

Can anything be said about how Jesus understood himself within his theocentric message? Not much. Attempts to do a psychoanalysis of Jesus and ferret out his self-consciousness founder on the lack of sufficient data. If Jesus claimed to be the Son of God or if he had any kind of awareness of divine sonship, we know nothing of such claims or awareness from the New Testament record. Hick is right; Jesus gave us no christology. Of all the titles that came to be bestowed on him, none of them was self applied—with the possible and acutely controversial exception of "the Son of Man."[8]

Theologians such as Hick, however, are stretching the New Testament data when they imply that because none of the christological titles has Jesus' own seal of approval, they can be discarded or freely traded in for new ones. Although Jesus did not neatly define himself for us, he did give us—New Testament scholars agree—some idea of how he saw his mission. He understood his role in bringing about this already-yet-still-to-come kingdom to be pivotal. The arrival of the kingdom and membership in it would be determined by how his fellow Jews responded to his message.

There are grounds, therefore, to conclude that Jesus understood himself as exercising a special, a unique, role in God's plan. Even though we cannot be certain that he did present himself as the Son of Man and as the suffering servant of Isaiah, the total picture of what he said and did indicates that he most likely experienced himself as *the eschatological prophet*—the final prophet (Deut. 18:15–19) who was anointed specially by God's Spirit, who was to complete the mission of the earlier prophets by announcing and enacting the good news of God's final rule.[9]

If this was how he grasped his mission, we can draw conclusions concerning how he understood his personal relationship with God. Schillebeeckx makes an elaborate and convincing argument that Jesus' "original Abba-experience" provides the "source and secret of his being, message and manner of life." Jesus seemed to feel and to claim a special intimacy with God, a special sonship. This is perhaps as close as we can come to penetrating his self-consciousness.[10] His deep awareness of God as his Father was in line with Jewish tradition; it does not automatically imply exclusivity. It does, however, indicate specialness, uniqueness. This must be respected in all contemporary interpretations of Jesus.[11]

Still, it should be remembered that in his awareness of himself as the eschatological prophet, in whatever titles he might have given himself (the Son of Man, suffering servant), Jesus remained profoundly theocentric. Whenever christology forgets this, it opens Christian consciousness to a "myopic christocentrism," to a "jesusology," to a reductionism that absorbs God into Jesus.[12] Christocentrism without theocentrism easily becomes an idolatry that violates not only Christian revelation but the revelation found in other faiths.

From Kingdom of God to Son of God

Why did the proclaimer become the proclaimed? How did Jesus' original message about the kingdom of God come to be translated into the early communities' proclamation of Jesus as Messiah, Lord, Christ, Word, Savior, Son of God? An overview of how contemporary New Testament scholars are trying to answer those questions offers valuable help for our own efforts to understand the uniqueness of Jesus in contemporary interreligious dialogue.

From what both the scholars and common sense tell us, it is clear that all New Testament christology, all the titles and proclamations about Jesus, have their origin in the *saving experience* of Jesus by individuals and the community. We must be careful not to distinguish experience and interpretation too neatly, as if it were possible to have a naked experience without any interpretation. Still, when we try to grasp the constellation of New Testament interpretations of Jesus, we find that they originated in a big-bang experience that transformed persons' lives, an experience of what can be called salvation. In their encounter with this man, they met the power and the reality of God, a reality that enabled them to feel, understand, and act differently from before. They had hope now, for this life and the next.

Such a saving experience of Jesus was an experience of *revelation*. Jesus made something known to them, something that not only satisfied their minds but transformed their entire being. This experience of a saving power or revelation was the source and sustenance of all the interpretations of Jesus found in the New Testament: "It was the sense that they found what they were looking for in Jesus that started the whole christological ball rolling."[13]

In tracing the course of this christological ball, in unraveling the development of the plethora of titles applied to Jesus, recent scholarship has corrected earlier misunderstandings. Today it is recognized that the various images used to understand Jesus cannot be clearly categorized chronologically or geographically. It is impossible to verify the widespread view that there was a clear progression in understanding Jesus, from Jewish models to Greek-pagan models. Scholars had tried to locate this progression geographically in the different early communities: the Palestinian Jewish community (using Jewish images, especially that of the Messiah to come), Jewish communities in the Diaspora (using the Jewish-gentile model of Lord, presently active in the community), and gentile Christian communities (adopting the pagan notion of "divine men" and son of God). Hick followed such a questionable scheme when he implied (as we saw in chap. 8) that belief in the incarnation and divinity of Jesus came solely or primarily from Greek influence and that in embracing such pagan models of "divine men" or gods becoming human, the Greek Christians were injecting something brand-new into Christian consciousness.[14]

Today, thanks to such pioneer research as that of Martin Hengel, Helmut Koester, and James Robinson, a unilinear view of the development of New Testament christology, from Jewish titles to Greek titles, has for the most part been abandoned.[15] The cultural world of the early church was hybrid. Judaism, some two centuries before Jesus, was permeated by Greek thought; and neither before nor after Paul was there any such thing as a purely Hellenistic gentile Christian community; Jewish influence was everywhere. Even such Jewish images as *Mareh* (Lord) and "Son of God," therefore, could well have carried, for the Palestinian community, clear connotations of sharing in divinity, before any further Greek influence via Paul or John. Also, the Greek concepts of "Logos" or "divine miracle worker" or "incarnation" were not used by New Testament authors uncritically; such mythic models were adjusted to blend with and expand on Jewish images; they were not introduced into Christian beliefs as brand-new or totally different insights.[16]

Instead of using clearly defined titles in a neat chronological development, New Testament scholars are adopting the category of "trajectories" to understand how the early Christians came to speak about Jesus. These were various creedal perspectives, differing according to different social contexts, which, for the most part, developed simultaneously and with intermingling influence. With caution, four such trajectories can be distilled from the complex cultural context of the early church:

1) The *maranatha* ("Come Lord Jesus") or *parousia* christologies envisioned Jesus as the lord of the future and judge of the world, he who brings the approaching fullness of salvation. This model, an expansion on the earliest creed, which saw Jesus as the final prophet, arose in the social context of Jewish apocalypticism with its intense desire for the final restitution of God's rule for Israel. Its principal titles were *Mareh* or *Mar* (lord) and "the Son of Man." According to Schillebeeckx, this christology, as found in the Q tradition (an earlier source used by both Matthew and Luke), does not mention the resurrection or any of the postresurrection appearances; Mark's use of this christology presupposes the resurrection, but only as a condition for the final coming in the parousia. The focus in this image of Jesus is predominantly on the future.[17]

2) The *divine man (theios aner)* christology presented Jesus as a divine agent, able to perform wondrous deeds; it was the inspiration behind the many collections of miracle stories. This christology feeds many scholarly controversies, yet most of the experts admit that when the early Christians applied the divine man model to Jesus, they did not necessarily hold him to be a divine person. The Greek concept of *theios aner,* though very much part of

the cultural air, was itself not very well defined. Even though often associated with the ability to work extraordinary feats, it served as a rather vague honorific epithet and often conveyed little more than the idea of an "inspired" figure. Scholars insist that when the first Jesus-followers used this model, they did so cautiously and with critical adjustments. The essence of Jesus was not to be found in divine miraculous powers.[18]

3) The *wisdom* and *logos (word)* christologies made use of another image that was part of the pre-Christian "spirit of the age," both Jewish and Greek. In its Jewish context, wisdom stood for God's activity in the world, creative, revelatory, and redemptive; wisdom often assumed elements of personality, without jeopardizing Jewish insistence on monotheism. Applied to Jesus, it expressed the believers' experience of him as the servant, bringer, and teacher of divine wisdom. In the Q tradition, Jesus is seen as the messenger of wisdom; in Matthew and in Paul, he is identified with wisdom, without, some scholars say, any clear notions of preexistence. Wisdom christology, therefore, served as the origin of the full-blown doctrine of incarnation that took shape especially when the author of John's Gospel combined the Jewish image of wisdom with the Greek symbol of the universal logos. For the Greeks, especially in the philosophy of Stoicism, the logos pervaded the universe, providing it with order, intelligibility, purpose. In John's prologue we find a clear affirmation of a preexistent divine reality coming down and taking flesh (John 1:1ff.; Heb. 1:3–4).[19]

4) The *paschal* or *Easter* Christology stressed the reality of Jesus' crucifixion and resurrection and, even more, the effects of this reality on the community of believers. This christology called upon Jesus as Christ or Messiah, and it balanced the *maranatha* christology by emphasizing that in his resurrection, even before the Final Coming, Jesus had accomplished everything; his followers can now share in it. Easter christologies are less concerned about the words and deeds of the historical Jesus than about his risen presence, forming and activating the community. Although Paul is its main proponent, this understanding of the fulfilled risen Lord was already present before Paul's influence.[20]

Christology from the Beginning: Dialogical, Pluriform, Evolutionary

Scholars continue to wrangle over the birth records and precise content of these different christologies. What the experts generally admit, however, is that the New Testament is "the end result and merger of different trajectories and images of Jesus, each having a specific context, presupposition, and implication."[21] What this means, and what is significant for our efforts to reinterpret the uniqueness of Jesus, is that christology, from its very beginnings, was diverse, in process, and the fruit of dialogue.

To state that New Testament christology is the fruit of dialogue is not to suggest that the early Christians merely dressed up their understanding of

Jesus in the various images available from the storehouse of current Jewish and gentile thought. Many of these images were not as clearly defined and readily available as earlier scholars had thought; and none of these symbols provided a perfect fit for what the early Christians experienced in Jesus and for what they ended up saying about him. When the early communities adopted symbols from other religions to express who Jesus was for them, it was always a cautious, critical adaptation.

Recognizing all this, scholars can still admit that "New Testament christology is built out of material which was part of the cultural heritage of the period."[22] Or, to put it more cautiously with A.D. Nock, "the impact of the figure of Jesus crystalized elements which were already there."[23] The Greek notion of the universal logos, the Jewish understanding of wisdom active in creation, were current cultural thought patterns. As even conservative New Testament scholars such as James D.G. Dunn admit, during the last three decades of the first century and the beginning of the second, images of preexistent "divine redeemers" or "sons of God" and "heavenly beings," who "descended" to aid humankind, were also part of the cultural-religious milieu. Even though it is probable that Christianity itself influenced the development of such images, it is also true that the influence was mutual.[24] The conclusion that I think can be drawn is that, although New Testament christology was not *determined* by Jewish or gentile influences, it would not have taken the form that it did without this influence—without this implicit dialogue with the philosophical, religious thought and experience of the time.

There is, furthermore, the diversity of New Testament christology. Such diversity signifies more than merely different facets of a clearly visible jewel. The differences in how Jesus was understood are real, and although they are not contradictory, neither are they smoothly complementary. This diversity must be preserved, especially when assessing the importance of the incarnational model, which, it can be said, represents the final fruits of New Testament christology and which, in the early councils of the fourth and fifth centuries, became the criterion for orthodoxy.

There were and still are other New Testament symbols, besides that of the incarnation, by which the meaning of Jesus can be expressed: the eschatological prophet (which Schillebeeckx holds to be the first and "fundamental interpretation of the life of Jesus"),[25] the man appointed Son of God in the resurrection, the coming Son of Man, the new Adam, the Wisdom of God. Dunn summarizes the conclusion of a majority of New Testament experts:

> Christology should not be narrowly confined to one particular assessment of Christ, nor should it play off one against another, nor should it insist on squeezing all the different NT conceptualizations into one particular "shape," but it should recognize that from the first the significance of Christ could only be apprehended by a diversity of formulations which, though not always strictly compatible with each other, were not regarded as rendering each other invalid.[26]

Finally, the diverse christologies of the New Testament can be coherently understood only as part of a process, a gradual unfolding. There is some scholarly dispute as to whether this process is best described as a "development" or as an "evolution." C.F.D. Moule contends that there was no evolution away from Jesus, no "successive additions of something new," but rather a making explicit of what was implicitly given, a *development* of "new insights into the meaning of what was there all along" in the original message and person of Jesus. [27]

Moule is correct in insisting that the New Testament did not run wild in its interpretations of Jesus, producing images of him that had little to do with what he really was or with what his followers first thought of him. Still, to portray New Testament christology as a development that merely rendered explicit what was implicitly known is to blur the picture of what really happened; it is also to blunt the contemporary significance of that picture. There was a genuine evolution of understanding; new species of symbols and images were employed. Although in continuity with the communities' original experience of Jesus, they were genuinely different from what was earlier understood.

As already pointed out, this evolution did not take place neatly, as a linear progression; it was more like a spiral of gradually advancing comprehension of the mystery encountered in this man Jesus. A clear example of this evolution, and one that throws light on our efforts to understand the uniqueness of Jesus, is the way the early churches came to recognize Jesus as divine, as the incarnate Son of God.

We have already heard the experts telling us that "there was no real evidence in the earliest Jesus-tradition of what could fairly be called a consciousness of divinity [in Jesus], a consciousness of sonship rooted in preexistent relationship with God." [28] It also seems certain that after the overpowering experience of the resurrection, believers did not immediately and unambiguously proclaim Jesus as the Son of God, equal to the Father. [29] Yes, the title "Son of God" was used from the beginning, and it did have implications of sharing in or mediating divinity. Yet the authors who used this title—Mark, Luke, Matthew—were still a long way from the notion of a preexistent incarnate Son. This is true also of Paul. He was far more interested in soteriology than in christology—more interested in spelling out the saving power of Jesus' death and resurrection for humankind than in explaining who Jesus was or what he said. It might be said that what was important for Paul was Christ's incarnation in Christians, not so much God's incarnation in Christ. [30]

As the early church grew into its second generation, there was a groping, multiphased evolution from what can be called an understanding of Jesus' eschatological sonship to an affirmation of his preexistent sonship. First-generation believers held to a certain becoming or development in Jesus' relationship with God. Especially in his resurrection, he became the Son of God who was then to come, finally, in the parousia. Such a view of divine sonship is contained in the wisdom christologies of Matthew and especially of Paul.

Jesus was the expression, even the identification, of God's eternal wisdom and thus was given a cosmic, mystical presence in the unfolding of history. Such eschatological wisdom christology was future-oriented and did not yet clearly affirm the preexistence of Christ; yet it was "the womb from which incarnational christology emerged."[31]

This emergence took place during the second generation of Christianity, when there was "a backward extension of the Son of God language—from resurrection to the beginning of Jesus' ministry (baptism in the Jordan), to his conception and birth, to a timeless eternity."[32] It was only under the influence of the author of John's Gospel that a sonship of degrees or stages was left behind and a full-blown belief in incarnation took place: "the author of John 1:1-16 was the first to take that step which no Hellenistic-Jewish author had taken before him, the first to identify the word of God as a particular person . . . the fourth Evangelist was the first Christian writer to conceive of the personal preexistence of the logos-Son and to present it as a fundamental part of his message."[33]

So we have the end point of an evolution from a predominantly functional, eschatological understanding of Jesus as Son of God to an incarnational, even ontological, proclamation of his divinity. It was John's incarnational christology that dominated the christology of the second and third centuries. Indeed, "in a real sense, the history of christological controversy is the history of the church's attempt to come to terms with John's christology."[34]

Even if some of the details in this selective summary of New Testament christology are debatable, the general picture is clear enough to provide some insights into the task of interpreting Jesus' uniqueness with a view to interreligious dialogue. I suggest that the first two generations of Christians offer us the following guidelines:

1) The christological trajectories and titles are not definitions but *interpretations* of who Jesus was for his early followers. These pictures are better understood not as photographs, but as impressionistic paintings. Each is conditioned by its historico-cultural context and concerns; each makes use of mythic models or symbolic images drawn from the Jewish and Hellenistic environment.

These images, like all mythic-symbolic language, are not to be taken literally; but they are to be taken seriously. As Bernard Lonergan might put it, we do not understand the christological models merely by "taking a look at them."[35] Rather, we must enter into the interpretive process ourselves, by feeling the symbolic power of these images, by understanding them in their historical contexts, by judging and reinterpreting their meaning in our own situations.

Proponents of the theocentric model for a theology of religions are correct when they look upon New Testament christological statements as myth; the purpose of such language is not to define or limit our understanding of Christ but to give us access to the mystery of Christ. Because it is undefinable, it must be understood ever anew.

2) No single New Testament trajectory or image of Jesus should be absolutized and allowed to absorb the others. The diversity of early christology should be preserved. This is not to say that all the images were equally relevant during the first centuries of the church or are so now. But all do preserve a validity and, as the situation warrants, must balance and complement each other. As historical contexts change, some models might have to be toned down and others played up.

Again, this is what many of the advocates of a new christology in dialogue with other religions are attempting. John Hick warns against understanding Jesus only or primarily according to a literal interpretation of the incarnation. Raimundo Panikkar attempts to resurrect the logos or wisdom christology of the early church as a more tolerant and inclusive expression of who Jesus was and is. Rosemary Ruether and other theologians in dialogue with Judaism are seeking to restore the meaning of Jesus as the eschatological prophet for the same reason. No one New Testament image of Jesus says it all.

3) Nor do all the New Testament images of Jesus, *taken together,* say everything about who this man was and what he means for Christians and for the world. We must be on guard against absolutizing the entire New Testament witness about Jesus. The evolutionary process of interpretation that makes up the New Testament must continue today in the same manner in which it took place then: in continuity with what went before, preserving the past without embalming it, faithful to the past without being limited by it. Christians will be faithful to the New Testament images of Jesus, they will truly believe in these images, by allowing them to give birth to new symbols and models of who this Jesus is and how he saves. Again, this is the intent of the theocentric model: a christology that will be genuinely but not totally new, a christology that will preserve the past by renewing it.

4) The continuing evolution of christology will need to make use of one of the main forces that moved it forward in the New Testament period: dialogue with other cultures and other religions. As was pointed out, the discovery of the meaning of Jesus by the early communities was dependent on, though not determined by, what Jews and gentiles had already discovered. Through such an open and critical dialogue with Hinduism, Buddhism, and Islam, theologians of the theocentric model are open to new images of Jesus that will make him more meaningful to them as well as to persons of other faiths. Their efforts are but the continuation of what Christians of the first two centuries were doing.

5) In our efforts to carry on the evolution of christology, what is especially needed is a renewal or return to the theocentrism that marked Jesus' understanding of his mission and, as far as we can tell, of himself. Any contemporary christology that loses this theocentric basis violates its origins; it will

also violate any effort to understand, value and dialogue with other religions. The theocentric model for understanding Christ and religions, therefore, is consistent both with the heritage of Christianity and with the "signs of the times."

UNIQUENESS AND EXCLUSIVENESS

There is another feature of New Testament christology that the previous section did not treat. Besides being diverse, evolutionary, and dialogical, much of what the New Testament says about Jesus is also *exclusive,* or at least *normative.* Jesus is the "one mediator" between God and humanity (1 Tim. 2:5). There is "no other name" by which persons can be saved (Acts 4:12). Jesus is the "only begotten Son of God" (John 1:14). No one comes to the Father except through him (John 14:6). Just as all died in one man, Adam, so all will be brought to life in one man, Christ (1 Cor. 15:21–22). What took place in him was "once and for all" (*epaphax*) (Heb. 9:12). He is the final prophet, providing the normative, final word for all who preceded or may follow.

To close one's eyes to such proclamation is either psychologically to repress or dishonestly to deny what one does not wish to face. It is also either dishonest or naive to argue that the early Christians really did not mean or believe what they were saying, as if they were conscious of the "historical relativity" or "mythic conditioning" of such language. When the early Jesus-followers announced to the world that Jesus was "one and only," they meant it.

Yet if christology was and is evolutionary, if it is in enduring need of reinterpretation, it can be asked whether such "one and only" or "final" language really does belong to the main content of what the early church experienced and believed. Here I should like to take up the question that faced us in chapters 5 and 6: the nature of such exclusivist language. Haddon Willmer poses the question succinctly when he asks "whether the development of such claims [about the exclusivity or finality of Jesus] depends not on what Jesus actually was but on the accident of the language in which he was described."[36] I shall suggest that all the "one and only" qualifiers to the various christological titles pertain more to the *medium* used by the New Testament than to its core *message.*

The Historico-Cultural Context

All christological reflection began, as the previous section explained, with a profound personal-communitarian experience of how the man Jesus and his message turned lives around and set them in new directions. Given the cultural context in which such experiences took place, it was natural, even necessary, that when persons tried to speak about such experiences, they did so in terms of finality and exclusivity. To an extent, there was no other way, no other language, for them to talk about what Jesus had done in their lives. To understand why this is so, we can examine three characteristics of the cultural neighborhood in which early Christianity grew up.

1) The Christian communities of the first and second centuries— indeed, Christianity throughout most of its history—were part of what contemporary theologians have come to call *classicist culture.* Like all culture, it pervaded their consciousness, formed their mind-set, colored their way of experiencing the world. As described in greater detail at the end of chapter 2, classicist culture, in distinction from contemporary *historical culture,* took it for granted that truth was one, certain, unchanging, normative. For anything to be true, to be reliable, it had to bear these qualities.[37] Certainly, the early Christians were aware that there were many truth-claims in the world around them. For the most part, however, they felt that if any one of these claims really were true, it had to either conquer or absorb the others. That is what truth did. Unavoidably, then, when they encountered the overwhelming truth of Jesus, they would *have* to describe it as the only or the final truth. Today, however, in the world of historical consciousness, coupled with a new experience of pluralism, it seems possible for Christians to feel and announce the saving truth about Jesus and his message without the requirements of classicist culture—that is, without having to insist that Jesus' truth is either exclusive or inclusive of all other truth.

2) Also, given the *Jewish eschatological-apocalyptic mentality* that marked especially the first generation of Christians, it was natural that they should interpret their experience of God in Jesus as final and unsurpassable. As Don Cupitt has pointed out (see chap. 8, above), the particular philosophy of history that the first Christians inherited from their Jewish mother religion led them to expect a new and definitive stage of history.[38] And it was a stage that was to break forth on the world only from Jerusalem. So when they encountered the transforming presence of God in Jesus, the spontaneous conclusion was that this stage had arrived.

One of the earlier christological trajectories, the *maranatha* model, expected the end of history, the fullness of the kingdom, to be around the corner. Naturally, possibilities of other revelations or prophets were simply beyond one's consideration. There was no time. When the final end did not arrive and as Christians came to realize that history still had a longer march than they had thought, they paid greater attention to other christologies (the wisdom/logos and Easter trajectories). Still, even in these other models, Jewish eschatologial convictions were preserved; Jesus was proclaimed as he who had already achieved and anticipated what was to come, for all, at the end of history. As Rosemary Ruether and Tom Driver explained, the finality of the *end* shifted to the *center* of history.[39]

The contemporary understanding or philosophy of history differs from the Jewish-apocalyptic model. History is experienced today not only as ongoing, open-ended, and painfully ambiguous, but also as moving along a plurality of cultural, evolutionary paths. This opens the question whether the influence of early apocalyptic ideas on christology can and should be recognized as time-conditioned and therefore in need of reinterpretation. Jesus need not be proclaimed as the absolutely *final* prophet, or as the *only center* of history; and still he can be affirmed as a universally meaningful savior who gives both promise and power to work for an eschatological future, for a kingdom that will be the transformation of the world as we know it now.

3) Another aspect of the historical context of the early church was its *minority status* within the larger Jewish community and especially within the vast, threatening Roman Empire. Cultural and religious pluralism was experienced otherwise than it is today. During the first centuries of its precarious growth, the community of Christians faced the danger either of being stomped out by larger groups for whom it was a threat or a nuisance, or of being absorbed by an all-consuming syncretism. To defend itself against these dangers, the community needed to arm itself with clear identity and total commitment. It did this especially through its beliefs, particularly its christological beliefs.

Such doctrinal language, therefore, can be called "survival language"; it was necessary for the survival of the community. By defining Jesus Christ in absolute terms, by announcing him as the one and only savior, the early Christians cut out for themselves an identity different from that of all their opponents or competitors. Such language also evoked a total commitment that would steel them in the face of persecution or ridicule.

Understood from such a sociological perspective, the absolute and exclusive quality of New Testament christology tells us more about the social situation of the early church than about the ontological nature of Jesus. This language was more moral than metaphysical. Its purpose was more to define identity and membership within the community than to define the person of Jesus for all time.[40]

This of course does not imply that there is no truth-content, no ontology at all, within early christology. The early Christians were proposing a worldview that included a definite view of Jesus. Yet if we understand the absolute, one-and-only descriptions of Jesus as insuring the survival of the community rather than as offering a once-and-for-all definition of Jesus, we can today still adhere to the basic worldview of early Christianity without insisting on its absolute, exclusive adjectives. In fact, in our present pluralistic situation, this seems to be what Christians are called to do.

"One and Only"—Trait of Confessional Language

The previous comments on the sociological function of christology reveal what I think is the basic nature of the exclusivist language about Jesus in the New Testament. All the "one and only" adjectives used to describe Jesus belong "not to the language of philosophy, science, or dogmatics, but rather to the language of confession and testimony."[41] In talking about Jesus, the New Testament authors use the language not of analytic philosophers but of enthusiastic believers, not of scientists but of lovers. It is, as Krister Stendahl urges, "religious language"—that is, "love language, caressing language."[42] In describing Jesus as "the only," Christians were not trying to elaborate a metaphysical principle but a personal relationship and a commitment that defined what it meant to belong to this community.[43]

Exclusivist christological language is much like the language a husband would use of his wife (or vice versa): "You are the most beautiful woman in the world . . . you are the only woman for me." Such statements, in the context of the marital relationship and especially in intimate moments, are certainly true. But the husband would balk if asked to take an oath that there is absolutely no other woman in the world as beautiful as his wife or no other woman whom he could possibly love and marry. That would be using a different kind of language, in a very different context. It would be transforming love language into scientific or philosophical language.[44] Christian dogmatic definitions, in the way they have been understood and used, have perhaps done just that to the love language of the early church. The languages of the heart and the head are not necessarily contradictory, but they are different. And their differences must be respected.

If we read some of the classic exclusivist New Testament texts as confessional rather than philosophical language, they sound different; and they take on an even more demanding personal challenge. In Acts 4:12, the apostles, after having cured the lame man in the name of Jesus, cried out "there is no other name by which we can be saved," not to rule out the possibility of other saviors, but to proclaim that this Lord Jesus was still alive and that it was he, not they, who was working such wonders in the community. The text, therefore, is abused when used as a starting point for evaluating other religions.[45]

The many texts that present Jesus as "the Son of God," even "the only begotten Son" (John 1:14), will also be heard differently. Their primary intent will not be to exclude anyone else as a possible son or daughter of God, but to urge all hearers to take this Jesus seriously, as authoritative. The point these texts are making is that just as any son can tell us much about his father, so Jesus is a reliable revelation of God. In translating the Greek, *uios tou Theou* ("son of God"), therefore, we must not insist on the definite article "the"; it does not appear in the original Greek and the phrase could as well be translated "*a* son of God." And the descriptive qualifier "only begotten" could perhaps be better rendered according to the Hebrew usage as "firstborn" or "beloved" (as it is in Mark 1:11, 9:7; Matt. 17:5; Luke 9:35). It could then be understood not to affirm the exclusivity but the reliability, the urgency, of Jesus' role as God's instrument. In this sense, Israel too was called the "firstborn" of God (Exod. 4:22; Sirach 36:11; Jer. 31:9).

Throughout the New Testament, others share in a family relationship with God.[46]

Even when Jesus is presented as "the one mediator between God and humankind" (1 Tim. 2:5), the adjective "one" will be heard not to imply "absolutely the only," but "the one whom we must take seriously," to whom all persons must listen, if they are truly to understand the God who, as the previous verse reminds us, "wants all people to be saved and come to know the truth." Like all Christians, the author of this passage was excited about Jesus; his principal concern was that all others experience the truth and salvation of this Jesus. The author was not out to condemn all other mediators or all those who did not know Jesus.

If Christians could reclarify and repossess the original and enduring intent of christological language—that is, if "one and only" could mean "I'm fully committed to you" rather than "no one else is worthy of commitment" —then many Christians would feel more honest about their faith, and doors would be opened more widely to dialogue with other believers equally committed to their saviors.

UNIQUENESS AND CONTEMPORARY UNDERSTANDINGS OF INCARNATION

So far in this chapter, I have tried to show that in light of New Testament christology, its pluriform evolution and its exclusivist language, a reinterpretation of the uniqueness of Jesus is not at all impossible. The specialness of Jesus need not require that he be either exclusive or inclusive of all other religious figures; the Christian does not have to enter interreligious dialogue with such claims. In this section, I should like to push the case further by showing that much of modern christology, both Catholic and Protestant, is moving toward just such a reinterpretation, even if the authors involved do not realize it or are reluctant to follow the momentum of their own thought.

I shall focus on two contemporary and respected attempts to understand the christological model that, though apparently a latecomer in the New Testament, has become the touchstone of christological orthodoxy: the incarnation. The so-called transcendental christology of Karl Rahner and the process christology of theologians such as John Cobb and Norman Pittenger have successfully shown how belief in the myth of the incarnation can be intellectually and personally relevant for twentieth century persons. In so doing, they have also, willy-nilly, set the stage for a theocentric reform of the traditional understanding of Jesus' uniqueness.

Transcendental Christology

Karl Rahner proposed his "transcendental christology" in the 1950s. Basically a retrieval of the Johannine model of incarnation as elaborated by the

Council of Chalcedon, transcendental christology has become one of the most elaborate and influential approaches of contemporary theology to the meaning of Christ. It has aided innumerable Christians to make sense of belief in the incarnation. Rahner's own christological writings, together with the commentaries and elaborations of his followers, are immense.[47] Here I offer only an aerial view of his thought in order to draw out its implications for the question of Jesus' uniqueness.

For Rahner, the essential Christian claim that Jesus is divine— one person with both a divine and a human nature—cannot be a mystery that we must accept on external authority or naked faith. Although it will always be beyond full comprehension, it must make sense on the basis of our experience of ourselves and our world; it "must possess for man a genuine intelligibility and desirability."[48] Rahner's well-constructed case for the meaningfulness and coherence of belief in the incarnation amounts to this: what happened in Jesus of Nazareth represents the fulfillment of what we are as human beings.

The title of Rahner's first well-known publication incorporates what he believes all human beings experience themselves to be: "Spirit in world."[49] The word "spirit" encapsulates his transcendental analysis of human nature. Expressed in our infinite desire to know, in our need to love and be loved, in our capacity to be responsible and faithful even when it hurts, in our ability and need to hope even when the future is uncertain—in all this ordinary stuff of human life is an openness, an orientation, a dynamic pull toward infinite mystery. A "fundamental act of transcendence constitutes the essence of man."[50] We are always reaching beyond ourselves to the More. This means that "a direct presence to God belongs to the nature of the spiritual person."[51]

To say that this spirit, this divinity within us, is "in the world," is to recognize, for Rahner, that we are thoroughly historical beings and that therefore we can experience our natural orientation toward God only in and through the events and persons of our own history. The spirit is not poured directly into our hearts; the pouring runs through the peaks and pits of our personal-social histories.

More significant for christology is a further implication of our being "in the world": "man in virtue of his history and his temporal character seeks the ultimate and definitive fulfillment of his existence precisely in history."[52] We are longing for the realization of the divine potential of our nature within time; we are looking for a perfected divine-human unity in this world. Rahner concludes that human nature, in the way it is put together and acts, is an "inquiring christology"; in our very being we are searching for "God's free epiphany in history," for "an absolute savior"—that is, for the kind of event that took place in Jesus of Nazareth.[53]

This is how Rahner makes sense of the incarnation. That God has taken on flesh in Jesus is not a freak event in history; it is not something totally unexpected. Rather, it is the almost natural or logical fulfillment of the awesome, mysterious nature that is ours as humans.

Rahner's descriptions of the incarnation are themselves awesome: in Jesus, human nature "simply arrived at the point to which it always strives by virtue of its essence." The incarnation of God in the man of Nazareth is "the realization of the highest possibility of man's being . . . the unique, supreme, case of the total actualization of human reality. . . . Christ is most radically man."[54]

Jesus, in other words, is the symbol of what human beings really are. As a symbol, he provides the assurance that the infinite hopes and strivings of our nature are not reaching out into an empty nothingness. God and the world can be one. The dream is a real possibility, for it has already been realized.[55] In light of the *fact* of the incarnation, Rahner comes to an even clearer and hope-filled reading of what human nature is: humanity was created, from the beginning, to be the vehicle, the symbol, of God's self-communication. God created the human being for the purpose of divine incarnation:

> God's creative act always drafts the creature [human being] as the paradigm of a possible utterance of himself. . . . We could now define man . . . as that which ensues when God's self-utterance, his Word, is given out lovingly into the void of god-less nothing. . . . [The] code-word for God is man. . . . If God wills to become non-God, man comes to be, that and nothing else we might say.[56]

Even though Rahner locates the incarnation, within the universal history of humanity, as the culmination of what human nature is meant to be, even though he states that the divine self-communication constituting the hypostatic union in Jesus is "intended for everyone,"[57] he still insists that this culmination/fulfillment has taken place and can take place *only once*. I find it difficult to get a firm grasp of his reasons why this is so.

In one context, Rahner seems to argue that the eternal Word has been and can be identified with only one human being: "For 'what' he [Jesus] is as the self-expression of the Logos and 'what' we are is the same. We call it 'human nature.' But the unbridgeable difference is constituted by the fact that this 'what' in him is spoken as his self-expression, and this is not the case with us."[58] This means that Jesus is "the offer for us" of God's divinizing grace; we are "the recipients of God's offer to us."[59] Elsewhere, Rahner implies that to claim that incarnation can be a possibility for all human beings would be to reduce it "to the level of nature, to the level of what is given always and everywhere. The truth of a divine humanity would be mythologized if it were simply a datum of every person always and everywhere."[60]

In both arguments, Rahner seems to believe that to allow incarnation, as it took place in Jesus, to possibly happen elsewhere would be to jeopardize what did take place in Jesus. To make the incarnation into a myth applicable to all humanity would be to undermine its historicity.

Process Christology

In chapter 7 we already saw something of the process theologians' understanding of Christ.[61] Again, I offer here only a bare sketch of how this view fits into their broader efforts to reinterpret the myth of the incarnation. With Rahner, they try to show that belief in divine enfleshment, far from being a matter only of pure faith, is thoroughly consistent with our experience of ourselves and the world. Their perspective on contemporary experience, however, is not Rahner's transcendental analysis of the human person's openness to the infinite, but Whitehead's model of all reality as a vast process made up not of beings but of free relationships (actual entities or occasions of experience), animated by a creative lure toward ever more complexity, harmony, and beauty.

Such an experience of a world in process leads to a *panentheistic* experience of God's relationship to the world. God is not identified with the world (pantheism), but everything and everyone in the world exists *in* God. Such a view is not, I should say, opposed to Rahner's understanding of divinity within us; but it does make for a tighter bond between the infinite and the finite. In the process model, divinity, in a limited but real sense, is dependent on the world for the unfolding of its being.[62]

Panentheism can be more clearly understood under one of its synonyms: incarnation. The world in God and God in the world means that all of creation is the arena of divine incarnation. This is what Cobb means (see chap. 7, above) with his vision of the universal Logos (Christ) incarnating itself throughout history; everytime there is a "creative transformation," whether among molecules or societies, God, in different degrees, has taken on flesh.[63] Norman Pittenger is even more lucid:

> God is ever incarnating himself in his creation, which means that he is ever entering into it—not as if he were absent from it and intervened now and again in it, but in the deeper sense that he who is unexhausted in himself, ever energizes in nature and in history, and above all in the lives of men, expressing himself more and more fully, until the whole created order becomes, in some sense, "the body of God." . . . It is *all* incarnation, in fact; but it is not on some uniformitarian level, for there are heights and depths, a more or a less, a here and a there, in the process.[64]

The central agent by which this process of divine incarnation takes place is the only power that can promote the kind of interrelations that make for authentic unity and justice: love. Within all creation, God "is there as the omnipresent lure, the omnipresent aim, the omnipresent agency for effecting love in the world. Thus every occasion, in its quality and in its own degree, is an incarnation of the divine dynamic which we call by the name of God."[65]

Within such a panentheistic, incarnational model of the God-world relationship, as within Rahner's transcendental analysis of the person, the
enfleshment of God in Jesus stands, not as a historical anomaly, but as a full
realization of what is going on throughout history. In the life of Jesus of
Nazareth, the process "worked." What God is up to in all history and in
every life was fully achieved in this man. Jesus is "the one in whom God
actualized in a living human personality the potential God-man relationship
which is the divinely-intended truth about every man."[66] Jesus is the "clue,"
the "primordial example," the "re-presentation," the symbol of what God
wants to accomplish in and through the entire process of evolution.[67] Process
theologians therefore can claim a universal *importance* for Jesus. The word
has a peculiar meaning in their technical vocabulary. It implies that Jesus is
an event that all persons must know if they are properly to grasp what God
has done in past history, what God is up to in the present, and especially what
can be the hopes and the projects for the future.[68]

Yet, as was indicated in chapter 7, all the process theologians, like Rahner
and his followers, go on to claim that Jesus is not only the full realization of
what God is up to in history, but the *only* such full realization. In other
words, they hold to a uniqueness of Jesus that, though not exclusive, is definitely inclusive and normative for all other revelations and religions. Process
theologians divide up and follow two different paths to this same conclusion.
Some (Cobb, Griffin, Ford) argue that Jesus is different from all other humans because God provided him with a particular revelation and possibility
(an "initial aim") given to no other. This was the call to unique divine sonship. Jesus responded freely, totally, with his whole being.[69]

Others (Mellert, Pittenger) refrain from claiming a special divine call given
to Jesus and to no one else; this, they feel, is too arbitrary and ends up making
Jesus an artificial insertion into history. Yet they do affirm that Jesus, like no
other human, responded to the divine lure totally and consistently. In this
view, Jesus is not different from us "in essence," but certainly "in degree"—
that is, in the way he responded to the divinity that is offered to all of us.[70]

Both views end with an image of Jesus in which his human person is totally
"oned" with and constituted by the divine lure—that is, by the personal
Logos. He is truly human, like all of us; but he is also truly and totally divine,
unlike all of us.[71] Schubert Ogden stands outside the mainstream of process
christology in his express refusal to make any historical claims about how
much Jesus himself responded to the divine lure; still, he advances the *existential* and the *ontological* claim that according to the normative New Testament witness, it is "solely through Jesus" that all peoples can find "the
decisive re-presentation of the meaning of ultimate reality."[72]

What They Say and What They Imply

Much of what these contemporary theologians—transcendental and
process—are saying about the incarnation confirms what we found in the

theocentric model for a theology of religions. First, they respect and treat belief in the incarnation as a true *myth,* a meaningful *model,* for expressing what Christians have experienced Jesus to be. These theologians take the myth seriously, but not literally. So they avoid the incredible (for many) and exclusivistic understanding of Jesus as a preexistent divine being who comes down from heaven, takes on a human nature (without a human personality), does his work of redeeming, and then goes back to heaven. Such a literal understanding tends not only to dehumanize Jesus, but so to humanize God as to confine deity to Jesus. Rahner and the process theologians respect the myth and so avoid such excesses.

Secondly, in taking the myth of incarnation seriously, in trying to reappropriate its truth, the christologies we have just reviewed lend support to an issue that has teased us throughout this study. Transcendental and process christologies interpret the myth of God's incarnation in Jesus as an expression of the *nondualistic* unity between divinity and humanity. Their interpretation of the myth affirms a given, at least potential, at-one-ment between God and humanity, which can be realized and lived by all.

This is what Troeltsch and Toynbee perceived with their view of God as coterminous with history, what Jung suggested with his own myth of our divine unconscious, what the conservative Evangelicals and mainline Protestants miss in their stress on the gulf between God and world, what the Catholic model holds with its notion of the supernatural existential, what Panikkar asserts with his "cosmotheandric principle." Incarnation is not a one-time event. Rather, it is an ideal for all, an ideal rooted in the ancient Christian belief in the one, universal logos or wisdom of God.

All this is what Rahner and the process theologians *say* in order to show how belief in the incarnation resonates with human experience. Yet they hold back from facing what seems to me to be the clear *implications* of what they are saying: that there can be *other incarnations,* other individuals who achieved (or were granted) the same fullness of God-human unity realized in Jesus. Some commentators are trying to force a confrontation with such implications: "From this point of view [Rahner's christology], the challenging question about the incarnation is not 'whether,' but 'why only once?' "[73] "May we legitimately speak of [God's] many 'incarnations' through which his saving presence, action, suffering, and revelation come effectively into human life and transform it?"[74]

The reasons why Rahner and process theologians cannot admit other incarnations leave me, and I think others, confused. It seems Rahner has not squarely faced the question why the eternal Word cannot be fully incarnated in more than one person. The Council of Chalcedon stressed that, although the union between the divine and human natures in Jesus was complete, the differences between them remain.[75] That would imply that the Word is free for other incarnations. Also, why must God's full and irrevocable offer of grace be given only once? Granted the huge number of potential recipients, a plurality of offers would seem to make sense. Finally, why would the possibility of other incarnations minimize the historicity and the saving significance of incarnation in Jesus?

For truth to be truth, for truth to call forth total commitment, must it be the *only* truth? And to the assertions of the process theologians, either that Jesus was given an "initial aim" granted to no one else or that the response of Jesus to the general divine lure surpassed "in degree" that of everyone else, the simple question can be posed: How can they be so sure? What is their data, their experiential reference, for making such sweeping claims?[76]

The very arguments that the transcendental and process theologians use successfully to *increase* the coherence and relevance of traditional Christian belief in divine incarnation in Jesus also serve, implicitly, to *decrease* the coherence and relevance of traditional claims that such incarnation can take place only in Jesus. If we follow through the implications of these christologies, we must, it seems to me, recognize at least the possibility, perhaps even the probability, that what happened in Jesus has happened or can happen elsewhere. Both Rahner and the process thinkers see the incarnation of the Word in Jesus as the full realization of what is the *potential,* the God-given, goal of all human beings. The unavoidable question is: If this is the potential for all, why should its complete actualization be limited to only one human being?

These contemporary christologies, therefore, lend even greater coherence and validity to the nonnormative reinterpretation of Christ proposed by the theocentric theologians studied in chapter 8. Rahner and the process theologians have shown that Christians can claim that incarnation *really* took place in Jesus, that Jesus *really* is "important" (in the process sense of the term) for all ages; but they have also implicitly shown that Christians can make such claims without having to add that this is true *only* of Jesus. If Christians can proclaim that "in him [Jesus] all the fullness of God was pleased to dwell" (Col. 1:19), they must also recognize that "you [others!] may be filled with all the fullness of God" (Eph. 3:19).

Any assertion that Jesus is the only incarnation should not be "dogmatically mediated"—that is, made only on the basis of Christian experience and doctrine. Rather, such "one and only" claims, if they are to be made at all, must be "critically mediated"—that is, open to examination and verification through concrete dialogue with other religions. As the next chapter will argue, we cannot, and we need not, assert that there are "no others" until we have tried to know and experience the others.

UNIQUENESS AND LIBERATION CHRISTOLOGY

In chapter 8 we saw how First World liberation theologians make use of an "ethical hermeneutics" to question the finality of Jesus.[77] Here I should like to offer a skeletal summary of the broader theological method of liberation christology (especially Latin American) in order, again, to show how these theologians, whether they realize it or not, are advancing a convincing case for the possibility of a theocentric, nonnormative reinterpretation of Christ.

In discussing liberation christology, we are, I believe, on "the cutting edge of contemporary theological reflection."[78] Just as liberation/political theology in general is alerting more and more Christians to the abstract, dangerously individualistic, naively ideological and apolitical qualities of much European and North American theology, so also Latin American christologies are pointing out these same features in both transcendental and process christology.

This does not mean that the liberation theologians deny the basic content of what Rahner and process theologians are saying. Rather, the liberationists argue from their own Third World experience that to extol the incarnation as the symbol of the God-world relationship and to hold up Jesus as the full realization of human potential is too neat, too easy, too certain. As we shall see, liberation theologians are convinced that before one can make such lofty claims, before one can know whether such claims are really so, one must get one's hands dirty in the actual human situation of suffering, oppression, and the struggle for liberation. One must be involved in the nitty-gritty praxis of trying to live and carry out this God-world relationship, this full realization of human potential. Things may not work just the way one thinks they do—which means the truth of one's theory may not be what it was thought to be.

The Primacy of Praxis

As was mentioned briefly in chapter 8, praxis is the heart of the method of liberation theology and christology. Praxis is not only the application or goal of theory; it is "theory's own originating and self-correcting foundation."[79] One does not first know the truth and then apply it in praxis; it is in action, in doing, that truth is really known and validated. The doing, or praxis, that liberation theologians are talking about is basically the effort to confront and transform the evil that clings to the human condition, an evil that, today, is enfleshed most evidently and destructively in injustice and oppression.

For these theologians, therefore, any experience of truth, especially God's truth, is not primarily a disclosure or an intellectual event consisting in an "adequation between the intellect and the object." Rather, the transcendent God is known, truly known, only in a transformative experience in which the "knower" acts differently and thus changes the world. In Christian terms: "Only in and through the process of conversion and *practical* change do we have access to the God of Jesus Christ."[80]

Such a theological method, based on such an epistemology, has sent transformative tremors through much of the traditional understanding of theology. The primacy of praxis leads to "the primacy of the anthropological

over the ecclesiastical, of the utopian elements over the factual . . . of the
social over the personal.''

Especially pertinent to our concerns for understanding the uniqueness of
Jesus is the call of liberation theology for a primacy ''of the critical element
over the dogmatic,'' or ''of orthopraxis over orthodoxy.''[81] Gutiérrez puts it
more sharply: ''the subject of liberation theology is not theology but liberation.''[82] This means that the dogmatic or scriptural formulations of the past,
though remaining normative, are not absolute norms. The ''truth'' of dogma
and tradition must be constantly exposed to the ''ultimate arbiter'' of truth—
that is, ''the transformative response of Christian praxis.''[83] ''Right knowing'' (orthodoxy) without ''right doing'' (orthopraxis) does not exist. This
means not only that orthodoxy must be adjusted under the pressure of orthopraxis but that one can more comfortably bear with uncertainty about what is
orthodox as long as one is able to make the responsible effort to bring about
transformation and liberation in the world.

The primacy of praxis also sets up a defense system against the persistent
danger of the decay of doctrine into ideology. By submitting their cherished
beliefs to the test of praxis, Christians are better able to recognize how much
such beliefs—for example, in the exclusivity of salvation in Christ—are possibly nurtured more by the desire to maintain power and privilege than by the
desire to promote truth and freedom. In so unmasking ideology and in submitting orthodoxy to the constant criticism of orthopraxis, liberation theologians clear the ground for a more fertile dialogue:

> Many ecclesiastical traditions and ecclesial institutions were functional
> at one time but today have become obsolete. They are centers of a con-
> servatism that locks the door to dialogue between faith and the world,
> the church and society. Criticism refines and purifies the core of the
> Christian experience so that it can be made incarnate within the histori-
> cal experience we are living.[84]

Not only is the ground for dialogue cleared, but an effective launching pad
is provided. To begin, and to maintain dialogue, it is not necessary that all
partners agree on certain universal truths—for instance, whether there is one
savior/incarnation or many. The mutual starting point will be how Christians and others can struggle, together, against those things that threaten
their common humanity. Only in the praxis of such struggle can clarity on
universal truths emerge.

Orthopraxis before Orthodoxy

The way liberation theologians such as Jon Sobrino, Leonardo Boff, Rosemary Ruether apply their general theological method to christology might be

so summarized: we cannot begin to know who this Jesus of Nazareth is unless we are following him, no matter what that demands. That is the starting point. Furthermore, everything we know or say about him must be repossessed and reclarified in the praxis of following him through the changing contexts of history. That is a never ending process.[85]

In establishing the praxis of following Jesus as the lens and litmus test for all christological statements, liberation theologians offer a further angle on the theocentrism found in the original message of Jesus: "Systematically speaking, we can say that the historical Jesus did not preach about himself or the church or God but rather about the kingdom of God."[86] Therefore, what is most important is to put this kingdom in the center of concern and to work toward building it; doctrinal purity and clarity about the church, the nature of God and Jesus himself, will follow. Christians must keep their priorities clear.[87]

Such priorities throw light on how Christians are to understand and use the titles given to Jesus in the New Testament. These titles are calls to action, not final, absolute statements about who Jesus is. They were the fruits of the early Christians' efforts to practice what they had experienced in the message and person of Jesus.

Agreeing with the lessons that we drew earlier in this chapter from New Testament christology, Boff warns against the "danger that christology may assimilate the biblical titles of Christ *uncritically,* without an awareness of their historical relativity." Worse, there is the danger of "ideologizing the titles of Christ," using them as a christological "justification" for "social and religious status." Therefore, "no title conferred on Christ can be absolutized."[88] Each must be understood in all its limitations and reexamined under the lens of praxis.

This means, too, that Christians must be open to new titles that will carry on, more meaningfully, the praxis called for by the old. In doing this, though, followers of Jesus should remember that to enter the kingdom of God, what is most important is not to be able to proclaim "Lord, Lord" or "only Savior, only Savior," but to work toward the liberation of the kingdom (Matt. 7:21-23).[89]

The implications that such a praxis-based christology carries for our question of the uniqueness of Jesus are many. I suggest some that seem most evident:

1) Liberation christology clarifies what are the conditions for the possibility of claiming any kind of exclusive or inclusive uniqueness for Jesus. What Sobrino states about the universality of Jesus applies equally well to uniqueness or finality: "his universality cannot be demonstrated or proved on the basis of formulas or symbols that are universal in themselves: e.g., dogmatic formulas, the kerygma as event, the resurrection as universal symbol of hope, and so forth. The real universality of Jesus shows up only in its concrete embodiment."[90] In other words, Christian conviction and proclamation that

Jesus is God's final or normative revelation cannot rest only on traditional doctrine or on personal experience. Such uniqueness can be known and then affirmed only "in its concrete embodiment," only in the praxis of historical involvement.

2) When Christians look at such praxis, at such concrete embodiment, there is reason to admit that not all the conditions for the possibility of claiming finality or normativity for Jesus have been fulfilled. I think Ruether has a point:

> By restoring the kingdom to the center of the gospel, liberation theology also throws into question much of the language of finality that the Christian church has been wont to use of Jesus. We cannot speak of Jesus as having "fulfilled" the hopes of Israel, for these were hopes for the kingdom of God. The kingdom of God has not been established on earth in any final or unambiguous form, either in the time of Jesus or through the progress of the Christian churches or nations.[91]

The concrete data from praxis, that of Jesus and of the church, is not sufficient, in other words, to establish any kind of absolute finality for Jesus. One might respond by arguing that Jesus, in himself, realized a final and normative anticipation or "prolepsis" of that future kingdom, even though the kingdom itself has not yet been realized in time. Even then it would be difficult to satisfy the required criteria from praxis.

Have Christians actively learned from and especially worked with other religions to such a degree that they can know, with certainty, that there is no other like Jesus? Has their "praxis" of these other religions been extensive enough to make the universal claim that Jesus' revelation surpasses and is therefore normative for these other faiths? I think not.

3) If the method of liberation christology shows why normative claims for Jesus are not presently possible, it also makes clear why they are not necessary. For liberation theology, the one thing necessary to be a Christian and to carry on the job of theology is commitment to the kingdom vision of liberating, redemptive action. What Christians *do* know, on the basis of their praxis, is that the vision and power of Jesus of Nazareth *is* a means for liberation from injustice and oppression, that it *is* an effective, hope-filled, universally meaningful way of bringing about God's kingdom. Not knowing whether Jesus is unique, whether he is inclusive or normative for all others, does not interfere with commitment to the praxis of following him. Such questions may be answered in the future. In the meantime, there is much work to be done.

4) Finally, liberation christology allows, even requires, that Christians recognize the possibility of other liberators or saviors, other incarnations. If liberating praxis is the foundation and norm for authentic divine revelation and truth, then Christians must be open to the possibility that in their dia-

logue with other believers they may encounter religious figures whose vision offers a liberating praxis and promise of the kingdom equal to that of Jesus. In view of their fruits of praxis, such saviors would have to be recognized and affirmed. Again, their existence would in no way have to jeopardize the universal relevance of Jesus' vision or lessen one's total commitment to it. "Anyone who is not against us, is with us" (Mark 9:40).

WHAT ABOUT THE RESURRECTION?

The preceding arguments that New Testament and contemporary christology can allow for a new and nonnormative understanding of Jesus' uniqueness might be thought to be neatly negated by a central "fact" in the Christian message: the resurrection. If the christological trajectory or myth of incarnation can admit of "others," what about the Easter trajectory? No other human being, it would seem, was ever raised from the dead, never to die again.[92] Does not the resurrection establish not only an inclusive but exclusive uniqueness for the man from Nazareth? Such questions lead us into some of the most tangled terrain of contemporary christology. All I shall attempt here is a brief summary of one reputable, though controversial, understanding of the resurrection, in order to show how it allows for a nonexclusivist, nonnormative christology.

The analysis and interpretation of the resurrection accounts offered by such Christian scholars as Edward Schillebeeckx, Reginald Fuller, Norman Perrin, Hans Küng, Bruce Vawter, James Mackey, and Dermot Lane differ in approach and particular conclusions.[93] They all harmonize, however, in their efforts to crack the dichotomy of views that hold the resurrection to be either an *objective* or a *subjective* event. Those arguing the "objectivity" of the resurrection insist that it was essentially an event that took place *in front of* the disciples; in his appearances the risen Jesus stood before a select group of disciples and thus brought forth their Easter faith. The subjective approach presents the resurrection as an event that took place *in* his followers: Jesus arose in their faith, in their renewed conviction that his message is still valid and must go on. In this view, the resurrection did not cause faith; faith caused the resurrection.[94]

The authors named above trace a cautious but clear path between such either-or, objective-or-subjective, views of the resurrection. For them, the Easter event is both. The resurrection, one might say, happened both *in* and *to* the disciples. Faith in the risen Lord was not simply caused by an objective event taking place in front of them; neither, however, was it created or concocted by the disciples' personal convictions or wishes or hallucinations. The Easter event was caused by something outside the witnesses (objective), and yet took place within them and was dependent on their personal perceptions and response (subjective). The resurrection, according to this interpretation, was first known as something that happened in and to the disciples. It was *their* experience, and yet it was brought about by something that was more than their experience. On the basis of this experience, they knew that something had happened to Jesus after his death.[95]

What was this experience? What was the objective reality that brought it about? The authors I am surveying generally admit "the impossibility of adequately describing what really happened after the death of Jesus."[96] Negatively, the Easter experience should not be understood as some kind of "incursion from above," a "supernatural intervention," a matter of "hocus pocus."[97] This means that it should not be understood only or even primarily as an encounter with a physical person standing "over there." As the Greek word *ophthe* used in one of the earliest accounts of the paschal experience indicates (I Cor. 15:5), Jesus was not simply "seen" by the first Christians, but was "revealed," made known, to them.[98]

These authors, therefore, generally conclude that belief in the resurrection originated from a deeply personal faith experience, which can be described as a "revelation" or "conversion" experience. Like any authentic faith or conversion experience, it was brought about by the objective reality of grace, the power of God, the Spirit. But this grace was mediated through "psychological realities and human experiences." Certainly "the productive remembrance of Jesus' basic message" and the disciples' previous faith in his role as the eschatological prophet played a crucial role. The early disciples found themselves amazingly reconverted and enabled to renew their faith in Jesus; he was still among them in a new, a transformed, presence.[99]

More detailed suggestions as to how this conversion experience took place differ and complement each other. Schillebeeckx suggests that the resurrection experience could well have been an experience of forgiveness, offered first to the guilty Peter and then shared by the others. Lane seems to agree and describes the first encounters with the risen Lord as an experience of "gracious fellowship, a personal reconciliation and a divine solidarity which did in fact disarm and surprise, lift and renew, change and transform their lives."[100] For Küng, the resurrection experience was a "vocation received in faith," a vocation to "shape one's own life out of the effective power of the life of this Jesus."[101]

Mackey offers a more general description and indicates the objective content of the Easter experience more clearly. Following Paul, he understands the experience of the risen Jesus to be an experience of "the Spirit of Jesus," "the life-giving Spirit," "the power or spirit in our lives, enabling us to overcome destructive evil, enhancing ourselves with faith and love and a hope that defies death."[102] It is suggested that such experiences most likely took place in "sacramental" situations: in breaking bread (Luke 24:13–25; John 21:1–14), forgiveness of sins (John 20:21–23), the solidarity of the Spirit (Matt. 28:16–20; John 20:22).[103]

However difficult it is to define the originating experiences of the risen Jesus, it is clear from these descriptions that such encounters were not essentially different from what Christians can and should experience today. The first meetings with the Living One were not magical, miraculous intrusions coming from above. Rather, they were intense, originating instances of how believers through the ages can encounter the real presence of Christ as they break bread, recall his story, live his message. Rahner offers an encapsulating statement:

> So far as the nature of this experience [of the resurrection] is accessible to us, it is to be explained after the manner of our experience of the powerful Spirit of the living Lord rather than in a way which either likens this experience too closely to mystical vision of an imaginative kind in later times, or understands it as an almost physical sense experience.[104]

According to such an interpretation of the resurrection, the accounts of appearances of the risen Jesus, as well as of the empty tomb, are interpreted as attempts to express and give more tangible form to these conversion experiences rather than as photographic statements of what took place. One must remember that the appearance stories "are scarcely reflections of the earliest preaching of the risen Christ."[105] They were offered as illustrations, stories, not as *proofs* of what had happened. The experience of the living Jesus was already there. Such stories, therefore, need not be taken literally, but they should be taken seriously.[106]

Often forgotten is the "punch line" of the story of the risen one's appearance to the disciples at Emmaus; Jesus was not recognized through his physical form but in the symbolism of the breaking of bread (Luke 24: 36–43). More clearly, Thomas is told that he would be better off among "those who have not seen but have believed" (John 20:29).

This is not to dilute the New Testament witness but to accept it for what it is—a richly mythic account, with an amazing variety of often contradictory detail, of experiences that could never be photographed. This understanding of the resurrection experience recognizes not only the appearances but also the resurrection model itself as symbolic attempts to express, to "picture," what had happened. As mentioned earlier, some of the earliest christologies do not make explicit mention of the resurrection but use the symbols of exaltation and parousia to express the conversion experiences that did take place.[107] Most importantly, this interpretation does justice not only to the nature of the New Testament accounts but to the nature of resurrection faith itself, which was not and is not a matter of historico-physical proofs but of deeply personal-communitarian experience and commitment.

If such an understanding of the resurrection is valid—and I think it is— then once again we have a contemporary christological interpretation that makes room for the nonnormative christology proposed by the theocentric model. Perhaps without clear awareness, the theologians and Christians who find this conversion or revelation model of the resurrection coherent with their own faith set up the further question: Must the reality behind the Easter stories be limited only to an experience of Jesus? Is not such a conversion or faith experience essentially what countless men and women have felt in their experience of other archetypal religious leaders after the deaths of these leaders?

Gautama the Buddha can serve as an example. Did not his disciples undergo a further, a continued, "vocation received in faith," a personal transformation after his death? Have they not continued to sense his spirit, his real presence, in their midst? Certainly, Buddhists did not speak of the resurrected Buddha. That makes sense. The resurrection of the dead was not an interpretive myth or model available in their culture and experience, as it was for the first Jewish Jesus-followers. Just as it seems that some early Christians could speak about their experience of the living Jesus without use of the resurrection model, so might Indians, had the Christ event taken place among them, have interpreted his abiding reality in other models.

In addition, even though other believers do not interpret their founders in terms of resurrection, this does not imply that nothing happened to these founders after their death as must have happened to Jesus. These founders, too, continue to live on in a transformed, spiritual, but *real* way. They were not overcome by death. Such a consideration might be pressed all the more meaningfully in the Trikaya myth of Mahayana Buddhism, in which Buddha came to be "deified" and was said to have, now, a "glorified body" (*Sambhogakaya*) by which he is really present to those who believe in him.[108]

What happened, therefore, to the early Christians and to Jesus after his death might possibly have happened to other believers and their saviors. The resurrection of Jesus, in all its authentic mystery and power, does not necessarily imply "one and only."

CONCLUSION: UNIQUENESS AND PERSONAL COMMITMENT

This chapter has tried to show that in light of New Testament christology, of New Testament exclusivist language, of contemporary transcendental, process, and liberation christologies, and of the nature of resurrection faith, it is possible for Christians to follow the lead of the *kairos* of today; they can endorse a theocentric theology of religions, based on a theocentric, nonnormative reinterpretation of the uniqueness of Jesus Christ.

In this concluding section, I should like to propose how, on the basis of my own and others' faith experience, such a move need in no way diminish one's personal and full commitment to Jesus as incarnation of God's saving purpose and presence.[109] On the contrary, a theocentric understanding of Jesus can confirm and intensify one's commitment to him by rendering it more intellectually coherent (better theory) and more practically demanding (better praxis).

The Psychology of Faith

Some, perhaps many, Christians will feel their faith threatened by the suggestion that Jesus may or may not be God's definitive, normative revelation, that there may be other saviors and other incarnations. Such feelings must be respected. The issue is a delicate one. I suggest to these believers that if they examine the psychological processes of how they came to believe in Jesus the Christ, they will find that such anxiety is unwarranted. The feeling of being threatened by "other saviors" arises not from the spontaneous voice of faith but from deep-seated attitudes of classicist consciousness (see chap. 2) or from unquestioned presuppositions of much Western philosophy to the effect that truth is always a matter of either-or, this-or-that. Deep down we still feel that for something to be really true and worthy of our commitment, it must be the only truth. And when this attitude merges with the traditionally North American mentality that only what is biggest and best—from automobiles to hamburgers to saviors—merits our purchase, naturally we shall be threatened by others who might be equally true and valuable.

The psychology of faith, however, does not require this. As has already been suggested in this chapter, especially by the liberation theologians, what brings a person to faith in and commitment to Jesus is a transforming experience; Jesus so empowers the heart and illumines the mind that one can now feel and know and, especially, act differently. The experience of faith necessarily includes the conviction that Jesus *is* God's revelation and grace. It does not necessarily include the conviction that he *alone* is this revelation and grace. Therefore, as John Macquarrie has urged, one can be totally committed to Jesus and at the same time genuinely open to the possibility of other revealers and saviors.[110] Or as the liberation theologians might suggest, one can give all one's heart and mind to the praxis of building the kingdom and at the same time recognize that this praxis is being realized along other paths.

To expand on an analogy used earlier, one can be totally and faithfully committed to one's spouse, even though one well knows that there are other persons in this world equally as good, intelligent, beautiful—yes, even when one makes the acquaintance of and enjoys the friendship of such persons. Absolute exclusivity, in attitude or practice, is neither honest or healthy in any commitment.

I even suggest that the ability to be open to others can serve as a gauge for the depth of one's commitment to Jesus. Sociologists point out that the more a group is secure in its own identity and the more it is committed to its unifying vision, the more it will be able to tolerate, even accept, other visions— what sociologists call "cognitive dissonance."[111] Perhaps this is why the early Christian communities could bear and actually thrive on so many different, seemingly contradictory, christologies; they were basically secure in their central commitment to following Jesus. Again, the analogy with marriage applies: the deeper the commitment to one's spouse and the more secure the marriage relationship, the more one will be able to appreciate the truth and beauty of others. Therefore, not only does commitment to Jesus not exclude openness to others, but the greater the commitment to him, the greater will be one's openness to others.

This proportionality also works in reverse: Might Christians' anxiety about the possibility of "other Christs" be a symptom of an underlying insecurity concerning their own identity and praxis?

Tension between Universality and Particularity

The challenge and the difficulty of maintaining total commitment to one revealer together with genuine openness to others can be better understood and embraced when seen as part of the intrinsic, creative tension between the particular and the universal. It is a tension inherent in all authentic religious experience. As was argued against the "common essence" approach to religious pluralism, there is no such thing as an essence that can be purely distilled from any one religion or from all of them together. This is because, for the great majority of humankind (Zen Buddhists claim exception), the divine mystery is not experienced directly, without some form of mediation. God is generally encountered through a mediator—a symbol, a sacrament, an incarnation. In other words, human beings need *particular* revealers or saviors.

Furthermore, as was pointed out in the chapter on historical relativism (chap. 2), when such particular experiences of divinity truly occur, they move the individual or community to feel not only that this particular revelation or symbol is "decisive for me"—that is, offering a new mode of acting in the world and therefore requiring a total response—it also includes the conviction that this revelation has something to say to all peoples; it is universally relevant. When truth, especially God's, is encountered, it can never be truth "only for me."[112]

As all this happens, however, as the experience of God through a particular savior or mediator deepens, a tension sets into the psychology of faith. There is a direct proportionality between the appropriation by a community of the power of its *particular* mediator and the confrontation of the community with the *universal* reality or mystery mediated through that savior. The more the community realizes that its savior *really* does make God known, the more it realizes that this God is a mystery ever more than what has been made known—the *Deus semper major,* the God ever beyond. In other words, the more the particular mediator's efficacy is realized, the more its relativity is recognized. Such a tension is creative because it constantly beckons the community to hold to and remain faithful to its mediator, without, however, allowing this mediator to become an idol. More concretely, this means that the community must never slip into the false security of thinking it knows what its mediator has revealed; for Christianity this implies that the task of christology, of interpreting the Christ event, is never finished.

In our present age of religious pluralism, the creative tension between the particular and the universal also requires that each religious community recognize that there can be, and most likely are, other particular mediators of this divine mystery, a mystery that can be captured, definitively, by no one mediator.

Open-ended Confession

Some practical advice as to how Christians can maintain their commitment and fidelity to Jesus the Christ and at the same time preserve the creative tension between the particular and the universal comes from a suggestion made by H. Richard Niebuhr in 1941. Niebuhr urged that Christians adopt a *confessional* approach to others—that is, that they confess and make known what they have experienced God to have done for them and the world in Jesus, *without* making any claims about Jesus' superiority or normativity over other religious figures.

According to Niebuhr, to take the apologetic tack, to make denigrating comparisons, works incalculable harm not only on other religions but on Christianity itself. He describes what he often finds among his fellow Christians:

> We not only desire to live in Christian faith but we endeavor to recommend ourselves by means of it and to justify it as superior to all other faiths. Such defense may be innocuous when it is strictly subordinated to the main task of living towards our ends, but put into the first place it becomes more destructive of religion, Christianity, and the soul than any foe's attack can possibly be.[113]

Instead, Niebuhr proposed that Christians reach out to others "by stating in simple, confessional form what has happened to us in our community, how we came to believe, how we reason about things and what we see from our point of view."[114] And leave the rest to God!

With such a confessional christology and approach to other faiths, Christians can hold to their personal, total commitment to the universal relevance of Jesus. In fact, it seems that only such a confessional stance will enable them to persuade others that what God has done in Jesus is meaningful for all human beings. We are persuaded by those who speak with deep conviction of what their savior has done for them. We are not persuaded by those who tell us, with deep conviction, that "my savior is bigger than yours."

A confessional approach, then, will be both certain and open-ended. It will enable Christians to take a firm position; but it will also require them to be open to and possibly learn from other positions. It will allow them to affirm the *uniqueness* and the universal significance of what God has done in Jesus; but at the same time it will require them to recognize and be challenged by the *uniqueness* and universal significance of what the divine mystery may have revealed through others. In boldly proclaiming that God has indeed been defined in Jesus, Christians will also humbly admit that God has not been confined to Jesus.[115]

How such a confessional approach, which is the practical application of a theocentric, nonnormative christology, can actually be carried out in dialogue with adherents of other faiths will be the concern of the final chapter.

Chapter X

Doing before Knowing—The Challenge of Interreligious Dialogue

Our conclusion from chapter 9—still a tentative conclusion, in need of criticism from the broader Christian community—was that Christians, in their approach to persons of other faiths, need not insist that Jesus brings God's definitive, normative revelation. A confessional approach is a possible and preferred alternative. In encountering other religions, Christians can confess and witness to what they have experienced and come to know in Christ, and how they believe this truth can make a difference in the lives of all peoples, without making any judgments whether this revelation surpasses or fulfills other religions. In other words, the question concerning Jesus' finality or normativity can remain an open question.

But how does one actually go about the process of dialogue with such a confessional approach? How can one converse with other believers so as truly to understand and learn from them? Also, how can one engage in dialogue as a means of answering, possibly, the open question of Jesus' uniqueness? These are the central questions that will lead us through this final chapter.

First and fundamentally, I suggest that we consider dialogue a means of *doing before knowing*. I shall outline an understanding and method of dialogue that allows it to be a praxis that illumines theory rather than a praxis that is predetermined by theory. Secondly, I shall try to show that for such an understanding of dialogue to work, it needs to be based on a model of truth that, for the most part, differs from past views concerning what truth is and how it is determined. Finally, I shall indicate that such an understanding of dialogue and truth calls for an expanded view of the nature and task of Christian theology.

DIALOGUE AS A HERMENEUTICS OF PRAXIS

What follows is an application, in a new direction, of the basic principle of liberation theology, as outlined and endorsed in chapter 9: to know the truth,

205

one must do it. Praxis is not simply the outcome of what is already known to be true; rather, it is "the originating and self-correcting foundation" of the truth. We saw how liberation theologians apply this hermeneutical method, this principle of interpretation, to christology. Only in the actual following of Jesus, only in practicing and living his message in our concrete situation, can we really know who he is and what he means.[1]

My contention is that one of the principal forms of praxis necessary today for discovering the truth of Christian revelation is not only the socio-political praxis of liberation, but also the *praxis of dialogue* with peoples of other faiths. Such an interreligious dialogue can serve as a *hermeneutics of praxis* that will throw ever greater light on the theoretical questions that have mounted throughout these pages. These questions are the central issues for any Christian theology of world religions: Is there revelation and salvation in other religions? What is the content and extent of such revelation? What is the place of Christianity among the religions of the world? Is Christian truth the corrective, the fulfillment, of other religions?

I am suggesting that answers to such questions, like all answers, are not simply "given" in the Christian scriptures and tradition; they must be worked out through the praxis of dialogue between Christian tradition and that of other religions. To fashion a theology of religions outside the praxis of dialogue would be as inappropriate as it would be for a tailor to make a suit without taking the customer's measurements.

In the past, for most of the history of Christianity, the situation may have been different. Interreligious dialogue was not an available form of praxis whereby the theory and truth of Christian revelation, as well as that of other religions, could be known. But as has been repeatedly stated throughout this study, extensively in chapter 1, the world of today is different. Today we live in an age of religious pluralism in which the opportunity for a new form of praxis, a "new originating and self-correcting foundation" for Christian belief, is present.

Thomas Merton, in lecture notes jotted down shortly before his death, recognized this clearly: "I am convinced that communication in depth, across the lines that have hitherto divided religious and monastic traditions, is now not only possible and desirable, but most important for the destinies of twentieth-century Man."[2] John Dunne expresses the same conviction more graphically: "The holy man of our time, it seems, is not a figure like Gotama or Jesus or Mohammed, a man who could found a world religion, but a figure like Gandhi, a man who passes over by sympathetic understanding from his own religion to other religions, and comes back again with new insight to his own. Passing over and coming back, it seems, is the spiritual adventure of our time."[3] Such a spiritual adventure is not only a new possibility but a new necessity; without the praxis of dialogue, Christians cannot adequately carry out the task of understanding what God has revealed in Jesus Christ.

More specifically, in the praxis of dialogue—I should say, *only* in this praxis—can the open theoretical question of Jesus' uniqueness be clarified.

The spiritual adventure of dialogue, an adventure that will take time and that Christians are only now really beginning, will provide the praxis that can verify *or* qualify the traditional Christian claim that in Jesus of Nazareth God has "surprised" us and offered the fullest expression of divine truth, the symbol that will confirm, complete, and correct all other religious symbols and thus unify humankind. Without dialogue, such a truth might be suspected and suggested, but it cannot be known.

The Nature and Presuppositions of Dialogue

Before we can go about the practice of dialogue, we must have some agreement as to what it means and what are its presuppositions. In recent years, much has been written on the subject.[4] I think this working description would meet with general agreement: dialogue is the exchange of experience and understanding between two or more partners with the intention that all partners grow in experience and understanding.

If one accepts this general description of dialogue, one would also have to accept certain presuppositions that are necessary if such an understanding of dialogue is actually to be carried out. We might call these presuppositions the "conditions for the very possibility of interreligious dialogue"; they are naturally implied by or contained in the given description. I shall outline three such general presuppositions. Each of them, in turn, contains further theological premises that are necessary if the general presuppositions are to be honestly affirmed and practiced. These theological premises are the attitudes—or perhaps "hypotheses"—that all the partners in the dialogue must recognize in their own theology before they can begin, much less carry out, a conversation with a believer of another faith. I shall add such theological premises to each of the basic presuppositions for dialogue. All of these presuppositions and premises have already been advanced and grounded in different sections of this study. What follows is but a summary.

1) *Dialogue must be based on personal religious experience and firm truth-claims*. The very nature of interreligious dialogue demands that it be conducted by *religious* persons, those who have had what can in general be termed religious experience, an encounter with the holy. If this is not so, one might be able to study other religions and learn much about their history and teachings; but one could not converse or dialogue with them. Without personal religious experience, there is no way of grasping what the dialogue is all about. Scholars of comparative religions are admitting today that even their study of religions cannot take place only on the intellectual level of doctrinal/ philosophical analysis or historical research. Such hard intellectual homework is, of course, vital for both study and dialogue; it dare not be minimized. Yet it must rest on or be completed by the deeper level of religious experience.[5]

Further, the partners, on the basis of their religious experience, must be able to take firm positions as to what they believe. These positions need to be affirmed not only as true for the individual but also as true, at least to some degree, for the other partners. According to the nature of truth (as was argued against Ernst Troeltsch and the relativists, in chap, 2),[6] whatever is really experienced to be true cannot be true "only for me." If it could, there would, again, be nothing about which to dialogue. The conversation would be nothing more than an exchange of information with no possibility of personally "growing in experience and understanding" from that exchange.

This general presupposition for dialogue must be based on a theological premise that, I think, is recognized by most of the world religions: to be religious and therefore to be able to participate in the dialogue, one must belong, in some form, to a particular religious tradition. Those who can experience and live in harmony with the divine individualistically, outside society and history, are rare souls, if there are any of them at all. As has previously been argued, the *universal* reality of the divine is encountered and made known through particular mediations. Ordinarily, it is only through the telescope of one's own particular religion that one catches a glimpse of the reality that constitutes the ground and goal of what John Hick has called the universe of faiths. Only through my religion and my savior can I come to know the God who, possibly, is beyond my religion.

Therefore those who, especially in the recent past, would urge a religious dialogue built on *epoché*—that is, a stepping outside one's religion and a suspension of one's own religious experience and beliefs—are removing the heart of religious dialogue.[7] It would be like calling a group of astronomers together to discuss their common findings with the preliminary requirement that they not use their telescopes. Partners in religious dialogue must bring *themselves* to that dialogue—most importantly, their *religious* selves.[8]

2) *Dialogue must be based on the recognition of the possible truth in all religions; the ability to recognize this truth must be grounded in the hypothesis of a common ground and goal for all religions.* Our description of the nature of dialogue also requires that the partners listen authentically to each other. This is more difficult than it sounds. Authentic listening requires a total openness to the possible truth of what the other person is pressing. In fact, it requires each partner to presume the truth of the others' positions: "I can never understand another's position as he does . . . unless I share his view; in a word, unless I judge it to be true."[9]

Authentic listening is therefore not possible if one partner presumes that the others have only an "incomplete" truth or that they can possess truth only insofar as it conforms with the norm of "my truth." Furthermore, authentic listening demands extreme caution in coming to the conclusion that one understands what the other means. Therefore a rule of thumb for dialogue: "No interpretation of any religion is valid if the followers of that religion do not recognize it as such."[10]

This presupposition for dialogue—namely, that one recognize and listen to the truth of the assertions of another religion—requires that the theology of all the partners take as a *hypothesis* that there is a common ground and goal for all religions.

Certainly a common goal is found in the concern of all religions to promote the unity of humanity and to offset the danger of world destruction. Yet that goal cannot really be worked toward or achieved unless the insights and efforts of the various religions are rooted in a deeper common ground—a ground that sustains their efforts toward world transformation and that allows them to be talking, in different ways, about *the same reality* when they talk to each other. Without this deeper sharing in something beyond them all, the religions do not have a basis on which to speak to each other and work together.

The deepest level of dialogue cannot be a matter of "apples and oranges." To try to formulate what this means, we can say that there must be the same ultimate reality, the same divine presence, the same fullness and emptiness— in Christian terms, the same God— animating all religions and providing the ultimate ground and goal of dialogue. If this is not so, then, ultimately, humanity is apples and oranges. Division, the fertilizer of discord and destruction, will have the final word.

There are dangers in proposing the hypothesis of a common ground and goal for all religions. John Cobb points them out when he warns that in recognizing "that every religion centers on one ultimate reality," one can all too easily impose one's own definition of that reality on another religion. To insist, for instance, that the Buddhist notion of emptiness is really what Christians mean by God can be as arrogant and offensive as calling Buddhists "anonymous Christians."[11]

These dangers must be taken seriously. That is why I propose the recognition of a common ground and goal as a *hypothesis* for interreligious dialogue. As a hypothesis, it must be used cautiously; partners in dialogue cannot verify it or truly grasp its contents outside the process of dialogue. This means that before engaging in dialogue, one will be hesitant to *define* the common ground as either God or emptiness; and in dialogue, one will be open to the necessity of expanding or reforming one's own notion of what the ultimate really is. If the recognition of a common ground and goal within all religions be used as a hypothesis, then the dangers of adopting such a recognition can be avoided while its fruits are gleaned.

On the basis of the Christian belief in a *universal divine revelation* within all religions, Christians not only can but should hypothesize about a common ground and goal for the history of religions. Previous chapters have shown how the recognition of such a universal revelation is proposed from various quarters inside and outside Christianity (by Troeltsch, Toynbee, Jung, mainline Protestants, Roman Catholics). Does not a universal revelation form the basis for the possibility of a common source and direction for all faiths? To recognize one ultimate reality revealing itself through all religions does not mean that all religions share a common essence, which would make them merely different models of the same product. The dangers in such a simplistic view were pointed out in chapter 3.[12]

How this universal revelation is perceived in the many religions, *how* the ultimate is experienced, unfolds in markedly and importantly different ways. (Perhaps these ways are so different that one might speak, with John Cobb, of different though always related ultimates.)[13] Also, the possibility of misunderstanding, of violating, the divine presence must be admitted. Still, *what* is being experienced can well be the same ineffable reality.

To propose the hypothesis of a common source based on a universal revelation within all religions is, in more simple yet more personal terms, to admit the possibility of a *universal faith* running through the astounding variety of the religious history of humankind: "Here, with the acknowledgment of a single faith expressed in contrasting and perhaps even contradictory beliefs, dialogue would start."[14]

Recognition of a universal faith, a common source and substance, to all world religions, sheds further light on why it is important that all partners in the dialogue begin with a deep experience of their own religion. If the same unspeakable reality, in splendid variety and color, is coming into view in the different religions, then the more I have perceived this reality in the color of my own tradition, the more are my eyes trained to sense it in other, even unexpected, colors. The more I have mastered one language, the more I am able to enter into the complexity and spirit of another. The more I have experienced love in my own life, the more I can sense its presence in the lives of others. To have penetrated, partially, into the divine mystery within my own religion prepares me to be surprised by the uncontainable richness of that mystery elsewhere.[15]

But if this recognition of a possible common source behind all religions is to have any practical payoff, if partners in dialogue are to be able to touch this source in each others' religions, a further theological premise seems necessary. The theology of all involved must also admit to the possibility and necessity of *entering into the religious experience of another tradition*. In fact, only when this is attempted does the conversation really get off the ground. I cannot begin the dialogue from my own religious experience and then look at the other religion only as a set of doctrines. Somehow, I must also be able to penetrate the faith-experience behind and within the doctrines.

Interreligious dialogue, in other words, must be *intra*religious dialogue; it must involve my entire religious being and "proceed from the depths of my religious attitude to these same depths in my partner."[16] A true encounter with another tradition cannot take place "from the outside"; I cannot expect truly to grasp another religion by standing outside it and looking in. Somehow, I must enter and be "inside" the other tradition by sharing its religious experience.[17]

Thomas Merton spoke about the need of all interreligious communication to originate from a *communion,* a communion that comes about when the partners "penetrate the ultimate ground of their beliefs," a communion that is rooted "in the silence of an ultimate experience." It will be " 'communion' beyond the level of words, a communion in authentic experience which is shared not only on a 'preverbal' level but also on a 'postverbal' level." Such a communion, such a sharing in the ground of each other's faith-experience, will illuminate all the words and, perhaps, will penetrate the evident verbal differences in doctrine, revealing the "great similarities and analogies in the realm of religious experience."[18]

Panikkar, in a personal confession, lays bare the content and difficulties of what is being suggested: "I 'left' as a Christian; I 'found' myself a Hindu; and I 'return' as a Buddhist, without having ceased to be a Christian. Granting my good faith, some people nevertheless doubt whether such an attitude is objectively tenable or even intelligible."[19]

Such a sharing in another faith, such "becoming a Hindu," is necessary for dialogue. But is it possible? With a growing number of contemporary practitioners of dialogue, I urge that it is. What in the past perhaps was only theoretically or potentially possible can today be realized. In an age in which the world is "shrinking" and cultures can know and touch each other as never before, persons can be aware as never before of what from the beginning was always real: their common humanity and the many manifestations of the one ultimate mystery. Today, as never before, "it may be that all the basic spiritual experiences of mankind can be re-enacted somehow in our individual lives."[20]

Today, what has been called "double belonging" is possible for religious persons, at least for some; they can belong to, share in, more than one religion.[21] Unless the theology of the partners in dialogue recognizes this, unless they make some attempt at it, their dialogue will perhaps be an informative conversation, but it cannot become a transformative encounter.

3) *Dialogue must be based on openness to the possibility of genuine change/conversion*. If our description of interreligious dialogue is going to work, all partners must be genuinely open to the possibility of accepting insights into divine truth that they previously either never realized or had rejected. So they must be ready to reform, change, perhaps even abandon, certain beliefs in their own religion. This in turn implies what has already frequently been stated: dialogue is not possible if any partners enter it with the claim that they possess the final, definitive, irreformable truth. Claims of finality set up a roadblock to any real growth in experience and understanding.

This recognition of the possibility of change opens the issue of conversion. Certainly, in taking clear positions, in holding to the "universal relevance" of any truth-claim, persons seek to convert their partners to their own understanding of truth. This is the nature of truth, what the experience of truth makes one want to do. Yet one must also be sincerely open to being converted to the partner's truth. The experience of truth, especially nowadays, also brings the recognition that the truth always overspills one's particular portion of it. The conversion intended by dialogue, therefore, is always a two-way street. In other words, the conversion that each partner seeks is not primarily conversion to one's own belief or religion, but conversion to God's truth, as it is made known in dialogue. What this implies for each religion, how much one will be converted to the other, can be known only in dialogue itself.

If openness to change/conversion is going to be both a theoretical and practical possibility, the partners in dialogue will have to recognize, as another theological premise, the *distinction between faith and beliefs*. Most religions would, it seems to me, accept this distinction. It has been analyzed in rich detail by a number of contemporary religious scholars.[22] Basically, they urge both an important distinction and an unbreakable bond between the experience of faith and its articulation in beliefs. Today, in the minds of many religious persons, the distinction between faith and beliefs is blurred, and faith is understood as a subscription to a set of propositional statements. Still, the distinction, as well as the bond, between the two can be stated simply and will resonate with what most religious persons feel "deep down."

The word "faith" indicates both the personal experience and the ineffable content behind all authentic religion. It is the intuitive contact with, the grasping and being grasped by, the ultimate; it generally takes shape in an act of trust by which we feel ourselves part of a larger reality, whether this reality is felt to be personal or impersonal. The act of faith has been described in many different ways; all such descriptions are, necessarily, poetic. Rahner presents faith as the handing over of oneself to ultimate mystery; Lonergan describes it as "falling in love unrestrictedly," without necessarily or clearly knowing with what one is in love; for Tillich, faith is the profoundly personal experience of "the courage to be," whereby we simply "accept the fact that we are accepted."[23] For the Buddhist, faith is the new awareness and new way of being that overwhelms one in enlightenment. Faith has a noetic content; it tells us something. But what it tells is ever more than what we can fully know or clearly state—the "known unknown."

Faith is different from beliefs, but it cannot exist without them. Thus, the unbreakable bond between faith and beliefs. Beliefs are the cultural, intellectual, emotional embodiment of faith—the effort to say, to share, to strengthen what has been experienced. Beliefs are necessary because we are embodied beings; faith, too, must be embodied. To claim that one can have faith without beliefs would be to claim that one can love without ever putting that love into words or deeds. Yet—and here is the point that is often missed by both "common believers" and hierarchs—no belief or set of beliefs can "say it all." Faith, in its experience and in its content, is transcendent, ineffable, and ever open. It cannot be fully or definitively expressed in beliefs; if it could, the object of faith would be fastened and made finite and thus the very nature and content of faith would be eviscerated. Although we need beliefs therefore, although we feel the need to be loyal to them, we must be ever ready to revise and move beyond them. Expressed more pointedly: if we are really willing to *die for* our faith, we must be ready to *die to* our beliefs.

This dynamic, in-flux relationship between faith and beliefs provides both the starting line and the goal of religious dialogue. The partners in dialogue start with a faith experience that, because it is recognized as a universal reality, allows for sharing and "double belonging." Acknowledging this distinction between faith and beliefs, one can more readily enter into and feel the deeper meaning, the intent, of otherwise strange beliefs.

Bernard Lonergan sees great promise in such a starting point:

> By distinguishing faith and belief we have secured a basis both for ecumenical encounter and for an encounter between all religions with a basis in religious experience. . . . Beliefs do differ, but behind this difference there is a deeper unity. For beliefs result from judgments of value, and the judgments of value relevant for religious belief come from faith, the eye of religious love, an eye that can discern God's self-disclosures.[24]

One discerns not only the other's beliefs, but also one's own. This discerning is a deepening that is always a questioning.

> If interreligious dialogue is to be real dialogue . . . it must begin with my questioning myself and the *relativity* of my beliefs (which does not mean their *relativism)*, accepting the challenge of a change, a conversion, and the risk of upsetting my traditional patterns.[25]

The questioning and the risk of change that are always involved in dialogue do not stem from an insecurity or lack of commitment to one's own beliefs; rather, they result from the experience of faith itself, an experience that by its very nature tells us that "our understanding is always partial," that "further insight is always possible."[26] The questioning faced by the person in dialogue, the risk of change and of conversion—even "of a conversion so thoroughgoing that the convictions and beliefs [one] has held hitherto may vanish or undergo a far-reaching change"[27]—is experienced not as a fearful ordeal but as an exciting adventure into the divine mystery ever beyond our comprehension.

How to Do It?—The Role of Imagination

What we have been talking about so far still pertains to the theory of dialogue—its nature, intent, presuppositions. The practical question has not yet been answered: how actually to do it? This how-to question comes up especially in view of the assertion that partners in dialogue must enter into each other's experience and share a universal faith. The exhortations to penetrate "the ultimate ground of beliefs" and enter into the "depths of the other's religious attitudes" seem sometimes to be wrapped in such a "cloud of unknowing'' as to make it difficult for the person in the trenches of dialogue to know just what it all means and how it can all be done.

One might feel surrounded in such a cloud, for example, when hearing Panikkar assert that dialogue should not proceed primarily out of *logos* (intellectual propositions) or *mythos* (symbol), but out of the inexpressible *pneuma* (spirit) that breathes where it will within all religions. Similar obscurity can result from Panikkar's claim that the mystical experience out of which dialogue should flow will be a center that is void: "No center can be found. That center has to be void, [as] in a *chakra;* all the hobs and spokes have to turn around an immobile point. Only a void center can coincide with all the movements of the circumference.''[28]

Certainly Panikkar's imagery contains an important concern. The content of any genuine religious experience will be mystical and in a sense "void"— beyond any word or symbol, any *logos* or *mythos*. Yet if the *pneuma* or spirit of personal faith and of shared religious experience is the foundation for authentic dialogue, there is a real danger in talking about this foundation so mystically that one cannot get at it and use it. How can we enter into this center? How can we look into and feel the depths of the faith of others through their eyes? Unless we are able to offer a more defined method or means of access to religious experience, our own and especially that of another, we shall be hamstringing dialogue in its first steps.

The religious imagination seems to be such a point of entry into the heart of another's personal faith. In recent years, there has been much talk among theologians and religious educators about the necessity of a fertile and active religious imagination. The light of revelation, it has been realized, is received along the conduit of imagination, so that the imagination plays a vital role in the origin and continued life of all religion. If our religious imaginations become dull and dry, our personal religious lives and our institutional religious practices cannot but lose their vital meaning.[29]

Crucial for the spirituality of the individual and of the community, the religious imagination can also be the springboard from which we can project ourselves into another person's religious world. The imagination, which bounds beyond the structures of the intellect and yet does not lose itself in the "void" clouds of the mystic, offers a tool for personally entering into the content of the stammering words and elusive symbols of another person's religious experience. That this tool has been effective is indicated by a number of veterans of dialogue who have achieved notable successes in entering other religious worlds; these veterans make use of the imagination, even though they may not describe their method in precisely these terms.

One of the most popular and proven methods of listening to and learning from another religion is John Dunne's process of *passing over*. Dunne offers a general description of what he sees as "the spiritual adventure of our time":

> Passing over is a shifting of standpoint, a going over to the standpoint of another culture, another way of life, another religion. It is followed

by an equal and opposite process we might call "coming back," coming back with new insight to one's own culture, one's own way of life, one's own religion.[30]

From his more detailed description of this technique—and from the way he actually carries it out in his explorations of other lives, cultures, and religions—it is clear that Dunne's whole effort pivots on the use of imagination. One enters into the feelings of other believers by allowing the symbols and stories of their religion to set off images in one's own imagination. One then runs with the images, following them wherever they might lead. From this exercise in imagination, one has something to think about—data for possibly new insights, new "theory." One then comes back to one's own religion with these new theories and tests them, perhaps appropriates them, in the praxis of one's own life:

> The technique of passing over is based on *the process of eliciting images* from one's feelings, attaining insights into the images, and then turning insight into a guide of life. What one does in passing over is to try to enter sympathetically into the feelings of another person, become receptive to the *images* which give expression to his feelings, attain insight into those images, and then come back enriched by this insight to an understanding of one's own life which can guide one into the future.[31]

Dunne points out that the possibility of such passing over to other religions rests on the recognition of the relativity of all beliefs or standpoints. No matter what I already know, there is always more to know. No standpoint can be the end point. This recognition of relativity, according to Dunne, does not throw open the doors to religious relativism. On the contrary, the very experience of passing over guards against the conclusion that, inasmuch as every belief is relative, one cannot really know anything and must be skeptical about all religious knowledge. Passing over proves that although one never attains a final answer, one can come to more answers, real answers. The imagination is persistently excited; new insights are born; the horizon of knowledge expands.

Interreligious dialogue, like all life, is seen not as a nervous pursuit of certainty but a freeing, exciting pursuit of understanding: "If I keep in mind the relativity of standpoints as I pass over from one standpoint to another, therefore, I effectively hold myself open toward mystery."[32]

Passing over, although it is mainly the work of the imagination, also requires some hard intellectual homework. Eliciting images from the symbols and teachings of another religion may not be as easy as it sounds. Usually some preparatory work must be done before the imagination can correctly grasp and be touched by very different religious imagery. This preparatory step requires the usual historical, socio-cultural, semantic study necessary for approaching any person or classic of another time or culture. If we are deal-

ing with a myth or doctrine, we will first have to try to grasp the basic contours of its meaning by situating and trying to understand it in its *text,* its
place within a broader literary work—and in its *context,* its historico-cultural
world. We then turn this general grasp of its vision and images over to our
imagination—and let our imagination take us where it will: possibly to new
insights, to new images of the world, ourselves, our God, to new modes of
being in the world, to surprisingly different perspectives on the symbols and
beliefs of our own tradition.

Panikkar, for all his occasional mystical evasiveness, clearly holds up
mythos as the main data for dialogue, data that can be grasped and felt only
through the imagination. The creative way his own imagination plays with
and learns from the symbols and images of other religions is evident throughout his works, especially in his monumental *The Vedic Experience —
Mantramanjari.*[33]

One of the most scholarly and convincing cases for the central role of the
imagination in attempting a conversation with a person or classic foreign to
us has recently been made by David Tracy in his *The Analogical Imagination.*[34] Especially his chapters on ''The Classic'' and ''Interpreting the Religious Classic'' might be read as a handbook of guidelines on the nature of
dialogue with other traditions and the pivotal role of the imagination in such
dialogue. For Tracy, the effort to interpret and converse with a classic, either
of our own tradition or of another, is essentially the same as the experience of
a genuine work of art. In it we must risk playing a ''game,'' a game in which
we have to abandon our intellectual control and our own self-consciousness
and let our feelings and imagination take over: ''In every game I enter the
world where I play so fully that finally the game plays me.''[35]

This game of conversing with a classic or another religion will lead us into
an ''intensification process'' by which we find ourselves, through our imaginations, participating in a reality that perhaps we did not realize existed. This
intensification process and the insights it delivers lead to a reflective ''dis-
tancing'' from the experience itself by which we realize, with even greater
clarity, the relativity and inadequacy of all religious beliefs; thereby we are
freed and motivated to return to the beliefs of our own religion in order to see
and interpret them anew.[36]

In his Epilogue, Tracy explicitly recognizes ''the possibilities of approaching the conversation among the religious traditions through the use of an
analogical imagination.''[37] The analogical imagination will always be a limited tool, for it recognizes that its images are analogies, telling us something
but never telling us everything; yet it will be *the* means by which we can gain
access to the experience and different worlds of other religions. In fact, our
religious imaginations will compel us to dialogue: ''if I have already lived
by an analogical imagination within my own religious and cultural heritages, I am much more likely to welcome the demand for further conversation.''[38]

DIALOGUE BASED ON A NEW MODEL OF TRUTH

I have described a view of dialogue, its nature, conditions, and methods, that, if followed, can serve as a Christian *praxis* that will throw new light on Christian *theory*—that is, on the understanding that Christianity has of itself. Yet for dialogue to attain its intended fruits, especially in order to recognize the possible truth in another religion and to grow in grasping the truth of one's own tradition, conversation must be anchored in what can be called a "new model" of truth. This new model views the general nature of truth and the criteria for discovering it quite differently from what has been the case for the West in general and for Christianity in particular. The new model offers a different kind of telescope with which to explore the universe of truth.

The Former Model

The old telescope with which philosophers have searched for truth has been in use since the time of ancient Greece. Most of the philosophical enterprise in the West has been pursued on the basis of certain first principles that, Aristotle claimed, the mind grasps intuitively, immediately, without any proof. The first of these is *the principle of contradiction*. In its logical form, it states that "of two propositions, one of which affirms something and the other denies the same thing, one must be true and the other false." In other words, a thing cannot be and not be at the same time, in the same way.[39] Truth, therefore, is essentially a matter of either-or. It is either this or not this; it cannot be both.

This means that truth—really the identity of all existing entities—was defined *through exclusion*. This is what the very word "de-finition" means: to determine the limits, to set off one thing from another. I am I because I am not you. This is what it is because it is not anything else. Defining truth through exclusion gives it an *absolute* quality. For something to be true, it has to be, in its category, the only, the absolute truth. One can know it is true by showing how it *excludes* all other alternatives—or, more recently, how it absorbs and includes all other alternatives.

If this has been the Western understanding of truth in general, it was especially so for religious truth. A religion is true because it either excludes or includes all others.

Such a model for truth has, no doubt, served the Western mind well. It has supported schools of precise logic, creative metaphysical systems, and a science and technology that have enriched humanity. Also, some theologians argue, only such absolute, either-or truth can truly satisfy the deepest needs of the human heart. According to Karl Rahner, human freedom, confronted with a multiplicity of possible truths and choices, is possessed of an inner dynamism toward a decision of final and definitive value. Humans want to make an absolute commitment; and that requires knowledge of an absolute, of a clearly defined, truth. We are led by a "searching memory," a prim-ordially innate desire, to discover and affirm one, final truth. We are searching for the definitive, historical presence of the Absolute. Rahner sum-marizes his argument and draws his conclusion: ". . . in the concrete it is only possible to live, religiously speaking, in absolute affirmation, and . . . among all religions only Christianity has the courage seriously to make an absolute claim."[40]

Today such a model of defining truth by exclusion, by making either-or, absolute judgments, has been opened to criticism from various fronts. This book has already expressed much of that criticism. Our contemporary his-torical consciousness has recognized the ongoing, pluralistic nature of truth. Persons have painfully experienced how final, absolute judgments break down in face of new discoveries from scientific research or of new insights from other cultures. On the scientific front, it has been especially the new physics, with its relativity theories and principle of uncertainty, that has re-minded moderns of the limitations, the relativity, of all knowledge. Science today, as has already been noted, no longer pursues "certain knowledge through causes," but "the most probable hypothesis."[41] Concerning the in-nate needs of the human heart, persons are realizing what John Dunne sug-gested above: if we look on life as a pursuit of certainty, if we hold back commitments until we have absolute, one-and-only truth, we are condemn-ing ourselves to a life of frustration. If, rather, we see life as a pursuit of increasing understanding, as a journey on an expanding horizon, we gain the peace and excitement of a common pilgrimage.

The model of absolute, either-or truth has been placed in question also because of the effects it has had on the Christian community. Roman Cathol-icism can serve as an example. Whatever may be the human need to posit a "definitive and absolute" act of freedom, it seems that one of the principal causes of the malaise, even rebellion, among Roman Catholics today has been the definitive and absolute statements they hear from their pastors and educators. Catholics indeed look to their pastors (priest, bishop, or pope) for firm, inspiring guidance in their faith lives, but they are turned away by direc-tives insisting that doctrine, or ethics, or liturgical practices, must be under-stood in "this and no other way." More and more Catholics have come to realize that such insistence on truth-through-exclusion easily atrophies per-sonal faith and reduces faith to doctrine, morality to legalism, ritual to super-stition. Catholics have also seen how such concern for absolute truth denigrates the value of other religious traditions.

So today, because of the continued insistence on absolutist claims by many church officials, there is a growing number of "anonymous Catholics" within Christian cultures—persons who personally identify with the truth and values of Catholicism but cannot number themselves among its mem-bers. As John Shea has pointed out, many Catholics, since the mid-1960s, have come to realize that the only way to affirm their religion, authentically and maturely, is to go through a perhaps painful process of *disenchant-*

ment—that is, to realize and accept that, although their Christian symbols, doctrines, moral codes, liturgical forms are true and reliable mediators of mystery, they are not mystery itself. "Mystery, the transcendent meaning of which Christians call God, remains Mystery. No finite reality, either the person of Jesus or the church, lays exclusive claim to it."[42] Catholics, like Christians in general, are realizing that for something to be true, it need not be absolute.

The New Model

In our world of historical consciousness, scientific relativity, and pluralism, human consciousness is being called to let go of its former securities and to affirm a new understanding of truth, including religious truth. For many Christians, this can well be a threat to the validity of their faith; therefore in proposing such a new model for truth, caution and pastoral sensitivity are necessary. In the new model, truth will no longer be identified by its ability to exclude or absorb others. Rather, what is true will reveal itself mainly by its ability to *relate* to other expressions of truth and to *grow* through these relationships—truth defined not by exclusion but by relation.

The new model reflects what our pluralistic world is discovering: no truth can stand alone; no truth can be totally unchangeable. Truth, by its very nature, needs other truth. If it cannot relate, its quality of truth must be open to question. Expressed more personally, I establish my identity, my uniqueness, by showing not how I am different from you but how I am part of you. Without you, I cannot be unique. Truth, without "other" truth, cannot be unique; it cannot exist. Truth, therefore, "proves itself" not by triumphing over all other truth but by testing its ability to interact with other truths—that is, to teach and be taught by them, to include and be included by them.

Such a model of relational truth undercuts what W.C. Smith calls "the big bang theory" of religion, which understands each religion to have originated in a kind of great seismic event, the force of which sends its shock waves through history. Each religion is all there, essentially, in its beginning; it preserves its identity by preserving faithfully the content, or the essence, of this first event.

The new model of religious truth is more consonant with a theory of the "continuous creation" of all religions. Each religion certainly originates in a powerful revelatory event or events. But the identity of each religion is not given in such events; rather, the identity of a religion develops through its ability, grounded in the originating event, to grow through relationships with other similar ongoing events. Religion, like all creation, is evolving, in constant flux; and the evolution takes place through ever new relationships.[43]

More importantly, the model of truth-through-relationship allows each religion to be unique; such uniqueness can even be called—if we are willing to redefine our terms—absolute. Each religion contains something that belongs to it alone, separately, distinctively, decisively: its particular grasp of divine truth. The truth it contains is uniquely important; it must not be lost. This uniqueness can be affirmed as absolute insofar as it calls for total personal commitment and claims universal relevance. But, in the new model of religious truth, a further quality of "absolute truth" is added; absoluteness is defined and established not by the ability of a religion to exclude or include others, but by its ability to relate to others, to speak to and listen to others in genuine dialogue. The more the truth of my religion opens me to others, the more I can affirm it as absolute. Admittedly, the new model of truth requires that we stretch traditional language and fill it with new meaning.

The relationship with others demanded by the new model of truth will not always be smooth and irenic. It will not shrink from challenging and correcting; it will not eschew telling partners where one thinks they are in error. Yet the emphasis in the new understanding of "absolute" relational truth will be on the *need* that each religion has of the other as they move, together, into a fuller understanding and living of the mystery that "is always present as nameless and indefinable, as something not at our disposal."[44] According to the new model for truth, a unique and absolute religion will not have to be founded on the absolutely certain, final, and unchangeable possession of divine truth; rather, it will be rooted in an authentic experience of the divine that gives one a secure place to stand and from which to carry on the frightening and fascinating journey, *with other religions,* into the inexhaustible fullness of divine truth.[45]

Implications for Religious Experience and Missionary Activity

The new model of relational truth provides the framework and incentive to strive toward what in chapter 1 was suggested as the direction of our new religious age: a unitive pluralism of religions.[46] The understanding of truth-as-relational confirms what has been hinted throughout this book: that, although there are real and important differences among the religions, differences that must be affirmed and confronted if dialogue is to bear fruit, these differences are, fundamentally, not contradictions but "dialogical tensions and creative polarities."[47] The world religions, in all their amazing differences, are more complementary than contradictory.

What this complementarity implies extends beyond the imagination of most Westerners. The import of the new model of relational truth goes beyond the recognition that the view of the Absolute enshrined in each religion is limited, beyond the admission that each religion is a map of the territory but not the territory itself. In asserting that the maps are *really* different and that these differences are necessary in order to know the territory, the new model of truth implies that all religious experience and all religious forms are, by their very nature, *dipolar.*

For Westerners, this dipolarity opens a new, perhaps perplexing, perspective on what it means to experience God and to talk about that experience. A proverb of the Duala people, in Cameroon, states it simply: "To make oneself understood, two sounds are needed."[48] "Two sounds" are needed, also, to penetrate and express what is contained in every encounter with the ultimate. The Taoist ontological principle of yin-yang tries to state this same dynamic "coincidence of opposites" that makes up all reality, especially ultimate reality.[49]

As we deepen our awareness of what we have encountered in our faith experience, as we search after the hidden face of God, we realize that every discovery, every insight, must be corrected or balanced by its opposite. As we discover the personality of God, we realize that God is beyond personality. As we penetrate into the immanence of divinity we become aware of its transcendence. As we awaken to the "already" of God's kingdom in this world, we become ever more conscious of its "not yet." Every belief, every doctrinal claim, must therefore be clarified and corrected by beliefs that, at first sight, claim the contrary. Realizing all this, we are disposed to look on different religions, with their "contrary" experiences and beliefs, not as adversaries but as potential partners.

The West is awakening to this necessary dipolarity of religious experience and identity. Paul Tillich saw it in his proposed "dipolar typology" for interpreting the entire history of religions.[50] W.C. Smith encapsulates it in his assertion that "in all ultimate matters, truth lies not in an either-or but in a both-and."[51] More recently, John A.T. Robinson argues the same in his elaborate case that "truth is two-eyed," and that Western Christianity, with its emphasis on the personality of God, the historicity of faith, the importance of the material world, has been peering into the mystery of God with only one eye.[52] John Cobb, in his proposal for a mutually transformative dialogue between Buddhism and Christianity, shows that the "profoundly different" experience of Buddhists and Christians are not contradictions but "mutually enriching contrasts."[53] Contained in this growing awareness is the insight that all religious experience and all religious language must be two-eyed, dipolar, a union of opposites. The stereotypical differences between the West and the East are in need of each other.

More concretely, the Christian doctrine of the trinity *needs* the Islamic insistence on divine oneness; the impersonal Emptiness of Buddhism needs the Christian experience of the divine Thou; the Christian teaching on the distinction between the ultimate and the finite needs the Hindu insight into the nonduality between Brahma and atman; the prophetic-praxis oriented content of the Judeo-Christian tradition needs the Eastern stress on personal contemplation and "acting without seeking the fruits of action." "These contrasting affirmations can no more cancel one another than the day cancels the night or vice versa. That is why the religions must witness to themselves, in their diversities, so that they may assume their full meaning."[54]

Many will feel, and vigorously object, that this new model of truth, especially with its implications about the dipolarity of religions, undermines the long and cherished Christian tradition of missionary activity.[55] Undoubtedly, the relational understanding of religious truth demands a thorough overhauling of the traditional model of missionary work—its primary goals, methods, and motivation.

Precisely through this overhauling—so runs the counterclaim—the missionary apostolate can be given a clarified integrity and renewed élan. This renewal of missionary purpose dovetails with what was outlined in chapter 7 as the new understanding of the nature and mission of the church. Christian theology, both Protestant and Catholic, admits that the church is not to be identified with God's kingdom. The kingdom, God's revealing-saving presence in the world, is much broader than the church and also operates through means other than the church. The primary mission of the church, therefore, is not the "salvation business" (making persons Christian so they can be saved), but the task of serving and promoting the kingdom of justice and love, by being sign and servant, wherever that kingdom may be forming.[56]

In order to promote the kingdom, Christians must witness to Christ. All peoples, all religions, must know of him in order to grasp the full content of God's presence in history. This need is part of the purpose and motivation for going forth to the ends of the earth. But in the new ecclesiology and in the new model for truth, one admits also that all peoples should know of Buddha, of Muhammad, of Krishna. This, too, is part of the goal and inspiration for missionary work: to be witnessed to, in order that Christians might deepen and expand their own grasp of God's presence and purpose in the world. Through this mutual witnessing, this mutual growth, the work of realizing the kingdom moves on.

In such an understanding of mission, conversion remains a valid, meaningful concern. But it is no longer the primary goal, the raison d'être, of missionary endeavors. If others are converted to the Christian community, the missioner will rejoice, as long as the conversion has taken place freely and as an integration of the person's personal-cultural identity. But if conversion to Christianity does not take place, the missionary's spirit need not wilt. The central purpose of mission is being realized as long as, through mutual witnessing, all are converted to a deeper grasp and following of God's truth. This is what insures the growth of the kingdom. So it can be said that the goal of missionary work is being achieved when announcing the gospel to all peoples makes the Christian a better Christian and the Buddhist a better Buddhist.[57]

This proposed revision of missionary work can inspire Christian missioners with a further, more specific goal, a goal that responds to an urgent need in contemporary Christianity. Today, as historical consciousness pervades the churches and sensitizes them to the value of other cultures and the limitations of their own, Christians are becoming aware that "catholic" (with a small *or* capital *C*) Christianity is not very catholic at all. The reality signified by the word "Christianity" is not a "catholic" religion—that is, a religion embodied in the whole world, in the different cultures of the nations. Rather, it is, for the most part, the message of the Jew, Jesus the Christ, as it has meaningfully and fruitfully taken shape within Western culture: "Christianity is, sociologically speaking, certainly one religion; it is the ancient paganism, or to be more precise, the complex Hebrew, Graeco, Latin, Celtic, Gothic, modern religion converted to Christ with more or less success.''[58] When this Western-Christian religion was planted in other cultures through missionary work, most of the seedlings came from Europe or North America; very little grafting onto local stock was allowed.

Contemporary missiologists and Christians in general are recognizing what has been called "the Latin captivity of the church."[59] The embodiment of Christianity predominantly in Western culture is called a captivity because such a limitation contradicts the very nature of the gospel; the good news is for "all nations" (Matt. 28:19), all cultures. Also, in the estimation of some, Christianity, in its Western captivity, is running dry; perhaps because it clings too tightly to its past cultural heritage of creed, code, and cult, perhaps because Western culture itself, in its superiority complex and isolation, is breaking down. Whatever the reason, traditional Western Christianity is losing its ability to speak to the hearts and minds of many contemporaries. Panikkar may overstate the case as he indicates a solution:

> The almost self-evident fact [is] that the Western-Christian tradition seems to be exhausted, I might almost say effete, when it tries to express the Christian message in a meaningful way for our times. Only by cross-fertilization and mutual fecundation may the present state of affairs be overcome; only by stepping over present cultural and philosophical boundaries can Christian life again become creative and dynamic.[60]

A central purpose of missionary work is to free the Church from its "Latin Captivity." Or expressed more positively, if missionary work is understood according to the new model of relational truth, if it is seen as the effort to cross-fertilize all religions and enable them to perceive and live the dipolar, indeed multipolar, character of divine truth, then the missions will be a powerful instrument in truly incarnating the message of Christ in other cultures.[61] Missionaries will be among the prime agents in bringing about what Karl Rahner, as mentioned in chapter 1, calls a third stage in the evolution of Christianity. The "Jewish Christian church" (the earliest form of Christianity), which gave birth to the "Western church" (Christianity through most of its history), will become a truly *world church*.[62] This will be an authentically *catholic* church, no longer only a European-American religion but an Indian, Chinese, Japanese religion. Such a world church is already taking shape in what the Christian churches of the southern hemisphere are demanding and doing.[63]

THE NEED FOR A GLOBAL THEOLOGY

What has been said so far about the nature and conditions of interreligious dialogue and about the new model of relational truth deposits some clear, urgent demands on the doorstep of the professional Christian scholar, the theologian. These demands are in no way peripheral to the general concern of this chapter that the praxis of dialogue yield abundant theoretical fruit for Christian consciousness and life. In fact, unless the theologians lend their hands to the task of dialoguing with others and of exploring the new horizons of relational truth, the fruits of the praxis of dialogue cannot be properly processed and passed on to the lifeblood of the Christian community, its leaders and its laity. But for theologians to make their contribution—this is the point I wish to stress in this section—they must understand "the theological enterprise" differently from how it has been understood in the past.

To state it succinctly, theologians today must recognize, theoretically and practically, that theology can no longer be "studied" or "done" from within only one religious tradition. Certainly theologians must be rooted in the faith of one religion; but if they stay only within this one religion, they will not be up to what their job requires of them. They will not be doing theology in the world, the pluralistic world of today; they will not be pursuing truth that includes rather than excludes others. Theologians, in other words, will not be assuming what in chapter 1 was presented as the growing obligation of all peoples in the shrinking, interdependent world of today: personal identity through world citizenship, or critical consciousness that is also "corporate" consciousness.[64] Today one cannot be in search of truth, one cannot really know oneself or one's own religion, unless one knows others.

There is an incipient, growing awareness among contemporary Christian theologians that a new method for a "global" or "world" theology is urgently needed.[65] Paul Tillich sensed this in 1965, in a lecture delivered shortly before his death; he expressed the desire to rewrite his *Systematic Theology* "oriented toward, and in dialogue with, the whole history of religions."[66] W.C. Smith, in 1961, prophesied:

> The time will soon be with us when a theologian who attempts to work out his position unaware that he does so as a member of a world society in which other theologians equally intelligent, equally devout, equally moral, are Hindus, Buddhists, Muslims and unaware that his readers are likely perhaps to be Buddhists or to have Muslim husbands or Hindu colleagues—such a theologian is as out of date as is one who attempts to construct an intellectual position unaware that Aristotle has thought about the world or that existentialists have raised new orientations, or unaware that the earth is a minor planet in a galaxy that is vast only by terrestrial standards. Philosophy and science have impinged so far on theological thought more effectively than has comparative religion, but this will not last.[67]

Ewert Cousins, writing in 1979, echoes a mounting consensus that Smith's prophecy must be fulfilled:

Christian systematic theology has remained engulfed within Western culture and its intellectual history. . . . To this day, Christian theology remains uninfluenced and unenriched by the majority of world religions. This is no longer possible. . . . The encounter of world religions calls for the forging of a Christian systematic theology that will encompass within its horizons the religious experience of mankind. . . . This is an unprecedented task. Never before in the history of Christianity has this challenge been raised.[68]

John Carmody uses more graphic imagery to announce the same need:

Today, athletes of the Christian spirit grow lazy, and probably untruthful, if they attend only a western gymnasium. I would hope that my tradition, Roman Catholicism, might send more of its scholars beyond the gymnasium, to the university of world religions. Studying there, they would be drawn, perhaps even forced, to a seriousness and honesty, a depth and simplicity, not now regular. This would be hard, but exciting.[69]

These calls for a global or interreligious theology recognize a kind of Teilhardian religious evolution that I described in chapter 1 and that undergirds this entire study. Christianity, along with all other world religions, is evolving out the *micro phase* of religious history in which the various traditions grew and consolidated in relative isolation from each other. The direction today is toward a *macro phase* of history in which each religion will be able to grow and understand itself only through interrelating with other religions.[70] To continue with a "micro theology" in a "macro world" is to run from what has traditionally been understood to be the nature of theology: faith seeking understanding, seeking this understanding by "correlating" faith/tradition with one's experience of the world as one finds it and as one tries to improve it.

As John Carmody admitted, such a new way of doing theology will be exciting, but hard. Something needs to be said about how one goes about it. First, the Christian theologian must know something about other religions. (Of course, the same must be said about the Buddhist or Hindu theologian; I am speaking here to Christians.) No theologians should consider their education complete without some courses on other faiths. Nor should theologians feel they are "keeping up with the literature" unless their reading includes something about other religions.

This is not to say that the Christian theologian must be a historian or a phenomenologist of religion. No one can be a specialist in all fields. The theological task, especially today, is carried out by individual experts in various "functional specialties."[71] Yet a global theology requires the theologian to know something about what the major world religions have experienced and said about the nature of the Ultimate, the phenomenon of religious experience, the constitution of the self, the problem with the human condition, the solution to this problem, the value of this world and of action in it. For the theologian, to draw Christian conclusions on any of these topics without some awareness of what other traditions have contributed would be as intellectually and ethically questionable as it would be for the anthropologist to arrive at conclusions concerning human nature from a study of only one culture.

It is not sufficient, however, for the theologian to know something, even a great deal, about other religions. Factual knowledge about the history, beliefs, practices of other faiths is necessary, but not enough. As already stated, one cannot really know another religion "from the outside," no matter how charitably or tolerantly one looks at it. This has been the blight and the embarrassment of much of what Christians have written about other religions; as is being admitted today, Christians have so often missed the point. One does not get a religious point by knowing it; one must also feel it.

What was laid out, therefore, as a condition for the possibility of dialogue applies even more stringently for the global theologian.

Theologians must "pass over" to the experience, to the mode of being in the world, that nurtures the creeds and codes and cults of other religions. Christian theologians must imaginatively participate in the faith of the other religions: "Faith can be theologized only from the inside."[72] "Christian theologians must reach out and enter into the very subjectivity of the other traditions in their distinct variety, and must bring this into the structure of a systematic theology."[73] The requirements of a global theology are indeed "hard." They call for more than expanded knowledge. More radically, "this new theology calls for *a new kind of theologian* with a new type of consciousness—a multi-dimensional, cross-cultural consciousness."[74]

A very practical aid in developing this new consciousness would be to attempt to pass over to other faiths together with persons who are living those faiths. It is much easier to pass over to the faith experience of a friend or colleague than to the experience behind a doctrine. Ideally, departments of theology or religious studies should number among their members Hindus or Muslims or Buddhists—persons with whom Christian theologians not only can test their insights but with whom they can share faith, with whom, perhaps, they can pray and meditate and celebrate.

With what Christian theologians have learned from their efforts to pass over to other faiths, they "pass back" to their own task. What might it all mean for Christian theology, for understanding the message of Jesus Christ? Clear, elaborated answers to this question, of course, cannot be given. A global theology is still taking its baby steps. I offer now only some methodological suggestions as to what a global approach might look like in what are recognized as the three major branches of Christian theology: fundamental, systematic, and practical theology.

Global Fundamental Theology

There is a good deal of scholarly controversy today over the function of *fundamental theology*. Most theologians, I think, would agree with this basic description of the fundamental theologian's role: to lay out the *praeambulum fidei,* the preamble of faith—the foundation, starting points, presuppositions for Christian faith as these are found within the human condition.[75] The *global* fundamental theologian recognizes that this task cannot be properly done within only one religious tradition or culture: "If fundamental theology is to have any relevance in our time of worldwide communication, it has to address itself to a radical cross-cultural problematic."[76]

A confrontation with others who think differently and who have different starting points can reveal, to the Christian fundamental theologian, the hidden, perhaps limited, presuppositions in Christian starting points:

> Only they [the others] can help me discover my presuppositions and the underlying principles of my science. In brief, *das Ungedachte,* the unthought, can be disclosed only by one who does not "think" like me, and who helps me discover the unthought magma out of which my thinking crystalizes.[77]

In becoming more clearly aware of my presuppositions, I can see their limitations. For instance, Christian fundamental theology asserts that human nature is radically historical and that in this historicity persons can experience an I-Thou relationship with divinity. Such presuppositions might have to be rethought when the Christian realizes that "two-thirds of the world's population today does not live in the myth of history; half the people on this earth (believers and nonbelievers) do not share the Abrahamic conception of God; one-third of mankind is unconscious of separated individuality."[78]

From this recognition of different presuppositions and the limitations of one's own, fundamental theologians of different religions can attempt to work out common, shared starting points—a fundamental theology for all the religions. It sounds like a utopian ideal, but this seems to be the opportunity offered by our new world. Again, I offer only a suggested "for instance" of what such a global fundamental theology might contain. Theologians and scholars from all the religions might be able to agree that a religion cannot be understood and, a fortiori, a theology cannot be undertaken, unless the theologian has, in Bernard Lonergan's terms, been personally *converted*— that is, has had some kind of religious or mystical experience.[79] Such an experience would be recognized as both real and beyond clear conception, as embracing a reality that might be symbolized in both personal and transpersonal images, as effecting in the individual both a destruction and transformation of the self. All religions, I suggest, could recognize such mystical experience (grace, enlightenment, *samadhi, satori*) as the bedrock for all religion and for all reflection on religion. It could serve as a common starting point to explore doctrine (systematics) and ethics (practical theology).

Global Systematic Theology

The function of *systematic theology* is to interpret the tradition in the changing contexts of history. A global perspective would certainly inspire and enrich this interpretive task. By passing over to other religious doctrines or myths that are analogous or homologous (serving similar existential functions) to Christian beliefs, the systematic theologian can return to Christian beliefs and see them differently, become aware of their limitations or unsuspected depths. Examples of such relatable beliefs: Brahma and Yahweh, karma and historicity, Isvara and Christ, avatar and incarnation, the anatman (no-self) and the new self, reincarnation and purgatory.

But the task and promise of a global systematic theology is richer and more challenging. Its hope is not simply to understand Christianity better by understanding other religions. It also aims at so understanding and presenting Christian beliefs that they will be not only internally intelligible and coherent, but also, at least to some degree, meaningful and true for persons of other faiths! In other words, a global systematic theology works from the persuasion that the cognitive claims of Christian tradition must somehow be true also for those of other religions if these claims are genuinely to be true for Christians! (Again, the same applies to the Hindu or Buddhist theologian.)

This sounds even more utopian than the suggestions made for fundamental theology. Yet Christian theologians today are urging just such a utopia. W. C. Smith, admitting that his vision is still an unrealized dream, writes:

> No statement about Christian faith is valid to which in principle a non-Christian could not agree. Theologians have not usually adopted such a principle. . . . Ideally the theology of comparative religion [i.e., global theology], when constructed, should be acceptable to, even cogent for, all humankind. We may dream, may we not?[80]

Raimundo Panikkar, speaking from the Hindu-Christian dialogue, proposes for theologians:

> [an] attitude of not wanting to hold to any position that cannot be submitted to the analysis and criticism of another. . . . This attitude constitutes the initial position for a Hindu-Christian theology. What we are looking for here is not a Christianization of Hinduism or a Hinduization of Christianity, but insofar as it is possible a genuinely valid theology for both Hindu and Christian.[81]

By pursuing the conviction that what is true for me must in some way also be true for others and that it is really possible to share religious truths, Chris-

tian systematic theologians can carry out their task of interpreting and drawing new meaning out of the gospel with new dynamism and possibilities. That
these possibilites may not be so difficult or distant is indicated by the new
systematic theologies of God and of Christ that are being proposed by the
Christian churches of Asia in dialogue with Hinduism and Buddhism.[82]

Global Practical Theology

As recent discussions on theological method are making clear, the role of
practical theology is not simply to apply what a religion holds true to particular ethical questions (theory leading to praxis), but also, more importantly, to
use those concrete questions as a means of understanding and revising what a
religion believes (praxis leading to theory). Ethics is not simply a "tail" for
systematic theology.[83]

If the relationship of theory to praxis be so understood, it is not difficult to
imagine what a *global* practical theology would look like. In fact, it is in the
arena of ethics or practical theology that the most encouraging steps toward
an interreligious theology have already been taken. Confronted by the evident evil and the "forced options" present in the worldwide realities of
hunger, exploitation, dwindling resources, and ecological devastation, representatives from different religions have already attempted to join forces in
order to build a better world.[84] On the basis of this common praxis of political
liberation and social transformation, the religions can continue to speak to
each other, challenge and criticize each other, as to how their beliefs, their
view of the world, of the ultimate and the self, can contribute to removing the
evil wrought on human beings and on the earth.

One of the clearest examples of how such a global practical theology can
contribute to a transformation of both the world and the religions themselves
is found in the interreligious discussions about the relationship between action and contemplation in socio-political liberation. Western Christian
theologians, having passed over to the East, see again (or for the first time)
that liberating action will be short-lived, in both personal dedication and in
results, unless it flows from the enlightenment of individuals and of the
community—from an experience (coming in many forms) of union with
something more that unites all humankind and animates all action. And the
East, having passed over to the "this-worldly" concerns of Christianity, is
realizing that unless enlightenment is nurtured by and leads to transformative
action in behalf of others and of the world, the content of enlightenment is
either faulty or false.

A global practical theology is telling Christian social prophets that they
must be more contemplative, and Eastern mystics that they must be more
prophetic. As John A.T. Robinson concluded from his passing over to Hinduism: "The mystical center needs the prophetic center if it is not to become
airborne. . . . But equally the prophetic center needs the mystical center if it is
not to become arrogant, narrow, and unlovely."[85]

WHAT WILL COME? IS JESUS UNIQUE?

What has been described in this chapter has only begun to be assimilated into the body of Christian consciousness and life: interreligious dialogue in which all partners genuinely share and grow, a model of relational truth and its implications for mission, a global theology. One cannot say where it will all lead. It is too early. The vision and hope of the coming "world church," however, does offer some forecast of what seems to be around the corner for Christianity.

If Christians, trusting God and respecting the faith of others, engage in a new encounter with other traditions, they can expect to witness a growth or evolution such as the church has not experienced since its first centuries. This growth will paradoxically both preserve the identity of Christianity and at the same time transform it. Such paradox is no mystery; we are acquainted with it in our own personal lives as well as in nature:

> Growth means continuity and development, but also implies transformation and revolution. Growth does not exclude mutation; on the contrary, there are moments, in the biological realm also, where only a real mutation can account for further life. . . . Growth does not exclude break and internal or external revolution. We know what the growth of an adolescent means only once the evolution is complete.[86]

Christianity, together with the other world religions, is on the edge of such mutation, transformation, even revolution. The changes to come in church practice and doctrine will follow the process of growth that has always characterized Christian life (all religious life) in the world—a process powerfully symbolized in "the paschal mystery" or in the "law of the cross": a process of life coming forth from death, of fuller life from the pain of letting go of the present to trust and move into the mysterious future.

Part of this transformative growth will be, I have suggested, a clarification of the theoretical question that has occupied us throughout this book: the uniqueness of Jesus Christ. In chapters 8 and 9, I tried to show that it is not necessary for Christians, in their own faith and in their conversation with other believers, to claim the "finality" or "normativity" of Jesus. But I also added that, though such a claim, at the present stage of interreligious encounter, need not and cannot be made, it may still be true. Perhaps something has happened in the historical event of Jesus Christ that surprisingly surpasses all other events. Perhaps God's historical revelation in Jesus—limited and relative like all history—contains and explains all other relative historical revelations. Perhaps what took place in the history of Jesus goes beyond anything found in the collective unconscious and myths of humankind.

This chapter has urged that to explore this list of possibilities, to try to answer the open question concerning the uniqueness of Jesus, the praxis of interreligious dialogue is necessary. Yet this is more easily said than done. To use dialogue as a means of trying to grasp the uniqueness of Jesus will involve some form of comparative evaluation. As Troeltsch warned (chap. 2, above), cross-cultural and interreligious judgments are difficult and fraught with possibilities of illusions and ideological impositions. Perhaps it is better not to intend such judgments but simply to let them happen as they will.

In any case, if authentic dialogue takes place between Christians and other believers, if genuine passing over to other religious experiences is carried out, the partners in dialogue can apply the general guidelines or criteria for determining the truth-value of any religion or religious figure. We touched on such criteria in our discussion of Jung in chapter 4.[87] They might be summarized as follows: 1) *Personally,* does the revelation of the religion or religious figure—the story, the myth, the message—move the human heart? Does it stir one's feelings, the depths of one's unconscious? 2) *Intellectually,* does the revelation also satisfy and expand the mind? Is it intellectually coherent? Does it broaden one's horizons of understanding? 3) *Practically,* does the message promote the psychological health of individuals, their sense of value, purpose, freedom? Especially, does it promote the welfare, the liberation, of all peoples, integrating individual persons and nations into a larger community?

In the actual praxis of dialogue, the application of these guidelines, by which the truth of any myth or religion can be evaluated, will perhaps help Christians, as well as Buddhists, Hindus, and Muslims, to come to see (and not be forced to see) what Christianity in the past has affirmed and what Christians today may deeply suspect. Perhaps Jesus the Nazarene will stand forth (without being imposed) as the unifying symbol, the universally fulfilling and normative expression, of what God intends for all history.

In carrying on the dialogue among religions, however, Christians must bear in mind that if such a recognition of Jesus does eventually result from the praxis of dialogue, it will be a "side effect" of the dialogue. Whether the question of Jesus' uniqueness is answered, whether Jesus does or does not prove to be final and normative, is not, really, the central issue or the primary purpose of dialogue. The task at hand, demanded of Christianity and all religions by both the religious and the socio-political world in which they live, is that the religions speak and listen to each other, that they grow with and from each other, that they combine efforts for the welfare, the salvation, of all humanity.

If this be done, then the central hopes and goals of all religions will come closer to being realized. Allah will be known and praised; Lord Krishna will act in the world; enlightenment will be furthered and deepened; God's kingdom will be understood and promoted.

Notes

Preface

1. Some of the most significant works from this period are: Hendrick Kraemer, *Religion and the Christian Faith* (Philadelphia: Westminster, 1956); E. L. Allen, *Christianity among the Religions* (Boston: Beacon, 1960); Paul Tillich, *Christianity and the Encounter of the World Religions* (New York: Columbia University Press, 1963); Heinz Robert Schlette, *Towards a Theology of Religions* (London: Burns and Oates, 1966); *Christian Revelation and World Religions,* Joseph Neuner, ed. (London: Burns and Oates, 1967); Charles Davis, *Christ and the World Religions* (New York: Herder and Herder, 1971); Robley Edward Whitson, *The Coming Convergence of World Religions* (Westminster, Md.: Newman, 1971).

2. *The Meaning of Other Faiths* (Philadelphia: Westminster, 1983).

3. Bühlmann, *God's Chosen Peoples* (Maryknoll, N.Y.: Orbis, 1983); Camps, *Partners in Dialogue: Christianity and Other World Religions* (Orbis, 1983); Cobb, *Beyond Dialogue: Toward a Mutual Transformation of Christianity and Buddhism* (Philadelphia: Fortress, 1982). Drummond's work is soon to be published by Orbis Books.

4. At the time of my writing, Drummond's work was available only in manuscript; for his understanding of Jesus' "consciously vicarious-redemptive role" for all religions, see his last chapter. For my interpretation of Cobb, see chap. 7, pp. 137–38, esp. note 84; chap. 9, pp. 189–92.

5. Race, *Christian and Religious Pluralism: Patterns in the Christian Theology of Religions* (Maryknoll, N.Y.: Orbis, 1983).

6. I do not believe, as Race seems to, that Jesus can be said *a priori* to be decisive for *only* one culture or that the final ground for religious truth is subjective appropriation. See my comments on Race's study, chap. 8, above, note 33; chap. 10, note 87.

Chapter 1

1. See Eric J. Sharpe, *Comparative Religion: A History* (New York: Scribner's, 1975), esp. chap. 1 and 2.

2. See Harvey Cox, *Turning East* (New York: Simon and Schuster, 1977).

3. *Christ and the World Religions* (New York: Herder and Herder, 1971), p. 25.

4. Wilfred Cantwell Smith, *The Faith of Other Men* (New York: Harper and Row, 1962), p. 11.

5. Wilfred Cantwell Smith, *Towards a World Theology* (Philadelphia: Westminster, 1981), p. 180.

6. Walbert Bühlmann, *The Coming of the Third Church* (Maryknoll, N.Y.: Orbis, 1977), p. 143. David Barrett, in his massive *World Christian Encyclopedia* (New

York: Oxford University Press, 1982), figures the Christian percentage of the world population in 1980 to be 32.8%. He holds that during the twentieth century "Christianity has surged ahead in the world's less developed countries from 83 million in 1900 to 643 million by 1980." Affirming that this surge will continue, Barrett predicts that by the year 2000 Christians will make up 32.3% of the world population (pp. 3–4). He does admit, however, to the "gradual numerical decline [of the number of Christians] when expressed as percentages of the world population" (p. 5).

7. Burlan A. Sizemore, Jr., "Christian Faith in a Pluralistic World," *Journal of Ecumenical Studies,* 13 (1976) 411.

8. Kenneth Scott Latourette, *Advance through Storm* (New York: Harper and Brothers, 1945), pp. 479–80.

9. Smith, *Faith of Other Men,* pp. 119–20.

10. Nicholas Lash, *Theology on Dover Beach* (New York: Paulist, 1979), p. 71.

11. Raimundo Panikkar, "The Myth of Pluralism: The Tower of Babel—A Meditation on Non-Violence," *Cross Currents,* 29 (1979) 217.

12. Ibid., p. 226.

13. Ibid., p. 201.

14. Alfred North Whitehead, *Process and Reality* (New York: Free Press, 1969). Charles Hartshorne, *The Divine Relativity* (New Haven: Yale University Press, 1948). Pierre Teilhard de Chardin, *The Phenomenon of Man* (New York: Harper and Row, 1961); idem, *The Future of Man* (New York: Harper and Row, 1969). Bernard Lonergan, *Insight* (New York: Longmans, 1957), pp. 115–39. *The Essential Aurobindo,* Robert A. McDermott, ed. (New York: Schocken, 1973).

15. David Bohm, *Wholeness and the Implicate Order* (London: Routledge and Kegan Paul, 1980).

16. See Fritjof Capra, *The Tao of Physics* (New York: Bantam, 1977).

17. See Robley Edward Whitson, *The Coming Convergence of World Religions* (Westminster, Md.: Newman, 1971), pp. 52–53.

18. For a concise summary of Kohlberg's theory of moral development, see Ronald Duska and Mariellen Whelan, *Moral Development: A Guide to Piaget and Kohlberg* (New York: Paulist, 1975), chap. 2.

19. Charles Davis, "Our New Religious Identity," *Studies in Religion,* 9 (1980) 36.

20. *Towards a World Theology,* p. 102; see also pp. 59–79.

21. Ibid., p. 79.

22. Lash, *Dover Beach,* p. 71.

23. Panikkar, "Myth of Pluralism," pp. 213, 203.

24. Charles Hartshorne, "Beyond Enlightened Self-Interest," in *Religious Experience and Process Theology,* Harry James Cargas and Bernard Lee, eds. (New York: Paulist, 1976), p. 315.

25. "New Religious Identity," p. 34.

26. See Richard Falk, "Satisfying Human Needs in a World of Sovereign States: Rhetoric, Reality, and Vision," in *World Faiths and the New World Order,* Joseph Gremillion and Joseph Ryan, eds. (Washington, D.C.: Interreligious Peace Colloquium, 1978), pp. 109–40.

27. Michael Foreman, *Dinosaurs and All that Rubbish* (New York: Crowell, 1972), pp. 26–27.

28. See Wilfred Cantwell Smith, "Divisiveness and Unity," in *Food/Energy and the Major Faiths,* Joseph Gremillion, ed. (Maryknoll, N.Y.: Orbis, 1978), pp. 71–85.

29. *Faith of Other Men,* p. 127; idem, "Divisiveness and Unity," p. 76.

30. See Ralph Wendell Burhoe, "The Source of Civilization in the Natural Selection of Coadapted Information in Genes and Cultures," *Zygon,* 11 (1976) 263-303; idem, "Religions' Role in Human Evolution: The Missing Link between Ape-Man's Selfish Genes and Civilized Altruism," *Zygon,* 14 (1979) 135-62; Donald T. Campbell, "On the Conflicts between Biological and Social Evolution and between Psychology and Moral Tradition," *Zygon,* 11 (1976) 167-208.

31. In the Foreword to *Food/Energy,* p. viii.

32. Wilfred Cantwell Smith, *Religious Diversity,* Willard G. Oxtoby, ed. (New York: Harper and Row, 1976), p. 113.

33. "Christianity and the Non-Christian Religions," in *Theological Investigations,* vol. 5 (Baltimore: Helicon, 1966), pp. 118, 116.

34. *Faith of Other Men,* pp. 132-33.

35. See chap. 10, below, pp. 223-29.

36. *The Intrareligious Dialogue* (New York: Paulist, 1978), p. 58.

37. *The Christian Debate: Light from the East* (London: Gollancz, 1964), p. 22.

38. Quoted in Smith, *Faith of Other Men,* pp. 120-21.

39. See note 6, above.

40. "Towards a Fundamental Theological Interpretation of Vatican II," *Theological Studies,* 40 (1979) 716-27.

Chapter 2

1. Paul H. Santmire, "Ernst Troeltsch: Modern Historical Thought and the Challenge to Individual Religions," in *Critical Issues in Modern Religion* (Englewood Cliffs, N.J.: Prentice-Hall, 1973), p. 367.

2. See Ernst Troeltsch, *Gesammelte Werke,* vol. 2 (Tübingen, 1913), pp. 731-33.

3. "The Place of Christianity among the World Religions," in *Christianity and Other Religions,* John Hick and Brian Hebblethwaite, eds. (Philadelphia: Fortress, 1980), p. 12.

4. In James Luther Adams, "Ernst Troeltsch as Analyst of Religion," *Journal for the Scientific Study of Religion,* 1 (1961/62) 109; see Santmire, "Ernst Troeltsch," p. 377.

5. *Gesammelte Werke,* vol. 2, p. 764.

6. See his "Die Selbständigkeit der Religion," *Zeitschrift für Theologie und Kirche,* 5 (1895) 367-436; also *Gesammelte Werke,* vol. 2, p. 340.

7. See his *Psychologie und Erkenntnistheorie* (Tübingen: 1905), pp. 26, 46; *Gesammelte Werke,* vol. 2, pp. 756, 494, 339.

8. See his *The Absoluteness of Christianity* (Richmond: John Knox, 1971), pp. 98-106.

9. See *Absoluteness,* pp. 86ff.; Adams, "Ernst Troeltsch," pp. 10-12.

10. *Absoluteness,* pp. 71, 85.

11. Ibid., pp. 131-63.

12. Ibid., pp. 94-106.

13. Ibid., pp. 92-93.

14. Ibid., p. 117; see also pp. 107-16.

15. Ibid., p. 114.

16. Ibid., pp. 114-15.

17. See the criticism of Michael Pye, "Ernst Troeltsch and the End of the Problem

about 'Other' Religions," in *Ernst Troeltsch and the Future of Theology,* John Powell Clayton, ed. (Cambridge University Press, 1976), pp. 172–95.

18. "Place of Christianity," p. 25.

19. Ibid., p. 23.

20. Ibid., p. 24.

21. Ibid., p. 30.

22. Ibid., pp. 30, 28.

23. *Absoluteness,* p. 123.

24. "Place of Christianity," p. 31.

25. Ibid.

26. Pp. 7–8.

27. Bernard Lonergan, "Dimensions of Meaning," in *Collection* (New York: Herder and Herder, 1967), p. 259.

28. Bernard Lonergan, "Belief: Today's Issue," in *Second Collection* (Philadelphia: Westminster, 1974), p. 92; idem, "The Transition from a Classicist World-View to Historical-Mindedness," ibid., pp. 1–10. See also Langdon Gilkey, *Reaping the Whirlwind* (New York: Seabury, 1976), pp. 188–208; David Tracy, *Blessed Rage for Order* (New York: Crossroad, 1975), pp. 3–21.

29. "Belief," pp. 94, 98.

30. See John S. Dunne, *The Way of All the Earth* (New York: Macmillan, 1972), pp. 42–49. See below, chap. 10, pp. 217–19.

31. See Vatican II, *Lumen Gentium,* chap. 7.

32. Pp. 12–13.

33. T. S. Eliot, *The Four Quartets,* Quartet 1/I.

34. See Russell F. Aldwinckle, *Jesus—A Savior or the Savior?* (Macon, Ga.: Mercer University Press, 1982); Oscar Cullmann, *Christ and Time* (London: SCM, 1951), part 2; Walter Kasper, *Jesus the Christ* (New York: Paulist, 1976), part 3.

35. Adams, "Ernst Troeltsch," p. 18.

36. Pp. 9–13.

37. See Tracy, *Blessed Rage,* pp. 121–22; idem, "The Particularity and Universality of Christian Revelation," in *Revelation and Experience (Concilium,* 113), Edward Schillebeeckx and Bas van Iersel, eds. (New York: Crossroad, 1979), pp. 106–16.

Chapter 3

1. *Change and Habit* (New York: Oxford University Press, 1966), p. 184.

2. See *A Study of History,* vol. 7 (New York: Oxford University Press, 1954).

3. See L. S. Betty, "The Radical Pluralism of Arnold Toynbee—Its Implications for Religion," *Journal of Ecumenical Studies,* 9 (1972) 820.

4. *An Historian's Approach to Religion* (New York: Oxford University Press, 1956), p. 262.

5. Ibid., p. 273; see also pp. 263, 272.

6. Ibid., pp. 274–77.

7. Ibid., p. 264.

8. "What Should Be the Christian Approach to the Contemporary Non-Christian Faiths?", in *Attitudes toward Other Religions,* Owen C. Thomas, ed. (London: SCM, 1969), p. 159.

9. *Historian's Approach,* pp. 269–70.

10. Ibid., pp. 271–72.

11. Ibid., p. 4.

12. "What Should Be," p. 154.

13. See chap. 1, above, p. 15.

14. "What Should Be," pp. 153–54.

15. Ibid., p. 160.

16. Ibid., p. 163.

17. Ibid., pp. 170–71.

18. *Change and Habit,* p. 192.

19. "What Should Be," pp. 165–66.

20. *Study of History,* vol. 7, p. 428.

21. Ibid., pp. 723ff.; see also Betty, "Radical Pluralism," pp. 825–27.

22. See the Supplementary Readings for this chapter, pp. 272–73.

23. See *The Meaning and End of Religion* (New York: New American Library, 1964), chap. 1–3, esp. pp. 16–17, 36–38, 43–44, 50.

24. Ibid., p. 141.

25. Ibid., chap. 6.

26. Ibid., pp. 141, 342, 170–71.

27. Ibid., p. 173.

28. See *Towards a World Theology* (Philadelphia: Westminster, 1981), chap. 6.

29. *Questions of Religious Truth* (New York: Scribner's, 1967), p. 68; see also p. 79.

30. See chap. 1, above, p. 11.

31. Below, pp. 223–29.

32. See *Meaning and End,* p. 335.

33. See *Towards a World Theology,* pp. 175–76.

34. Aldous Huxley, *The Perennial Philosophy* (New York: Harper and Brothers, 1945); Huston Smith, *Forgotten Truth: The Primordial Tradition* (New York: Harper and Row, 1976); idem, *Beyond the Post-Modern Mind* (New York: Crossroad, 1982), esp. pp. 31–57; Seyyed Hossein Nasr, *Knowledge and the Sacred* (New York: Crossroad, 1981).

35. Quoted in Huston Smith's Introduction to Frithjof Schuon, *The Transcendent Unity of Religions* (New York: Harper and Row, 1975), p. ix.

36. See *Transcendent Unity,* chap. 3, esp. pp. 35–36.

37. Ibid., pp. 37–38.

38. See Huston Smith's Introduction to *Transcendent Unity,* pp. xiii–xiv.

39. "Des stations de la Sagesse," *France-Asie* (Saigon, 1953, no. 85–86), pp. 507–13.

40. Smith's Introduction to *Transcendent Unity,* p.xxiv.

41. Ibid., p. xxviii.

42. Ibid., p. 44.

43. Ibid., p. 15.

44. Ibid., p. xxvi.

45. Ibid., p. xxxi.

46. Ibid., chap. 8, esp. pp. 118–29.

Chapter 4

1. C. G. Jung, *Memories, Dreams, Reflections,* Aniela Jaffe, ed. (New York: Vintage, 1965), p. 59.

2. For a concise treatment of Jung's views on God and religion, see James Heisig, "La Nozione di Dio secondo Carl Gustav Jung," *Humanitas,* 10 (1971) 777-802. Peter Homans shows how Jung's concepts of religion and of God are rooted in Jung's own early religious experience, which Homans describes as "personal-mystical-narcissistic" *(Jung in Context: Modernity and the Making of a Psychology* [University of Chicago Press, 1979], pp. 115-32).

3. See James Heisig, *Imago Dei: A Study of C. G. Jung's Psychology of Religion* (Lewisburg, Pa.: Bucknell University Press, 1979), pp. 110-22.

4. *The Varieties of Religious Experience* (New York: New American Library, 1958), p. 188.

5. See Victor White, *God and the Unconscious* (Chicago: Regnery, 1953), p. 37.

6. *Collected Works of Carl G. Jung,* vol. 12, *Psychology and Alchemy* (London: Routledge and Kegan Paul, 1953), p. 6.

7. See C. G. Jung, *Psychology and Religion* (New Haven: Yale University Press, 1938), p. 63.

8. *Collected Works,* vol. 8, p. 158.

9. "The Spiritual Problem of Modern Man," in *The Portable Jung,* Joseph Campbell, ed. (New York: Viking, 1971), p. 470.

10. Jolande Jacobi, *The Way of Individuation* (New York: Harcourt, Brace and World, 1967), p. 34.

11. *Collected Works,* vol. 12, pp. 10-11.

12. *The Myth of Meaning: Jung and the Expansion of Consciousness* (New York: Penguin, 1975), p. 54.

13. See Frank M. Bockus, "The Archetypal Self: Theological Values in Jung's Psychology," in *The Dialogue Between Theology and Psychology* (University of Chicago Press, 1968), pp. 237-42.

14. See Gebhard Frei, "On Analytical Psychology: The Method and Teaching of C. G. Jung," in White, *God and the Unconscious,* p. 247.

15. *Collected Works,* vol. 12, p. 10.

16. Ibid., p. 13.

17. Ibid., pp. 14, 17.

18. *Two Essays in Analytical Psychology* (London: Bailliere, 1928), p. 70.

19. In Raymond Hostie, *Religion and the Psychology of C. G. Jung* (New York: Sheed and Ward, 1957), p. 160.

20. *Psychology and Religion,* pp. 113-14.

21. Dated Sept. 22, 1944, quoted in Frei, "Analytical Psychology," p. 248.

22. See *Collected Works,* vol. 12, p. 9. Peter Homans shows that Jung's general assessment of religion and of the reality of God consists of a "double movement of reduction and retrieval of meaning." Jung did "reduce" God to psychological functions, but then he went on to show that these functions and their contents are essential to psychological health. See Homans, *Jung in Context,* pp. 182-92.

23. *Psychology and Religion: West and East (Collected Works,* vol. 11) (New York: Pantheon, 1958), p. 74.

24. See *Collected Works,* vol. 12, p. 17.

25. Quoted in Regina Bechtle, "C. G. Jung and Religion," in *Psyche and Spirit,* John J. Heaney, ed. (New York: Paulist, 1973), p. 69. See also Wallace B. Clift, *Jung and Christianity: The Challenge of Reconciliation* (New York: Crossroad, 1982), p. 43.

26. *Collected Works,* vol. 12, pp. 11-13; see also Clift, *Jung and Christianity,* pp. 113-28.

27. *Collected Works,* vol. 12, p. 18.

28. Ibid., p. 15.

29. Ibid., p. 19.

30. See Heisig, "La nozione," pp. 794–95. Heisig, drawing on Jung's personal correspondence, clarifies terminological coordinates that are not so clear in Jung's technical writings: for Jung the religious symbol of God corresponds to the unconscious, especially in its collective aspect; Christ symbolizes the self, the achieved unity between the individual and God; incarnation corresponds to individuation; and the Holy Spirit represents the fullness of incarnation, i.e., the possibility that all can share in it.

31. See *Psychology and Religion: West and East,* p. 157; see also pp. 273, 88; Bockus, "Archetypal Self," pp. 239–41.

32. *Collected Works,* vol. 12, p. 36.

33. Ibid., p. 17.

34. C. G. Jung, Foreword, in D. T. Suzuki, *An Introduction to Zen Buddhism* (New York: Grove, 1964), p. 26.

35. See *Modern Man in Search of a Soul* (London: Kegan Paul, Trench, Trubner, 1933), p. 221; "Differences between East and West," in *Portable Jung,* pp. 487–89.

36. "Spiritual Problem of Modern Man," in *Portable Jung,* p. 476.

37. "Differences between East and West," in *Portable Jung,* p. 490.

38. Foreword to *Introduction to Zen,* p. 22.

39. "Differences between East and West," p. 489.

40. *Modern Man in Search,* p. 221; see also "Differences between East and West," pp. 501–2.

41. See *Varieties of Religious Experience,* p. 61.

42. Ibid., pp. 61, 65, 71, 73.

43. Ibid., pp. 386, 388–89.

44. Ibid., p. 389.

45. Ibid.

46. Ibid., pp. 380–81.

47. Ibid., p. 368.

48. See Abraham Maslow, *Religions, Values, and Peak-Experiences* (New York: Viking, 1970), pp. 69–71.

49. See William Thompson, "A Spiritual Journey within the Psychoanalytic Tradition," *The Ecumenist,* 15 (1977) 49–53.

50. Ibid., pp. 51–52.

51. *Religions, Values, and Peak-Experiences,* pp. 59–68.

52. See *The Psychology of Science* (Chicago: Regnery, 1966), p. 124.

53. *Religions, Values, and Peak-Experiences,* p. 19.

54. Ibid., p. 20.

55. In his earlier writings Maslow looked upon the institutional forms of religion as inimical to this inner experience; later he was to admit that the need for community and therefore for formal religion was "itself a basic need" (ibid., p. xiii).

56. Ibid., p. 28.

57. Roberto Assagioli, "Transcendental Experiences and Meditation," in *Psyche and Spirit,* John J. Heaney, ed. (New York: Paulist, 1973), p. 127. See also Roberto Assagioli, *Psychosynthesis* (New York: Hobbs, Dorman, 1965); "Roberto Assagioli: The Rebirth of the Soul," an interview in *Intellectual Digest,* Aug. 1973, pp. 8–10.

58. *Man Becoming: God in Secular Experience* (New York: Herder and Herder, 1971), pp. 3–13.

59. See Martin Buber, *Eclipse of God* (New York: Harper and Row, 1952), pp. 104-20.

60. See Paul Knitter, "Thomas Merton's Eastern Remedy for Christianity's 'Anonynous Dualism'," *Cross Currents*, 31 (1982) 285-95.

61. Just what makes for "good psychology" is, admittedly, an extremely complex question. It ties into the question concerning what is the fulfillment and goal of human nature; and this leads to the broader and even more controverted epistemological problem: what is truth and how do we know it? An attempt at an answer would have to include elements of Lonergan's understanding of the structures of human consciousness, the Marxist additive concerning truth as praxis, and the process philosopher's model of truth and reality as constantly in process. Elements of such an attempted answer will be worked out in chap. 10, below.

62. See Eugene Bianchi, "Jungian Psychology and Religious Experience," *Anglican Theological Review*, 61 (1979) 187.

63. See Clift (note 25, above) pp. 105-7.

64. See David Tracy, *Blessed Rage for Order* (New York: Crossroad, 1975), pp. 204-23; Norman Perrin, *The New Testament: An Introduction* (New York: Harcourt Brace Jovanovich, 1974), pp. 21-34; John Shea, *Stories of God: An Unauthorized Biography* (Chicago: Thomas More, 1978), pp. 66-74.

65. See Karl Rahner, "Salvation," in *Sacramentum Mundi*, vol. 5, pp. 429-32.

Chapter 5

1. Martin Marty, *A Nation of Behavers* (University of Chicago Press, 1976), p. 80.

2. Martin Marty, "Tensions within Contemporary Evangelicalism: A Critical Appraisal," in *The Evangelicals*, David F. Wells and John D. Woodbridge, eds. (Nashville: Abingdon, 1975), p. 172.

3. In fact, Martin Marty suggests as a "first clue" for defining the Evangelicals: "the Evangelicals are people who find evangelist Billy Graham or his viewpoints acceptable" (*Nation of Behavers*, p. 83).

4. See Richard Quebedeaux, in his Introduction to Arthur Carl Piepkorn, *Profiles in Belief*, vol. 4 (New York: Harper and Row, 1979), p. xvi. See also James Barr, *Fundamentalism* (Philadelphia: Westminster, 1978), p. 1.

5. See George Ladd, *The New Testament and Criticism* (Grand Rapids: Eerdmans, 1967); Richard J. Coleman, *Issues of Theological Warfare: Evangelicals and Liberals* (Eerdmans, 1980), pp. 10-11.

6. The growth of the New Evangelicals, esp. their move to the political left, has been recorded by Richard Quebedeaux in *The Young Evangelicals* (New York: Harper and Row, 1974) and *The Worldly Evangelicals* (New York: Harper and Row, 1978).

7. New York, Oxford University Press, 1982, p. 71.

8. Ibid. Also Deane William Ferm, *Contemporary American Theologies: A Critical Survey* (New York: Seabury, 1981), pp. 99-100.

9. Thomas Clancy, "Fundamental Facts about Evangelicals," *America*, May 31, 1980, pp. 454-55.

10. *Christianity Today*, Dec. 21, 1979.

11. Ibid., Jan. 17, 1978.

12. Quebedeaux, *Worldly Evangelicals*, p. xi; Clancy, "Fundamental Facts," p. 454.

13. *Christianity Today*, 14 (1970) 843.

14. For all these citations, see the full text of the Frankfurt Declaration in *Christianity Today*, 14 (1970) 844–46.

15. Harold Lindsell, "Missionary Imperative: A Conservative Evangelical Exposition," in *Protestant Crosscurrents in Mission: The Ecumenical-Conservative Encounter*, Norman A. Horner, ed. (Nashville: Abingdon, 1968), p. 57.

16. Donald G. Bloesch, *Essentials of Evangelical Theology* (San Francisco: Harper and Row, 1968), vol. 1, pp. 245–46. See also Henricus Berkhof, *Christian Faith* (Grand Rapids: Eerdmans, 1979), pp. 532–33. Quebedeaux notes among Ecumenical Evangelicals a "subtle shift in the direction of belief in universal salvation." See "The Evangelicals: New Trends and New Tensions," *Christianity and Crisis*, Sept. 30, 1976, p. 202. See also Bernard Ramm, *After Fundamentalism: The Future of Evangelical Theology* (New York: Harper and Row, 1983), pp. 165–72.

17. Rodger C. Bassham, *Mission Theology: 1948–1975. Years of Worldwide Creative Tension Ecumenical, Evangelical, and Roman Catholic* (Pasadena: William Carey Library, 1979), p. 209.

18. Quebedeaux, *Worldly Evengelicals*, p. 59.

19. "Lausanne Congress, 1974," in *Mission Trends No. 2: Evangelization*, Gerald A. Anderson and Thomas F. Stransky, eds. (New York: Paulist, 1975), p. 241. Pages 239–48 contain the 15-point "Covenant" that summarizes the conclusions of the congress.

20. Ibid., p. 242.

21. "Dialogue, Encounter, Even Confrontation," in *Mission Trends No. 5: Faith Meets Faith*, Anderson and Stransky, eds. (New York: Paulist, 1981), pp. 168, 162; see also David J. Hesselgrave, "Evangelicals and Interreligious Dialogue," ibid., p. 126.

22. Barth has been staunchly attacked by Carl Henry, Francis Schaeffer, and especially Cornelius Van Til. Barth is especially criticized for his use of the historico-critical method and for his devaluing of scripture as the word of God by his concept of revelation as personal experience. See Gregory Bolich, *Karl Barth and Evangelicalism* (Downers Grove, Ill.: InterVarsity Press, 1980).

23. Ferm, *Contemporary American Theologies*, p. 106; Quebedeaux, *Worldly Evangelicals*, p. 100.

24. Coleman, (note 5, above), pp. 4–5. See also Waldron Scott, *Karl Barth's Theology of Mission* (Downers Grove, Ill.: InterVarsity Press, 1978). For the most recent proposal for a revision of Evangelical theology on the basis of Barth's theology, see Bernard Ramm, *After Fundamentalism* (note 16, above).

25. See David Tracy, *Blessed Rage for Order* (New York: Crossroad, 1975), pp. 27–31; Wilhelm Pauk, *Karl Barth: Prophet of a New Christianity?* (New York: Harper, 1931).

26. George W. Hunt, "Karl Barth—Ten Years Later," *America*, Nov. 4, 1978, p. 302.

27. Engl. trans. by G.T. Thomason and Harold Knight (Edinburgh: Clark, 1956), pp. 280–361. German original published in 1938.

28. Although Barth, in later volumes of *Church Dogmatics*, spoke of "other words and other lights outside the walls of the church" and came to view creation as "the external ground of the covenant," he continued to affirm that such positive content in other religions can be known and assume its value *only* in and after the revelation of Christ. Those who argue that Barth later reversed the negative verdict of paragraph 17 on the religions seem to ignore this. See Paul F. Knitter, *Towards a*

Protestant Theology of Religions (Marburg [W. Germany]: N.G. Elwert, 1974), pp. 32–36. See also Alan Race, *Christians and Religious Pluralism: Patterns in the Christian Theology of Religions* (Maryknoll, N.Y.: Orbis, 1983), pp. 14–16.

29. See Hendrick Kraemer, *The Christian Message in a Non-Christian World* (London, 1938); idem, *Religion and the Christian Faith* (London: Lutterworth, 1956). See also Race, *Religious Pluralism*, pp. 17–25.

30. *Church Dogmatics*, vol. 1/2, p. 301.

31. Ibid., p. 301–2.

32. Ibid., p. 306.

33. Ibid., p. 307.

34. Ibid.

35. Ibid., p. 300.

36. Ibid., pp. 299–300.

37. Ibid., pp. 295–96; 303. See also pp. 280–94.

38. Ibid., p. 327.

39. Ibid.

40. Ibid. See also pp. 352–54.

41. Ibid., p. 325.

42. Ibid., pp. 325–26.

43. Ibid., pp. 326–27.

44. Ibid., p. 338.

45. Ibid., p. 297.

46. Ibid., p. 348.

47. Ibid., p. 356; see also pp. 344, 285.

48. Ibid., p. 388. Once it is clearly recognized that the truth of Christianity does not reside in its content or activity as a religion, Barth admits that the grace of God does bring about certain secondary changes in Christianity. These changes do make it different from other religions. In Christianity "God is really known and worshiped, there is a genuine activity of man as reconciled with God. . . . And it alone has the commission and the authority to be a missionary religion. . . . It is formed and shaped by it [revelation]. It becomes the historical manifestation and means of its revelation" (ibid., pp. 344, 357–58). And yet Barth continually insists that such positive, empirical characteristics in Christianity are only "the site and symptoms" of a reality that is constantly beyond it and never identified with it (ibid., p. 339). They in no way can be "evidence" for the truth of Christianity or for the truth of any other religion.

49. Ibid., p. 343; see also pp. 340–42.

50. Ibid., p. 339.

51. See the Lausanne statement in *Mission Trends No. 2*, p. 241. Also, Kenneth S. Kantzer, "Unity and Diversity in Evangelical Faith," in *The Evangelicals: What They Believe, Who They Are, Where They Are Changing*, David F. Wells and John D. Woodbridge, eds. (Nashville: Abingdon, 1975), pp. 48–52. Avery Dulles agrees that according to the Evangelical model, one cannot really speak about revelation in other religions: "Conservative Evangelicalism, while it makes use of the distinction between general and special revelation, tends to look on extrabiblical religion not as revealed but as a 'depraved answer to the revelation of God' " (*Models of Revelation* [New York: Doubleday, 1983], p. 178). Dulles refers to G.C. Berkouwer, "General and Special Divine Revelation," in *Revelation and the Bible*, C.F.H. Henry, ed. (Grand Rapids: Baker Book House, 1958), p. 27.

52. *Essentials of Evangelical Theology*, vol. 2 (New York: Harper and Row, 1979), p. 287; see also vol. 1 (1978), pp. 88–119.

53. Tracy, *Blessed Rage*, p. 28.

54. Reinhold Niebuhr interprets the ethics of Jesus as such an "impossible possibility"—i.e., as a relevant but impossible ethical ideal (*An Interpretation of Christian Ethics* [New York: Seabury, 1979]).

55. Hunt (note 26, above), p. 303.

56. See Alfred C. Krass, "Accounting for the Hope That Is in Me," in *Christian Faith in a Religiously Plural World*, D.G. Dawe and J.B. Carman, eds. (Maryknoll, N.Y.: Orbis, 1978), pp. 155-67, esp. p. 165.

57. *The Analogical Imagination: Christian Theology and the Culture of Pluralism* (New York: Crossroad, 1981), pp. 376-89.

58. Gadamer, *Wahrheit und Methode: Grundzüge einer philosophischen Hermeneutik* (Tübingen: Mohr, 1965), pp. 289-90; Tracy, *Blessed Rage*, pp. 73-79.

59. The theological method briefly described here is what David Tracy calls "a revisionist method of theology." The individual critiques and the final proposals of the present study are grounded in this understanding of the nature and task of theology. See Tracy, *Blessed Rage*, pp. 43-63.

60. See chap. 10, below, pp. 223-29.

61. *Christ in a Changing World: Toward an Ethical Christology* (New York: Crossroad, 1981), pp. 66, 73; the *"sic"* is Driver's.

62. See Paul Althaus, "Sola fide numquam sola—Glaube und Werk in ihrer Bedeutung für das Heil bei M. Luther," *Una Sancta*, 16 (1961) 227-35; Knitter, *Towards a Protestant Theology*, pp. 224-25.

63. See V. Pfnür, *Einig in der Rechtfertigungslehre?* (Weisbaden, 1970), pp. 385-99; Hans Küng, *Rechtfertigung: Die Lehre Karl Barths und eine katholische Besinnung* (Paderborn, 1957), pp. 267-76.

64. See Paul Knitter, "Christianity as Religion: True and Absolute? A Roman Catholic Perspective," in *What is Religion? An Inquiry for Christian Theology* (*Concilium*, 136), Mircea Eliade and David Tracy, eds. (New York: Seabury, 1980), pp. 12-13.

65. Pp. 186-90.

66. *Church Dogmatics*, vol. 1/2, p. 338.

67. See note 28, above.

Chapter 6

1. Althaus, professor of systematic theology at the University of Erlangen (1925-1956), was rooted deeply in the Lutheran tradition. Brunner, who taught systematic and practical theology at the University of Zurich (1924-1953), was a member of the Swiss Reformed Church. Personal friend of Barth, he was one of the co-founders with Barth of neo-orthodox or "dialectical" theology but broke with him in 1934 on the issue of general revelation. Both Althaus and Brunner represent a "middle way" between the extremes of liberal theology and neoorthodoxy.

2. Paul Althaus, *Die christliche Wahrheit* (Gütersloh: Gütersloher Verlagshaus, 7th ed., 1966), pp. 37-94; Emil Brunner, "Revelation and Religion," in *Attitudes toward Other Religions*, Owen C. Thomas, ed. (London: SCM Press, 1969), p. 120-22 (first published in *Revelation and Reason: The Christian Doctrine of Faith and Knowledge* [Philadelphia: Westminster, 1948]); Paul Tillich, *Systematic Theology*, vol. 1 (Digswell Place: James Nisbet, 1968), pp. 53-60; combined vols. 1-3, pp. 118-31.

3. Brunner, "Revelation," pp. 121–22.

4. See Althaus, *Christliche Wahrheit*, p. 44; idem, *Grundriss der Dogmatik,* vol. 1 (Gütersloh: Bertelsmann, 1947), p.124; Brunner, "Revelation," p. 121.

5. *Christliche Wahrheit*, pp. 61–62.

6. Ibid., pp. 61–96; *Grundriss der Dogmatik*, vol. 1, pp. 19–25.

7. Althaus, *Christliche Wahrheit*, p. 53; Brunner, "Revelation," pp. 117–19.

8. See *Christianity and the Encounter of World Religions* (New York: Columbia University Press, 1963), p. 4; *Systematic Theology*, vol. 1, pp. 153–55.

9. See Peter Beyerhaus, "Zur Theologie der Religionen im Protestantismus," *Kerygma und Dogma*, 15 (1969) 98–99.

10. "Die Religionen und das Christentum," in *Der christliche Glaube und die Religionen*, C.H. Ratschow, ed. (Berlin: Töpelmann, 1967), pp. 89, 94–95; idem, "Die Möglichkeit des Dialogs angesichts des Anspruchs der Religionen, *Evangelischer Missions-Jahrbuch*, 1970, p. 116.

11. See *Revelation as History*, Wolfhart Pannenberg, ed. (London: Macmillan, 1968), pp. 3–21; 125–58.

12. *Basic Questions in Theology*, vol. 2 (Philadelphia: Fortress, 1971), p. 112.

13. Ibid., pp. 88, 95–96; see also *Theology and the Philosophy of Religion* (London: Darton, Longman and Todd, 1976), pp. 310–26.

14. Every *Erkenntnis* of God in Christ is always a *Wiedererkenntnis* (*Christliche Wahrheit*, pp. 61–62; *Um die Wahrheit des Evangeliums* [Stuttgart: Calwer, 1962], p. 139).

15. See "The Nature of a Theological Statement," *Zygon* (1972) 6–19; *Theology and the Philosophy*, pp. 316–26, 358–71. Tillich makes basically the same argument in "Missions and World History," in *The Theology of the Christian Mission*, Gerald H. Anderson, ed. (Nashville: Abingdon, 1961), pp. 281–89.

16. See Althaus, *Grundriss*, vol. 1, p. 19; idem, *Christliche Wahrheit*, p. 62.

17. See *The Idea of God and Human Freedom* (Philadelphia: Fortress, 1973), pp. 111–15.

18. Ratschow, "Möglichkeit," p. 113; idem, "Religionen," pp. 118–20, 123–24; Althaus, *Christliche Wahrheit*, pp. 140, 408.

19. Althaus, *Grundriss*, vol. 2, p. 34.

20. Althaus, *Christliche Wahrheit*, pp. 137–39; idem, "Mission und Religionsgeschichte," *Zietschrift für systematische Theologie*, 5 (1927–28) 181.

21. *Basic Questions*, pp. 69–70.

22. "Die Inflation des Begriffs der Offenbarung in der gegenwärtigen Theologie," *Zeitschrift für systematische Theologie*, 18 (1941) 143.

23. "Mission und Religionsgeschichte," pp. 192–94; *Grundriss*, vol. 1, pp. 26–29; *Christliche Wahrheit*, pp. 93, 141–43.

24. Brunner, "Revelation," pp. 122–25.

25. See Ratschow, "Religionen," pp. 125–26, 128; *Der angefochtene Glaube* (Gütersloh, 1957), pp. 260–61, 286–87.

26. See Brunner, "Revelations," pp. 122–23, 128; Althaus, *Christliche Wahrheit*, pp. 388, 136–37.

27. *Systematic Theology*, vol. 1, pp. 160–62; vol. 2, pp. 191–94; vol. 3, pp. 148–50; Paul Tillich, *The Future of Religions*, Jerald C. Brauer, ed. (New York: Harper and Row, 1966) p. 181.

28. See *What is Religion?* (New York: Harper and Row, 1969), pp. 88–97; *Systematic Theology*, vol. 2, pp. 91–111, 136–59, 191–208.

29. Braaten, *The Future of God* (New York: Harper and Row, 1969), pp. 42–46, 58–66.

30. Even Israel, according to Pannenberg, is caught in this "finitization" of God: although the Jews experienced God as a God of history, "Israel continued to seek the fundamental revelation of its God in the events of the past, in the giving of the law at Sinai, and not in the future of God's reign" (*Basic Questions*, pp. 113, 107–10).

31. *Basic Questions*, p. 115; see also pp. 225–26, 232–33; "The Revelation of God in Jesus," in *Theology as History*, J.M.Robinson and J.B. Cobb, Jr., eds. (New York: Harper and Row, 1967), pp. 109–10, 118.

32. Althaus, *Christliche Wahrheit*, pp. 596–607, 277–89, 462–78. Emil Brunner, *The Christian Doctrine of Creation and Redemption* (Philadelphia: Westminster, 1952), pp. 98–107, 281–97. It must be pointed out that Althaus, occasionally, speaks about a universal activity of Christ outside Christianity, which he then strains to keep tied to the historical fact of Jesus: see *Christliche Wahrheit*, pp. 102–7.

33. "The Uniqueness and Universality of Jesus Christ," in *Faith Meets Faith: Mission Trends No. 5*, Gerald H. Anderson and Thomas F. Stransky, eds. (New York: Paulist, 1981), pp. 74–75.

34. Ibid., p. 79.

35. Ibid., p. 80.

36. *The Flaming Center* (Philadelphia: Fortress, 1977), p. 108.

37. Ibid., p. 117.

38. Ibid.

39. Ibid., p. 118.

40. See Russell Aldwinckle, *Jesus—A Savior or the Savior? Religious Pluralism in Christian Perspective* (Macon, Ga.: Mercer University Press, 1982), pp. 180–81.

41. Althaus, *Christliche Wahrheit*, pp. 599–601; idem, *Gundriss der Dogmatik*, vol. 1, pp. 28, 41–48; idem, "Das Kreuz Christi," *Zeitschrift für systematische Theologie*, 1 (1923) 122–23.

42. Brunner, "Revelation," p. 131.

43. Althaus, *Christliche Wahrheit*, pp. 145–46; Brunner, "Revelation," pp. 130–31.

44. Brunner, *Christusbotschaft im Kampf mit den Religionen* (Stuttgart, 1931), p.15.

45. *Systematic Theology*, vol. 1, p. 159.

46. "Christianity and the Encounter," pp. 81–82; *Systematic Theology*, vol. 1, p. 150.

47. It must be pointed out that in the last lecture before his death Tillich admitted that the attainment of the "religion of the Concrete Spirit . . . can happen . . . here and there . . ." within other religions (*The Future of Religions*, p. 81–89). From this faint suggestion, expressed just a few days before he died, one cannot conclude that Tillich recognized the possibility that there could be "other Christs" in other religions. In his analysis of Tillich, Alan Race implies such a conclusion. He holds that Tillich would not want to "prejudge" the history of religions in light of Jesus Christ as the symbol of the "Concrete Spirit." Race maintains that Tillich "leaves open the possibility that there may be a central event in the history of religions which has universal significance even for a historically conscious world." That is a misleading understatement! For Tillich, the central event did take place in Jesus the Christ. I suggest that Race is misreading Tillich (or not reading him enough) when he ranks Tillich alongside John Hick and Wilfred Cantwell Smith in what Race calls the school

of "pluralism" (which is equivalent to what, in chap. 8, I call "the theocentric model").

48. *Basic Questions*, p. 114; see also *Jesus—God and Man* (London: SCM Press, 1968), pp. 334–37.

49. *Jesus—God and Man*, pp. 130–31; see also p. 36.

50. *Flaming Center*, pp. 96–98.

51. Braaten, "Uniqueness," p. 78.

52. Tillich, *Systematic Theology*, vol. 1, p. 154.

53. *Flaming Center*, p. 109.

54. By showing how these four theologians fall into the mainline Protestant model, I am not saying that this is the case for all contemporary Protestant mission theologians. The next chapter will show how some Third World Protestant thinkers make use of what I shall call the Catholic model.

55. Lesslie Newbigin, *The Open Secret: Sketches for a Missionary Theology* (Grand Rapids: Eerdmans, 1978), pp. 197–98.

56. See Stephen Neill, *Christian Faith and Other Faiths: The Christian Dialogue with Other Religions* (New York: Oxford University Press, 1970), pp. 230–32.

57. Newbigin, "The Centrality of Jesus for History," in *Incarnation and Myth: The Debate Continued*, Michael Goulder, ed. (Grand Rapids: Eerdmans, 1979), p. 209; see also his "The Basis, Purpose and Manner of Inter-Faith Dialogue," in *Interreligious Dialogue*, Richard W. Rousseau, ed. (Scranton: Ridge Row, 1981), p. 17.

58. Newbigin, *Open Secret*, p. 199.

59. Ibid.

60. Ibid., pp. 73–75.

61. Neill, *Christian Faith*, p. 17.

62. Newbigin, "The Basis," pp. 21–22; see also *Open Secret*, pp. 200–201.

63. Neill, "Christian Faith," p. 12.

64. Ibid., pp. 10–11.

65. Newbigin, "Centrality," p. 210; see also his *The Finality of Christ* (London: SCM Press, 1969), pp. 65–87.

66. "Centrality," pp. 203, 205; also *Open Secret*, pp. 76–80.

67. *Open Secret*, pp. 200–201, 205; "The Basis," pp. 24–25. Newbigin urges us to affirm the necessity of Christ and to leave the question of how those who do not know him are saved "to the wise mercy of God" (The Basis," pp. 19–20). In *The Open Secret* he argues that Christians must hold both to a universalism of salvation and to the real possibility of damnation (pp. 87–91).

68. Newbigin, "Centrality," p. 208.

69. J. Verkuyl, *Contemporary Missiology: An Introduction* (Grand Rapids: Eerdmans, 1978), p. 266.

70. M. M. Thomas, *The Acknowledged Christ of the Indian Renaissance* (London: SCM Press, 1969), pp. 308, 301; idem, "Modern Man and the New Humanity in Christ," in *The Human and the Holy: Asian Perspectives in Christian Theology*, Emerito P. Nacpil and Douglas J. Elwood, eds. (Maryknoll, N.Y.: Orbis, 1980), pp. 313–17.

71. See Paul Devanandan's study of Hinduism, *The Concept of Maya* (London: Lutterworth, 1950).

72. "Modern Man," pp. 327–33.

73. Thomas, "Modern Man," pp. 329–30; see also Paul Devanandan, *The Gospel and Renascent Hinduism* (London: SCM Press, 1959); Marcus Braybrooke, *The Un-*

discovered Christ: A Review of Recent Developments in the Christian Approach to Hindus (Madras: Christian Literature Society, 1973), pp. 7–8.

74. "Christ-Centered Syncretism," *Religion and Society*, 26 (1979) 33, 35.

75. Thomas, "Modern Man," p. 318; see also p. 308.

76. Ibid., p. 320.

77. *Preparation for Dialogue*, Nalini Devanandan and M.M. Thomas, eds. (Bangalore: CISRS, 1964), p. 153.

78. Thomas, "Theological Insights for a Secular Anthropology," in *Asian Christian Theology: Emerging Themes*, Douglas J. Elwood, ed. (Philadelphia: Westminster, 1980), pp. 291–93.

79. Ibid., p. 295.

80. Thomas, "Theological Insights," p. 294.

81. *Preparation for Dialogue*, p. 167.

82. "Christ-Centered Syncretism," p. 35.

83. Ibid., p. 27; also "Theological Insights," p. 294. Another well-known Indian Protestant theologian, D.P. Niles, agrees essentially with Devanandan's and Thomas's bottom-line assessment of other religions. Niles clearly recognizes a universal revelation in other religions made possible by the universal presence of Christ. Yet when he explains the finality of Christ and shows how Christianity differs from other religions, he implies that salvation, if present, is fundamentally inadequate. He argues that only Christianity affirms a really this-worldly salvation; "the Scriptures of other religions deal fundamentally either with the interior life or the life after death." Also, he holds, with Pannenberg, that "whereas in all other religions and systems of belief the present is determined by the past, in Christianity the present is determined by the future." See "The Christian Claim for the Finality of Christ," in *The Finality of Christ*, Dow Kirkpatrick, ed. (Nashville: Abingdon, 1966), pp. 13–31, esp. pp. 19 and 30; idem, *The Preacher's Task and the Stone of Stumbling* (New York: Harper and Brothers, 1958), pp. 32–33.

84. J. Daniélou, *Le Mystère du salut de nations* (Paris, 1948); idem, *Prayer as a Political Problem* (New York: Sheed and Ward, 1967), chap. 6, "Religion and Revelation"; Hans Urs von Balthasar, "Catholicism and the Religions," *Communio*, 5 (1978) 6–14; Joseph Ratzinger, "Christianity and the World Religions," in *One, Holy, Catholic, Apostolic*, H. Vogrimler, ed. (New York: Sheed and Ward, 1968), pp. 297–336; Max Seckler, "Sind Religionen Heilswege?," *Stimmen der Zeit*, 9 (1970) 187–94; Bernard Stöckle, "Die ausserbiblische Menschheit und die Weltreligionen," *Mysterium Salutis*, vol. 2, pp. 1049–74.

85. "Christianity and the Encounter," p. 62; *The Future of Religions*, p. 81.

86. *The Christ: The Experience of Jesus as Lord* (New York: Seabury, 1980), p. 646.

87. Althaus, *Grundriss der Dogmatik*, vol. 2, p. 34.

88. *Systematic Theology,* vol. 3, pp. 104–13.

89. "Uniqueness," p. 75.

90. *Christliche Wahrheit*, p. 139. Hans Küng speaks about "salvation only in a relative sense" in other religions (*On Being a Christian* [New York: Doubleday, 1976], p. 104).

91. See John 1:1–14; Col. 1:12–20; Eph. 1:22–23, 4:9–10. See also Bruce Vawter, *This Man Jesus: An Essay Toward a New Testament Christology* (New York: Doubleday, 1973), pp. 171–78.

92. See *Offizieller Bericht der 4. Vollversammlung des lutherischen Weltbundes, Helsinki, 1963* (Berlin, 1965), p. 514.

93. Thoman Merton, *Zen and the Birds of Appetite* (New York: New Directions, 1968), pp. 137-38. Concerning what the Christian notion of history can gain from Hinduism, see Samuel Rayan, "Indian Christian Theology and the Problem of History," in *Asian Christian Theology* (note 78, above), pp. 125-32. For examples of what Christian theologians are learning from Eastern religions regarding the nature of God, human nature, and the meaning of salvation, see Paul F. Knitter, "Horizons on Christianity's New Dialogue with Buddhism," *Horizons*, 8 (1981) 40-61; Heinrich Dumoulin, *Christianity Meets Buddhism* (LaSalle, Ill.: Open Court, 1974); John Dunne, *The Way of All the Earth* (New York: Macmillan, 1972); Bede Griffiths, *Return to the Center* (Springfield, Ill.: Templegate, 1977); John A. T. Robinson, *Truth is Two-Eyed* (London: SCM Press, 1979); Richard Drummond, *Gautama the Buddha: An Essay in Religious Understanding* (Grand Rapids: Eerdmans, 1974).

Chapter 7

1. "Response to Pietro Rossano," in *Christ's Lordship and Religious Pluralism*, Gerald H. Anderson and Thomas F. Stransky, eds. (Maryknoll, N.Y.: Orbis, 1981), p. 110.

2. Denzinger-Schönmetzer (hereafter: DS), *Enchiridion Symbolorum Definitionum et Declarationum*, 331-33, 340.

3. Origen, *In Jesu Nave*, 3, 5; Cyprian, *De Unitate Ecclesiae*, 6.

4. Justin, *I Apologia*, 46; *II Apologia*, 10, 13; Clement of Alexandria, *Stromata*, 1, 13; 5, 87, 2; idem, *Protreptikos*, 6, 68, 2ff.; Origen, *Commentarium in Joannem*, I, 39.

5. *Apologia*, 17, 4-6.

6. *Retractationes*, 1, 13, 3; *Epistola 102*, 2.

7. *Enchiridion*, 107.

8. *De Fide ad Petrum*, 38, 79.

9. See Paul Tillich, *Christianity and the Encounter of World Religions* (New York: Columbia University Press, 1963), pp. 37-39; Walbert Bühlmann, *God's Chosen Peoples* (Maryknoll, N.Y.: Orbis, 1983), pp. 97-99.

10. *Summa Theologica*, II-II, q. 2, art. 5, ad 1; III, q. 61, art. 1; II, q. 2, art. 7; *Quaestiones Disputatae de Veritate*, q. 14, art. 11. "Therefore St. Thomas is not persuaded that each and every person after original sin is called to salvation" (M. Flick, *De Gratia Christi* [Rome: Gregorian University Press, 1964], p. 188).

11. DS 802.

12. DS 870-72.

13. DS 1351.

14. DS 1524, 1542.

15. The implicit *Votum Ecclesiae* ("desire for the church") is expressly appealed to in Pius XII's *Mystici Corporis* and in the rejection by the Holy Office of the views of Leonard Feeney, S.J., who held that only Catholics are admitted to heaven (DS 3821, 3869-71).

16. See Maurice Eminyan, *The Theology of Salvation* (Boston: St. Paul Editions, 1960), pp. 167-81.

17. "The Church and Non-Christian Religions," in *The Meaning of the Church*, D. Flanagan, ed. (Staten Island, Alba House, 1966), p. 95. A notable exception to this ignoring of other religions is the Renaissance thinker and churchman Nicholas of Cusa (d. 1464). He saw the one divine *Logos* behind all religions which establishes

the essential concord and harmony of them all (*De Pace Fidei*, 10–12, 16–18, 68). The Jesuit missionary-theologians Matteo Ricci in China (d. 1610) and Robert de Nobili in India (d. 1656), in their recognition of truth and value in other religions, are also notable exceptions to the general ignoring of other religions.

18. *Lumen Gentium*, 16.

19. *Nostra Aetate*, 2. Because of "the spiritual bond linking the people of the New Covenant with Abraham's stock," the declaration has special praise for Judaism (ibid., 4).

20. Hans Waldenfels, "Das Verständnis der Religionen, und seine Bedeutung für die Mission in katholischer Sicht," *Evangelische Missionszeitschrift*, 27 (1970) 131–35; Walbert Bühlmann, "Die Theologie der nichtchristlichen Religionen als ökumenishes Problem," in *Freiheit in der Begegnung*, J.L. Leuba and H. Stirnimann, eds. (Frankfurt, 1969), pp. 459–60; Paul Hacker, *Theological Foundations of Evangelization* (St. Augustin: Steyler Verlag, 1980), pp. 70–72.

21. Heinz Robert Schlette, "Theology of Religions," *Sacramentum Mundi*, vol. 5, p. 283.

22. "Christ's Lordship and Religious Pluralism in Roman Catholic Perspective," in *Christ's Lordship* (note 1, above), p. 103.

23. *Lumen Gentium*, 14; *Unitatis Redintegratio*, 3.

24. See Richard McBrien, *Do We Need the Church?* (New York: Harper and Row, 1969), pp. 151–53.

25. See *Theological Investigations*, vol. 5, pp. 115–34. It should be noted that already in the 1930s there was a lone Roman Catholic voice calling Christians "to recognize the religious values in other religions" and to see them as "channels of grace and salvation" (Otto Karrer, *Religions of Mankind* [New York: Sheed and Ward, 1936]; see esp. pp. 183–91, 264–65).

26. See *Schriften zur Theologie*, vol. 8, p. 357. Rahner's positive evaluation of cultural and religious pluralism has been severely, sometimes caustically, criticized by a number of Catholic theologians who feel that he has opened the doors of the Roman Church to the confusion and relativism of the modern world. See Paul Hacker, *Theological Foundations of Evangelization*, pp. 61–70. H. Van Straelen, *The Catholic Encounter with World Religions* (London: Burns and Oates, 1966), pp. 95–132.

27. *Theological Investigations*, vol. 5, pp. 123–24; *Schriften*, vol. 8, pp. 193–96, 357–59.

28. See "Observations on the Concept of Revelation," in *Revelation and Tradition* (New York: Herder and Herder, 1966), pp. 9–25; *Theological Investigations*, vol. 6, pp. 390–98; *Schriften*, vol. 8, pp. 209–10, 360–62.

29. *Method in Theology* (New York: Seabury, 1972), pp. 101–7.

30. Schlette, *Towards a Theology of Religions* (New York: Herder and Herder, 1965), pp. 63–77; Schoonenberg, "The Church and Non-Christian Religions," in *The Evolving Church*, D. Flanagan, ed. (Staten Island: Alba House, 1966), pp. 89–109; idem, *God's World in the Making* (Pittsburgh: Duquesne University Press, 1964), pp. 61–105; Bühlmann, *The Chosen Peoples* (note 9, above), pp. 202–10.

31. See "The World Religions in God's Plan of Salvation," in *Christian Revelation and World Religions*, Joseph Neuner, ed. (London: Burns and Oates, 1967), pp. 37–47.

32. Rahner, *Foundations of Christian Faith* (New York: Crossroad, 1978) p. 315; see also pp. 40–41, 145, 154; *Theological Investigations*, vol. 5, pp. 128–30. This "sociological link" is an argument used by most representatives of the Roman Catho-

lic model. See Schlette, *Towards a Theology*, p. 77; Küng, *On Being a Christian* (New York: Doubleday, 1976), pp. 90–91; Eugene Hillman, "Evangelism in a Wider Ecumenism: Theological Grounds for Dialogue with Other Religions," *Journal of Ecumenical Studies*, 12 (1975) 1–12.

33. *Theological Investigations*, vol. 5, pp. 121, 125; italics added.

34. Rahner comments that only Christianity is equipped with such an authority structure that it can require believers either to accept a particular erroneous doctrine or be excommunicated (*Theological Investigations*, vol. 5, pp. 126–27).

35. Bühlmann (note 9, above), pp. 222–26; Arnulf Camps, *Partners in Dialogue: Christianity and Other World Religions* (Maryknoll, N.Y.: Orbis, 1983), pp. 44–48.

36. *Method in Theology*, pp. 108–11, 115–19.

37. Schlette, *Towards a Theology*, pp. 80–81; Küng, "The World Religions in God's Plan of Salvation," pp. 51–53.

38. *Catholicism,* Minneapolis: Winston, 1981, pp. 269–71, 290.

39. See *Theological Investigations*, vol. 5, 131–34; *Schriften*, vol. 6, pp. 551–53; vol. 8, p. 187.

40. See *Theological Investigations*, vol. 5, pp. 119–21.

41. Ibid., pp. 118, 122.

42. See *Theological Investigations*, vol. 6, pp. 393–95; "Christianity," in *Sacramentum Mundi*, vol. 1, p. 302; *Foundations*, pp. 178–203, 318.

43. *Theological Investigations*, vol. 6, pp. 390–91, 393–95; vol. 5, p. 118.

44. See *Theological Investigations*, vol. 5, p. 132; *Schriften*, vol. 6, pp. 546–47; vol. 9, pp. 498–501.

45. *Theological Investigations*, vol. 5, p. 133.

46. See *Schriften*, vol. 9, pp. 513–14.

47. "Christ's Lordship" (note 22, above), pp. 99–101.

48. *Redemptor Hominis*, 14.

49. See McBrien, *Catholicism*, pp. 274, 691–99, 709–15; Edward Schillebeeckx, "The Church and Mankind," *Concilium*, 1 (1965) 36, 43–47; Johannes Feiner, "Kirche und Heilsgeschichte," in *Gott in Welt*, vol. 2 (Freiburg, 1964), pp. 325–26; Küng, "The World Religions," pp. 57–66.

50. *Theological Investigations*, vol. 5, p. 122.

51. See *On Being a Christian*, p. 98; idem, "The World Religions," pp. 31–37. Inasmuch as Küng is also against vaporizing Christ, inasmuch as he insists on the essential link between Christ and the historical Jesus, the implication (which he does not state) is that neither is Christ necessary for salvation. For other criticisms of Rahner's theory of anonymous Christianity, see Schlette, Küng, Rahner, "Anonymous Christianity: A Disputed Question," *Theology Digest*, 24 (1976) 125–31; *Christentum innerhalb und ausserhalb der Kirche*, Elmar Klinger, ed. (Freiburg: Herder, 1976).

52. See chap. 8, below, pp. 159–63.

53. Gregory Baum, "Christianity and Other Religions: A Catholic Problem," *Cross Currents*, 16 (1966) 461.

54. Schoonenberg, "The Church and Non-Christian Religions," pp. 97–99; Eugene Hillman, *The Wider Ecumenism* (New York: Herder and Herder, 1968), pp. 60–61; Bühlmann, "Die Theologie" (note 20, above), pp. 472–73.

55. Schoonenberg, "The Church and Non-Christian Religions," pp. 100–107; Rahner, "Towards a Fundamental Theological Interpretation of Vatican II," *Theological Studies*, 40 (1979) 716–27; Bühlmann, *The Coming of the Third Church* (Maryknoll, N.Y.: Orbis, 1976).

56. See Schlette, *Towards a Theology*, pp. 83–93; Hillman, *Wider Ecumenism*, pp. 81–109.

57. M. Zago, "Evangelization in the Religious Situation of Asia," *Concilium*, 114 (1979) 74; Hillman, *Wider Ecumenism*, pp. 110–58; Roger Haight, "Mission: The Symbol for Understanding the Church Today," *Theological Studies*, 37 (1976) 620–48; McBrien, *Do We Need the Church?* pp. 14–15, 112–13, 158–66, 169–73.

58. J. Peter Schineller, "Christ and the Church: A Spectrum of Views," *Theological Studies*, 37 (1976) 556–57. In this quotation, Schineller adds "unsurpassable" after "unique." This appears to be inaccurate. Although this new view denies that Jesus is the unique or only mediator of salvation, it still holds that he is the unsurpassable mediator. Otherwise, he would not be the norm for all others.

59. Küng, *On Being a Christian*, pp. 123–24.

60. Ibid., p. 110, see also pp. 106–9.

61. Ibid., pp. 111–15.

62. Ibid., pp. 113, 447; italics added.

63. Ibid., pp. 110, 114. Alan Race ends his analysis of Küng's attempt at a more open dialogue by expressing his "impression" that Küng views "Christianity as the final arbiter of religious truth." It should be more than an "impression"! (Race, *Christians and Religious Pluralism: Patterns in the Christian Theology of Religions* [Maryknoll, N.Y.: Orbis, 1983], pp. 63–64). For a more extensive criticism of Küng's theology of religions, see Paul F. Knitter, "World Religions and the Finality of Christ: A Critique of Hans Küng's *On Being a Christian,* " *Horizons*, 5 (1978) 151–64.

64. *Method of Theology*, pp. 112–13, 119.

65. *Towards a Theology*, pp. 93–94, 96. The ultimate normativity of Christ is also affirmed in Teilhard's notion of Christ as the Omega Point for all history and religions and in William Thompson's more recent call for a "transcultural consciousness" available in the risen Christ. See Ursula King, "Religion and the Future: Teilhard de Chardin's Analysis of Religion as a Contribution to Inter-religious Dialogue," *Religious Studies*, 7 (1971) 307–23; William Thompson, "The Risen Christ, Transcultural Consciousness and the Encounter of the World Religions," *Theological Studies*, 37 (1976) 381–409.

66. Bühlmann, *The Chosen Peoples*, p. 207; see also pp. 219–22.

67. See *Lumen Gentium*, 16; *Ad Gentes*, 9; *Nostra Aetate*, 2; Rahner, *Lexikon für Theologie und Kirche*, vol. 2, pp. 1104–5.

68. See Camps (note 35, above), pp. 33–34, 48, 54, 113, 155. Avery Dulles, in recent statements, clearly holds to a view of Christ as constitutive and normative for all revelation/salvation in other religions. See *Models of Revelation* (New York: Doubleday, 1983), pp. 189–92; idem, "Contemporary Approaches to Christology," *The Living Light*, 13 (1976) 143–44.

69. See M.A.C. Warren, *I Believe in the Great Commission* (Grand Rapids: Eerdmans, 1976), pp. 153–70; John V. Taylor, "The Theological Basis of Interfaith Dialogue," in *Christianity and Other Religions*, John Hick and Brian Hebblethwaite, eds. (Philadelphia: Fortress, 1981), pp. 212–33, esp. 222–23; K. Cragg, *Christianity in World Perspective* (London, 1968); idem, *The Christian and Other Religions* (London: Mowbrays, 1977), pp. 63–64. Anglicans John A. T. Robinson and John Macquarrie (in his earlier writings) will be mentioned in the next chapter; they represent efforts to move toward a new model for understanding other religions.

70. "Christianity in a Pluralist World—The Economy of the Holy Spirit," in *Living Faiths and the Ecumenical Movement*, Stanley J. Samartha, ed. (Geneva:

WCC, 1971), pp. 131–42; see also Paul Verghese, "Christ and All Men," ibid., pp. 159–64.

71. See chap. 6, note 54, above.

72. See "Adam in Deep Sleep," in *The Human and the Holy: Asian Perspectives in Christian Theology*, E. P. Nacpil and D. J. Elwood, eds. (Maryknoll, N.Y.: Orbis, 1978), pp. 36–61, esp. p. 43.

73. "Theology of the Incarnation," in *Asian Voices in Christian Theology*, Gerald H. Anderson, ed. (Maryknoll, N.Y.: Orbis, 1976), pp. 147–60; *Third-Eye Theology* (Orbis, 1979), pp. 116–117.

74. "Christian Mission and the Peoples of Asia," *Missiology*, 10 (1982) 291–95; "Towards a Framework for 'Doing' Theology in Asia," in *The Human and the Holy*, pp. 281–83.

75. See C. S. Song, "The Divine Mission of Creation," in *Asian Christian Theology: Emerging Themes*, Douglas J. Elwood, ed. (Philadelphia: Westminster, 1980), pp. 187–88. The works of John S. Mbiti, speaking for African theology, are in basic agreement with these Asian theologians. See his "Some African Concepts of Christology," and "Some Reflections on African Experience of Salvation Today," in *Living Faiths and Ultimate Goals: A Continuing Dialogue*, S. J. Samartha, ed. (Maryknoll, N.Y.: Orbis, 1975), pp. 108–19.

76. Koyama, *Waterbuffalo Theology* (Maryknoll, N.Y.: Orbis, 1974), pp. 178–84; Song, "The Decisiveness of Christ," in *What Asian Christians Are Thinking*, Douglas J. Ellwood, ed. (Quezon City, Philippines: New Day Publ., 1976), pp. 240–64.

77. "Theology of the Incarnation," p. 157.

78. "From Israel to Asia: A Theological Leap," in *Mission Trends No. 3*, Gerald Anderson and Thomas Stransky, eds. (New York: Paulist, 1976), pp. 212–33, esp. p. 216.

79. See *Christ in a Pluralistic Age* (Philadelphia: Westminster, 1975), chap. 3 and 4.

80. *Christ without Myth* (New York: Harper and Brothers, 1961) pp. 156–57, 160–61; *The Reality of God* (New York: Harper and Row, 1963), pp. 164–87.

81. *The Lure of Divine Love* (New York: Pilgrim, 1979), pp. 87–99; *Catholic Faith in a Process Perspective* (Maryknoll, N.Y.: Orbis, 1981), pp. 23–32.

82. See *Christ in a Pluralistic Age*, pp. 20–21. Christian exclusivism was the main criticism that Ogden leveled at Bultmann's existential interpretation of the New Testament. See *Christ without Myth*, pp. 111–26.

83. *Christ in a Pluralistic Age*, pp. 24, 100–110, 138–39, 171.

84. Ibid., p. 142. In his more recent book on Christian-Buddhist dialogue, Cobb argues for the "centrality" of Jesus by claiming that Jesus provides a historical basis for the Buddhist experience of Ultimate Reality as gracious; such a firm historical basis, according to Cobb, is lacking in Buddhism. The argument seems to be that Jesus accomplished something in history that neither Buddha nor anyone else did. See *Beyond Dialogue: Toward a Mutual Transformation of Christianity and Buddhism* (Philadelphia: Fortress, 1982), pp. 136–40.

85. *The Reality of God*, p. 173, 203; see also "The Point of Christology," *Journal of Religion*, 55 (1975) 378–79, 387, 391. Ogden sometimes seems to limit his claims for the uniqueness of Christ to Christians, allowing for the possibility that other final norms may be valid for other religions. Although Pittenger, in a recent book, admits the possibility of other unique saviors for other religions, he holds to a normative

christology that sees Jesus as "the focal statement" of God's universal presence (*The Divine Lure*, pp. 164–65, 100–25; idem, *Catholic Faith*, pp. 73–101). Other contemporary Protestant theologians who do not adopt the model of process philosophy but who still hold to a normative christology are Gabriel Fackre and Eugene TeSelle. Fackre urges Christian recognition of the salvific value of other religions but insists on "the scandalous singularity of divine deliverance and reunion" in Jesus; the gospel of Jesus remains "the primal norm" ("The Scandals of Particularity and Universality," *Mid-Stream: An Ecumenical Journal*, 22 [1983] 32–52, esp. pp. 44–53). TeSelle summarizes his view of the universal saving activity of God and of Jesus as the normative focus of that activity: "The humanity of Jesus, although it is shaped by and attests to the Word, neither exhausts the Word nor is the sole means of access to it, for the Word is both knowable and efficacious elsewhere. The uniqueness of Jesus . . . will consist, then, in being the touchstone by which other responses are judged, the achievement by which their deficiencies are overcome, the center of gravity around which they cluster" (*Christ in Context: Divine Purpose and Human Possibility* [Philadelphia: Fortress, 1975], p. 164; see also pp. 146–69).

86. "Christian Encounter with Men of Other Beliefs," *Ecumenical Review*, 16 (1964) 451–55; "Christians in Dialogue with Men of Other Faiths," *International Review of Mission*, 56 (1967) 338–43. Also, *New Delhi Speaks about Christian Witness, Service, Unity*, W. A. Vissert't Hooft, ed. (New York: Association Press, 1962). For an overview of the various consultations with other religions, see Gerard Vallee, "The Word of God and the Living Faiths of Men: Chronology and Bibliography of a Study Process," in *Living Faiths*, pp. 165–82; *Dialogue with People of Living Faiths and Ideologies* (Geneva: WCC, 1980), pp. 57–61.

87. Stanley J. Samartha, "Guidelines on Dialogue," *Ecumenical Review*, 31 (1979) 155–56.

88. Ibid., pp. 155, 157.

89. *Guidelines on Dialogue with People of Living Faiths and Ideologies* (Geneva: WCC, 1979), pp. 11–12.

90. Ibid., p. 13.

91. In a letter to the author, April 18, 1983.

92. *Beyond Dialogue* (note 84, above), p. 21.

93. Henri Maurier, "The Christian Theology of the Non-Christian Religions," *Lumen Vitae*, 21 (1976) 59, 66, 69, 70.

Chapter 8

1. *Christ in a Changing World: Toward an Ethical Christology* (New York: Crossroad, 1981), p. 43.

2. "Christian Faith and Life in a World of Religious Pluralism," in *True and False Universality of Christianity* (*Concilium*, 135), C. Geffre and J. P. Jossua, eds. (New York: Seabury, 1980), p. 103.

3. "Christ and Church: A Spectrum of Views," *Theological Studies*, 37 (1976) 565.

4. *Society and the Sacred: Toward a Theology of Culture in Decline* (New York: Crossroad, 1981), p. 144.

5. See *God Has Many Names* (London: Macmillan, 1980), pp. 1–5. Hick first announced his revolution in *God and the Universe of Faiths* (New York: St. Martin's Press, 1973).

6. "Whatever Path Men Choose is Mine," in *Christianity and Other Religions*, John Hick and Brian Hebblethwaite, eds. (Philadelphia: Fortress, 1980), pp. 180–81; *God and the Universe*, pp. 120–31.

7. *God and the Universe*, p. 131; *Many Names*, pp. 5–6.

8. Hick follows Karl Jaspers's notion of the "axial period" of humankind. See "The Outcome: Dialogue into Truth," in *Truth and Dialogue in World Religions: Conflicting Truth Claims*, John Hick, ed. (Philadelphia: Westminster, 1974), pp. 149–51; idem, "Whatever Path," pp. 182–83.

9. "Whatever Path," p. 178; *God and the Universe*, p. 139; *Many Names*, p. 6. In his more recent statements, Hick is careful not to call the common content of all religions "God." He is aware that such a theistic interpretation is not adequate to religions such as Buddhism. He now prefers terms such as "the Real," "the True," or simply "Reality." See "On Grading Religions," *Religious Studies*, 17 (1981) 452–53, 467.

10. See D. B. Forrester, "Professor Hick and the Universe of Faiths," *Scottish Journal of Theology*, 29 (1976) 65–72; J. Lipner, "Christians and the Uniqueness of Christ," ibid., 28 (1975) 359–368; idem, "Does Copernicus Help? Reflections for a Christian Theology of Religions," *Religious Studies*, 13 (1977) 243–58; Peter Byrne, "John Hick's Philosophy of Religions," *Scottish Journal of Theology*, 35 (1982) 289–301.

11. "Towards a Philosophy of Religious Pluralism," *Neue Zeitschrift für systematische Theologie und Religionsphilosophie*, 22 (1980) 133.

12. Ibid., pp. 135–42, 148–49. See also Hick, "Pluralism and the Reality of the Transcendent," *Christian Century*, 98 (1981) 46–47.

13. "On Grading Religions," (note 9, above), p. 451.

14. Ibid., p. 463.

15. Ibid., pp. 464–65, 453.

16. Ibid., pp. 463, 467.

17. Ibid., pp. 462, 465–67.

18. "The Outcome," pp. 152–53.

19. *God and the Universe*, pp. 146–47; "Whatever Path," pp. 188–89; "The Outcome," pp. 151–52.

20. *Many Names*, p. 6.

21. *God and the Universe*, p. 148.

22. The myth of the incarnation, therefore, is much like the *Trikaya* myth with which Mahayana Buddhists attempted to speak about the Mystery they had encountered in Buddha. In fact, Hick speculates that had Christianity moved eastward into India instead of westward into the Roman Empire, Jesus most likely would have been interpreted as a *Bodhisattva*, as the one who had realized the fullness of nirvana and then lived out his life trying to show others the way to this same experience (*God and the Universe*, p. 117; "Jesus and the World Religions," in *The Myth of God Incarnate*, John Hick, ed. [London: SCM Press, 1977], pp. 168–69).

23. "Whatever Path," p. 184; *God and the Universe*, pp. 113–14.

24. "Jesus and the World Religions," p. 174.

25. Ibid., pp. 172, 175–76; *God and the Universe*, pp. 116.

26. "Whatever Path," pp. 185–86; "Jesus and the World Religions," pp. 179–80.

27. "Jesus and the World Religions," pp. 183–84.

28. Ibid., pp. 177–78; *The Center of Christianity* (New York: Harper and Row, 1968), p. 32.

29. "Jesus and the World Religions," p. 172; *God and the Universe*, pp. 114–16.

Hick in other words affirms that Jesus actually did realize in his own life the vision of God and way of life that he preached: "If Jesus had not lived in accordance with his own teaching, but had been seen by those who began to follow him to be selfish, cynical, deceitful, and unscrupulous, then the Jesus movement would never have developed as it did into the great world faith which we know as Christianity" ("On Grading Religions," p. 459).

30. *God and the Universe,* pp. 148–58.

31. Ibid., p. 159.

32. *Truth Is Two-Eyed* (London: SCM Press, 1979), pp. 104, 120. Robinson points out the dangers of relativism he finds in Hick's approach to other religions; and in no way does he wish to jettison the doctrine of the incarnation as, he thinks, Hick and other contributors to *The Myth of God Incarnate* (note 22, above) seem to. Still, with Hick, he interprets the mythic language of the incarnation to mean not that Jesus is "of one substance" *(homoousios)* but "of one love" *(homoagape)* with the Father (ibid., pp. 102, 116–17, 119–21). Whereas Robinson is staunchly opposed to "an absolutist, exclusivist, or triumphalist assertion of the uniqueness of Jesus as the Christ," he makes the "humble confession" that for him Jesus of Nazareth incarnates and expresses the divine *agape* "more fully than . . . any other such focal figure." But he insists that this is a personal confession, not a metaphysical declaration. It, like Christ himself, bears an inescapable "provisionality." The Christian's personal confession that Jesus is the clearest focus of God's love is "always to be clarified, completed, and corrected in dialogue" (ibid., pp. 125–29; see also *The Human Face of God* [Philadelphia: Westminster, 1973], chap. 7).

33. For Race's overall presentation of his "action christology," see *Christians and Religious Pluralism: Patterns in the Christian Theology of Religions* (Maryknoll, N.Y.: Orbis, 1983), pp. 127–37; the quotations given in our text are on pp. 129, 135–36. With his exclusion of all metaphysical claims and with his insistence that Jesus is a decisive focus for only "one cultural setting," Race seems to end up with the "wretched historicism" and relativism that he warned against in his analysis of Troeltsch (pp. 81–82).

34. Ewert H. Cousins, "Raimundo Panikkar and the Christian Systematic Theology of the Future," *Cross Currents,* 29 (1979) 143.

35. "The Category of Growth in Comparative Religion: A Critical Self-Examination," *Harvard Theological Review,* 66 (1973) 115, 131; "Have 'Religions' the Monopoly on *Religion?",* *Journal of Ecumenical Studies,* 11 (1974) 517; *The Intrareligious Dialogue* (New York: Paulist, 1978), pp. 2–23.

36. *The Unknown Christ of Hinduism* (Maryknoll, N.Y.: Orbis, 1981, rev. ed.), p. 23.

37. Ibid., pp. 24, 19.

38. "Have 'Religions' the Monopoly," p. 517.

39. *Unknown Christ,* pp. 75–96. Panikkar states that he would have liked to be "much more radical" in this new edition but, for the sake of continuity and "the rhythm of history," held back (p. 30).

40. *Salvation in Christ: Concreteness and Universality, The Supername* (Santa Barbara, 1972, privately published), p. 48. The main portion of these privately published lectures was reprinted as "The Meaning of Christ's Name in the Universal Economy of Salvation," in *Evangelization, Dialogue, and Development,* Mariasusai Dhavamony, ed. (Rome: Gregorian University Press, 1972), pp. 195–218.

41. "Category of Growth," p. 127.

42. "Christianity and World Religions," in *Christianity* (Patiala, India: Punjabi University, 1969), pp. 86–91. Panikkar's notion of the Christ also enables us to grasp more clearly what he means by "the fundamental religious fact."

43. *Unknown Christ,* p. 27.

44. See "Category of Growth," pp. 115–16; *Unknown Christ,* p. 27; *The Trinity and the Religious Experience of Man* (Maryknoll, N.Y.: Orbis, 1973), pp. 71, 74.

45. *Trinity,* pp. 74–75.

46. *Unknown Christ,* p. 169.

47. Ibid., pp. 48–49, 155–59, 165, 169; *Trinity,* pp. 53, 73. Panikkar understands the Spirit to be the immanent dimension of God, distinguished from the personal quality of the Logos; this immanence is the dynamism by which all returns to the Source (*Trinity,* pp. 58–69).

48. *The Unknown Christ of Hinduism* (London: Darton, Longman and Todd, 1964), p. 145; *Trinity,* p. 55.

49. This turning point was signaled in "Christianity and World Religions" (note 42, above), pp. 78–127, and then carried out in "The Category of Growth" (note 35), *Salvation in Christ* (note 40), and esp. in the completely revised 1981 edition of *The Unknown Christ* (note 36).

50. *Salvation in Christ,* pp. 62, 51; *Unknown Christ* (1981), pp. 8–9.

51. *Salvation in Christ,* pp. 70–71; *Unknown Christ,* p. 83.

52. "Christianity and World Religions," p. 114.

53. *Salvation in Christ,* p. 64; *Unknown Christ,* p. 7.

54. *Trinity,* p. 53; *Unknown Christ,* pp. 14, 27; *Salvation in Christ,* pp. 52–62; "Christianity and World Religions," p. 100.

55. See *Trinity,* pp. 53–54; *Unknown Christ,* pp. 27, 48.

56. "Christianity and World Religions," p. 101; *Salvation in Christ,* pp. 71–72.

57. Wilfred Cantwell Smith, *Towards a World Theology* (Philadelphia: Westminster, 1981), p. 175. For Don Cupitt, the notion of the finality and absoluteness of Christ is a discardable element in the mythic model with which Jesus was first understood, part of the "eschatological scheme . . . a view of time peculiar to the Jews." In his own reinterpretation of Christ, Cupitt explicitly adopts a logos model. Instead of a christology of Jesus as the final, only begotten Son of God, he proposes a christology of Jesus as the Word of God. With such a model, Jesus is not final in himself but "because of the way he bears witness to what is final and unsurpassable." Cupitt urges "that talk of Christ must either break away from an exclusive association with Jesus of Nazareth or be severely pruned back" ("The Finality of Christ," *Theology,* 78 [1975] 618–22, 626–27; "One Jesus, Many Christs?" in *Christ, Faith, and History,* S. W. Sykes and J. P. Clayton, eds. [Cambridge University Press, 1972], pp. 137–39). John Macquarrie, esp. in his earlier writings, holds that for Christians to claim that their "particular revelation . . . is the touchstone and norm by which all other revelations whatsoever must be judged" is "not only morally but intellectually objectionable. . . . The notion of a normative revelation must be rejected" ("Christianity and Other Faiths," *Union Seminary Quarterly,* 20 [1964] 39, 44). In more recent statements, Macquarrie calls Jesus "the definitive focus of God's acting and presence in the world" (i.e., the Logos), but it is clear that he intends this "definitiveness" to describe the quality of Christian commitment to Christ ("Commitment and Openness: Christianity's Relation to Other Faiths," *Theology Digest,* 27 [1979] 347–55). See also Thor Hall, *The Evolution of Christology* (Nashville: Abingdon, 1982), pp. 124–25. Christopher Duraisingh, with his claim that Jesus' uniqueness should be un-

derstood only as a "paradigmatic decisiveness," agrees essentially with Panikkar's christology ("World Religions and the Christian Claim for the Uniqueness of Jesus Christ," *Indian Journal of Theology,* 30 [1981] 169–85).

58. See *Courage for Dialogue: Ecumenical Issues in Inter-Religious Relationships* (Maryknoll, N.Y.: Orbis, 1982), p. 144; see also "Religious Pluralism and the Quest for Human Community," ibid., pp. 15–34.

59. "Dialogue as a Continuing Christian Concern," in *Living Faiths and the Ecumenical Movement,* S. J. Samartha, ed. (Geneva: WCC, 1971), pp. 153–57.

60. See *The Hindu Response to the Unbound Christ* (Bangalore: Christian Institute for the Study of Religion and Society, 1974). In this study, originally published in German in 1970, Samartha speaks of "the lordship of the crucified and risen Christ" as a "declaration of the universality of the unbound Christ" (pp. 199–200). Yet already he implies that the cosmic or unbound Christ cannot be expressed normatively, even in the historical Jesus.

61. "The Lordship of Jesus Christ and Religious Pluralism," in *Christ's Lordship and Religious Pluralism,* Gerald H. Anderson and Thomas F. Stransky, eds. (Maryknoll, N.Y.: Orbis, 1981), p. 35.

62. *Courage for Dialogue,* pp. 151–52; "Lordship," pp. 29–30.

63. "Lordship," p. 29.

64. *Courage for Dialogue,* p. 153; "Lordship," p. 36.

65. "Lordship," p. 27; *Courage for Dialogue,* p. 152. In a recent lecture, Samartha clearly adopts Panikkar's distinction between the universal Christ and the particular Jesus, and calls Christians to recognize "that the risen and living Christ is larger than Jesus of Nazareth. . . . The living presence of the risen Christ includes Jesus of Nazareth but goes beyond him" ("The Other Side of the River," manuscript of lecture for the Alumni Association of the Gurukul and the United Theological College, Bangalore, Sept. 2, 1982, pp. 16–18. This lecture will appear in *The Other Side of the River* [Madras: CLS, forthcoming]).

66. "Lordship," pp. 30, 33–34, 36.

67. See Howard R. Burkle, "Jesus Christ and Religious Pluralism," *Journal of Ecumenical Studies,* 16 (1979) 457–71. Burkle's article is one of the most coherent contemporary statements of how Christians might recognize the relativity of Jesus and all religious figures without necessarily denying their "decisiveness" and universal relevance (see esp. pp. 459–60, 462, 464). Dawe and Gilkey would agree: Donald G. Dawe, "Christian Faith in a Religiously Plural World," in *Christian Faith in a Religiously Plural World,* Donald G. Dawe and John B. Carman, eds. (Maryknoll, N.Y.: Orbis, 1978), pp. 13–33; Langdon Gilkey, *Society and the Sacred* (note 4, above), pp. 139–44. Gilkey, however, is not clear as to how far one can go in applying radical relativity to Jesus (ibid., pp. 157–70).

68. For a review of theologians who still hold to this supersessionist model, see Michael B. McGarry, *Christology after Auschwitz* (New York: Paulist, 1977), pp. 64–72.

69. John T. Pawlikowski, *Christ in the Light of the Christian-Jewish Dialogue* (New York: Paulist, 1982), p. 7; idem; "Christ and the Christian-Jewish Dialogue," *Chicago Studies,* 16 (1977) 367–68.

70. See Pawlikowski, *Christ in the Light,* pp. 8–35. McGarry follows the same "double" or "single" covenant framework in *Christology,* pp. 73–98.

71. Monika Hellwig, "Christian Theology and the Covenant of Israel," *Journal of Ecumenical Studies,* 7 (1970) 37–51. Paul van Buren, *The Burden of Freedom* (New

York: Seabury, 1976); idem, *Discerning the Way* (New York: Seabury, 1980). A. Roy Eckardt, *Elder and Younger Brothers* (New York: Schocken, 1973). J. Coos Schoneveld, "Israel and the Church in Face of God: A Protestant Point of View," *Immanuel,* 3 (1973/74) 80–83.

72. Rosemary Ruether, *Faith and Fratricide* (New York: Seabury, 1974); idem, "An Invitation to Jewish-Christian Dialogue: In What Sense Can We Say that Jesus Was 'The Christ'?," *The Ecumenist,* 10 (1972) 17–24. Gregory Baum, Introduction to Rosemary Ruether's *Faith and Fratricide,* pp. 1–22; idem, "Rethinking the Church's Mission after Auschwitz," in *Auschwitz: Beginning of a New Era?,* Eva Fleischner, ed. (New York: KTAV, The Cathedral of St. John the Divine, Anti-Defamation League of B'nai B'rith, 1977), pp. 113–28. James Parkes, *Prelude to Dialogue: Jewish-Christian Relationships* (New York: Schocken, 1969). J. Coert Rylaarsdam, "Jewish-Christian Relationship: The Two Covenants and the Dilemmas of Christology," *Journal of Ecumenical Studies,* 9 (1972) 249–70. E. P. Sanders, *Paul and Palestinian Judaism* (Philadelphia: Fortress, 1977). John Pawlikowski, *Christ in the Light.*

73. Pawlikowski, "Christ and the Christian-Jewish Dialogue," p. 376; Rosemary Ruether, *To Change the World: Christology and Cultural Criticism* (New York: Crossroad, 1981), p. 43.

74. Ruether, "An Invitation," p. 22; Hellwig, "Christian Theology," p. 49.

75. See Ruether, *Faith and Fratricide,* pp. 64–182; idem, "Theological Anti-Semitism in the New Testament," *Christian Century,* 85 (1968) 194ff.

76. *Faith and Fratricide,* p. 249.

77. Ibid., p. 256; "An Invitation," p. 22; *To Change the World,* pp. 42–43.

78. "Christian Theology," p. 49. In a more recent work, Hellwig is much more reserved about reinterpreting the uniqueness of Jesus. She suggests that some kind of affirmation of Jesus' exclusive centrality is intrinsic to Christian experience and tradition (*Jesus, the Compassion of God* [Wilmington, Del.: Michael Glazier, 1983], see pp. 127–41).

79. *Christ in the Light,* pp. 114–15.

80. Ibid., pp. 116–18, 76–107.

81. Ibid., p. 122. Here Pawlikowski is approvingly quoting A. Roy Eckardt.

82. Ibid., p. 122.

83. Ibid., p. 149.

84. Ibid., pp. 122–23; "Christ in the Christian-Jewish Dialogue," pp. 385–87; Ruether, *To Change the World,* pp. 38–39.

85. See "Response to Pietro Rossano," in *Christ's Lordship* (note 61, above), pp. 118–19.

86. I well realize that many stress the important differences between "liberation" and "political" theologies and between the ways such theologies are actually carried out by First and Third World theologians. Here I join liberation and political theologians in what I think is their basic agreement in methodological theory. See Francis Fiorenza, "Political Theology and Liberation Theology: An Inquiry into Their Fundamental Meaning," in *Liberation, Revelation, and Freedom: Theological Perspectives,* Thomas M. McFadden, ed. (New York: Seabury, 1975), pp. 3–29.

87. See Gustavo Gutiérrez, *A Theology of Liberation* (Maryknoll, N.Y.: Orbis, 1973), pp. 1–19; Juan Luis Segundo, *Liberation of Theology* (Orbis, 1976), chap. 1 and 3.

88. See Driver, *Christ in a Changing World* (note 1, above), p. 22; Ruether, *To Change the World* (note 73, above), p. 4.

89. Driver, *Christ in a Changing World,* p. 23.

90. Ibid., pp. 16, 29.

91. Ibid., pp. 58, 60.

92. *To Change the World,* p. 31.

93. Driver, *Christ in a Changing World,* p. 3.

94. Ibid., pp. 20, 143; Ruether, *To Change the World,* pp. 45–56.

95. Driver, *Christ in a Changing World,* p. 40.

96. Ibid., pp. 64–65.

97. *True and False Universality of Christianity* (note 2, above), p. vi. This entire volume is an expression of missionary dissatisfaction with the Christian claims of superiority or normativity; see the article by Ignace Puthiadam, pp. 99–112. Also Burlan A. Sizemore, Jr., "Christian Faith in a Pluralistic World," *Journal of Ecumenical Studies,* 13 (1976) 405–19. Aloysius Pieris divides the dominant Asian christologies into two camps: the "Christ against religion" view (= the conservative Evangelical and mainline Protestant models) and the "Christ of religions" view (= the Catholic model, esp. in its anonymous Christianity form). Both impose a Western theology on Asian churches and prevent a real listening to the cultural and religious situation of Asia. He calls on Asian theologians to abandon claims about the uniqueness of Christ and to allow a truly Asian christology to develop from an authentic dialogue with Asian religiosity and poverty. See "Speaking of the Son of God in Non-Christian Cultures, e.g., in Asia," in *Jesus, Son of God?* (*Concilium,* 153), Edward Schillebeeckx and Johannes-Baptist Metz, eds. (New York: Seabury, 1982), pp. 65–70. For the negative effects that a normative christology has on missionary efforts, see Alexandre Ganoczy, "The Absolute Claim of Christianity: The Justification of Evangelization or an Obstacle to It?" in *Evangelization in the World Today* (*Concilium,* 114), Norbert Greinacher and Alois Mueller, eds. (New York: Seabury, 1979), pp. 19–29; Michael Singleton and Henri Maurier, "The Establishment's Efforts to Solve the Evangelical Energy Crisis: The Fourth Roman Synod and *Evangelii Nuntiandi,"* in *Concilium,* 114, pp. 113–19; Henri Maurier, "The Christian Theology of the Non-Christian Religions," *Lumen Vitae,* 21 (1976) 59–74. See also Eugene Hillman, "Towards the Catholicization of the Church," *American Ecclesiastical Review,* 168 (1974) 122–34; idem, *The Wider Ecumenism* (New York: Herder and Herder, 1968), pp. 143–58.

Chapter 9

1. See chap. 1, above, pp. 18–20. See also John W. O'Malley, "Reform, Historical Consciousness, and Vatican II's Aggiornamento," *Theological Studies,* 32 (1971) 573–601.

2. Chap. 5, p. 91.

3. See Raimundo Panikkar, *Salvation in Christ: Concreteness and Universality, The Supername* (Santa Barbara, 1972, privately published), pp. 2–5.

4. "The kingdom of God is at hand" is an announcement found in five different New Testament traditions: that of Q, the Marcan tradition, the source peculiar to Matthew, that peculiar to Luke and in the Johannine tradition. See Edward Schillebeeckx, *Jesus: An Experiment in Christology* (New York: Crossroad, 1979) p. 140; Norman Perrin, *The Kingdom of God in the Teaching of Jesus* (Philadelphia: Westminster, 1963), pp. 158–206.

5. See Schillebeeckx, *Jesus,* pp. 229–56; Alexandre Ganoczy, "The Absolute Claim of Christianity: The Justification of Evangelization or an Obstacle to It?"

Concilium, 114 (1979) 23–25; Hans Küng, *On Being A Christian* (New York: Macmillan, 1976), pp. 214–26.

    6. See Raymond E. Brown, *Jesus, God and Man* (Milwaukee: Bruce, 1967), pp. 23–38.

    7. See Jean Milet, *God or Christ: The Excesses of Christocentricity* (New York: Crossroad, 1981), pp. 1–35.

    8. See Joseph A. Fitzmyer, "Jesus the Lord," *Chicago Studies,* 17 (1978) 97–101; James D. G. Dunn, *Christology in the Making* (Philadelphia: Westminster, 1980), pp. 65–97; Reginald H. Fuller, *The Foundations of New Testament Christology* (New York: Scribner's, 1965), pp. 119–29.

    9. See Dunn, *Christology,* pp. 253–54; Schillebeeckx, *Jesus,* pp. 154–229, 441–515; James Mackey, *Jesus the Man and the Myth* (New York: Paulist, 1979), pp. 121–72. Schubert Ogden argues that "the earliest Jesus kerygma" presents Jesus as the eschatological prophet *(The Point of Christology* [New York: Harper and Row, 1982], pp. 115–18).

    10. Schillebeeckx, *Jesus,* pp. 256–71.

    11. This is what the historical record tells us about Jesus' self-understanding. What is often not recognized by theologians is that, on the basis of the historical record, we cannot conclude that Jesus actually *was* what he thought himself to be. Whether his consciousness actually corresponded to reality is a question that can be answered not by the historian but by believers who have experienced this Jesus in their own life. See Dennis Nineham, "Epilogue," in *The Myth of God Incarnate,* John Hick, ed. (Philadelphia: Westminster, 1977), pp. 194–95; Ogden, *Point of Christology,* pp. 41–63.

    12. Dermot A. Lane, *The Reality of Jesus: An Essay in Christology* (New York: Paulist, 1975), p. 142.

    13. Frances Young, "A Cloud of Witnesses," in *Myth of God,* p. 19; Schillebeeckx, *Interim Report on the Books Jesus and Christ* (New York: Crossroad, 1981), pp. 10–27; C. F. D. Moule, *The Origin of Christology* (New York: Cambridge University Press, 1977), pp. 7, 9, 136. Ogden claims that all the christologies of the New Testament originated from a "constitutive christological assertion" or experience, i.e., from the fact that Christians found Jesus to be for them "of decisive significance for human existence because he is the decisive re-presentation of the meaning of ultimate reality for us" (*Point of Christology,* pp. 148–49; see also pp. 76, 81, 129).

    14. See chap. 8, pp. 149–50.

    15. See Martin Hengel, *Judaism and Hellenism* (Philadelphia: Fortress, 1974); James Robinson and Helmut Koester, *Trajectories through Early Christianity* (Philadelphia: Fortress, 1971), esp. pp. 1–19, 269–79.

    16. See Larry W. Hurtado, "New Testament Christology: A Critique of Bousset's Influence," *Theological Studies,* 40 (1979) 306–17; Frances Young, "Two Roots or a Tangled Mass?" in *Myth of God,* pp. 104–5, 110; I. H. Marshall, "Palestinian and Hellenistic Christianity: Some Critical Comments," *New Testament Studies,* 19 (1972–73) 271–87; Moule, *Origin of Christology,* pp. 11–46.

    17. See Schillebeeckx, *Jesus,* pp. 405–23.

    18. Ibid., pp. 424–29; Young, "Two Roots," pp. 100–102.

    19. See Schillebeeckx, *Jesus,* pp. 429–32; Dunn (note 8, above), pp. 209–12; Fuller (note 8), pp. 222–27; A. C. Bouquet, "Revelation and the Divine Logos," in *The Theology of the Christian Mission,* Gerald H. Anderson, ed. (Nashville: Abingdon, 1961), pp. 184–89.

20. See Schillebeeckx, *Jesus,* pp. 432–36.

21. Francis Fiorenza, "Christology after Vatican II," *The Ecumenist,* 18 (1980) 86.

22. Young, "Cloud of Witnesses," pp. 15–16.

23. Quoted in Young, "Two Roots," p. 118.

24. See Dunn, *Christology,* pp. 251–61; Young, "Two Roots," pp. 118–19.

25. Schillebeeckx, *Jesus,* pp. 441, 473.

26. Dunn, *Christology,* pp. 265–67, also p. 62. See also Young, "Cloud of Witnesses," p. 13; Schillebeeckx, *Jesus,* p. 436.

27. *Origin of Christology,* pp. 3–4, 135.

28. Dunn, *Christology,* p. 60.

29. See Fitzmyer, "Jesus the Lord" (note 8, above), p. 102.

30. Ibid., p. 91; Dunn, *Christology,* pp. 60–64; Young, "Cloud of Witnesses," pp. 19–22.

31. Dunn, *Christology,* pp. 256, 60–64.

32. Ibid., pp. 254–56.

33. Ibid., p. 249, also 257–58; Fitzmyer, "Jesus the Lord," pp. 91–92; Fuller (note 8, above), pp. 232–33.

34. Dunn, *Christology,* p. 250.

35. *Method in Theology* (New York: Crossroad, 1972), pp. 238–39.

36. In Moule, *Origin of Christology,* p. 165.

37. See chap. 2, above, pp. 31–32.

38. See chap. 8, note 57.

39. See chap. 8, p. 165.

40. See Gregory Baum, "Is There a Missionary Message?," *Mission Trends No. 1,* Gerald Anderson and Thomas Stransky, eds. (New York: Paulist, 1974), pp. 81–84; Robert J. Schreiter, "Response to Stanley Samartha," in *Christ's Lordship and Religious Pluralism,* Anderson and Stransky, eds. (Maryknoll, N.Y.: Orbis, 1981), pp. 50–51.

41. Young, "Cloud of Witnesses," p. 13.

42. "Notes for Three Bible Studies," in *Christ's Lordship,* pp. 14–15.

43. Again, this is not to imply that there was no metaphysical truth in what the early Christians said or that they were conscious of this distinction between metaphysical and confessional language. If they could have made such a distinction, they most likely would have said that the cognitive or metaphysical content of their confessional language was that there was no one else like Jesus. I am suggesting that given the nature of their language, such metaphysical claims are not intrinsic to that language. Today, Christians can hear and use the same language with different metaphysical content.

44. See Stendahl, "Notes," pp. 14–15.

45. Ibid., pp. 12–15; John A. T. Robinson, *Truth Is Two-Eyed* (Philadelphia: Westminster, 1980), pp. 105–6. See Peggy Starkey's illuminating reexamination of scriptural exclusivistic language in "Biblical Faith and the Challenge of Religious Pluralism," *International Review of Mission,* Jan. 1982, pp. 68–74.

46. See Robinson, *Truth Is Two-Eyed,* pp. 107–12; C. H. Dodd, "A Hidden Parable in the Fourth Gospel," in *More New Testament Studies* (Manchester University Press, 1968), pp. 30–40.

47. Some representative statements by Rahner: "Current Problems in Christology," *Theological Investigations,* vol. 1, pp. 149–200; "On the Theology of the In-

carnation," ibid., vol. 4, pp. 105–20; "Christology within an Evolutionary View of the World," ibid., vol. 5, pp. 157–92; "Two Basic Types of Christology," ibid., vol. 13, pp. 213–23; "Incarnation," in *Sacramentum Mundi,* vol. 3, pp. 110–18; "Jesus Christ," ibid., pp. 192–200, 203–9; *Foundations of the Christian Faith* (New York: Crossroad, 1978), pp. 176–321.

48. *Sacramentum Mundi,* vol. 3, p. 114, also p. 203.

49. *Geist in Welt* (Innsbruck, 1939).

50. *Sacramentum Mundi,* vol. 3, p. 116.

51. "Dogmatic Reflections on the Knowledge and Self-Consciousness of Christ," in *Theological Investigations,* vol. 5, p. 209; *Foundations,* pp. 208–11.

52. *Sacramentum Mundi,* vol. 3, p. 199.

53. Ibid., p. 195; *Theological Investigations,* vol. 1, p. 187; *Foundations,* pp. 193–95.

54. *Theological Investigations,* vol. 4, pp. 109–10, 117; *Theological Investigations,* vol. 1, 183; *Foundations,* pp. 217–18.

55. *Theological Investigations,* vol. 4, p. 111.

56. Ibid., pp. 115–16; *Foundations,* pp. 224–27.

57. *Foundations,* p. 201.

58. Ibid., p. 224; *Theological Investigations,* vol. 4, p. 116.

59. *Foundations,* p. 202.

60. Ibid., p. 218; *Theological Investigations,* vol. 4, p. 112.

61. Chap. 7, pp. 137–38.

62. John B. Cobb, Jr., and David Ray Griffin, *Process Theology: An Introductory Exposition* (Philadelphia: Westminster, 1976), pp. 13–29, 41–62; Norman Pittenger, *The Lure of Divine Love* (New York: Pilgrim, 1979), pp. 87–99; Schubert M. Ogden, "Toward a New Theism," in *Process Philosophy and Christian Thought,* Delwin Brown et al. (Indianapolis: Bobbs-Merrill, 1971), pp. 173–87.

63. John B. Cobb, Jr., *Christ in a Pluralistic World* (Philadelphia: Westminster, 1975), pp. 62–94; idem, *Process Theology,* pp. 98–99.

64. *God in Process* (London: SCM Press, 1967), pp. 19–20.

65. Norman Pittenger, *Christology Reconsidered* (London: SCM Press, 1970), p. 141.

66. Ibid., p. 114.

67. Robert B. Mellert, *What Is Process Theology?* (New York: Paulist, 1975), pp. 85–86; Pittenger, *Divine Love,* pp. 109–13; Bernard Lee, *The Becoming of the Church: A Process Theology of the Structures of Christian Experience* (New York: Paulist, 1974), pp. 109–19.

68. Norman Pittenger, "Process Thought and the Significance of Christ," in *Process Theology: Basic Writings,* Ewert H. Cousins, ed. (New York: Paulist, 1971), pp. 211–12.

69. John B. Cobb, Jr., "A Whiteheadian Christology," in *Process Philosophy* (note 62, above), pp. 388–94; idem, "The Finality of Christ in a Whiteheadian Perspective," in *The Finality of Christ,* Dow Kirkpatrick, ed. (Nashville: Abingdon, 1966), pp. 144–47; David R. Griffin, *A Process Christology* (Philadelphia: Westminster, 1973), pp. 206–27; Lewis Ford, "The Power of God and the Christ," in *Religious Experience and Process Theology,* Harry James Cargas and Bernard Lee, eds. (New York: Paulist, 1976), pp. 83–90.

70. Mellert, *Process Theology?* pp. 81–88; Pittenger, *Christology Reconsidered,* pp. 87–101.

71. Cobb-Griffin, *Process Theology,* pp. 102–6; Griffin, *Process Christology,* pp. 228–32; Norman Pittenger, *Catholic Faith in a Process Perspective* (Maryknoll, N.Y.: Orbis, 1981), pp. 87–101.

72. Schubert Ogden, *The Point of Christology* (New York: Harper and Row, 1982), pp. 83–84, 148–49; idem, "On Revelation," in *Our Common History as Christians: Essays in Honor of Albert C. Outler,* John Deschner, Leroy T. Howe, and Klaus Penzel, eds. (New York: Oxford University Press, 1975), pp. 281–85. As already pointed out in chap. 7, note 85, Ogden considers this the claim every Christian *must* make in order to be faithful to the New Testament witness. He implies, however, that although a Christian must always hold Jesus to be *the,* and not *a,* decisive revelation of God, the Christian is open to recognizing that other revealers may be *the* decisive revelation for other persons.

73. Otto Hentz, in a seminar paper read at the American Academy of Religion Convention, 1974.

74. Donald Gray, "The Divine and Human in Jesus Christ," *Proceedings of the Catholic Theology Society of America,* 1976, p. 25.

75. Denzinger-Schönmetzer, *Enchiridion Symbolorum,* 302.

76. Cobb seems more and more inclined to admit the possibility of other incarnations; see chap. 7, above, p. 138; idem, "Is Christianity a Religion?" in *Concilium,* 136, pp. 8–10. Still, in his more recent book, *Beyond Dialogue* (Philadelphia: Westminster, 1982), Cobb criticizes John Hick, W. C. Smith, and Paul Knitter for abandoning christocentrism for theocentrism. In Cobb's estimation, "to see Jesus as one savior among others" would lead to abandoning "the universal meaning and truth of Christ" (p. viii). When Cobb goes on to explain his own christocentric position, however, it seems to be only terminologically different from theocentrism. For Cobb, a christocentric faith affirms God not as a "noumenal Absolute," but as a reality to be found "in ourselves and in our world" (pp. 44–45); but so does a theocentric faith as explained in the present chapter. Cobb also has no difficulty in recognizing the fundamental identity between Christ and Amida (pp. 123–28). Such a Christ would seem in no way to be tied to Jesus or necessarily fully and finally revealed in Jesus.

77. Chap. 8, pp. 163–65.

78. Fiorenza, "Christology after Vatican II" (note 21, above), p. 88.

79. David Tracy, "Theologies of Praxis," in *Creativity and Method: Essays in Honor of Bernard Lonergan,* Matthew L. Lamb, ed. (Milwaukee: Marquette University Press, 1981), p. 36; Lamb, "Dogma, Experience, and Political Theology," *Concilium,* 113 (1979) 81; idem, "The Theory-Praxis Relationship in Contemporary Christian Theologies," *Proceedings of the Catholic Theological Society of America,* 1976, p. 171.

80. Leonardo Boff, *Jesus Christ Liberator: A Critical Christology for Our Time* (Maryknoll, N.Y.: Orbis, 1978), p. 279; Lamb, "Dogma," p. 83; David Tracy, *The Analogical Imagination* (New York: Crossroad, 1981), pp. 390–98.

81. Boff, *Jesus Christ,* pp. 44–47.

82. Quoted in Rosemary Ruether, *To Change the World* (New York: Crossroad, 1981), p. 27.

83. Lamb, "Dogma," p. 87.

84. Boff, *Jesus Christ,* p. 45.

85. See Boff, ibid., pp. 32–48; Jon Sobrino, *Christology at the Crossroads* (Maryknoll, N.Y.: Orbis, 1978), pp. xxiv, 35, 391.

86. Boff, ibid., p. 280.

87. Ibid., pp. 281-95; Ruether, *Change the World,* p. 21.

88. See Boff, ibid., pp. 229-31.

89. Ibid., pp. 156-57.

90. Sobrino, *Christology,* pp. 9-10.

91. *Change the World,* p. 23.

92. It might validly be argued that a physical resurrection does not necessarily imply either the divinity of Jesus or his absolute uniqueness (see John Hick, *The Center of Christianity* [New York: Harper and Row, 1978], p. 30). Jesus was raised, not by his own power, but by the power of God; and God can well do the same for others, even before the "final judgment." Still, the resurrection of Jesus, understood literally and physically, has been used as an argument for his exclusive uniqueness, and it is this argument that I am now examining.

93. See Schillebeeckx, *Jesus,* pp. 328-97; idem, *Interim Report,* pp. 74-93; Reginald H. Fuller, *The Formation of the Resurrection Narratives* (New York: Macmillan, 1971); Norman Perrin, *The Resurrection According to Matthew, Mark, and Luke* (Philadelphia: Fortress, 1977); Hans Küng, *On Being a Christian* (note 5, above), pp. 343-84; Bruce Vawter, *This Man Jesus* (New York: Doubleday, 1973), pp. 33-51; Mackey (note 9), pp. 86-120; Lane (note 12), pp. 44-81. For a helpful overview of the contemporary discussion on the resurrection, see William P. Lowe, "The Appearances of the Risen Lord: Faith, Fact, and Objectivity," *Horizons,* 6 (1979) 177-92.

94. This latter view is generally assigned to Bultmann, Marxsen, and Tillich. See Rudolf Bultmann, *Kerygma and Myth,* Hans Werner Bartsch, ed. (New York: Harper and Row, 1961), pp. 35-43; Willi Marxsen, "The Resurrection of Jesus as a Historical and Theological Problem," in *The Significance of the Message of the Resurrection for Faith in Jesus Christ,* C.F.D. Moule, ed. (London: SCM Press, 1968), pp. 15-50; Paul Tillich, *Systematic Theology,* vol. 2 (University of Chicago Press, 1957), pp. 183-90. See Joseph Smith, "Resurrection Faith Today," *Theological Studies,* 30 (1969) 395-98.

95. See Mackey (note 9, above), pp. 102, 105; Schillebeeckx, *Interim Report,* pp. 78-80; Vawter, *This Man,* pp. 50-51; Fuller, *Resurrection Narratives,* pp. 22-23.

96. Lane (note 12, above), p. 61; Vawter, *This Man,* p. 46.

97. Schillebeeckx, *Interim Report,* pp. 76-77; Küng (note 5, above), p. 346.

98. See Fuller, *Resurrection Narratives,* pp. 30-31; Schillebeeckx, *Jesus,* pp. 346-48.

99. See Schillebeeckx, *Interim Report,* pp. 75-77.

100. Schillebeeckx, *Jesus,* pp. 385-92; Lane (note 12, above), pp. 60-61.

101. Küng (note 5, above), p. 380.

102. Mackey (note 9, above), pp. 99, also 97, 104-5, 111.

103. Lane (note 12, above), p. 61.

104. *Foundations,* p. 276. See also Mackey (note 9, above), p. 97; Fuller, *Resurrection Narratives,* p. 183.

105. Fitzmyer (note 8, above), p. 94; Fuller, ibid., pp. 28-29.

106. Schillebeeckx, *Interim Report,* pp. 78, 80-90; idem, *Jesus,* pp. 352-60; Fuller, ibid., pp. 171-79; Mackey (note 9, above), pp. 105-13, 119; Perrin, *Resurrection,* pp. 9-13.

107. See Fitzmyer (note 8, above), p. 94; Schillebeeckx, *Jesus,* pp. 392-97; Mackey (note 9), pp. 117-19.

108. See Edward Conze, *Buddhism: Its Essence and Development* (New York: Harper and Row, 1959), pp. 34–38, 171–73.

109. In other words, I very much disagree with Avery Dulles's contention: "Christian theology must keep the spotlight on the utter uniqueness and transcendence of what happened in the career of Jesus Christ. If this is obscured, the Christ event will not elicit the kind of worship and thanksgiving needed to sustain the Christian community in its vibrant relationship to God" *(The Resilient Church: The Necessity and Limits of Adaptation* [New York: Doubleday, 1977], p. 78). I hope that in this section (and in this entire chapter) I am sufficiently meeting the concern that Frans Jozef van Beeck expresses in his criticism of Schoonenberg's christology—i.e., that all reinterpretations of Christ must be such that they be able to elicit "an act of total surrender, in worship and witness" *(Christ Proclaimed: Christology as Rhetoric* [New York: Paulist, 1979], p. 389, also 385–95).

110. See *Principles of Christian Theology* (London: SCM Press, 1966), pp. 155–58.

111. Schreiter (note 40, above), p. 48; Lewis Coser, *The Functions of Social Conflict* (New York: Free Press, 1956).

112. David Tracy, *Blessed Rage for Order* (New York: Crossroad, 1975), pp. 121–23; idem, "The Particularity and Universality of Christian Revelation," *Concilium,* 113 (1979) 112–15.

113. *The Meaning of Revelation* (New York: Macmillan, 1962), p. 39.

114. Ibid., p. 41.

115. See Robinson, *Truth Is Two-Eyed* (note 45, above), pp. 125–27.

Chapter 10

1. See chap. 9, above, pp. 192–94.

2. *The Asian Journal of Thomas Merton* (New York: New Directions, 1973), p. 313.

3. *The Way of all the Earth* (New York: Macmillan, 1972), p. ix.

4. See Raimundo Panikkar, *The Intrareligious Dialogue* (New York: Paulist, 1978); *Guidelines on Dialogue with People of Living Faiths and Ideologies* (Geneva: World Council of Churches, 1979); *Truth and Dialogue in World Religions: Conflicting Truth Claims,* John Hick, ed. (Philadelphia: Westminster, 1974); *Interreligious Dialogue,* Richard W. Rousseau, ed. (Scranton: Ridge Row Press, 1981); S. J. Samartha, *Courage for Dialogue* (Maryknoll, N.Y.: Orbis, 1982).

5. See Panikkar, *Intrareligious Dialogue,* pp. 25–52; Mircea Eliade, "Crisis and Renewal," in *The Quest: History and Meaning in Religion* (University of Chicago Press, 1969), pp. 54–71; W. C. Smith, "Comparative Religion: Whither—and Why?," in *Religious Diversity,* Willard G. Oxtoby, ed. (New York: Harper and Row, 1976), pp. 138–57.

6. Chap. 2, p. 36. Peter Berger maintains that dialogue can be profitably carried out only by "people who are not safely grounded in any tradition" and who are "unsure of their position" ("The Pluralistic Situation and the Coming Dialogue between the World Religions," *Buddhist-Christian Studies,* 1 [1981] 39, 36). Berger's point, stated somewhat extremely, does not contradict mine. When I advocate that partners take "clear" positions, that does not mean absolute, final positions. All involved in religious dialogue must recognize the intrinsically "unsafe" and "unsure" quality of all positions. There is always more to experience and learn. That, I think, is Berger's point.

7. See Panikkar, *Intrareligious Dialogue,* pp. 39–52.

8. What is argued in this section does not deny the importance of dialogue between religious believers and advocates of nonreligious ideologies. In such a dialogue, of course, one cannot require an explicit religious faith or commitment. Also, what is stated about the necessity of belonging to a religious community in order to engage in religious dialogue in no way negates the fact that, from a theological point of view, there is much genuine, though perhaps implicit, faith outside religious communities among professed atheists and agnostics.

9. Raimundo Panikkar, "Faith and Belief: A Multireligious Experience," *Anglican Theological Review,* 53 (1971) 225.

10. Panikkar, *Intrareligious Dialogue,* p. 64; see also W. C. Smith, *Towards a World Theology* (Philadelphia: Westminster, 1981), p. 97.

11. John B. Cobb, Jr., *Beyond Dialogue: Toward a Mutual Transformation of Christianity and Buddhism* (Philadelphia: Fortress, 1982), pp. 41–44.

12. See chap. 3, pp. 51–54.

13. After having insisted that the Mahayana Buddhist experience of emptiness and the Christian experience of God point to two different realities (and that therefore one should not talk about a common ground for both religions), Cobb goes on to show convincingly that the two realities are necessarily complementary and in need of each other. (Cobb calls emptiness "Ultimate Reality" and God "Ultimate Actuality.") This seems to indicate that *ultimately* both emptiness and God have *something in common.* If they did not, Cobb's project of Christian-Buddhist dialogue would be impossible. See *Beyond Dialogue,* pp. 42–43, 86–90, 110–14. Also, John Cobb, "Buddhist Emptiness and the Christian God," *Journal of the American Academy of Religion,* 45 (1979) 11–25.

14. Panikkar, "Faith and Beliefs," p. 225.

15. See Panikkar, *Intrareligious Dialogue,* pp. xix–xxvii. See also Merton, *Asian Journal,* p. 315; Eugene Hillman, *The Wider Ecumenism* (New York: Herder and Herder, 1968), p. 65.

16. Panikkar, *Intrareligious Dialogue,* p. 50, also pp. 40–44.

17. See W. C. Smith, *Towards a World Theology,* chap. 6, esp. pp. 111, 125–26.

18. *Asian Journal,* pp. 311, 315.

19. "Faith and Beliefs," p. 220.

20. Dunne, *Way of All the Earth,* p. xi.

21. Joseph J. Spae, *East Challenges West: Towards a Convergence of Spiritualities* (Chicago Institute of Theology and Cultures, 1979), pp. 62–64.

22. See W. C. Smith, *Faith and Belief* (Princeton University Press, 1979); Bernard Lonergan, *Method in Theology* (New York: Crossroad, 1972), pp. 115–24; Panikkar, "Faith and Belief" (note 9, above), pp. 219–37. For a brief but excellent summary of the discussion, see Dermot A. Lane, *The Experience of God: An Invitation to Do Theology* (New York: Paulist, 1981), pp. 55–62.

23. Rahner, *Foundations of Christian Faith* (New York: Seabury, 1978), pp. 44–89; Lonergan, *Method in Theology,* pp. 105–9; Tillich, *Dynamics of Faith* (New York: Harper and Row, 1957), pp. 1–29; idem, *The Courage to Be* (New Haven: Yale University Press, 1952), pp. 155–90. For faith in Buddhism and Hinduism, see W. C. Smith, *Faith and Belief,* pp. 20–32, 53–68.

24. *Method in Theology,* p. 119.

25. Panikkar, *Intrareligious Dialogue,* p. 40.

26. Dunne, *Way of All the Earth,* p. xi.

27. Panikkar, "Faith and Belief," pp. 228–29. See also John Cobb, *Beyond Dialogue,* pp. 47–53.

28. Panikkar, "The Myth of Pluralism: The Tower of Babel—A Meditation on Non-Violence," *Cross Currents,* 29 (1979) 193–94; idem, *Myth, Faith, and Hermeneutics* (New York: Paulist, 1979), pp. 336–48. The *chakras* are the six energy centers in the body that, when freed in mediation, promote spiritual experience.

29. See William Lynch, *Images of Faith* (University of Notre Dame Press, 1973); William J. O'Brien, *Stories to the Dark* (New York: Paulist, 1977); *University of Dayton Review,* Fall, 1980: the entire issue studies the religious imagination.

30. *Way of All the Earth,* p. ix.

31. Ibid., p. 53; italics added. Other studies in which Dunne carries out his method of passing over: *A Search for God in Time and Memory* (University of Notre Dame Press, 1977); *The City of the Gods* (University of Notre Dame Press, 1978).

32. *Search for God,* p. 7, also p. ix; see also "Spiritual Adventure: The Emergence of a New Theology," interview with John Dunne in *Psychology Today,* Jan. 1978, p. 48.

33. *Vedic Experience,* Berkeley: University of California Press, 1977. See also the creative way his imagination works with the Hindu symbols of Brahma and Isvara in *The Unknown Christ of Hinduism* (Maryknoll, N.Y.: Orbis, 1981), pp. 97-162.

34. *Analogical Imagination,* New York: Crossroad, 1981.

35. Ibid., pp. 113–15.

36. Ibid., pp. 173–78.

37. Ibid., p. 449.

38. Ibid., p. 451.

39. Aristotle, *Metaph.,* 1005 b 35ff.; Frederick Copleston, *A History of Philosophy,* vol. 1, part 2 (New York: Doubleday Image Books, 1962), p. 26.

40. Rahner, "Christianity," *Sacramentum Mundi,* vol. 1, p. 302.

41. See chap. 2, pp. 31–32.

42. *Stories of God* (Chicago: Thomas More, 1978), pp. 32–36.

43. See W. C. Smith, *Towards a World Theology,* pp. 154–55, 27.

44. Rahner, *Foundations,* p. 61.

45. For a different slant on the same new model for relational truth as a basis for religious dialogue, see Henri Maurier, "The Christian Theology of the Non-Christian Religions," *Lumen Vitae,* 21 (1976) 71–72.

46. Chap. 1, pp. 7–16.

47. Panikkar, "The Myth of Pluralism" (note 28, above), p. 226.

48. Quoted in Maurier (note 45), p. 72.

49. Jung Young Lee, "The Yin-Yang Way of Thinking: A Possible Method for Ecumenical Theology," *International Review of Mission,* 289 (1971) 363–70.

50. *Christianity and the Encounter of the World Religions* (New York: Columbia University Press, 1963), pp. 53–59.

51. *Faith of Other Men,* p. 17.

52. *Truth Is Two-Eyed.*

53. *Beyond Dialogue,* pp. 47–53, 140–43.

54. Maurier (note 45), p. 72.

55. See H. Van Straelen, *The Catholic Encounter with World Religions* (London: Burns and Oates, 1965), pp. 71–132; Peter Beyerhaus, *Missions: Which Way? Humanization or Redemption* (Grand Rapids: Zondervan, 1971); Harold Lindsell, *An Evangelical Theology of Missions* (Grand Rapids: Zondervan, 1970).

56. See chap. 7, above, pp. 132–33.

57. See Hubert Halbfas, *Fundamentalkatechetik* (Düsseldorf, 1968), pp. 240–42; Marcello Zago, "Evangelization in the Religious Situation of Asia," *Concilium,* 114 (1979) 74.

58. Raimundo Panikkar, "The Relation of Christians to Their Non-Christian Surroundings," in *Christian Revelation and World Religions*, Joseph Neuner, ed. (London: Burns and Oates, 1967), p. 168.

59. Robinson, *Truth Is Two-Eyed*, p. x.

60. *Intrareligious Dialogue*, p. 61.

61. See José Comblin, *The Meaning of Mission* (Maryknoll, N.Y.: Orbis, 1977).

62. See chap. 1, above, p. 20.

63. See *Asian Christian Theology: Emerging Themes*, Douglas J. Elwood, ed. (Philadelphia: Westminster, 1980); *The Human and the Holy: Asian Perspectives in Christian Theology*, Emerito P. Nacpil and Douglas J. Elwood, eds. (Maryknoll, N.Y.: Orbis, 1980); Choan-Seng Song, *Third-Eye Theology: Theology in Formation in Asian Settings* (Orbis, 1979); Robin Boyd, *An Introduction to Indian Christian Theology* (Madras: CLS, 1975).

64. See chap. 1, pp. 9–13.

65. John Hick proposes and carries out a "global theology" in *Death and Eternal Life* (New York: Harper and Row, 1976), esp. pp. 29–34; idem, *God Has Many Names* (London: Macmillan, 1980), pp. 6–9. W. C. Smith does the same in *Towards a World Theology*.

66. *The Future of Religions*, Jerald C. Brauer, ed. (New York: Harper and Row, 1966), pp. 31, 91.

67. *Faith of Other Men*, p. 123.

68. Cousins, "Raimundo Panikkar and the Christian Systematic Theology of the Future," *Cross Currents*, 29 (1979) 145–46. See also A. R. Gualtieri, "Confessional Theology in the Context of the History of Religions," *Studies in Religion*, 1 (1972) 347–60; Richard H. Drummond, "Christian Theology and the History of Religions," *Journal of Ecumenical Studies*, 12 (1975) 389–405; Peter Slater, "Towards a Responsive Theology of Religions," *Studies in Religion*, 6 (1977) 507–14; Carl A. Raschke, "Religious Pluralism and Truth: From Theology to a Hermeneutical Dialogy," *Journal of the American Academy of Religion*, 50 (1982) 35–48; Paul F. Knitter, "The Challenge of the World Religions: A New Context for Theology," *Verbum SVD*, 19 (1978) 34–56.

69. "A Next Step for Catholic Theology," *Theology Today*, 32 (1976) 381.

70. See Thomas Berry, "Religious Studies and the Global Community of Man," *An Integral View*, 1 (1980) 35–43.

71. Lonergan, *Method in Theology*, pp. 125–45.

72. W. C. Smith, *Towards a World Theology*, p. 124.

73. Cousins (note 68), p. 145.

74. Ibid., p. 146; italics added.

75. See Gerald O'Collins, *Fundamental Theology* (New York: Paulist, 1981), pp. 21–31; Heinrich Fries, "Fundamental Theology," *Sacramentum Mundi*, pp. 368–71; Johannes Baptist Metz, *Faith in History and Society: Towards a Practical Fundamental Theology* (New York: Crossroad, 1980), pp. 3–11; David Tracy, "The Task of Fundamental Theology," *Journal of Religion*, 54 (1974) 13–34.

76. Panikkar, *Myth, Faith, and Hermeneutics*, p. 325.

77. Ibid., p. 333.

78. Ibid., p. 330.

79. Lonergan, *Method in Theology*, pp. 237-44, 267-71. For Lonergan, the term "conversion" has a broad meaning. Religious conversion should include intellectual and moral conversion.

80. *Towards a World Theology*, pp. 101, 126.

81. "*Rtatattva*: A Preface to a Hindu-Christian Theology," *Jeevadhara: A Journal of Christian Interpretation*, 49 (1979) 13.

82. See Hans Waldenfels, *Absolute Nothingness: Foundations for a Buddhist-Christian Dialogue* (New York: Paulist, 1980); Raimundo Panikkar, *The Trinity and the Religious Experience of Man* (Maryknoll, N.Y.: Orbis, 1973); M.M. Thomas, *The Acknowledged Christ of the Indian Renaissance* (London: SCM, 1969); S. J. Samartha, *The Hindu Response to the Unbound Christ* (Madras, 1974); Klaus Klostermaier, *Kristvidya* (Bangalore, 1967).

83. See David Tracy, *Analogical Imagination*, pp. 390-98; Tom F. Driver, *Christ in a Changing World* (New York: Crossroad, 1981), pp. 12-31.

84. See *World Faiths and the New World Order*, Joseph Gremillion and William Ryan, eds. (Washington, D.C.: Interreligious Peace Colloquium, 1978); *Food/ Energy and the Major Faiths,* Joseph Gremillion, ed. (Maryknoll, N.Y.: Orbis, 1978). For a compendium review of the major issues and forced options facing the present world, see Roger Lincoln Shinn, *Forced Options: Social Decisions for the 21st Century* (New York: Harper and Row, 1982).

85. *Truth Is Two-Eyed*, pp. 64-65; Paul F. Knitter, "Horizons on Christianity's New Dialogue with Buddhism," *Horizons*, 8 (1981) 51-55.

86. Raimundo Panikkar, "The Category of Growth in Comparative Religion: A Critical Self-Examination," *Harvard Theological Review*, 66 (1973) 137-38.

87. Chap. 4, pp. 68-69. These working criteria for judging truth claims in interreligious dialogue focus a central difference between the conclusions I draw in this final chapter and the conclusions Alan Race makes in his final chapter (*Christians and Religious Pluralism: Patterns in the Christian Theology of Religions* [Maryknoll, N.Y.: Orbis, 1983], pp. 138-48). We both agree that religious truth-claims can be made only in the actual praxis of dialogue and that whatever claims are made, the mystery encompassing humanity will always be more than any religious truth can express. Race, however, insists that the criterion for verifying truth-claims within dialogue can be only subjective; any further verification can come only "eschatologically": "The genuineness of the encounter [with mystery] cannot be demonstrated by rational means, but can be verified only in terms of the extent to which it enables those who live in its wake to live according to the vision of life which it yields. Thereafter any verification will be eschatological" (p. 146). The criteria I have drawn from Jung and from the liberation theologians try to reach beyond such subjectivism; they are intended to examine whether the "vision of life" of a religion actually promotes the psychological welfare and the liberation of both individuals and societies. Such criteria, it is hoped, can be applied now, in this ambiguous and ever incomplete course of history, and do not have to wait for some kind of eschatological judgment at the end of time.

Supplementary Readings

Chapter 1

Cragg, Kenneth. *The Christian and Other Religions*. London: Mowbrays, 1977, pp. 1–30.

Davis, Charles. *Christ and the World Religions*. New York: Herder and Herder, 1971, pp. 13–48.

———. "Our New Religious Identity." *Studies in Religion*, 9 (1980) 25–40.

Folkemer, Lawrence D. "Dialogue and Proclamation." *Journal of Ecumenical Studies,* 13 (1976) 420–39.

Race, Alan. *Christians and Religious Pluralism: Patterns in the Christian Theology of Religions*. Maryknoll, N.Y.: Orbis, 1983, chap. 1: "The Problem."

Rupp, George. "Religious Pluralism in the Context of an Emerging World Culture." *Harvard Theological Review*, 66 (1973) 207–18.

———. *Beyond Existentialism and Zen: Religion in a Pluralistic World*. New York: Oxford University Press, 1979, pp. 3–26.

Samartha, Stanley. *Courage for Dialogue*. Maryknoll, N.Y.: Orbis, 1982, pp. 15–34, 121–28.

Sizemore, Burlan A. Jr. "Christian Faith in a Pluralistic World." *Journal of Ecumenical Studies*, 13 (1976) 405–19.

Smart, Ninian. *Beyond Ideology: Religion and the Future of Western Civilization*. New York: Harper and Row, 1981, pp. 17–68.

Smith, Wilfred Cantwell. "The Christian in a Religiously Plural World," in *Christianity and Other Religions*, John Hick and Brian Hebblethwaite, eds. Philadelphia: Fortress, 1980, pp. 87–107.

———. "Mankind's Religiously Divided History Approaches Self-Consciousness," in *Religious Diversity*, Willard G. Oxtoby, ed. New York: Harper and Row, 1976, pp. 96–114.

———. "Divisiveness and Unity," in *Food/Energy and the Major Faiths*, Joseph Gremillion, ed. Maryknoll, N.Y.: Orbis, 1978, pp. 71–85.

Thompson, William M. "The Risen Christ, Transcultural Consciousness, and the Encounter of the World Religions." *Theological Studies*, 37 (1976) 381–409.

Tillich, Paul. *Christianity and the Encounter of the World Religions*. New York: Columbia University Press, 1963, pp. 1–25.

Whitson, Robley Edward. *The Coming Convergence of World Religions*. Westminster, Md.: Newman, 1971, pp. 1–53.

Chapter 2

Adams, J. L. "Ernst Troeltsch as an Analyst of Religion." *Journal for the Scientific Study of Religion*, 1 (1961–62) 98–108.

Allen, E. L. *Christianity Among the Religions*. Boston: Beacon, 1960, pp. 83–93.

Braxton, Edward K. *The Wisdom Community*. New York: Paulist, 1980, pp. 17–50.

Coakley, Sarah. "Theology and Cultural Relativism. What is the Problem?" *Neue Zeitschrift für Theologie und Religionsphilosophie*, 21 (1979) 223–43.

Driver, Tom F. *Christ in a Changing World*. New York: Crossroad, 1981, pp. 57–81.

Gilkey, Langdon. *Reaping the Whirlwind*. New York: Seabury, 1976, pp. 188–208.

Johnson, Roger A. "Troeltsch on Christianity and Relativism." *Journal for the Scientific Study of Religion*, 1 (1961–62) 220–25.

Lonergan, Bernard. "The Transition from a Classicist World-View to Historical Mindedness," "Theology in Its New Context," "Belief: Today's Issue," "The Absence of God in Modern Culture," all in *A Second Collection: Papers by Bernard J. F. Lonergan, S. J.*, William Ryan and Bernard Tyrrell, eds. Philadelphia: Westminster, 1974.

Pye, Michael. "Ernst Troeltsch and the End of the Problem about 'Other' Religions," in *Ernst Troeltsch and the Future of Theology*, John Powell Clayton, ed. Cambridge University Press, 1976, pp. 172–95.

Quigley, Michael A. "Ernst Troeltsch and the Problem of the Historical Absolute." *Heythrop Journal*, 24 (1983), pp. 19–37.

Santmire, H. Paul. "Ernst Troeltsch: Modern Historical Thought and the Challenge to Individual Religions," in *Critical Issues in Modern Religion*. Englewood Cliffs, N.J.: Prentice-Hall, 1973, pp. 365–99.

Sykes, S. W. "Ernst Troeltsch and Christianity's Essence," in *Ernst Troeltsch and the Future of Theology* (see above), pp. 139–71.

Troeltsch, Ernst. *The Absoluteness of Christianity and the History of Religions*. Richmond: John Knox Press, 1971, esp. chap. 3 and 4.

———. "The Place of Christianity among the World Religions," in *Christianity and Other Religions*, John Hick and Brian Hebblethwaite, eds. Philadelphia: Fortress, 1980, pp. 11–31.

Chapter 3

Betty, L. S. "The Radical Pluralism of Arnold Toynbee—Its Implications for Religion." *Journal of Ecumenical Studies*, 9 (1972) 819–40.

Gualtieri, Antonio Roberto. "Faith, Tradition, and Transcendence: A Study of Wilfred Cantwell Smith." *Canadian Journal of Theology*, 15 (1969) 102–11.

Heiler, Frederich. "The History of Religions as a Preparation for the Co-operation of Religions," in *The History of Religions: Essays in Methodology*, Mircea Eliade and Joseph M. Kitagawa, eds. University of Chicago Press, 1959, pp. 132–60.

Hocking, William Ernest. "The Way of Reconception," in *Living Religions and a World Faith*. New York: Macmillan, 1940, pp. 190–208. Also in *Attitudes toward Other Religions*, Owen C. Thomas, ed. London: SCM Press, 1969, pp. 133–49.

Otto, Rudolph. *The Idea of the Holy*. New York: Oxford University Press, 1958, esp. chap. 1–6, 21.

Radhakrishnan, Sarvepalli. *The Hindu View of Life*. New York: Macmillan, 1973, pp. 11–44.

———. *Eastern Religions and Western Thought*. London: Oxford University Press, 1969, pp. 306–39.

Schleiermacher, Friedrich. "Religion and the Religions," in Thomas, *Attitudes toward Other Religions* (see above), pp. 49–69.

Schuon, Frithjof. *The Transcendent Unity of Religions*. New York: Harper and Row, 1975, esp. the Introduction by Huston Smith, pp. ix–xxvi.

Smith, Wilfred Cantwell. *The Meaning and End of Religion*. New York: New American Library, 1964, Chapters 6 and 7.

———. "Traditional Religions and Modern Culture," in *Religious Diversity*, Willard G. Oxtoby, ed. New York: Harper and Row, 1976, pp. 59–76.

Streiker, Lowell D. "The Hindu Attitude toward Other Religions." *The Ecumenist*, 6 (1968) 177–80.

Toynbee, Arnold. "What Should be the Christian Approach to the Contemporary Non-Christian Faiths?" in *Christianity among the Religions of the World*. New York: Scribner's, 1957, pp. 83–112. Also in Thomas, *Attitudes toward Other Religions* (see above), pp. 151–71.

———. "The Task of Disengaging the Essence from the Non-essentials in Mankind's Religious Heritage," in *An Historian's Approach to Religion*. New York: Oxford University Press, 1956, pp. 261–83.

Chapter 4

Assagioli, Roberto. "The Transcendental Experience and Meditation," in *Psyche and Spirit*, John J. Heaney, ed. New York: Paulist, 1973, pp. 125–35.

Bechtle, Regina. "C. G. Jung and Religion," in *Psyche and Spirit* (see above), pp. 57–80.

Bianchi, Eugene C. "Jungian Psychology and Religious Experience." *Anglican Theological Review*, 61 (1979) 182–99.

Bockus, Frank M. "The Archetypal Self: Theological Values in Jung's Psychology," in *The Dialogue between Theology and Psychology*, Peter Homans, ed. University of Chicago Press, 1968, pp. 221–47.

Clift, Wallace R. *Jung and Christianity*. New York: Crossroad, 1982 (esp. part 2).

Frankl, Viktor E. *The Unconscious God: Psychotherapy and Theology*. New York: Simon and Schuster, 1975, pp. 19–76.

Homans, Peter. *Jung in Context: Modernity and the Making of a Psychology*. University of Chicago Press, 1979, pp. 115–32, 182–92.

James, William. *The Varieties of Religious Experience* (various editions). Lectures 2, 3, 20.

Jung, C. G. *Psychology and Alchemy* (Collected Works, vol 12). London: Routledge and Kegan Paul, 1953, pp. 3–37.

———. *Psychology and Religion*. New Haven: Yale University Press, 1938, chap. 1, "The Autonomy of the Unconscious." Also in *Psychology and Religion: West and East* (Collected Works, vol. 11), pp. 5–33.

———. "The Spiritual Problem of Modern Man," in *Modern Man in Search of a Soul*. New York: Harcourt, Brace, 1955, pp. 226–54. Also in *The Portable Jung*, Joseph Campbell, ed. New York: Viking, 1971, pp. 456–79.

———. "The Difference betwen Eastern and Western Thinking,"in Collected Works, vol. 11 (see above), pp. 475–93. Also in *The Portable Jung* (see above), pp. 480–502.

Maslow, Abraham H. *Religions, Values, and Peak-Experiences*. New York: Viking, 1970, pp. 19–29, 59–68.

Thompson, William M. "A Spiritual Journey within the Psychoanalytic Tradition." *The Ecumenist*, 15 (1977) 49–53.

White, Victor. "The Unconscious and God." in *God and the Unconscious*. Chicago: Regnery, 1953, pp. 23–39.

Chapter 5

Barth, Karl. "The Revelation of God as the Abolition of Religion," in *Church Dogmatics*, 1/2. Edinburgh: Clark, 1956, pp. 280–361. Abridged version in *Christianity and Other Religions*, John Hick and Brian Hebblethwaite, eds. Philadelphia: Fortress, 1980, pp. 32–51.

Beyerhaus, Peter. "Mission and Humanization," in *Mission Trends No. 1: Critical Issues in Mission Today*, Anderson and Stransky, eds. New York: Paulist, 1974, pp. 231–45.

———. "Christianity and Other Religions." *Theology Digest*, 27 (1979) 121–24.

"The Frankfurt Declaration," in Peter Beyerhaus, *Missions: Which Way? Humanization or Redemption*. Grand Rapids: Zondervan, 1971, pp. 111–20.

Gualtieri, Antonio Roberto. "The Failure of Dialectics in Hendrik Kraemer's Evaluation of Non-Christian Faiths." *Journal of Ecumenical Studies*, 15 (1978) 274–90.

Hallencreutz, Carl F. *New Approaches to Men of Other Faiths*. Geneva: World Council of Churches, 1969, chap. 2 and 5.

Hesselgrave, David J. "Evangelicals and Interreligious Dialogue," in *Mission Trends No. 5: Faith Meets Faith*, Anderson and Stransky, eds. New York: Paulist, 1981, pp. 123–27.

Kraemer, Hendrick. *Religion and the Christian Faith*. Philadelphia: Westminster, 1956, pp. 340–65.

Krass, Alfred C. "Accounting for the Hope That Is in Me," in *Christian Faith in a Religiously Plural World*, D. G. Dawe and J. B. Carman, eds. Maryknoll, N.Y.: Orbis, 1978, pp. 155–67.

"Lausanne Congress, 1974," in *Mission Trends No. 2: Evangelization*, Anderson and Stransky, eds. New York: Paulist, 1975, pp. 239–48.

Packer, James I. "Are Non-Christian Faiths Ways of Salvation?" *Bibliotheca Sacra*, 130 (1973) 110–16.

Race, Alan. *Christians and Religious Pluralism*. Maryknoll, N.Y.: Orbis, 1983, pp. 10–37.

Scott, Waldron. " 'No Other Name' —An Evangelical Conviction," in *Christ's Lordship and Religious Pluralism*, Anderson and Stransky, eds. Maryknoll, N.Y.: Orbis, 1981, pp. 58–74.

Stott, John R. "Dialogue, Encounter, Even Confrontation," in *Mission Trends No. 5* (see above), pp. 156–72.

Chapter 6

Braaten, Carl. "The Uniqueness and Universality of Jesus Christ," in *Mission Trends No. 5: Faith Meets Faith*. Anderson and Stransky, eds. New York: Paulist, 1981, pp. 69–89.

———. "The Gospel of Salvation and the World Religions," in *The Flaming Center*. Philadelphia: Fortress, 1977, pp. 93–119.

Brunner, Emil. "Revelation and Religion," in *Revelation and Reason: The Christian Doctrine of Faith and Knowledge*. Philadelphia: Westminster, 1946, pp. 258–73.

Also in *Attitudes toward Other Religions*, Owen C. Thomas, ed. London: SCM Press, 1969, pp. 113–32.

———. "The Element of Truth in Historicism: Revelation and the History of Religion," in *The Philosophy of Religion*. London: James Clarke, 1958, pp. 114–49.

Burns, R. "Paul Tillich and the World Religions." *Angelicum*, 54 (1977) 394–416.

Lindbeck, George A. "Unbelievers and the 'Sola Cristi.' " *Dialog*, 12 (1973) 182–89.

Neill, Stephen. *Christian Faith and Other Faiths: The Christian Dialogue with Other Religions*. New York: Oxford University Press, 1970, pp. 1–19.

Newbigin, Lesslie. "The Basis, Purpose, and Manner of Inter-Faith Dialogue," in *Interreligious Dialogue*, Richard W. Rousseau, ed. Montrose, Pa.: Ridge Row Press, 1981, pp. 13–31.

———. "The Centrality of Jesus for History," in *Incarnation and Myth: The Debate Continued*, Michael Goulder, ed. Grand Rapids: Eerdmans, 1979, pp. 197–210.

———. *The Open Secret: Sketches for a Missionary Theology*. Grand Rapids: Eerdmans, 1978, pp. 181–214.

Pannenberg, Wolfhart. "Towards a Theology of the History of Religions," in *Basic Questions in Theology*, vol. 2. Philadelphia: Westminster, 1971, pp. 65–118.

Tillich, Paul. *Systematic Theology,* vol. 1, pp. 137–44, 218–30 (153–60, 242–54); vol. 2, pp. 78–88 (91–102); vol. 3, pp. 98–106 (104–13). Initial page numbers refer to the American edition (Chicago: University of Chicago Press, 1951–63); page numbers in parentheses refer to the British edition (Digswell Place: James Nisbet, 1968).

———. *What Is Religion?* New York: Harper and Row, 1969, pp. 56–97.

———. *The Future of Religions,* Jerald C. Brauer, ed. New York: Harper and Row, 1966, pp. 80–94.

Chapter 7

Bühlmann, Walbert. *God's Chosen Peoples*. Maryknoll, N.Y.: Orbis, 1983, chap. 10, "The Other Religions."

Fransen, Piet. "How Can Non-Christians Find Salvation in Their Qwn Religions?" in *Christian Revelation and World Religions*, Joseph Neuner, ed. London: Burns and Oates, 1967, pp. 67–122.

Glyn, Richard. "Towards a Theology of Religions." *Journal of Theological Studies*, 31 (1980) 44–66.

Guidelines on Dialogue with People of Living Faiths and Ideologies. Geneva: WCC, 1979. Also in *Mission Trends No. 5: Faith Meets Faith*, Anderson and Stransky, eds. New York: Paulist, 1981, pp. 128–54.

Hillman, Eugene. "Evangelism in a Wider Ecumenism: Theological Grounds for Dialogue with Other Religions." *Journal of Ecumenical Studies*, 12 (1975) 1–12.

Khodr, George. "The Economy of the Holy Spirit," in *Mission Trends No. 5* (see above), pp. 36–49.

King, Ursula. "Religion and the Future: Teilhard de Chardin's Analysis of Religion as a Contribution to Inter-religious Dialogue." *Religious Studies*, 7 (1971) 307–23.

Küng, Hans. "The Challenge of the World Religions," in *On Being a Christian*. New York: Doubleday, 1976, pp. 89–118.

———. "The World Religions in God's Plan of Salvation," in *Christian Revelation and World Religions* (see above), pp. 25–66.

McBrien, Richard P. *Catholicism*. Minneapolis: Winston, 1981, pp. 245–77.

Rahner, Karl. "Christianity and the Non-Christian Religions," in *Theological Investigations*, vol. 5, Baltimore: Helicon, 1966, pp. 115–34.

———. "Anonymous Christianity and the Missionary Task of the Church," in *Theological Investigations*, vol. 12. New York: Seabury, 1974, pp. 161–78.

———. "Observations on the Problem of the 'Anonymous Christian,' " in *Theological Investigations*, vol. 14. New York: Seabury, 1976, pp. 280–94.

———. "Jesus Christ in Non-Christian Religions," in *Foundations of Christian Faith*. New York: Seabury, 1978, pp. 311–21.

Rossano, Pietro. "Christ's Lordship and Religious Pluralism in Roman Catholic Perspective," in *Christ's Lordship and Religious Pluralism*, Anderson and Stransky, eds. Maryknoll, N.Y.: Orbis, 1981, pp. 96–110. Also in *Mission Trends No. 5* (see above), pp. 20–35.

Schineller, J. Peter. "Christ and the Church: A Spectrum of Views." *Theological Studies*, 37 (1976) 545–66.

Schlette, Heinz Robert. *Towards a Theology of Religions*. London: Burns and Oates, 1966, pp. 63–118.

Schoonenberg, Piet. "The Church and Non-Christian Religions," in *The Evolving Church*, D. Flanagan, ed. Staten Island: Alba House, 1966, pp. 89–109.

Taylor, John V. "The Theological Basis of Interfaith Dialogue," in *Mission Trends No. 5* (see above), pp. 93–110.

Chapter 8

Cupitt, Don. "The Finality of Christ." *Theology*, 78 (1975) 617–28.

———. "One Jesus, Many Christs?" in *Christ, Faith, and History*, S. W. Sykes and J. P. Clayton, eds. Cambridge University Press, 1972, pp. 131–44.

Dawe, Donald G. "Christian Faith in a Religiously Plural World," in *Christian Faith in a Religiously Plural World*, D. G. Dawe and J. B. Carman, eds. Maryknoll, N.Y.: Orbis, 1978, pp. 13–33.

Driver, Tom F. *Christ in a Changing World: Toward an Ethical Christology*. New York: Crossroad, 1981, chap. 3 and 4.

Hick, John. *God and the Universe of Faiths*. New York: St. Martin's Press, 1973, pp. 120–47.

———. "Jesus and the World Religions," in *The Myth of God Incarnate*, John Hick, ed. London: SCM Press, 1977, pp. 167–85.

———. "Whatever Path Men Choose is Mine," in *Christianity and Other Religions*, John Hick and Brian Hebblethwaite, eds. Philadelphia: Fortress, 1980, pp. 171–90.

———. "On Grading Religions." *Religious Studies*, 17 (1981) 451–67.

Macquarrie, John. "Christianity and Other Faiths." *Union Seminary Quarterly*, 20 (1964) 39–48.

———. "Commitment and Openness: Christianity's Relation to Other Faiths." *Theology Digest*, 27 (1979) 347–55.

Panikkar, Raimundo. "The Meaning of Christ's Name in the Universal Economy of Salvation," in *Evangelization, Dialogue, and Development*, Mariasusai Dhavamony, ed. Rome: Gregorian University Press, 1972, pp. 195–218.

———. *The Unknown Christ of Hinduism*. Maryknoll, N.Y.: Orbis, 1981 (rev. ed.), pp. 1–30.

———. "The Category of Growth in Comparative Religion: A Critical Self-Examination," in *The Intrareligious Dialogue*. New York: Paulist, 1978, pp. 53–73.

Pawlikowski, John T. *Christ in the Light of the Christian-Jewish Dialogue*. New York: Paulist, 1982, chap. 2 and 5.

Pieris, Aloysius. "Speaking of the Son of God in Non-Christian Cultures, e.g. in Asia," in *Jesus, Son of God?* (*Concilium*, 153), Edward Schillebeeckx and Johannes-Baptist Metz, eds. New York: Seabury, 1982, pp. 65–70.

Race, Alan. *Christians and Religious Pluralism: Patterns in the Christian Theology of Religions*. Maryknoll, N.Y.: Orbis, 1983, chap. 5, "Incarnation and the Christian Theology of Religions."

Ruether, Rosemary. "An Invitation to Jewish-Christian Dialogue: In What Sense Can We Say that Jesus Was 'the Christ'?" *The Ecumenist*, 10 (1974) 343–64.

Samartha, S. J. *Courage for Dialogue*. Maryknoll, N.Y.: Orbis, 1982, chap. 7 and 11.

Sizemore, Brian A., Jr. "Christian Faith in a Pluralistic World." *Journal of Ecumenical Studies*, 13 (1976) 405–19.

Chapter 9

Burkle, Howard R. "Jesus Christ and Religious Pluralism." *Journal of Ecumenical Studies*, 16 (1979) 457–71.

Cragg, Kenneth. "Islam and Incarnation," *Truth and Dialogue in World Religions: Conflicting Truth-Claims*, John Hick, ed. Philadelphia: Westminster, 1974, pp. 126–39.

Dunn, James D. G. *Christology in the Making*. Philadelphia: Westminster, 1980, pp. 251–68.

Ganoczy, Alexandre. "The Absolute Claim of Christianity: The Justification of Evangelization or an Obstacle to It?" *Concilium*, 114 (New York: Seabury, 1979), pp. 19–29.

Hick, John. *God and the Universe of Faiths*. New York: St. Martin's Press, 1973, pp. 148–79.

Nineham, Dennis. Epilogue, in *The Myth of God Incarnate*, John Hick, ed. London: SCM Press, 1977, pp. 186–204.

Robinson, John A. T. "The Uniqueness of Christ," in *Truth Is Two-Eyed*. Philadelphia: Westminster, 1980, pp. 97–129.

Schillebeeckx, Edward. *Jesus: An Experiment in Christology*, New York: Crossroads, 1979, pp. 401–38.

Schreiter, Robert. "Reply." in *Christ's Lordship and Religious Pluralism*, Maryknoll, N.Y.: Orbis, 1981, pp. 45–52.

Stendahl, Krister. "Notes for Three Bible Studies," in *Christ's Lordship and Religious Pluralism* (see above), pp. 7–18.

Watts, Alan. *Behold the Spirit*. New York: Vintage, 1971, pp. 64–87.

Young, Frances. "A Cloud of Witnesses," in *The Myth of God Incarnate* (see above), pp. 13–47.

———. "Two Roots or a Tangled Mess?" in *The Myth of God Incarnate* (see above), pp. 87–121.

On Transcendental Christology

Rahner, Karl. *Foundations of Christian Faith*. New York: Seabury, 1978, pp. 178-228.

A World of Grace: An Introduction to the Themes and Foundations of Karl Rahner's Theology, Leo J. O'Donovan, ed. New York: Seabury, 1980, pp. 92-199.

On Process Christology

Cobb, John B. Jr., and David Ray Griffin. *Process Theology: An Introductory Exposition*. Philadelphia: Westminster, 1976, pp. 95-110.

Pittenger, Norman. "Process Thought and the Significance of Christ," in *Process Theology: Basic Writings*, Ewert H. Cousins, ed. New York: Paulist, 1971, pp. 203-15.

Suchocki, Marjorie Hewitt. *God Christ Church: A Practical Guide to Process Theology*, New York: Crossroad, 1982, pp. 93-121.

On Liberation Christology

Boff, Leonardo. *Jesus Christ Liberator*. Maryknoll, N.Y.: Orbis, 1978, pp. 32-48, 264-95.

Sobrino, Jon. *Christology at the Crossroads*. Maryknoll, N.Y.: Orbis, 1978, pp. 346-95.

On The Resurrection

Küng, Hans. *On Being a Christian*. New York: Macmillan, 1976, pp. 343-84.

Mackey, James. *Jesus the Man and the Myth*. New York: Paulist, 1979, pp. 86-120.

Schillebeeckx, Edward. *Jesus* (see above), pp. 328-97.

Chapter 10

Ariarajah, S. Wesley. "Towards a Theology of Dialogue," in *Interreligious Dialogue*, Richard W. Rousseau, ed. Montrose, Pa.: Ridge Row Press, 1981, pp. 32-45. Also in *Ecumenical Review*, 29 (1977) 3-11.

Drummond, Richard H. "Christian Theology and the History of Religions." *Journal of Ecumenical Studies*, 12 (1975) 389-405.

Dunne, John S., *The Way of All the Earth*. New York: Macmillan, 1972, pp. ix-xiii.

——. "The Emergence of a New Theology: John Dunne Interviewed by Kenneth Woodward." *Psychology Today*, Jan. 78, pp. 47-50.

Franklin, R. L. "Religion and Religions." *Religious Studies*, 10 (1974) 419-32.

Hellwig, Monika Konrad. "Bases and Boundaries for Interfaith Dialogue: A Christian Viewpoint." *Interreligious Dialogue* (see above), pp. 68-87. Also in *Journal of Ecumenical Studies*, 14 (1977) 419-31.

Lee, R. Y. "Yin-Yang Way of Thinking: A Possible Method for Ecumenical Theology." *International Review of Missions*, 60 (1971) 363-70. Also in *Christianity and the Religions of the East*, Richard W. Rousseau, ed. Montrose, Pa.: Ridge Row Press, 1982, pp. 9-15.

Maurier, Henri. "The Christian Theology of the Non-Christian Religions." *Lumen Vitae*, 21 (1976) 59–74.

Merton, Thomas. *The Asian Journal of Thomas Merton*. New York: New Directions, 1968, pp. 309–17.

Panikkar, Raimundo. "Faith and Belief: A Multireligious Experience," in *The Intrareligious Dialogue*. New York: Paulist, 1978, pp. 1–23. Also in *Anglican Theological Review*, 53 (1971) 219–37.

———. "The Rhetoric of the Dialogue" and "The Rules of the Game in the Religious Encounter," in *Intrareligious Dialogue* (see above), pp. xi–xxxviii, 26–37.

———. "*Epoche* in the Religious Encounter," ibid., pp. 39–52.

———. Metatheology as Fundamental Theology," in *Myth, Faith, and Hermeneutics*. New York: Paulist, 1979, pp. 321–34.

Race, Alan. *Christians and Religious Pluralism: Patterns in the Christian Theology of Religions*. Maryknoll, N.Y.: Orbis Books, 1983, chap. 6, "A Question of Truth."

Raschke, Carl A. "Religious Pluralism and Truth: From Theology to a Hermeneutical Dialogy." *Journal of the American Academy of Religion*, 50 (1982) 35–48.

Sharpe, Eric J. "The Goals of Inter-Religious Dialogue," in *Truth and Dialogue in World Religions: Conflicting Truth-Claims*, John Hick, ed. Philadelphia: Westminster, 1974, pp. 77–95.

Smith, Wilfred Cantwell. *Towards a World Theology*. Philadelphia: Westminster, 1981, chap. 6 and 8.

———. "Comparative Religion: Whither—and Why?" in *Religious Diversity*, Willard G. Oxtoby, ed. New York: Harper and Row, 1976, pp. 138–57.

Index

Compiled by William Schlau

Schlette, Heinz Robert, 126, 127, 134, 233, 249, 250, 251
Schoneveld, J. Coos, 160
Schoonenberg, Piet, 123, 126, 250, 265
Schreiter, Robert J., 261, 265
Schuon, Frithjof, 44, 47-50, 52, 53, 54, 154
Science, 7-8, 20, 31, 32, 218
Scott, Waldron, 241
Seckler, Max, 247
Segundo, Juan Luis, 258
Sharpe, Eric J., 233
Shea, John, 71, 218
Shinn, Roger Lincoln, 269
Singleton, Michael, 259
Sizemore, Burlan, 165, 234
Slater, Peter, 268
Smith, Huston, 2, 47, 237
Smith, Wilfred C., 233, 234, 235, 245, 265, 266, 268; and the common essence approach, 44-47; on faith, 51, 127; on global theology, 224; and interreligious dialogue, 228; on Jesus, 157; on knowledge, 11; problems with ideas of, 52, 54; on religious pluralism, 17-18; theocentrism of, 263; and truth, 219, 221; and world fellowship, 14-15
Sobrino, John, 194, 195, 264
Sociology, 9-13
Sölle, Dorothee, 163, 164
Song, Choan-Seng, 136, 137, 268
Spae, Joseph J., 266
Starkey, Peggy, 261
Stendahl, Krister, 185
Stöckle, Bernard, 247
Stott, John, 80
Subconscious. *See* Unconscious
Suzuki, D.T., 239
Symbols, 57, 60, 61, 62, 66, 69, 70, 103, 107
Syncretism, 9, 79, 111
Systematic theology, 98-108, 228-29
Taylor, John V., 135-36
Teilhard de Chardin, Pierre, 7, 9, 251
Tertullian, 121
TeSelle, Eugene, 253
Theocentrism, 47, 131, 134, 145-67, 171-204, 263
Theophilus of Antioch, 121
Theravada Buddhism, 38, 39

Third Force, the, 64-66
Third World Protestant theologians, 110-13, 136-37
Thomas, M.M., 97, 108, 110-13, 117, 118, 247, 269
Thompson, William, 239, 251
Tillich, Paul, 233, 244, 246, 248, 264; and Devanandan, 111; on faith, 212; on global theology, 224; on interreligious dialogue, 114; on Jesus, 106-7, 110, 245; on *Kairos,* 18; and mainline Protestantism, 97; on the Protestant principle, 115; on revelation, 98-99; on revisions in Christianity, 143; on salvation, 101, 103, 118; and Thomas, 111; on truth, 221
Toynbee, Arnold: and the common essence approach, 37-44; and the common psychic origin approach, 65, 66; criticism of, 51-52, 53, 54; on the incarnation, 191; on Jesus, 71, 89, 171; and liberal theology, 76; on revelation, 49, 209; and Smith, 45, 47
Tracy, David, 31, 71, 90, 143, 145, 216, 236, 241, 243, 263, 265, 268, 269
Transcendental christology, 186-88, 190-92, 193, 200
Trent, Council of, 123
Troeltsch, Ernst: and Barth, 81; and the common psychic origin approach, 65, 66; historical relativism of, 23-36, 53, 88; on the incarnation, 191; and interreligious dialogue, 231; on Jesus, 71, 89, 171; and liberal theology, 76, 80; on revelation, 49, 209; Samartha on, 158; on truth, 42, 43, 208
Truth: Barth on, 82, 84-86, 95; and change, 19, 31; Christian claims to, 42; in classicist culture, 183; criteria for, 11, 29-31, 231, 269; Devanandan on, 111; and epistemology, 240; Evangelicalism and, 91; and historical relativism, 24, 27-29, 32, 33, 36, 93; and interreligious dialogue, 208, 211-12, 217-23; Jung on, 69; in liberation theology, 193, 194; in nonchristian religions, 102; as personal, 10, 11; religious, and psychology, 68-69; Roman Catholicism on, 132, 142;